FUNDAMENTALS
of INFORMATION
STUDIES SECOND EDITION

Understanding Information and Its Environment

June Lester and Wallace C. Koehler, Jr.

NEAL-SCHUMAN PUBLISHERS, INC.

NEW YORK   LONDON

Published by Neal-Schuman Publishers, Inc.
100 William St., Suite 2004
New York, NY 10038

Printed and bound in the United States of America.

The paper used in this publication meets the minimum requirements of American National Standard for Information Sciences—Permanence of Paper for Printed Library Materials, ANSI Z39.48-1992.

Library of Congress Cataloging-in-Publication Data

Lester, June, 1942–
    Fundamentals of information studies: understanding information and its environment / June Lester, Wallace C. Koehler, Jr.—2nd ed.

        p. cm.
    Includes bibliographical references.
    ISBN 978-1-55570-594-7
  1. Information science.   2. Information resources.   3. Information services.
  4. Information technology.   5. Information policy.   6. Information society.
  I. Koehler, Wallace C., Jr.   II. Title.
    Z665.L535 2007
    020—dc22   2007012846

Contents

List of Figures

Foreword

How do we make sense of information? From cave drawings and the Rosetta Stone to HTML and the Wayback Machine, people today see the study of information as a worthwhile enterprise. But information can seem to be a truly abstract concept easily confused with data, facts, and documents all mixed together in the maelstrom of knowledge creation. For many decades we looked to editors and publishers as the legitimizing forces who bestowed their stamp of approval on credible information, but now in the wide-open landscape of the Web, the quality of information is for the user to decide.

In this second edition of *Fundamentals of Information Studies*, June Lester and Wally Koehler take on the noble task of examining the theory and application of information concepts to clarify the history and current environment of information use, information applications, and information technology. The book's overt mission is to help students understand communication and information systems and how they have evolved and to provide a learning tool for introductory courses in information studies. Instead of plodding along in typical textbook fashion, the authors insert fascinating anecdotes and real-life examples to energize what could otherwise be merely a theoretical work. Theory in itself is important and not to be diminished, however, and to their credit, the authors build their chapters on a foundation of solid information science research. From the work of Otlet, Paisley, Buckland, and Briet, the book offers students concepts from the "names they should know" in the information field while still being an accessible text. At the same time the authors also provide an interesting read to all those who wish to understand a field that emerged in the twentieth century and continues in prominence in the twenty-first.

Those unfamiliar with the information field may not realize that there are many subdisciplines, such as information seeking, information retrieval, knowledge management, and informatics, among others, that are subject to primary research at major universities around the world. This text is ecumenical in scope, bridging a number of professional fields, including communication, computer science, library and information science, and information technology, and offering an international focus that commends it to those who see information studies as global by nature. University programs in information science and information technology (outside of computer science and engineering schools) are a relatively recent phenomenon, and there is a dearth of texts that unify the various concepts of information as well as information and communication technology (ICT). *Fundamentals of Information Studies* is an excellent starting point for students at the undergraduate and graduate levels, opening an intellectual door to the challenging and abiding questions that are integral to nascent fields of study such as information science whose applications change rapidly and continuously.

It is not just the theory and practice of information that gives value to this volume. The text introduces readers to the political side of information and the concomitant power relationships that exist in the access to information or the lack of it in everyday society. The analysis of power and information is a welcome addition to this updated version of the book, comprising a new chapter in the second edition. A chapter on the economic aspects of information and its distribution also provides a depth of thoughtful ideas related to a pluralistic and democratic society. The new edition has additional material on user behavior, a key aspect of the social informatics side of the informing sciences. Recognizing the human aspects of information and technology use is appropriate for a work that emanates from the library and information science field. Library professionals traditionally focus on the information needs of individuals, relevant information to meet those needs, and how people and organizations use information.

Lester and Koehler are seasoned faculty in the field of information studies with years of teaching experience and experience as administrators over decades of work within higher education. Their interests are broad and range from the arts and humanities to political science and information policy. Individually each author has held prestigious positions with information professional organizations and on editorial and directorial boards within the informing fields. It is only appropriate, then, that the book outlines the various professional roles that students who aspire to information professions can fill as they complete their studies on the university level. As a practical matter, this focus is important in professional schools where students see themselves on the path to a career that they will sustain over a lifetime, despite shifts and moves in various positions along the way.

I am impressed with the care and thoughtfulness with which the authors have approached the subject matter of all things related to information. They are courageous to take on material that potentially changes at every news conference announcing a new operating system or new e-gadget or i-device. In a world where "screenagers" live on the screen and are facile with online social networking, googling, and interactive digital video, a book that steps back to survey the information environment and its broad implications for society is welcome for those who wish to work with students and encourage them to be intelligent consumers and producers of information. The chapter on ethics is particularly useful in its offering of deep questions that touch the values that gird a society where organizations depend on quality information in order to function. It is not easy for those outside of the field of philosophy to write about ethics without appearing to be moralistic. The approach taken by Lester and Koehler works well by demonstrating that professionals in information environments across the board attempt to adhere to codes of ethics based on the moral norms expected of them by society. As the text concludes, looking toward information futures with allusions to popular and classic films about artificial intelligence, the authors suggest that understanding information and technologies may actually help us examine big ideas such as what makes us human and the responsibilities we must assume because of our humanity and those we can delegate to machines.

Claire McInerney, Associate Professor
Rutgers, the State University of New Jersey
School of Communication, Information and Library Studies

Preface

Information has become so central to our daily lives that we now live in an "information environment," a habitat that surrounds us as surely and completely as the ecosystem in which we live. This habitat expands constantly to encompass new sources of information and new information activities.

In writing *Fundamentals of Information Studies: Understanding Information and Its Environment, Second Edition*, we sought to combine theory and everyday examples to provide a broad-based introduction to the field.

We define information broadly as anything that changes the knowledge state of the receiver. Our focus here is on human information activity. We use the term "information environment" to connote not only information and information activity but also the social, political, economic, and cultural milieu. It is, in our view, impossible to separate information from the context in which it occurs.

Although *Fundamentals of Information Studies* focuses primarily on the contemporary information environment, we also strive to connect current information institutions to their historical roots and with their cultural, political, and economic settings. *Fundamentals of Information Studies* also examines what we consider key concepts and issues in information policy.

Throughout this book, we have tried to identify and trace general themes that the reader can track over time. The most prominent theme is the impact of the development of technology on access to and use of information and the changes that this development causes in the structure and operation of society. One question that pervades the entire book is whether the information issues and challenges we currently face are really new or just different manifestations of issues and concerns that have been with us since the beginning of recorded communication. Although we suggest answers, in the end, the reader is left to decide.

We believe that our duty as authors is to help the reader identify significant questions and to suggest ways in which the reader can ponder those questions. Thus, we are not necessarily trying to provide answers to the issues raised, but rather to help the reader to think about the questions and to look for answers on an ongoing basis. This is, of course, the primary purpose of education.

The ideas and concepts within the book have been shaped by experience and interaction with students and faculty colleagues and through our participation in the information profession over a long period of time. One of us has been teaching an introductory course in this area at the graduate level for over thirty years and the other has worked and taught in the area of politics and policy for almost that long.

Fundamentals of Information Studies is designed primarily for use as a textbook in introductory courses in undergraduate and graduate information studies programs. It also could be assigned as background or collateral reading for more narrowly focused undergraduate or graduate courses. We hope that nonstudents seeking background on the information society or wishing to gain perspective on this rapidly changing subject will also find that the work clarifies their understanding of how information affects us daily.

NEW IN THIS EDITION

One of the advantages of writing more than one edition of a book is that one can take into account the criticisms and comments of reviewers. Book reviews provide a valuable service to readers looking to select works of interest. They also offer valuable guidance to authors by helping to point out lacunae and other gaps in their material. We thank our reviewers for their guidance.

We have chosen to provide additional material in this second edition based upon two reviews of our first edition that we believe provide valuable insights. Based on a review by Elena Macevičiūtė (2004), we have added chapter 3, "Information Needs and Information Seeking Behavior," which offers a broad exploration of user behavior. Douglas Raber (2004) pointed out that the first edition, while not explicitly a Foucauldian analysis of the art, science, and practice of informing, fails to address the nexus between power and information. Raber is correct. Because we were writing an introduction of informing, we purposefully did not provide that level of analysis. On reflection, we have decided to offer an analysis of power and information in a new chapter 10. Other changes in this edition include expansions of several chapters and updates and revisions throughout. We wish to express our appreciation to those who have granted permission to use their materials.

We have also added two new features to each chapter:

- A "Learning Guide" that introduces important terms and issues and prepares the reader for the topic at hand. Instructors and students can use these guides to assess whether key concepts have been comprehended and retained.

- An "Information Idea" that draws attention to an interesting application or to supplemental material that enriches the chapter's content.

ORGANIZATION

- Chapter 1, "The Impact of Information in Society," provides an overview of information in our daily lives and in society as a whole.
- Chapter 2, "Fundamental Concepts of Information," defines information in several ways and considers characteristics of information, making a distinction between "information" and the "information record."
- Chapter 3, "Information Needs and Information Seeking Behavior," explores users' motivations for seeking information.
- Chapter 4, "History of Information Technology," traces the development of information technology and the social implications of major changes.
- Chapter 5, "Current Information Technology," introduces contemporary uses of information technology within the contexts of creating, transmitting, storing, retrieving, and preserving information and the information record.
- Chapter 6, "Societal Institutions for Creation, Distribution, and Management of Information," begins with a brief history and describes modern institutions that develop, produce, transmit, distribute, manage, and provide access to information records.
- Chapter 7, "The Information Professions," discusses four broad categories of information work (creation, transmission, management, and storage) across three traditions (oral, print, and electronic).
- Chapter 8, "The Impact of Information Cultures and Societies," focuses first on how one identifies an "information society" and then explores the impact of information and information technology in oral, print, and electronic environments.
- Chapter 9, "Economics of Information," defines key economics terms and explicates the role of the government in the economics of information.
- Chapter 10, "Information, Power, and Society," highlights the relationship between information and power and the various ways in which the two concepts interact.
- Chapter 11, "The Regulation and Politics of Information," examines the idea of information regulation and introduces a sample of the governmental, intergovernmental, and nongovernmental agencies that are either regulatory or policy-making bodies.
- Chapter 12, "The Areas and Issues of Information Policy," focuses on two key areas of current concern: copyright and privacy. It also inspects

policies related to generation and production, dissemination and access, and distribution of information.

- Chapter 13, "Information Ethics," gives examples of several professional codes of ethics and discusses current key issues in information ethics: privacy, intellectual freedom, equitable access, and intellectual property.
- Chapter 14, "Information Future(s)," concludes with speculation on where further development in the information society may lead.

We conclude each chapter with summary thoughts and with "Questions for Consideration." These questions are intended to stimulate thinking about the issues and concepts that have been introduced. While they might be assigned for discussion by a class or by small groups of students, they could also be assigned as individual essay questions to help develop students' critical thinking skills. In addition to the references given at the end of each chapter, most chapters include a list of additional sources that might be useful in pursuing the topic. When appropriate and available, Web sources are included. The appendixes include a glossary and a list of acronyms.

Since the information environment changes so rapidly, *Fundamentals of Information Studies* should be supplemented with sources that can provide the latest developments on the issues and concerns addressed. A companion Web site is provided for this purpose; see the copyright page for details. We also recommend that educators and students use a combination of the current professional literature, a national newspaper, and Web sites that give attention to the topics covered, many of which are listed in either the references or additional sources.

Through our years of experience, we have learned that one of the most difficult challenges in our field is finding a framework in which to place all of the information activities that occur and in which to make sense of the constant changes. The information environment often seems much like a kaleidoscope—the minute we think we have a fix on the patterns, everything seems to turn and change again. We hope to assist our readers in making sense of the information environment and to provide a background from which more specialized and detailed investigation can take place. If the pieces of the information puzzle make more sense after reading this book—and if there are still interesting questions that have not been answered—we will judge our efforts to have been successful.

References

Macevičiūtė, Elena. 2004. "June Lester and Wallace C. Koehler. Fundamentals of Information Studies: Understanding Information and Its Environment. New York: Neal-Schuman Publishers, Inc., 2003." *Information*

Research 9, no. 2. Available: http://informationr.net/ir/reviews/revs124 .html (accessed December 2006).

Raber, Douglas. 2004. "Fundamentals of Information Studies: Understanding Information and Its Environment." *Library Quarterly* 74, no. 4: 486–488.

DEDICATION

*This work is dedicated to our children
and to our grandchildren,
those with us and all yet to come.*

ACKNOWLEDGMENT

*We wish to express our appreciation to those who have
granted permission to use their materials.*

How does information, or the lack of information, affect one's daily life and activities? What impact does information have on the way a society functions? To prepare for this chapter, make a list of all of the activities that you have undertaken to this point in your day that have involved using information in some way. Then write a paragraph that describes your understanding of how information is used to help a society to function. At the end of the chapter, reread your list and your paragraph to see if you want to revise them based on what you have read.

Chapter 1

The Impact of Information in Society

Learning Guide

After reading this chapter, you should be able to

- identify the information devices you use on a daily basis;
- match devices for use or management of information to the mode in which the information is received;
- describe how information is used in society to control and influence behavior;
- discuss ways in which individuals differ in their ability to access and use information;
- explain how the use of information in today's society is changing.

When you have finished the chapter, return to this page to be sure you have learned what you need to know.

INTRODUCTION

We live immersed in an information environment that surrounds us as totally as the air we breathe. While we may not always deal with information on a conscious level, it is there; and we receive messages that we process, often without recognizing that we are doing so. To introduce this concept of pervasive information possibilities, this book begins with exploration of the information environment in the familiar space of daily life.

USES OF INFORMATION IN DAILY ACTIVITIES

In day-to-day activities, individuals are constantly interacting with information in one form or another. From the moment of awakening until going to sleep—and for many during sleep—information activities are occurring. Information is encountered in a variety of modes. It may be received

- *visually,* through the sense of sight, ranging from the print on this page to the messages sent in the clothes one wears to the way a living space is decorated;
- *aurally,* through hearing, as in the whistle of a train, the chirping of a bird, or the whirring of a lawn mower;
- *tactilely,* through the sense of touch, in such activities as stroking a cat or feeling the humidity in the air;
- *olfactorily,* through the sense of smell, which can provide information that coffee is brewing in the next room or that bacon is on the breakfast menu in a campus dining hall;
- *gustatorily,* through the sense of taste, which can inform one that milk has gone sour or that too much salt was added to a stew.

Some of each person's daily information activities involve transforming information from one format to another. For example, when a piano student sits down to learn a Chopin waltz, the learning session involves an information activity that transforms information from the written notation of music, received through visual means, to the sound produced by the keys of the piano striking the strings. At a later point in the piano student's progress, the information about the waltz will be stored in the student's memory and will be extracted from there to be transformed into the sounds of the piano made during a performance and received aurally by the listeners. When a building is constructed, information is transformed from the visual architectural and engineering drawings into a physical structure, information about which may then be received visually or tactilely.

The total amount of new information created is escalating. A recent study reported that new information produced in 2002 could form 37,000 libraries with collections the size of the Library of Congress, or approximately 800 MB for every person in the world. The rate of growth of new stored information since the previous study was conducted was estimated at 30 percent per year (Lyman and Varian, 2003). Based on these calculations, the projected production of digital data for 2006 is 20 exabytes (Deloitte Touche Tohmatsu, 2006).

With this constant inundation of an ever-rising tide of information from a wide variety of sources and types of media, the individual is continuously processing information using filtering techniques that have been unconsciously developed (Schement and Curtis, 1995: 117). Much of the information that is encountered is ignored; it simply does not register in one's consciousness, as a means of dealing with the overwhelming volume.

As one way of helping to gather and manage information, individuals use an increasing array and number of information sending, receiving, recording, tracking, and manipulation devices, as well as an expanding number of information services. For example, recent statistics indicated the average American home had 8 radios and 2.4 television sets (U.S. Census Bureau, 2006: 737). In 2004, more than 60 percent of U.S. households had computers and more than half of all American homes had Internet connections (U.S. Department of Commerce, 2004: 4). By 2005, 80 percent of adult Americans had Internet access in their homes or workplaces, indicating the rapid growth in Internet access in the United States (U.S. Census Bureau, 2006). By the same token, broadband penetration is increasing rapidly: in countries that are members of the Organisation for Economic Co-operation and Development, broadband subscriptions moved from 11.7 percent of inhabitants in June 2005 to 15.5 percent in June 2006, an increase over the period of 33 percent (Organisation for Economic Co-operation and Development, 2006). In 2006, it was not uncommon for an individual living in one of the developed nations to own and use most of the following information devices on a daily basis:

- clock
- watch
- radio
- television set
- telephone
- telephone answering machine
- cell phone
- PDA (personal digital assistant, e.g., Palm Pilot)
- computer

- printer
- scanner
- VCR
- book
- CD player
- DVD player/recorder
- MP3 player
- calendar
- fax machine
- camera
- calculator
- security or alarm system
- thermostat

Information Ideas

Information Devices around the World

Although one generally tends to think of the United States as the most infor-mation intensive nation in the world, this perception reflects a limited view of the reality of use of information devices in other nations as well as a limited concept of what constitutes information intensity. For example, according to statistics from the International Telecommunication Union (ITU), the United States in 2005 had 67.62 cell phone subscribers per 100 inhabitants com-pared to 122.65 per 100 in Hong Kong, 113.04 in Israel, 123.14 in Italy, and 115.22 in the Czech Republic, just to give a few examples. Other countries with subscriber rates similar to the United States were Croatia (65.55), South Africa (65.36), and Chile (67.79).

In the measure of broadband penetration (including DSL, cable modems, and other technologies), the United States ranked sixteenth worldwide, be-hind such nations as Iceland (first), Korea (second) the Netherlands (fourth), Canada (tenth), and Taiwan (twelfth). In the ITU's Digital Opportunity Index, a measure that combines information, communication, and technology afford-ability, coverage, tele-density (land and cell phones), Internet access, comput-ers and hand-held access devices, Internet usage, and quality of access, the United States in 2005 ranked twenty-first, with the top ten being (in order) Korea, Japan, Denmark, Iceland, Hong Kong, Sweden, the United Kingdom, Norway, Netherlands, and Taiwan.

While these measures of availability and use of information and communica-

(Continued on p. 5)

tion technology provide a different view of the U.S. position vis-à-vis information intensity, a different contrast can be seen between the United States and other developed economies and the rest of the world if one expands the concept of information in society to include the use of such information devices as African masks, the Ta Moko tattooing of the Maori, which provides information about the individual's life; the dances of Taiwanese aboriginal tribes; and the information-intense traditional clothing of the women of the village of Olympos on the Greek island of Karpathos, which indicates not only marital and economic status but also birth order in the family. When one considers the variety of means by which information has been conveyed throughout history, using both tangible, concrete symbols such as buildings and monuments and oral transmission through stories and songs, the idea that today's society is more information intensive than any other has been needs to be reconsidered, or at least put into perspective.

Sources

International Telecommunication Union. 2005. "Digital Opportunity Index (DOI): Ranking: Top 25 Digital Economies." Available: www.itu.int/osg/spu/statistics/DOI/results2005.html (accessed December 2006).

———. 2005. "Digital Opportunity Index (DOI): Structure." Available: www.itu.int/osg/spu/statistics/DOI/structure.phtml (accessed December 2006).

———. 2005. "Economies by Broadband Penetration, 2005." Available: www.itu.int/ITU-D/ict/statistics/at_glance/top20_broad_2005.html (accessed December 2006).

———. 2005. "Mobile Cellular, Subscribers per 100 People." Available: www.itu.int/ITU-D/ict/statistics/at_glance/cellular05.pdf (accessed December 2006).

In addition, the individual would likely have used one or more of the following information services:

- telephone service
- cable TV subscription
- satellite radio subscription
- Internet access
- security monitoring service
- wireless phone service

The use of information in daily activities continues to grow and expand, both in terms of hours of use and in the scope and variety of information devices and services. Total media usage per person per year for 2008 is projected to be 4,059 hours, with television viewing and radio listening continuing to lead the way with 1,669 hours and 1,032 hours respectively. While personal usage of some types of media, such as daily newspapers, magazines, and books is declining, use of other media is increasing, such as Internet and video games (U.S. Census Bureau, 2006: 736). A recent survey indicates that 73 percent of Americans use the Internet (Madden, 2006: 4).

The range of information devices has expanded to include the nearly ubiquitous portable MP3 player, the digital camera, and the more recent portable video players. In addition, the capabilities of already available devices change on an almost daily basis: witness the smartphone that combines the cell phone, camera, and PDA. Likewise, information services are expanding at an accelerated pace. The success of iTunes digital music service from Apple has generated competitors, downloadable movie services are increasingly prevalent, VoIP (Voice over Internet Protocol) is taking off, and cell phone service in flight is on the near horizon. Although perhaps not accurately labeled an information service, the blog (weblog) is one of the growth areas of information delivery, combining content and comment that can range from a personal diary to a community-building space. Whatever the topic of interest, there is likely a blog on it, including political races at local, state, and national levels.

Schement and Curtis refer to the proliferation of devices and services as a "tendency toward more dense personal media environments" (Schement and Curtis, 1995: 110). One result of this proliferation is an increased dependency on these information devices to structure daily life. Removal of the current information apparatus of the individual, however, would likely result, not in the reduction of dependence, but in the construction of another set of information tools for daily use, since, as will be discussed in chapter 4, dependence on information devices is not a new phenomenon. It is the form, nature, and capacity of these devices that have changed and that will continue to do so.

Information devices and services provide to the individual information that is used for a variety of purposes in the conduct of daily life. Information is used to

make decisions, both significant and mundane.

The information posted at the University of Oklahoma College of Arts and Sciences Web site about the course for which this textbook was initially written was used by students to make the decision on whether to enroll. Information in the entertainment section of the newspaper (another type of information device) is used to decide what movie to see. These two decisions vary in consequence and significance, but both are made because of, or with the assistance of, information. This decision making assisted by relevant information is an ongoing activity of daily life, in many cases done in such a ubiquitous manner that neither the acquisition of the needed information nor the decision activity is conducted at a conscious level.

Information is also used to

resolve uncertainty.

As with information assisting decision making, the use of information to revolve uncertainty is also often a nondeliberative, unobtrusive action. Consider, for example, the brief glance one makes at a clock when reading or studying for a test, both of which are more deliberate information activities. The information provided in that glance resolves the unarticulated uncertainty, experienced as a vague feeling, of whether it is time to stop reading so as to leave for an appointment or to stop studying and go to class. Information to resolve uncertainty, of course, may be deliberately pursued. That pursuit, however, requires:

- recognition that there is an uncertainty
- awareness that it may be resolvable with information
- analysis of the kind of information that would be useful
- knowledge of the availability of such information
- access to the information needed
- skills necessary to locate and interpret the information

Researchers have characterized the first phase, recognition that there is an uncertainty, in several ways. One particularly useful framework for thinking about this phase is found in the work of Carol Kuhlthau, who discusses the affective characteristics of "anxiety and lack of confidence" associated with the initial recognition that there is an uncertainty (Kuhlthau, 1993: 347). As one moves toward gaining the information needed to resolve the uncertainty, the affective symptoms change to confidence and satisfaction (Kuhlthau, 1993: 343, 352). Other ways in which the process of finding information to resolve uncertainty have been characterized are as a "gap" that has to be bridged through a process of "sensemaking" (Dervin, 1992) and as a resolution of an "anomalous state of knowledge" (Belkin, 1980).

However one conceptualizes the process of using information to resolve uncertainty, it is clear that not everyone has equal access to the information and information devices that can provide the needed information, nor is there equality of access for individuals to the skills necessary to locate and interpret information.

For many information pursuits, the assistance of an information professional is needed. The roles that information professionals play in this process will be discussed in chapter 7. On an individual basis, however, access to the information devices and services we considered above varies considerably, even within developed nations. We will examine these differences within and among countries on a more detailed level in chapter 13. For now, a few examples will serve to illustrate how divergent individual access to the means to find and process information needed in daily life can be, even within the United States. The largest proportion of Americans using the Internet are white non-Hispanics, 72 percent, whereas 58 percent of African Americans use it (Pew Internet & American Life Project, 2007). Of adults in the United States living with illness or disability, 61 percent are online as compared to the 74 percent of those without disability or illness (Fox, 2007: 5).

USES OF INFORMATION IN SOCIETY

Beyond the daily, individual uses of information, information is a powerful and pervasive force in the operation and functioning of society, regardless of where that society is situated in terms of historical time or economic development. Chapter 4 will trace the historical evolution of information use through changes in the technologies that enable information activities. In current, developed societies, information is used as an instrument of influence and control, in the lives of individual citizens, in the political structure of the country, and in the relationships among nations.

Within the economic sphere, information is used daily to influence behavior. The most obvious example is the use of advertising, wherein information is provided to consumers with the intent of changing behavior in a manner that will result in increased sales or use of the product or service about which information is presented. In the United States, recent figures show that $263,699,000,000 was spent on advertising, with the largest expenditures on ads in newspapers, direct mail, and broadcast television (U.S. Census Bureau, 2006: 813). The major targets in the attempts to change consumer behavior through information on television were automobiles (TNS Media Intelligence, 2006). However, the range of products and services about which information is provided is wide, from daily use goods like food and wearing apparel to special purpose purchases like prescription medicine (information about which has increased dramatically in recent years) and insurance.

At a more fundamental level, it is information that makes all other resources available for economic production. As McHale points out, "Material and energy resources are dependent on being recognised as such." And further, "All other resources are dependent upon [information and knowledge] for their evaluation and utilization" (McHale, 1976: 18). For example, it is information about the properties of oil that makes it such a valuable resource. Without information, oil would have no intrinsic value.

In the political sphere, information is used to influence behavior of citizens, particularly in their voting choices; to shape public opinion on national issues; and to inform and support public policy decisions. In this arena, both the provision of information and the withholding of information are used as elements of control; and the control of information is a key component in the establishment and maintenance of a political power base. While the practice of information dissemination and control by government may be more highly developed today than in previous centuries, the ability to disseminate information from the center to the hinterlands of the territory governed (occurring as a result of the invention of printing) is credited with facilitating the development of the nation-state (see discussion in chapter 8).

A key change that has occurred, however, is the rapidity with which information is disseminated, causing governments to lose what has been referred to as information float or the "time cushion" between an event or problem and the diffusion of widespread, global information about the event (McHale, 1976: 77). Such instantaneous information spread dictates an immediacy of response to increasingly complex domestic and international events. Take, for example, the sinking of the Japanese fishing trawler, the *Ehime Maru*, by the U.S. Navy nuclear submarine *Greeneville*, on 9 February 2001, or the in-flight collision of an American EP-3 surveillance plane with a Chinese F-8 fighter plane and the subsequent unauthorized landing of the U.S. spy plane at a Chinese air base on 1 April 2001. In both instances, information about the events was available around the world within hours, demanding reaction from both governments involved (Japan and the United States and China and the United States). Had similar incidents occurred in the nineteenth—or even the middle of the twentieth—century, information about them would have been days or weeks in being made available either to citizens of the countries involved or to other nations.

Information is and has always been also used for entertainment. Troupes of troubadours roamed Europe in medieval times entertaining but also carrying news and myths from one end of the continent to the other. Today information as entertainment is as powerful as ever, if not more so. We follow sporting events, from curling, baseball, cricket, bridge, track and field, wrestling—real and professional—to tiddlywinks. Hollywood and Bollywood produce uncounted films. Videos and video games are staples. The "older" arts are alive and well, too, from the novel to poetry to folksongs to kabuki to water puppets. Again, as is the case for the political and economic effects, entertainment is now available almost instantaneously from one place in the world to all others. We have heard Celine Dion and the Chicken Dance polka literally everywhere in the world. Lucille Ball is a cultural icon. This kind of information diffusion raises other concerns. There is now a fear in many countries that one culture, the American popular culture, may well overwhelm all others. Governments as far-flung as the French, the Canadian, and the Chinese have sought to stem that "inevitable tide." We will return to discussion of this issue in later chapters.

INFORMATION IN TRANSITION

Information may be undergoing a transformation. However "information" was perceived and treated in the past, it is being treated more and more as a commodity that can be owned, controlled, and traded in the marketplace. We know that information and technology march hand in hand, the one feeds on the other. We have extended the definition of information to encompass not only any communication between human beings, but also communication between human beings and machines and between machines. We include both the content and the means for transmitting that content within the context of information.

As we proceed through this book, we will see that information in all of its forms has become more "commodified"—turned into a product to be sold. We have become more concerned with the bottom-line economic value of information than with its social, developmental, and even entertainment value. This trend has been challenged by the likes of David Bollier (2002, 2005), Lawrence Lessig (2001, 2004), and Siva Vaidhyanathan (2001, 2004). They each conclude that if current trends in information economics and jurisprudences proceed, the end result will be the stifling of the creative process.

This fight over intellectual property rights is happening in all spheres. Perhaps the more obvious are in the entertainment arena: witness the Napster case or DVD (digital versatile disc) play protection. Essentially, the Napster case was a clash between the recording industry and those who wished to utilize peer-to-peer sharing of music files from CDs they had purchased or borrowed, raising the question of whether an information content owner can control all uses of that information. Some of the more important challenges are in the academic realm (McSherry, 2001), where questions of idea ownership revolve around the issue of who owns the intellectual output of faculty, the individual faculty member or the university.

That brings us to the most fundamental of questions: who or what should own or control ideas and, by implication, information? We take it as a given in the United States that everyone should have the right to communicate quickly, efficiently, and cheaply. This concept undergirds our notions of public education. It found early voice in the rural free delivery (RFD) philosophy of the postal service in the late nineteenth century and was further strengthened by the universal access for all customers required of the telephone company in the early twentieth century. We see it still in the concern over the digital divide and the Internet.

What, then, are the rights of information/idea creators, publishers, distributors, and users? We will suggest that these rights are in transition and have always been in transition. Moreover, different cultures even today treat these questions differently. Even within the same culture, there may be differences among different cultural domains. Consider, for example, the socio-philosophical arguments of Michel Foucault (1977), who asks, "What is an Author?" versus legal discourse. Foucault and others might conclude that the concept of authorship and the role of the author is in decline, while in the legal domain it is often central.

Foucault argued that "discourse" is a philosophical construct with a common focus or methodology. His interest lay in understanding the process of deriving understanding from texts with very different etiologies. His concern with authorship has not only to do with the creator of text but also with the relationship of "author" with the fluidity of the environment in which the text and author exist. Not only that, but Foucault "deconstructs" the notion of author as creator. Authors are the product of writing, of document creation, and not the other way around. The notion of "author" then becomes inextricably intertwined with "document," but with additional human baggage.

Author rights as Foucault might have defined them differ from the way in which most systems of jurisprudence would. Consider how Foucault might treat the notion of "copyright holder" or "creator" rather than "author." We have moved into a legal environment where the "rights" of the copyright holder trump not only the rights of author or creator, but also the rights of the "information container" owner. Legal discourse addresses these issues. The law may be fluid but it is nonetheless much more rigid than Foucault's discourse. Legal structures are complex and formal. But even legal discourse may yield to construct redefinition. For example, Bernard Hibbitts makes an interesting argument for the role of metaphor in legal discourse. Metaphor in some ways shapes our understanding of the law (Hibbitts, 1994: 241).

CONCLUSION

We are not going to try to answer these questions:

- *Who or what should own or control ideas and information?*
- *What are the rights of information/idea creators, publishers, distributors, and users?*

Rather, we would ask you to keep these concepts uppermost in your mind as you work through this text. This chapter has introduced some of the themes that will be pursued in later chapters. As may already be evident in this brief beginning foray into information ideas, it is not possible to discuss the information environment in a wholly sequential and segmented approach, for like the natural environment, the information environment is an interrelated, interactive, and dynamic space which, although it evolves and changes over time, is best examined holistically.

QUESTIONS FOR CONSIDERATION

1. The conduct of daily life is affected by the number of different information devices (for sending, receiving, recording, tracking, manipulating information) one owns or can access. Which of the information devices that you use would have been available to your parents when they were your age? How does having the information devices that you use make your life different from how theirs was?
2. Is information received in one mode, for example, visually, by reading print on a page, the same information when it is transferred to another mode, for example to an aural mode when someone reads that page to you?
3. The information devices we use on a daily basis change over time. What information devices have you added to your daily routine in the past year? Which ones have you discarded in the past two years? What is the oldest information device (in terms of when it became available) that you use?
4. From a news Web site, read one of the lead stories. In addition to the Web site posting, how else would you be able to get information about the event described in the story? How would the event or the dissemination of information about it have been different if it had occurred a hundred years ago? How would that difference have affected society's perception of the event?
5. Watch a commercial on television (your choice) and find an ad for the same product in a magazine. Is there "information" conveyed in the commercial that is different from that in the print ad? What was the advertiser trying to get the watchers of the commercial to think/believe/do? Was the advertiser trying to get the same result from the print ad?

REFERENCES

Belkin, Nicholas J. 1980. "Anomalous States of Knowledge as a Basis for Information Retrieval." *Canadian Journal of Information Science* 5: 133–143.
Bollier, David. 2002. *Silent Theft: The Private Plunder of Our Common Wealth*. New York: Routledge.

————. 2005. *Brand Name Bullies: The Quest to Own and Control Culture.* Hoboken, NJ: John Wiley.

Deloitte Touche Tohmatsu. "Technology, Media & Telecommunications." 2006. *TMT Trends: Predictions, 2006, A Focus on the Technology Sector.* London: Deloitte & Touche. Available: www.deloitte.com/dtt/cda/doc/content/us_tmt_techpredictions2006_020206(1).pdf (accessed December 2006).

Dervin, Brenda. 1992. "From the Mind's Eye of the User: The Sense-making Qualitative-Quantitative Methodology." In *Qualitative Research in Information Management*, edited by Jack D. Glazier and Ronald R. Powell, 61–84. Englewood, CO: Libraries Unlimited.

Foucault, Michel. 1977. "What Is an Author?" In *Language, Counter-Memory, Practice: Selected Essays and Interviews*, edited by Donald F. Bouchard, 113–138. Translated by Donald F. Bouchard and Sherry Simon. Ithaca, NY: Cornell University Press.

Fox, Susannah. 2005. "Digital Divisions." Washington, DC: Pew Internet & American Life Project, 5 October. Available: www.pewinternet.org/pdfs/PIP_Digital_Divisions_Oct_5_2005.pdf (accessed December 2006).

————. 2007. "Share of Americans Online by Disability Status." *My Health, Circa 2007.* Pew Internet & the American Life Project, 6 February. Available: www.pewinternet.org/ppt/Fox%20Ix%20Feb%206%202007%20with%20notes%20for%20upload.ppt (accessed February 2007).

Hibbitts, Bernard J. 1994. "Making Sense of Metaphors: Visuality, Aurality, and the Reconfiguration of American Legal Discourse." *Cardozo Law Review* 16: 229–356.

Kuhlthau, Carol C. 1993. "A Principle of Uncertainty for Information Seeking." *Journal of Documentation* 49 (December): 339–355.

Lessig, Lawrence. 2001. *The Future of Ideas: The Fate of the Commons in a Connected World.* New York: Random House.

————. 2004. *Free Culture: How Big Media Uses Technology and the Law to Lock Down Culture and Control Creativity.* New York: Penquin Press.

Lyman, Peter, and Hal R. Varian. 2003. "Executive Summary." *How Much Information? 2003.* Berkeley: University of California. School of Information Management and Systems, 27 October. Available: www.sims.berkeley.edu/research/projects/how-much-info-2003/execsum.htm (accessed December 2006).

Madden, Mary. 2006. "Internet Penetration and Impact." Washington, DC: Pew Internet & American Life Project, 26 April. Available: www.pewinternet.org/PPF/r/182/report_display.asp (accessed December 2006).

McHale, John. 1976. *The Changing Information Environment.* Boulder, CO: Westview Press.

McSherry, Corynne. 2001. *Who Owns Academic Work: Battling for Control of Intellectual Property.* Cambridge, MA: Harvard University Press.

Organisation for Economic Co-operation and Development. 2006. "OECD Broadband Statistics to June 2006." OECD, 13 October. Available: www.oecd.org/document/9/0,2340,en_2649_34223_37529673_1_1_1_1,00.html (accessed February 2007).

Pew Internet & American Life Project. 2007. "November 30–December 30, 2006 Tracking Survey." 11 January. Available: www.pewinternet.org/trends/User_Demo_1.11.07.htm (accessed February 2007).

Schement, Jorge Reina, and Terry Curtis. 1995. *Tendencies and Tensions of the Information Age: The Production and Distribution of Information in the United States.* New Brunswick, NJ: Transaction Publishers.

TNS Media Intelligence. 2006. "TNS Media Intelligence Reports U.S. Advertising Expenditures Increased 3.0 Percent In 2005." 27 February. Available: www.tns-mi.com/news/02282006.htm (accessed December 2006).

U.S. Census Bureau. 2006. "No. 1116. Media Usage and Consumer Spending: 2000 to 2008"; "No. 1117. Utilization of Selected Media: 1980–2003"; "No. 1265. Advertising Estimated Expenditures, by Medium: 1990–2004." *Statistical Abstract of the United States: 2006.* Washington, DC: Department of Commerce, 4 January. Available: www.census.gov/prod/2005pubs/06statab/infocomm.pdf (accessed December 2006).

————. Department of Commerce. Economics and Statistics Administration and National Telecommunications and Information Administration. 2004. *A Nation Online: Entering the Broadband Age.* Washington, DC: Department of Commerce, September. Available: www.ntia.doc.gov/reports/anol/NationOnlineBroadband04.pdf (accessed December 2006).

Vaidhyanathan, Siva. 2001. *Copyrights and Copywrongs: The Rise of Intellectual Property and How it Threatens Creativity.* New York: New York University Press.

————. 2004. *The Anarchist in the Library: How the Clash between Freedom and Control Is Hacking the Real World and Crashing the System.* New York: Basic Books.

ADDITIONAL SOURCE

Hofstadter, Douglas R. 1997. *Le Ton beau de Marot: In Praise of the Music of Language.* New York: Basic Books.

Before you read this chapter, take a few minutes to write your own definition of information. Keep it handy to compare it with the definitions that you will find in this section.

Chapter 2

Fundamental Concepts of Information

Learning Guide

After reading this chapter, you should be able to

- understand and define the following terms:
  - information
  - information artifact
  - document
  - semiotics
- identify the significance of the following in terms of information:
  - Rosetta Stone
  - Unicode
  - SETI Project
  - Biometrics
- articulate the differences among symbols, data, information, and knowledge;
- explain the differences between information transmission on a purely technical level and information transmission on a semantic level and identify the types of interference that may occur in each;
- distinguish between "information" and the medium that carries information or the "information record."

When you have finished the chapter, return to this page to be sure you have learned what you need to know.

INTRODUCTION

Information is a term that has become ubiquitous in today's society. It is encountered so frequently that one usually does not stop to question how it is defined. As with many terms that have more precise technical meanings in specific settings, the meaning of "information" in everyday parlance is assumed to be understood. However, information as a concept is found in a number of disciplinary contexts and is part of the theoretical structure of a variety of fields:

- communication theory, in both the technical aspects and in the study of communication among humans
- cybernetics, in the mathematically based study of feedback and its relationship to information system performance
- computer science
- physics, in the study of waves
- chemistry, in the structure and function of chemical molecules and in the study of use of chemical reactions in processing information
- biology, in the activity of neurons
- psychology, in the study of cognitive functions

The use of the term in many of these fields is relatively recent, dating from the 1950s.

Information and information activity are not associated just with humans, which is how we usually think of it. Our focus is primarily information as related to humans and human behavior, but we should always keep in mind the broader contexts of the term.

LEVELS AND FORMS OF INFORMATION

The precise definition of information used within various disciplines will help hone our intuitive understanding of what information is. However, before considering the various definitions of information, we need to consider the differences among several related terms, which can be thought of as designating different levels of related concepts. These are often described in a hierarchy and visually portrayed as a pyramid (see figure 2-1).

At the base of the pyramid are representational *symbols*: letters, numerals, other codes, such as signs.

At the next level are *data*, which are combinations of the symbols put together according to rules or conventions. In ancient civilizations—and not so ancient—these conventions often were understood only by an elite body. In modern times, most codes and data are open (e.g., the alphabet, the number system) and accessible, but not necessarily understood and used by all. How-

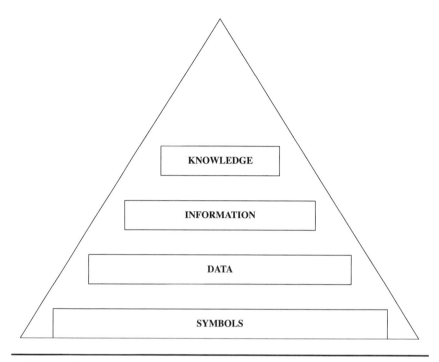

Figure 2-1 Information Pyramid

ever, understanding of the codes for symbol combination is critical in access to information. We call this understanding by the term "literacy." Data are our way of representing observed facts.

The next level is *information*, which is aggregated data, which become information when processed by the human mind. If the data do not change the knowledge state of the individual, they remain at the data level, i.e., data only become information when they are processed.

In understanding these concepts, a critical distinction that needs to be made is in the difference between "information" and the "information record." Information and its carrier or surrogate in form of symbols in some medium—paper, disc, etc.—are not the same thing. Allan Pratt uses the term "informative artifact" to describe this graphic record (Pratt, 1998: 28). These two concepts, "information" and the "information record," are often confused in our everyday usage, but they are different and have different properties. For example, information can be both retained and given away. One cannot do that with the physical surrogate without creating a second physical manifestation. Information does not necessarily diminish in value through use, but the information record may.

There is some controversy about what actually constitutes an "information record" or a "document." Michael Buckland discusses these aspects and sheds light on the issue. Are objects "documents" if we get information by observing them? The French documentalist, Suzanne Briet, distinguished the concept along the lines of whether an object is perceived of or intended as an information source and used the example of an antelope in the wild as contrasted to an antelope in the zoo. Briet drew a significant distinction between the antelope in the zoo and the one in the wild. The reason for an antelope in the zoo was for scientific, educational, or entertainment purposes. The animal in the wild was not *placed* there for any of those reasons; and from the perspective of documentation, its observation is to be considered *different*. Thus, not only is the *what* important (content) to understanding but also the *why* (context). Paul Otlet called these information sources three-dimensional documents (Briet cited in Buckland, 1997: 806; Otlet quoted in Buckland, 1997: 807).

The next level in our hierarchy of related concepts is *knowledge*, which is assimilated information. A possible way of thinking of the relationships among the terms is the following:

> Facts are processed into data, *which are processed into information.* INFORMATION IS INTEGRATED INTO KNOWLEDGE.

Knowledge, then, is what is used for used for decisions (Hayes, 1992: 270).

DEFINITIONS OF INFORMATION

There are difficulties with defining information, somewhat related to the difficulties of separating information from the concept of the "information record." We can describe the properties, effects, and behavior of information, which is pervasive in our lives.

Examples of Definitions

Definitions of information are sometimes either content or context specific. For example, information in the context of libraries traditionally has referred to or been defined as the collection. In banks, information would be the accounts held in the banks or would be other financial data. In the medical field, information may be thought of as readings from the human body as recorded by a variety of sophisticated instruments. Before proceeding to the next section, take a few minutes to think of (and perhaps make some notes about) definitions of information that you may have encountered in your reading and compare them with your own personal definition of information that you wrote as you began this chapter. Then go ahead and examine the examples of definitions of information given below.

Marc Porat defines information as
— "Information is data that have been organized and communicated" (Porat, 1977: 2).
Richard Derr, drawing on the work of theorists such as Warren Weaver and Claude Shannon, defines information as
— "a record of resolved uncertainty" (Derr, 1985: 498).
William Paisley's definition:
— "Information denotes any stimulus that alters cognitive structure in the receiver."
> Paisley goes on to say that something the receiver already knows is not information (Paisley quoted in Hayes, 1992: 272). This is an idea that we will encounter again.
The International Standards Organization's definition:
— "The meaning that a human assigns to data by means of the human conventions used in their representation" (Theiss, 1983: 88).
Debons, Horne, and Cronenweth:
— "The cognitive state of awareness (as being informed) given representation in physical form (data). This physical representation facilitates the process of knowing" (Debons, Horne, and Cronenweth, 1988: 8).

Sometimes information is defined in terms of how the information is represented, as in a computer record, memo, book or other form of document, microform, pictorial product, recording, etc. This approach, however, confuses representation of information with information.

Most of these definitions are based on the concept of information as a property that can reside in some transmission medium, be it a paper document, a set of electronic signals, or an oral message. An alternative way to consider information, one put forward by Allan Pratt in *Information of the Image*, is that information is a process that occurs that shapes our inward images. Thus the shaping that takes place is dependent on the current shape of the image and each "informative event," to use another term from Pratt, is different, even though it may have been occasioned by the same "informative artifact" (Pratt, 1998: 28).

Additional Aspects to Consider

There are several questions that considering information as a process or as an event leads to, which have been posed by the writer S. D. Neill in *Dilemmas in the Study of Information: Exploring the Boundaries of Information Science*.

- Does information exist external to or outside of the human mind?
- Does it somehow reside in the symbols (the graphic record) but become useful only when interpreted by the mind?
- What is the match between information (assuming it exists) and the reality (assuming that exists) it represents?
- Is there something external to the mind that the mind then does something with? (Neill, 1992: 5, 6, 9)

CHARACTERISTICS OF INFORMATION

Regardless of whether we think of information as an event, a process, or a commodity, as external and existing or not, information can be described as having certain characteristics.

- Information may be good or bad, correct or incorrect.
    - Data may be correct but incomplete, thus providing bad or misleading information.
    - Data may be correct but not useful in resolving a state of uncertainty, so are not good information.
    - Data may be accurate and of high quality but of a volume too large to be processed, so they do not provide "good" information.
    - Data may be accurate, of high quality, of appropriate volume so they can be processed into information and resolve an uncertainty but be thought of as "bad" because of the nature of that resolution.
- Information may be complete/incomplete, perfect/imperfect.
    - Information that we use is usually incomplete information. Decisions are made on the basis of imperfect information, but even the nature and extent of that imperfection is not known until later. The degree of "incompleteness" or "imperfection" depends on the individual and the individual's previous knowledge state.

INFORMATION AS PROCESS

To further consider information as a process that occurs, we need to look more closely at the way that information transfer happens. Information transfer can be defined as a "sequence of events leading to a transmission of information from a source to a destination" (Cleveland, 1992). The information transfer process or communication process has three key elements:

Source————Channel————Destination

The source may be an individual, a group, an institution, a government, or some other originating entity. The source puts the message into a form that can be received at the destination. The diagram oversimplifies what happens but illustrates the key elements.

Using the Pratt definition, there will be variation in the information event from person to person, even though the data transmitted are the same. The Vickery model of information transfer better illustrates this approach to information transfer.

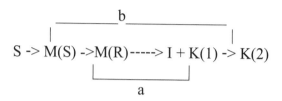

Figure 2-2   Vickery Information Transfer Model

Source: Adapted from Vickery, Brian, and Alina Vickery. Information Science in Theory and Practice, 42. Rev. ed. London: Bowker-Saur, 1992. © K. G. Saur Verlag, Munich. Used with permission.

In this diagram, S = the source of the message; $M(S)$ = the message sent; $\rightarrow$ = the channel through which the message is transmitted; $M(R)$ = the message that is received; I = the information extracted from the message, which changes the initial internal knowledge state $K(1)$ of the individual to $K(2)$. I, the information extracted, is dependent on both $M(R)$, the message that is received, and $K(1)$, the initial state of knowledge of the individual. The lower feedback loop (a) indicates that the channel may be adjusted to try to change any disparities between $M(S)$, the message sent, and $M(R)$, the message received. The upper loop (b) indicates feedback that tries to change the message sent $M(S)$.

There are other complexities in this process:

- Other competing messages may conflict with the message.
- The receiver needs to verify if what was received was what was sent.
- The channel—the medium or carrier of the message—may distort or lose information due to
    - technical problems;
    - social/psychological interference (interaction between the channel and the receiver);
    - ideological or political intervention in the channel.

For example, if there is static that disrupts a radio signal, the M(R) may not be identical to M(S). If the message is sent through a channel subject to governmental censorship, the M(R)—if it comes through at all—may not match the M(S).

Feedback may be

- positive: the message satisfied the information need
- negative: the message was inadequate to meet the information need

When the feedback is negative there may be a need to adjust the process so that the information (message) sent equals the information (message) received. The Vickerys indicate this happening in two ways:

1. change the relationship between M(S) and M(R) by changing something in the channel, e.g., increase volume
2. change the message sent, e.g., effect a change in the originator of the message (Vickery and Vickery, 1992: 41–42)

Feedback of type (2) is not always immediate and direct and depends on the distance between the sender and the receiver, on the channel, and on the nature of the message form. If the message was sent from one source to many recipients, the feedback to adjust the message is slower and more complicated. For example, feedback in a political situation, where the message sent is a political message, may take the form of opinion polls or votes. Where the message is an advertising message, the feedback can take the form of sales. On the other hand, if the message is from one source to one receiver, the feedback can be both immediate and direct, as in a personal conversation, when the individual receiving the message says, "I don't understand," and the source then restates the message in a different way.

The study of transmission of messages can be done on three levels:

- **technical level** (as in the work of Claude Shannon)

  This approach considers the physical transfer of symbols or the syntactic level (see Wigand, Picot, and Reichwald, 1997: 60) and asks questions about accuracy of transfer and disturbance in the channel.
- **semantic level** (Wigand, Picot, and Reichwald, 1997: 60)

  This approach asks, what is the meaning of the message? Was the meaning of the message received what the sender intended? If the sender and receiver are from different cultures, there could be very different use and interpretations of the same symbols. Differences in interpretations of the same symbols are particularly problematic when dealing with metamessages, as described in Deborah Tannen's work in use of metamessages in communication (Tannen, 1990). In some cases, it may not be possible to change the knowledge state of the receiver if there is too much difference in the way the symbols are used.

- **influential/pragmatic level** (as described in Wigand, Picot, and Reichwald, 1997: 60–61)

    This level considers the reaction of the receiver and the results of the message, and asks what the effect of the message was.

To look at these levels in application, consider again the Vickery model. At the technical level, we are concerned with whether the message sent is the same as the message received, or whether something interfered with the sending of the message to distort it. For example, in a cell phone conversation, the sounds received may have blips in the words that were not there in the spoken voice that originated the message. At the semantic level, an example may be seen in the confusion over a university administration promulgated dress code, which prohibited wearing thongs. The cultural gap between the administration, or sender of the message, and the intended receivers, the students, yielded quite different interpretations of the meaning of the message. Whereas the administration intended to reference a kind of footwear, students interpreted the symbols "thongs" to reference undergarments. At the pragmatic level, students questioned how the prohibition—the intended effect—could be enforced.

INFORMATION THEORY

Information theory as developed by Claude Shannon and others is concerned primarily with the engineering challenge of moving a signal, or, if you will, a message, from point A to point B. Shannon's signal contribution, first developed in his 1948 paper, "A Mathematical Theory of Communication," is concerned with noise and noise interference with information transmission. Information theory, let us stress, is not concerned with the content of the signal but with its integrity, that is, whether the signal remains unchanged in the transfer process. By improving signal integrity, Shannon recognized, uncertainty is reduced.

What does this mean and what is its application for analog and digital transmissions? Shannon recognized that for information transmission, the *how* of the transmission was everything and the *what* irrelevant. He was first to recognize that a binary signal (zeros and ones, on and off) could be used to encode anything. If indeed we can use binary, that is, digital code, to transmit information, it is easier to reduce system noise and maintain the integrity of the signal than with an analog wave.

Shannon's work has since been elaborated upon. In 1953, the Shannon-McMillan Theorem was elaborated to determine probabilities of string length (McMillan, 1953). The Kolmogorov complexity, an axiom of compression theory, is concerned with minimum code word length. Later work further elaborated compression theory and multiple sources (Slepian and Wolf, 1973; Ziv and Lempel, 1977).

Figure 2-3 is a very simplified "Shannon" model. The sender transmits to the receiver a message consisting of a binary code. The distance between sender and receiver is in some ways irrelevant, although distance itself can be considered as a source of noise. Distance is noise when and if signal degradation is a function of the distance between sender and receiver. There are certainly many other potential noise sources, including static. Consider what happens when you are watching television during a thunderstorm. Each time there is a lightening strike, the picture is distorted. That distortion is noise. If the receiver is sufficiently sensitive or if some form of signal enhancement is built into the system, signal quality may not be lost.

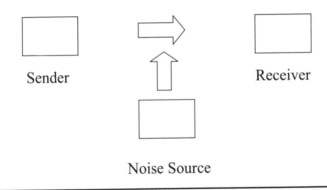

Sender   Receiver

Noise Source

Figure 2-3   Shannon Model of Information Transmission

Why then is digital better than analog for signal maintenance? Consider figures 2-4 and 2-5. If, over time or distance, an analog signal degrades, it is not possible to extrapolate the degraded wave back to the original signal.

Digital signals, on the other hand, are on or off. If a degraded signal passes through an enhancement point, a repeater, that degraded signal can be enhanced back to its original strength.

PERCEPTIONS OF INFORMATION

What is perceived as information and how it is perceived is related to the discipline in which one is operating. For example, in a biological model,

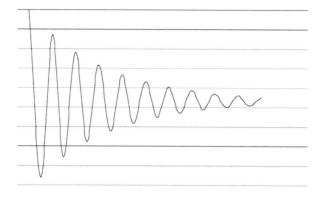

Figure 2-4   Analog Signals

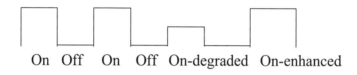

On   Off   On   Off   On-degraded   On-enhanced

Figure 2-5   Digital Signals

DNA is the basic information unit, the building block of the information system in living organisms. Genetic messages are sent (information transfer occurs) to provide instructions to build the organism. In the legal environment, information is perceived as property. In economics, information is perceived as a commodity. In philosophy, information is perceived as what can be known.

Perceptions of information by the individual are unique. For some theorists, like Brenda Dervin, information is a personal construct, i.e., it does not exist in the abstract. Dervin considers information to be "subjectively constructed" and part of personal sensemaking (Dervin, 1992). Considered this way, individuals are in a constant state of change: as we incorporate new information, our state of information changes, so we are constantly altering our "internal image" that Pratt talks about. John Perry Barlow discusses information as a relationship between the sender and the receiver, with each interchange being unique (Barlow, 1994: 15). His perception of information is as action existing in time, rather than something existing in physical space, and existing only in the time in which it is moving.

LINGUISTIC AND BIOLOGICAL APPROACHES TO INFORMATION

The influence of the context, and particularly of the discipline, in which information is perceived can be illustrated by examining some of the approaches to information taken in linguistics and in biology.

Memetics

Memetics is defined as the "theoretical and empirical science that studies the replication, spread and evolution of memes." The *meme* is defined as "an information pattern, held in an individual's memory, which is capable of being copied to another individual's memory" (Heylighen, 2001). Memes and genes are conceived as related concepts; one is the carrier of cultural traits while the other is the carrier of biological traits (Bonner, 1980). Meme transmission can be vastly more rapid than gene transmission, but it is also vastly more imprecise and fuzzy (Moritz, 1995).

In the information era, or what some now term the *digital era*, these self-contained knowledge units or memes (Dawkins, 1976) are disseminated at ever greater speeds and are therefore incorporated vertically and horizontally intra- and inter-culturally again ever more rapidly. Rapid meme change may be culturally destabilizing (Shepherd, 2004: 3). Differential rates of meme transmission and absorption may explain "different types and rates of socio-techno-economic transformation across the globe" (Shepherd, 2004: 3).

Memetics theory, sometimes referred to as mind virus, offers one explanation for the digital divide and varying rates of technological adaptation and use.

Semiotics

Semiotics is defined as the science of the understanding of the meaning of signs, or more particularly the meaning of signs as representations or icons of social life and behavior. Semiotics underlies linguistics, which in turn contributes substantially to information (see Saussure et al., 1983). Semiotic theory has been applied in a number of venues, from social anthropology (Claude Lévi-Strauss) and psychoanalysis (Jacques Lacan) to cultural studies (Roland Barthes). Umberto Eco (1976: 7) offers perhaps the broadest of definitions: "semiotics is concerned with everything that can be taken as a sign."

Signs and sign systems, then, are combined to form meaning. How we structure these signs is part of a larger discipline, linguistics. Linguistics is concerned not only with semiotics, but also with *semantics, syntactics,* and *pragmatics* (Morris, 1938). Morris defined semantics as the relationship of signs to what they represent, syntactics as the formal structures among signs, and pragmatics as the interplay between signs and their interpreters.

Information Ideas

Architecture and Location as Information Symbols

We use symbols and signs in a variety of ways. The Casa Rosada, or "Pink House," is the office of the President of Argentina in the Plaza de Mayo in Buenos Aires. Both the Casa Rosada and the Plaza de Mayo have many symbols of state associated with them.

Figure 2-6   Casa Rosada

(*Continued on p. 28*)

> The building is called the Casa Rosada because it is indeed painted a shade of pink, having been first painted that hue in the 1870s to celebrate the consolidation of two major political parties, the Federal party and the Unitarian party, whose colors were red and white respectively.
>
> The Plaza de Mayo likewise has symbolic importance. It commemorates Argentina's establishment of autonomous government following the revolution beginning 25 May 1810. More recently the Madres de la Plaza de Mayo (the mothers of the Plaza de Mayo) and now the Abuelas (grandmothers) led protests against the government of that day seeking information about the *desaparecidos*, their children and grandchildren who disappeared following the military coup d'etat and subsequent rule from 1976 to 1983. The Abuelas still stand watch in front of the Casa Rosada.
>
> Note that in the photograph there are two flags flying from the central flagstaff, both Argentine flags. The smaller, lower flag is a signal that the president is in residence. When he is away from the building, that flag is lowered.

SYMBOLS

Semioticians generally base their analyses on a *text*. Text is defined as a collection of signs. Text may be conveyed through a variety of general (e.g., TV, radio, books) or personal (conversation, e-mail, letters) communications media or *genre*. The channels may matter to meaning (Nöth, 1990).

Consider the sign meaning of the plaque that accompanied Pioneer 10 when it was launched into deep space by NASA in 1972 (see figure 2-7).

The human figures have been criticized as misrepresenting humankind. Why? Both appear more "white" than other races. The male figure, with arm raised, seems more outgoing in his greeting while the female figure seems more reticent. Or is that an interpretation of semiotic signs based upon an essentially Western orientation? What might we make of their hairstyles? The lack of body hair? What does it say about our culture to send such information into space in the first place? That we send it is a form of communication; that we are willing to send it, another perhaps more profound message.

The psychoanalyst Carl Jung theorized that human beings share a common symbol set or *archetypes of the collective unconscious*. The archetypical symbols are universally or almost universally recognized as laden with strong meaning. Moreover, we manifest certain behaviors—signs—based upon the roles we have assumed or have had thrust upon us: parson, cobbler, vicar's wife. Some of our archetypical behaviors are gender or sexually determined, others are deeper and are inherent in our basic humanness. Jung found that some symbols are universal, for example, star shapes and the cross and its variant, the swastika. Our response or reaction to the swastika has always been a

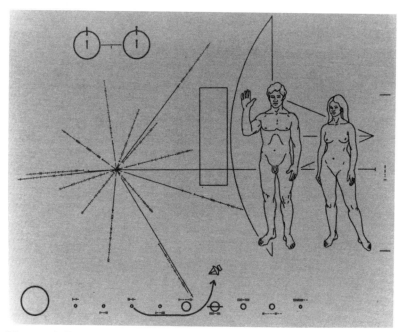

Figure 2-7   Pioneer 10 Plaque

Source: U.S. National Aeronautics and Space Administration. SpaceLink. "Pioneer 10 and 11 Missions." Available: www.nasa.gov/centers/ames/images/content/72418main_plaque.jpg. For further information, see www.nasa.gov/centers/ames/news/releases/2001/01images/Pioneer10/pioneer 10.html (accessed December 2006).

strong one. But it is only in recent years, since the 1930s when it was adopted by the Nazis in Germany as their symbol, that the general *Western* response has been a strong negative one. All cultures have yin and yang, good and evil symbols, often intertwined in some fashion.

Semiotics, whether culturally derived or inherent, influences the how, the where, and the why we communicate. The discipline has been applied widely to understand mass media (Bignell, 1997) and to the evolution of language (Fonagy, 2001). How we dress, speak, eat, interact all have a basis in semiotics and all are forms of information transfer.

UNICODE

A critical aspect of information transfer is the ability to translate information from one system of coding to another, which requires devices that make such conversion possible. The best-known historic instrument enabling such translation is the Rosetta Stone, uncovered in Egypt in July 1799 by Napoleon's army. It has the same text written in three languages: Egyptian hieroglyphs,

Demotic, and Greek. In 1822, Jean François Champollion, a French linguist and scholar, was able to use the Rosetta Stone to develop a dictionary to decipher hieroglyphs, theretofore unreadable in the modern era.

A modern counterpart of the Rosetta Stone is Unicode 4.0.0, published in August 2003, which supports more than 96,000 characters across more than fifty-five writing systems or scripts (see www.unicode.org/versions/Unicode 4.0.0).

The Script Encoding Initiative of the Department of Linguistics at the University of California at Berkeley was developed to promote broadening of Unicode across "non-popular" and "non-economic" alphabets (Erard, 2003). There are some eighty scripts currently in use that have yet to be encoded and an unknown number of historic or "dead" scripts that could be incorporated. According to the Script Encoding Initiative Web site, scripts as yet not encoded include "Balinese, Batak, Chakma, Cham, Fraser, Meithei Mayek, New Tai Lu, N'Ko, Pahawh Hmong, Pollard, Syloti Nagri, Tifinagh, and Vai. Scripts of historical significance include Aramaic, Avestan, Brahmi, Egyptian Hieroglyphics, Javanese, Kitan, Lanna, Lepcha, Old Permic, Pahlavi, 'Phags-pa, Phoenician, South Arabian, and Tangut" (University of California, 2006).

Efforts like the Script Encoding Initiative are important if universal translators, thesauri, crosswalks, or linguistic maps are to be built or if these languages are to be used at all in the digital era. Much of the development of Unicode has been underwritten by major corporations that see economic and commercial benefits to a standard digital code for the world's major languages but perceive little such advantage for the minor languages. As a result, a variation on the digital divide has emerged, one casting the lesser-used languages at a digital disadvantage to the more commonly used.

THE NEW "ROSETTA STONE"

The Rosetta Project (www.rosettaproject.org) was initiated by the Long Now Foundation to provide documentation for 1,000 of the world's some 7,000 "living languages" and has since been expanded to include 4000 languages. The Project's purpose is:

- to create an unprecedented platform for comparative linguistic research and education
- to develop and widely distribute a functional linguistic tool that might help with the recovery of lost or compromised languages in unknown futures
- to offer an aesthetic object that suggests the immense diversity of human languages as well as the very real threats to the continued survival of this diversity (Long Now Foundation, n.d.)

Figure 2-8   Rosetta Disk
Source: Rolfe Horn, courtesy of The Long Now Foundation. Used with permission.

The Rosetta Project has produced the "Rosetta Disk," print, and online media to archive key elements of its chosen languages. These resources have been distributed to interested individuals and institutions to promote language preservation and archiving. The Rosetta Project goal "is an open source 'Linux of Linguistics'—an effort of collaborative online scholarship drawing on the expertise and contributions of thousands of academic specialists and native speakers around the world" (Long Now Foundation, n.d.). A copy of the Rosetta Disk was included on the European Space Agency Rosetta comet probe, launched in February 2004 (see www.esa.int/export/SPECIALS/Rosetta).

THE SETI PROJECT

We are not only purposefully sending information into the galaxy about ourselves, as was done on Pioneer 11 and 12. We are also looking for evidence of intelligence in the universe, trying to determine if "information" or, more precisely, some form of information artifact is being transmitted from beyond earthly bounds. The Search for Extraterrestrial Intelligence Project at the University of California at Berkeley was designed to try to find evidence of extraterrestrial life. It does so by analyzing radio astronomy signals captured by astronomers. To date, the SETI Project has not identified any signals that are certain evidence of extraterrestrial life; but, it has identified a number of possible candidates. These candidates are further investigated using the Arecibo radio telescope in Puerto Rico.

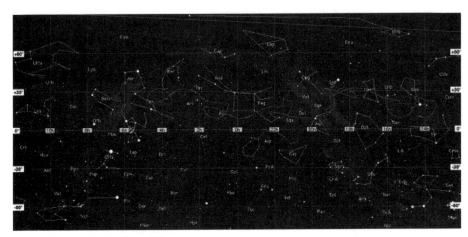

Figure 2-9   Sky Map
Source: SETI Project. Used by permission. Copyright by the SETI@home project, U.C. Berkeley.

SETI@home is an innovative way that the SETI Project has employed to analyze a very large data collection. Individuals subscribe to the Project who then make available to the Project their personal computers for data analysis. Raw data are sent to these computers and analyzed data returned to the Project over the Internet. The SETI Project's software examines the data for four different pattern types—Gaussian curves ("normal distribution" or "bell-shaped" curve), spikes, triplets, and pulses. The assumption is made that these regularities *may* represent evidence of intelligence and of agency. Thus extraterrestrial intelligence may employ a variety of regular signals that might also be detected and interpreted by another intelligence. For a discussion of how SETI defines signal candidates, see http://setiathome.berkeley.edu/sah_sci_newsletters.php?frag–news-13.inc.

Figure 2-9 represents the sky map produced by the SETI Project. The "cloudy" area represents the Milky Way. The small lines map constellations. The initials name the 88 "official" constellations. The "squiggly line" figure, running mostly through the center of the map, between 0° and 30° parallels, represents the area scanned by the Arecibo telescope. Further definition and a color version of the figure can be found at: http://setiathome.berkeley.edu/sah_glossary/images/skymap_sp_493.gif.

Biometrics

Biometrics represents identification systems for individuals based upon physical or biological characteristics. In a sense, biometric characteristics are "data" and only become "information" when we are able to identify their uniqueness, capture that uniqueness, and interpret it.

The use of biometrics for identification is as old as the concept of using physical characteristics for identification: appearance, gender, race, height, weight, coloring, voice characteristics, and so on. Finger- or palm prints were used in China in the third century BCE and in Persia as late as the fourteenth century as a means to sign documents. It was not until 1856, when an English magistrate in India, Sir William Hershel, began what started as a casual experiment, that fingerprinting—the first "captured" biometric—came into its own as a means for the absolute identification of individuals. Biometrics has now become far more sophisticated and includes facial thermograms, hand geometry, facial and ear characteristics, iris and pupil characteristics, palm prints, voice prints, gait, signature (Jain and Ross, 2004) as well as various genetic and DNA markers, not the least of which are blood and tissue typing. More recently "brain fingerprints" (Farwell and Smith, 2001) are being accepted as a form of lie detection.

Today, biometrics is a widely studied field with practical applications in identification and security technologies. The National Institute of Standards and Technology and other U.S. federal agencies conduct and support research in the field (U.S. National Institute of Standards and Technology, n.d.).

CONCLUSION

With these concepts to "inform" us, our personal understandings of what information is may begin to alter; and we begin to understand the extraordinary challenge faced in providing ways for others to access and use information. As this text continues, the use of the term "information" will not always be as precise as the definitions and distinctions made in this chapter. However, it will be important to note, as you continue reading, if it is really "information," as contrasted to "data" or "information record or container," that is the subject of the discussion.

QUESTIONS FOR CONSIDERATION

1. Can one have knowledge without having interacted with an information record? If you answer yes, explain how. If you answer no, then explain why not.
2. How can good data fail to lead to good information? What are specific examples where good data might fail to produce good information?

3. If you read the book, *The World Is Flat*, by Thomas L. Friedman, and then your best friend read the book, would the information the two of you received be the same? Why or why not? If you read that same book when it was originally published in 2005 and then reread it again this week, would the information be the same?
4. When is a car a document?
5. Language is one of the systems used by society to assist in transfer of information from one person to another. What are other systems or means of assisting in such transfer that you use on a regular basis?

REFERENCES

Barlow, John Perry. 1994. "A Taxonomy of Information." *Bulletin of the American Society for Information Science* 20 (June/July): 13–17.

Bignell, Jonathan. 1997. *Media Semiotics: An Introduction.* Manchester, UK: Manchester University Press.

Bonner, John T. 1980. *The Evolution of Culture in Animals.* Princeton, NJ: Princeton University Press.

Briet, Suzanne. 1997. *Qu est-ce que la documentation.* Paris: EDIT, 7–8. Quoted in Michael K. Buckland, "What Is a 'Document'?" *Journal of the American Society for Information Science* 48 (September): 806.

Buckland, Michael K. 1997. "What Is a 'Document'?" *Journal of the American Society for Information Science* 48 (September): 804–809.

Cleveland, Donald B. 1992. Lecture in LIS 5000, Foundations of Library and Information Science. Denton, TX: University of North Texas.

Dawkins, Richard. 1976. *The Selfish Gene.* Oxford: Oxford University Press.

Debons, Anthony, Esther Horne, and Scott Cronenweth. 1988. *Information Science: An Integrated View.* Boston, MA: G. K. Hall.

Derr, Richard L. 1985. "The Concept of Information in Ordinary Discourse." *Information Processing & Management* 21: 489–99.

Dervin, Brenda. 1992. "From the Mind's Eye of the User: The Sense-making Qualitative-Quantitative Methodology." In *Qualitative Research in Information Management*, edited by Jack D. Glazier and Ronald R. Powell, 61–84. Englewood, CO: Libraries Unlimited.

Eco, Umberto. 1976. *A Theory of Semiotics.* Bloomington, IN: Indiana University Press.

Erard, Michael. 2003. "Computers Learn New ABCs." *Technology Review* (September): 28. Available: www.technologyreview.com/read_article.aspx?id=13277&ch=infotech (accessed December 2006).

Farwell, Lawrence A., and Sharon S. Smith. 2001. "Using Brain MERMER

Testing to Detect Concealed Knowledge Despite Efforts to Conceal." *Journal of Forensic Sciences* 46 (January): 135–143.

Fonagy, Ivan. 2001. *Languages within Language: An Evolutive Approach.* Amstersdam: John Benjamins.

Hayes, Robert M. 1992. "Measurement of Information." In *Conceptions of Library and Information Science: Historical, Empirical, and Theoretical Perspectives,* edited by Pertti Vakkari and Blaise Cronin, 268–285. London: Taylor Graham.

Heylighen, Francis. 2001. "Memetics." *Principia Cybernetica Web.* Available: http://pespmc1.vub.ac.be/MEMES.html (accessed December 2006).

Jain, Anil, and Arun Ross. 2004. "Multibiometric Systems." *Communications of the ACM* 47 (January): 34–40.

Long Now Foundation. *The Rosetta Project.* Available: http://web.archive.org/web/20050208051240/http://www.rosettaproject.org/live/concept (accessed December 2006).

McMillan, Brockway. 1993. "The Basic Theorems of Information Theory." *Annals of Mathematical Statistics* 24: 196–219.

Moritz, Elan. 1995. "Metasystems, Memes and Cybernetic Immortality." In *The Quantum of Evolution: Toward a Theory of Metasystem Transitions,* edited by Francis Heylighen, Cliff Joslyn, and Valentin Turchin, 155–171. Special issue of *World Futures: The Journal of General Evolution* 45: 1–4. New York: Gordon and Breach.

Morris, Charles W. 1938. *Foundations of the Theory of Signs.* Chicago: University of Chicago Press.

Neill, Samuel D. 1992. *Dilemmas in the Study of Information: Exploring the Boundaries of Information Science.* New York: Greenwood.

Nöth, Winifried. 1990. *Handbook of Semiotics.* Bloomington, IN: Indiana University Press.

Otlet, Paul. 1997. *L'organisation internationale de la bibliographie et de la documentation.* IIB publ. 128. Brussels: Institut International de Bibliographie. Translated in *International Organization and Dissemination of Knowledge: Selected Essays.* FID 684, 197. Amsterdam: Elsevier, 173–203. Quoted in Michael K. Buckland, "What Is a 'Document'?" *Journal of the American Society for Information Science* 48 (September): 807.

Paisley, William. 1992. "Information and Work." In *Progress in Communication Sciences,* edited by Brenda Dervin and Melvin J. Voigt, 2 (1980): 118. Quoted in Robert M. Hayes, "Measurement of Information," 272. In *Conceptions of Library and Information Science: Historical, Empirical, and Theoretical Perspectives,* edited by Pertti Vakkari and Blaise Cronin, 268–285. London: Taylor Graham.

Porat, Marc Uri. 1977. *The Information Economy: Definition and Measurement.* Washington, DC: U.S. Department of Commerce, Office of Telecommunications.

Pratt, Allan D. 1998. *Information of the Image*, 2nd ed. Greenwich, CT: Ablex.

Rosetta Project. Available: www.rosettaproject.org (accessed December 2006).

Saussure, Ferdinand de, Charles Bally, Albert Sechehaye, and Albert Riedlinger. 1983. *Course in General Linguistics.* Translated by Roy Harris. London: Duckworth.

Shannon, Claude E. 1948. "A Mathematical Theory of Communication." *Bell System Technical Journal* 27 (July, October): 379–423; 623–656.

Shepherd, Jill. 2004. "Why the Digital Era?" In *Social and Economic Transformation in the Digital Era*, edited by Georgios I. Doukidis, Nikolaos Mylonopoulos, and Nancy Pouloudi, 1–18. Hershey, PA: Idea Group Publishing.

Slepian, David S., and Jack K. Wolf. 1973. "Noiseless Coding of Correlated Information Sources." *IEEE Transactions on Information Theory* 19 (July): 471–480.

Tannen, Deborah. 1990. *You Just Don't Understand: Women and Men in Conversation.* New York: Morrow.

Theiss, Helmut. 1983. "On Terminology." In *Information Science in Action: System Design*, edited by Anthony Debons and Arvid G. Larson, vol. 1, 84–94. The Hague: Martinus Nijhoff.

Unicode Consortium. 2006. The Unicode Standard, Version 4.0.0, defined by: *The Unicode Standard, Version 4.0* (Boston, MA: Addison-Wesley, 2003). Available: www.unicode.org/versions/Unicode4.0.0 (accessed December 2006).

United States National Institute of Standards and Technology. Information Technology Laboratory. *The Biometrics Resource Center Website.* Available: www.itl.nist.gov/div893/biometrics (accessed December 2006).

University of California. 2006. *SETI@Home.* Available: http://setiathome .berkeley.edu (accessed December 2006).

———. Department of Linguistics. 2006. "Script Encoding Initiative." 12 April. Available: http://linguistics.berkeley.edu/~dwanders (accessed December 2006).

Vickery, Brian, and Alina Vickery. 1992. *Information Science in Theory and Practice.* Rev. ed. London: Bowker-Saur.

Wigand, Rolf, Arnold Picot, and Ralf Reichwald. 1997. *Information, Organization and Management: Expanding Markets and Corporate Boundaries.* Chichester, UK: John Wiley.

Ziv, Jacob, and Abraham Lempel. 1977. "A Universal Algorithm for Sequential Data Compression." *IEEE Transactions on Information Theory* 23 (May): 337–343.

ADDITIONAL SOURCES

Blackmore, Susan. 1999. *The Meme Machine*. Oxford: Oxford University Press.

Brodie, Richard. 1996. *Virus of the Mind: The New Science of the Meme*. Seattle: Integral Press.

Madden, A. D. 2000. "A Definition of Information." *Aslib Proceedings* 52 (October): 343–349.

Pierce, John R. 1980. *An Introduction to Information Theory: Symbols, Signals and Noise*. 2nd rev. ed. New York: Dover.

Reza, Fazlollah M. 1994. *An Introduction to Information Theory*. New York: Dover.

Think of the last time you needed information. How did you become aware that you had that need? How did you go about seeking the information? How did you feel about the process? How and when did you know to stop looking, that you had what was needed? Is your process of looking for information the same regardless of the context? Answers to questions like these are important in understanding your own information behavior and, by extension, that of others. This chapter explores some of the ways these questions have been answered.

Chapter 3

Information Needs and Information Seeking Behavior

Learning Guide

After reading this chapter, you should be able to

- understand and define the following terms:
  - information need
  - anomalous state of knowledge (ASK)
  - sense making
  - information encountering
  - Dewey Decimal Classification
  - Library of Congress Classification
  - chain indexing
  - pertinence
  - relevance
  - salience
  - recall
  - precision
- identify a key idea from each of the following information behavior theorists:
  - Robert Taylor
  - Nicholas Belkin
  - Brenda Dervin
  - Sanda Erdelez
  - Carol Kuhlthau
  - Charles Atkin
- discuss the relationship of information needs to other types of needs;
- explain the relationship of feelings to information behavior;
- discuss the ways in which information usefulness can be measured;
- identify and describe the various bases used to classify or categorize information.

When you have finished the chapter, return to this page to be sure you have learned what you need to know.

INTRODUCTION

The exploration of information needs and information seeking focuses primarily on the user of information and secondarily on the information intermediary, the agent (human or otherwise) that assists the user in obtaining the information sought. It is less concerned with questions of the how of information formation and transmission. This exploration has both theoretical and practical implications. Theories have been offered to explain the basic meaning of information; the reasons humans seek information; and the ways in which information is assimilated, retained, and applied. From a more applied perspective, we are interested in developing systems that facilitate the assimilation of information. For example, it has been posited that human beings learn in different ways—some of us are more verbal, visual, or aural learners than others. Some of us have learning disabilities that inhibit assimilation of information. From a practical perspective, are there information interfaces that make information use easier, more efficient, easier to retain, and so on? In recent years, various GUIs (graphical user interfaces) have been introduced. Likewise, new technology has made possible a wider variety of learning tools beyond the classroom lecture and the linear printed text, assisting and diversifying the ways by which the process of acquiring information skills occurs.

A whole literature has grown up around the concept of information needs and wants and the means by which individuals seek or look for that information. Donald Case (2002), for example, has written a very useful discussion, review, and critique of prevailing thought. As Case informs us, a great deal is implied by information needs and information seeking behaviors. When do we know we have an information need? How do we know when that need is satisfied or satisficed? What do we do when we identify an information need? Has technology changed the way we seek to meet our information needs and, if so, for the better or for the worse? We consciously and unconsciously assimilate information. Some information assimilation is purposeful, some accidental, and still other assimilation may be inborn or somehow genetically encoded. Kalvero Järvelin and Peter Ingwersen offer the following definition: "Information seeking has been understood as a process in which the actor's understanding of his or her tasks or problems, information needs, relevance criteria, and the available information space evolve" (Järvelin and Ingwersen, 2004).

Moreover, as Case (2002) traces for us, there has been a virtual explosion in theories and explanations of information, information needs, and information seeking over the past five decades. We suspect that the growth in these explanations and theories will not wane, at least in the near future, given the identified importance of "information" in our society and economy. The good news is that we have begun to understand the limits of our definitions and to revise and refine our understanding. Brenda Dervin perhaps led the way when she inquired into and rejected much of the informed opinion by exploring ten "dubious assumptions" about information and information seeking. These include such long-standing bromides as "more information is better" and "relevant information" exists to meet all needs (Dervin, 1976: 325–29). Both internal and external information needs and stimuli help form information seeking behaviors.

To put the questions in a somewhat different way: are information needs a fundamental human drive or are information needs surrogates for fundamental human needs? What do we want information for? Assuming that we understand our information needs, how do we satisfy those needs?

Can we enumerate our needs? Clearly there are basic needs. If these needs go unsatisfied, there are dire consequences. At a minimum, we require oxygen, water, food. Without these basic inputs the organism fails in minutes, days, or weeks. Beyond these needs, we require shelter from the elements, the company of others, exercise, and intellectual and physical stimulation. Human beings, it is said, have basic drives, including survival, reproduction, and recognition. Everything we do is concerned with meeting our basic needs and drives. Thomas D. Wilson, for example, suggests that information seeking might be described as part of a human stress/coping response (Wilson, 1997: 571), which implies that we look for information to help address situations in which our needs are not being met.

This need/drive model is inherently simplistic. Why do we have shelter needs? What shelter needs do we have? Part of the answer is survival, part of the answer is comfort, and part of the answer is status. In large part our shelter needs are a function of environment. People who live in very cold environments have different shelter needs from those who live in temperate places and different from those who live in hot places. Humidity and access to water and fuel matter. Hence, how we meet our shelter needs depends, at least in part, on context.

Information does not shelter us, clothe us, warm or cool us, or feed us. It does not transport us or nurse us. Information, however, provides us with the means to find ways to shelter us, clothe us, feed us, heal us, and so on. Or it may provide us with a rationale and strategy to acquire shelter, clothing, food, or alternatively to forego some or all of the above. Given that we have needs and information provides us with a means to meet those needs, how do we differ from any other organism? Deer, whales, earthworms, redwoods, and viruses all have survival needs, and all have developed strategies to meet those needs.

Let us assume for the sake of argument that Jean Auel's tale *The Clan of the Cave Bear* correctly distinguishes between the Neanderthal's inherent knowledge and the Cro-Magnon's reasoning and learning. It would appear that some behaviors are inherent. Babies cry; moreover, babies have different cries. The different cries communicate different needs, very few of which are information needs. Babies tell us when they are bored, hungry, in pain, and little else. Perhaps a boredom cry is an information request, but the other cries seek other inputs or actions.

Inherent or genetically encoded knowledge may offer certain advantages in some circumstances, but the ability to reason and think may offer advantages in others. Are people, pigeons, and pigs all hard wired, or do we have adaptive abilities that transcend heredity? If we have these adaptive abilities, information seeking and interpretative behaviors contribute to our survival skills, but they may also cloud inherent knowledge. That said, how should we address hormonally driven behaviors? Should we define adolescent hormonal surges as "information" by some definition? If we accept an inborn definition, the human maturation process might be considered "information." Or perhaps that is "data." How we interpret these behaviors, within the context of various social systems, then express those interpretations might be "information."

There is anecdotal evidence to suggest that mammals, including some human beings described as "primitive," respond to nature's signals to protect themselves from catastrophe. Those of us considered "advanced" either disregard primal signals as noise or come to rely on instrumentation to replace lost skills. For example, certain indigenous peoples and many animals were somehow alerted to the tsunami that devastated South Asia on 26 December 2004. Perhaps some animals are better able to detect very low frequency vibrations from earthquakes or disturbances on the oceans than other animals and human beings. Or perhaps modern and postmodern humans have lost the ability to "read" nature that once they had (Kenneally, 2005). Clearly the ability to sense danger is an information need that meets an important purpose—survival of the individual or group. Contemporary humans have come to rely on technology rather than their own innate senses to detect danger or to enhance quality of life. Thus, we develop tsunami warning systems, use computers, replace our legs and animals with motorized vehicles, and on and on. In most societies, we substitute ability to overtly seek and use information, supported by a plethora of information devices, for the unconscious reception and interpretation of information on which our early ancestors relied and on which our animal cousins still depend.

ENTERTAINMENT AS INFORMATION

If we accept that food, water, air, shelter, health, and reproduction are basic human needs, can we include entertainment in that list? An inordinate proportion of our time, resources, and gross domestic product are allocated to entertainment. Is "entertainment" "information"? If "entertainment" is not information, is there "infotainment"; and where does one draw the lines among information, entertainment, and infotainment?

The distinctions drawn between information and entertainment are artificial at worst and a matter of semantics and interpretation at best. Newspapers make for an interesting case study. There are significant exceptions (e.g., *New York Times, USA Today, Wall Street Journal*), but most American newspapers contain gossip columns, "funnies," and astrological predictions. These newspapers may also carry bridge and chess columns, crossword and other puzzles; entertaining, yes, but perhaps instructional as well. These newspapers also carry full sections for sports, advertisements, society, and other "not quite real news" elements. Not information? We think not. Even if we could subjectively distinguish between entertainment with and without information content, the decision of precisely where that line of demarcation lies would be arrogant. Perhaps to paraphrase freely, a little bit of entertainment helps the information go down. Following that metaphor, entertainment may also be therapeutic, particularly for the stressed or the bored (Zillmann and Bryant, 1985: 155); that is to say, entertainment may be viewed as medicine.

Play theorists relate information seeking and play behaviors. Play theory helps explain why we elect to seek information from one set of sources over another (see, for example, Dozier and Rice, 1984; Shepherd, Duffy, Watters, and Gugle, 2001). The *New York Times* is generally considered the newspaper of record in the United States, yet not even in New York City do a majority of residents subscribe to it. Why not? Perhaps because it carries no funnies. Consider, in addition, one's current choices of television news sources. The number of news shows has proliferated from the three network programs that broadcast no more than fifteen minutes in the 1950s to the 24-7-365 cable programming beginning with CNN and now MS-NBC, Fox News Network, and so on. Many of these around-the-clock programs have long since abdicated any sense of objectivity. Whatever their information value, these programs and newspapers have sought to increase the entertainment content and value of their offerings.

INFORMATION NEEDS

An extended discussion on the definition of information is provided in chapter 2 and not recapitulated here. As already indicated, the question for this chapter is whether, in fact, human beings have information needs; or, are "information needs" actually surrogates for more fundamental requirements? Like the definitions for information, the explanations given for information needs are equally varied and sometimes contradictory. As a consequence, explanations for information seeking, information needs, and information uses depend in large part on the basic premises one accepts. "Information" may include every intrinsic and extrinsic impulse, impressions, opinions, wishes and dreams, activities, and so on. If you feel hungry or tired, are you receiving information? Do you satisfy or satisfice those urges by acknowledging, telling someone, reading books about eating and sleeping, or by eating and sleeping?

Some psychologists suggest that human beings have an instinctive need to know, to seek information (for example, Miller, 1983; Maslow, 1963; Rokeach, 1960). Although we have suggested that what we perceive to be needs for information are more accurately quests to satisfy more primal needs, it may be that human beings and perhaps other organisms are hardwired to need to know. Taking this approach, the need for information could be interpreted as an inherent definition of life or, more specifically, of being human. For example, Bosman and Renckstorf (1996) posit three interrelated motivations for what might be described as information needs: social utility, instrumental utility, and intrinsic utility. Information needs have also been described as fluid, changing as one's state of information changes (Harter, 1992). Yet another perspective, from Bryce Allen (1996), informs us that information seeking may serve to gratify noninformational needs.

Perhaps the idea that information needs are inherent is too sweeping to be useful, or perhaps information needs have other antecedents. Among the first to address these issues, Robert Taylor theorizes that information needs form out of an unconscious or conscious but inchoate sense of dissatisfaction. This sense evolves into a "mental description" of need followed by a more formalized expression. It is finally formed into an articulated request conditioned by the expectation of results and of the competencies of the responder. Taylor's analysis is limited to the patron-information intermediary transaction in a library setting (Taylor, 1962). It does, however, provide insights into the development of the recognition and expression of an information need in other contexts.

Charles Atkin (1973) defines information need more in terms of the cognitive state arising between a state of uncertainty and the information seeker's knowledge state, externalities, and the new knowledge state desired. In sum, it is a function of uncertainty reduction. These externalities, termed "environmental objects," include both extrinsic and intrinsic objects—people, places, things, ideas, feelings, time. Knowledge seeking is prompted by the internal knowledge state, however imperfect; perceived variances between the belief state and the observed; and the wish to reduce the perceived variances if and until perfect knowledge is achieved.

Nicholas Belkin (1978) blended in a way the thinking of Taylor and Atkin. For Belkin, information need is a visceral state arising out of uncertainty. Information need is termed in this paradigm as an "anomalous state of knowledge," or to employ the useful acronym, as an "ASK." An ASK prompts information seeking behavior to reduce uncertainty. Reducing the ASK might be analogous to scratching an intellectual itch.

There must be more to information seeking behavior than scratching itches, however powerful those itches might be. Brenda Dervin (1989) interpreted information need as sense making. Not only does the information seeker have an itch, there must be some acceptable reasonableness to the scratch. Another key aspect of Dervin's approach to information needs is that the need is situational, that is, it occurs in a specific context, and that it is the situation or context that in large part determines both what information will satisfy the need and how the information will be sought. In fact, Dervin talks in terms of information being constructed rather than being sought and found.

Others have been critical of the set of information need explanations offered by Taylor, Atkin, Belkin, and Dervin. In order to "know" the information need of another, it is necessary to have access to the mind, the cognitive processes of the seeker. The state of the information science art does not allow us to literally peer into the minds of others—or even, for that matter, into ourselves. Wilson (1981, 1997) acknowledges information need but argues that we can only effectively describe behaviors. However, what have been described as information needs are more accurately behaviors. Moreover, what we describe as information needs are better described as other needs manifested through information seeking behavior. Information needs are generalized surrogates for a broad range of social, biological, and psychological needs.

INFORMATION SEEKING BEHAVIORS

As we have seen, there are many reasons and theories to define information and to explain why humans have information needs. The next step in the process is to explore how humans seek information and ascertain when their information needs have been met.

Explanations of information seeking behavior are varied, and different theories examine different strategies and approaches. These include decision theory, problem solving, intake strategies, information avoidance, information overload, research methods, and others. Books have been written about each of these approaches, and our description is necessarily cursory.

How do most of us seek information? As already suggested, environmental information surrounds us, and we constantly receive and process information.

We might call this state of awareness "unconscious information seeking." We are socialized and trained to process these environmental information inputs in a more or less effortless way. When we place ourselves in unfamiliar environments, we recognize dissonances in our unconscious information acquisition. For example, when the English or Japanese travel to continental Europe or North America, they must attune themselves to traffic traveling to the right. North Americans or continental Europeans must attune themselves to traffic on the left in Australia and Barbados. Different people with different needs are sensitive to different information inputs. Daniel Boone, out in the backwoods of Kentucky in the eighteenth century, was far more sensitive to animal sounds, the winds, rustle of leaves, and animal spoor than most urban denizens of the twenty-first century. How would Daniel Boone or Louis XIV react to the urban environment of Bangkok, Baltimore, or Buenos Aires? None too well, we suspect; they would not understand traffic signals, police whistles, or car horns, not to mention the wide array of other environmental information.

There are also informal and formal explicit information seeking techniques. Numerous studies have demonstrated that most of us, as a first effort, will turn to our families, our peers, and our presumed knowledgeable neighbors to help resolve information needs. Trips to a library or even opening the previously ubiquitous home encyclopedia are frequently distant on the strategy chain. The Internet has modified our seeking practices somewhat, with the search engine becoming an important ally in the search process.

Whatever our individual information seeking paths may be, it has been concluded that individuals tend to repeat those information seeking strategies at least until a particular strategy is shown as inefficient (Gantz, Fitzmaurice, and Fink, 1991). We may also turn to professionals to address our information needs. Teachers and librarians leap to mind. But we just as (or more) frequently seek other experts—lawyers, accountants, engineers, translators, consultants, and physicians, for example—to meet certain specific information needs.

Most information searching behavior is "unsophisticated." We often engage in browsing and that, in turn, sometimes results in serendipitous finds. Browsing for information is analogous to shopping. One moves up and down the stacks in the library, bookstore, or video shop. Because libraries and shops are organized along some principle, once we locate ourselves in the general section that interests us, we may find titles or products we did not know existed but which turn out to fulfill an information need. Or we may learn something by chance from a conversation or even eavesdropping. Sometimes serendipity will lead us to information finds in old trunks or by skimming through various tomes.

However, browsing may be intentional or unintentional. You may intentionally go to the video store to select a mystery film, and by browsing in the mystery section you might encounter something that fulfills the criterion "mystery film"; but it may be something you otherwise knew nothing of. Or you may be walking around in the mall, decide on a whim to enter the video store, turn left rather than right, and stumble into the same section and the same film. Sanda Erdelez (1997, 2005) has provided us with the useful concept of "information encountering" to study the ways in which these kinds of accidental information acquisitions occur. As she explains, some of us are more attuned to such acquisition than others—more highly developed "information encounterers," as it were.

Another important aspect to information seeking behavior that we need to examine briefly is how one feels about the process. Using the concept of uncertainty, Carol Kuhlthau (1993, 2005a) has helped us understand the affective aspects of searching for information, especially when the information is necessary to complete an assignment for school or work. As she explains, our feelings about the seeking activity change as we progress through the phases of the process, what she calls initiating, selecting, exploring, formulating, collecting, and presenting information (Kuhlthau, 1993: 343–44). Affectively we move from "uncertainty" through "optimism" to "confusion, frustration, doubt," on to "clarity" and "sense of direction/confidence," and finally to "relief" and "satisfaction or disappointment," depending on the outcome (Kuhlthau, 2005a: 231). How one feels about searching for information impacts how one does the looking. As Kuhlthau puts it, "[f]eelings of anxiety at the beginning of a search affect the choices one makes as do feelings of confidence in later stages" (Kuhlthau, 1993: 351).

Information Ideas

Where Shared Purpose Leads to Shared Information
A very useful and instructive concept related to information needs and information seeking behavior is the idea of an "information grounds," developed primarily by Karen Fisher (also writing initially as Karen Pettigrew) and her colleagues. The idea of the information grounds is that a space for exchange of information is formed when individuals gather for some specific purpose and construct "a social atmosphere that fosters the spontaneous and serendipitous sharing of information" (Pettigrew, 1999: 811). This sharing of information in such a setting is unplanned, primarily informal (although it can be formal), and occurs via the social interaction in a one-off kind of situation. The information grounds dissolves when the group disperses and, depending on the

(*Continued on p. 48*)

setting, may not exist again in exactly the same configuration. As Fisher (2005) notes, this kind of information sharing in such gatherings is not new, just newly identified as such.

Historically there have been many such "information grounds," some segregated by gender and others not. One could think of such gatherings as barn raisings, ladies' sewing circles, church "all day preaching and dinner on the grounds," and community Fourth of July picnics all as potentially "information grounds." In today's society, information grounds might exist among the mothers gathered at soccer practice, volunteers working at a political headquarters, and travelers on a cruise.

Awareness of such settings for information exchange has led in some states to targeted programs to get specific information to those who need it but are unlikely to have opportunity to get it. A clear example of this kind of program (although not related to the development of the "information grounds" research) is one training hairstylists to recognize signs of domestic abuse and provide information on assistance and shelters available to battered women. The beauty salon is one place that such women may be able to go to without monitoring and share information about their plight without fear of their situation being disclosed. Programs training hairstylists to provide information to these women have been launched in Virginia, Florida, and Idaho (Perlman, 2005).

Sources

Fisher, Karen E. 2005. "Information Grounds." In *Theories of Information Behavior*, edited by Karen E. Fisher, Sanda Erdelez, and Lynne (E. F.) McKechnie, 185–190. Medford, NJ: Information Today.

Nguyen, Dong-Phuong. 2004. "Hair Salons to Look for Domestic Violence." *St. Petersburg Times*, 24 March. Available: www.sptimes.com/2004/03/24/Tampabay/Hair_salons_to_look_f.shtml (accessed December 2006).

Perlman, Ellen. 2005. "Shop Talk: Training Beauticians to Direct Battered Women toward Help." *Government Magazine* (February). Available: www.ncdsv.org/images/ShopTalkTrainingBeauticians.pdf (accessed December 2006).

Pettigrew, Karen E. 1999. "Waiting for Chiropody: Contextual Results from an Ethnographic Study of the Information Behavior among Attendees at Community Clinics." *Information Processing & Management* 35: 801–817.

Information Organization

There is another side to studying information seeking behaviors, the examination of strategies to improve information storage and retrieval. Much of this approach addresses the "how" of information storage and retrieval for the lay and the expert user. Consider how information is organized in retail stores, warehouses, university and public libraries, or in a computer. Let us take a video rental store, perhaps Blockbuster, for example. How are the products arranged? Organization is usually by media (tape or disc), by genre (comedy, mystery, action, children, XXX, foreign language), and often by recent release or classic. How are the films organized within categories? They are most often organized in alphabetic order by title and sometimes by cast. The study of information seeking behavior in this and other contexts can provide direction in organizing information for storage and retrieval in ways that will better accommodate users' innate information seeking behavior as opposed to behavior that must be learned to accommodate the system. In this example, for instance, an alternative organizing principle could be alphabetic order by the name of the director or the producing studio. In some contexts, such as a collection of videos for faculty and students in a film school, that organization might better follow the information seeking behavior of the users, although for a video rental store it would be a poor choice.

It is generally recognized that there is a certain amount of method to browsing and serendipitous information seeking. As already suggested, information and products are almost always organized according to some principle. Department stores are called department stores because products are segregated by departments: one expects to find men's clothing in the men's clothing section, from underwear and socks to suits and ties. Blenders, coffeepots, and flatware belong in household goods, and so on. One would probably not begin searching for bras in menswear or spark plugs in household goods. What prompts us to search for bras in women's clothing or spark plugs in the automotive section? At some point we learned that products, like information, are organized by some underlying principle and that bras and spark plugs are classed in certain ways.

Understanding how information is classed and how individuals understand how information is classed is the basis of much information seeking or retrieval research. A person may class information in ways another might not consider and vice versa. Part of understanding information classification is based upon one's understanding of the subject matter; other approaches depend upon how the information is presented. Information can be classed in any number of ways. One of the most common is "fact or fiction." The Dewey Decimal Classification, for example, lumps all fiction into a single class: "F." Another very common approach is "aboutness." Very complex classification systems or taxonomies have been developed to describe aboutness. A third approach is authority or who or what is responsible for the creation of the information artifact. Medium is also an organizing principle: is the artifact a film, microfiche, codex, stone sculpture? If it is a codex, was it handwritten, printed, engraved, on parchment or acid free paper? Is the artifact electronic; and, if so, is it in its original format or a copy? Which fonts were used, what point size, and so on? Date of publication is yet another classification element. Are there graphics or audio elements to the work? What is the size of the artifact and how is "size" determined? What color is it? Is it part of a set? In sum, anything that sets one artifact off from another can be used to classify that artifact.

Libraries use these more complex ordering practices, although in function they do not differ particularly from video stores. The Dewey Decimal Classification (DDC) System and the Library of Congress (LC) Classification provide the organizational schemes for information in libraries. Materials are categorized by content or meaning first, usually in categories far more detailed or granular than comedy, mystery, and romance. Complex numeric (DDC) and alphanumeric (LC) codes have been developed to describe "meaning" of the information in the artifacts (books, tapes, films, DVDs, CDs, and so on) being organized. Subsequent categorizations often follow authority and edition.

DDC- and LC-like systems are not the only categorization systems that have been developed. There are many others. Governments and international organizations frequently develop classification schemes based on the issuing organization and its subdivisions, date, and the type of document (report, white paper, order) rather than subject matter or human creator or author. The U.S. Federal Government uses the SuDoc or the superintendent of documents system. The United Nations follows a not too dissimilar format.

Another approach is chain indexing. Concepts are divided by subject and sub-subjects in "chain-link" order. The city of Orlando might be indexed as United States—Florida—Orlando. The popular portal and search engine Yahoo! uses chain indexing as part of the way it organizes information.

With the advent of information digitization, a plethora of new categorization schemes have been developed. Some schemes are bibliographic, which means they provide a standardized description of a work. Examples include abstracts, keyword lists, and online catalog entries. These bibliographic entries are often incorporated into some kind of bibliographic database, now nearly always created and accessible in digital format.

Pertinence and Relevance

One of the more interesting questions in user studies is the matter of information usefulness. Can empirical measures of information usefulness be developed; and, if so, what are those measurements? Furthermore, can these usefulness measures be incorporated into the various systems devised for information identification and retrieval?

There are two generally accepted terms used to define information usefulness: relevance and pertinence. Salience is a third, related concept. The relevance of any given "information object" has been defined within the context of information seeking and use as the degree of "aboutness," defined objectively, that the information object has in meeting the specific information needs of the interrogator. Information objects can be assessed as either relevant or not relevant to the query (see, for example, Belkin and Vickery, 1985). Ritchie has taken the concept a step further by suggesting that "[p]atterns with communicative potential are data, and data with relevance are information" (1986: 20). Hence, we might suggest that data without relevance are not information.

There are problems with these definitions. Who decides whether data have relevance or that some information object meets the needs of the user? These definitions have been amended to infer that only the *first* information object that fulfills an information need has relevance. Once the information need has been fulfilled, any additional similar information is not relevant to fulfilling the need because of its redundancy. Second and subsequent information objects might have been considered relevant if and only if they had been processed first. Information scientists like Alan Rees and Tefko Saracevic (1966) and Carlos Cuadra and Robert Katter (1967) emphasize the contextuality of human judgments. Cognitive processes, information needs, and the context of the query render absolutely objective assessment of relevance impossible. Harter (1992) has shown, for example, that information objects that are not strictly speaking a complete match between query and the object may, in fact, satisfy information needs. Furthermore, as Thomas Froehlich (1994) has argued, we generally mean pertinence when using the term relevance, where pertinence has to do with an information need rather than with the question posed. If an information object fulfills an information need, whether or not the information object is congruent with the expressed need (that is, the formal question), that object may be considered pertinent. Thus it is possible for an information object to be at the same time pertinent but not relevant, or relevant and not pertinent. Finally, Froehlich (1991) reminds us that an information object may have both multiple and overlapping meanings.

Let us throw an additional problem into these definitions. Not only must an information artifact potentially meet a need, the user must also be able to interpret the information object. Objectively speaking, an information artifact written in Chinese fulfills no information need if the user cannot understand

Chinese. That information object, presented in Chinese, may provide the definitive answer for an information need, but because it cannot be interpreted by the user, it is useless in that specific context. Or, from a positive perspective, consider the skills that backwoodsmen like Daniel Boone or Davy Crockett were alleged to possess. They were able to interpret the sights, sounds, and smells surrounding them in the forest to track animals or detect danger. Today we speak in terms of "street smarts" and the ability to survive in an urban setting by extracting information from what would not generally be recognized as standard information carriers.

Or to take another example: how many of us can identify the race, gender, and approximate age at death when confronted with skeletal remains? William Bass, a forensic anthropologist, has contributed significantly to our ability to read and interpret these and other data into information from the dead. Bass's account of the creation of the Body Farm at the University of Tennessee, Knoxville, informs us of how he and others learned to read corpses in ways heretofore unknown (Bass and Jefferson, 2003). Again, by reading the signs, data are converted into information.

Salience

The definition of salience includes not only relevance but applicability to the solution of problems (Johnson, 1997). To be salient, relevant information must have utility. Johnson explores, among other things, information in a cancer-related environment. A layperson might find highly relevant technical information on the treatment of cancer through surgery, chemotherapy, or radiation; but that information is not salient to any but oncologists. On the other hand, information on cancer prophylaxis through diet might be very salient: brussels sprouts, cabbage, and broccoli have been suggested to reduce the likelihood of colon cancer. We can all add these vegetables to our dinner tables if we so choose.

Recall and Precision

Recall and precision are relevance measures and offer a means by which the quality of information retrieval may be measured. Recall measures the ratio of relevant records returned in a search of a database to the total number of relevant records in that database.

Precision is a measure of the number of relevant records retrieved to relevant and nonrelevant records returned in a search in any given database.

$$\text{Recall} = (A/(A+B)) \times 100$$
$$\text{Precision} = (A/(A+C)) \times 100$$

where A = number of relevant records returned, B = number of relevant records not returned, and C = number of nonrelevant records returned.

There are several issues to be taken with these measures. First, it is assumed that in any given database the number of relevant and nonrelevant records or documents is known. For very large databases, it may not be possible to count or identify the number of relevant and nonrelevant records for any given search. For a database such as the World Wide Web, even estimates of the number of relevant and nonrelevant documents is impossible because of the size of the Web as well as its very fluid nature.

Second, defining relevance for any given search may be difficult. Documents may be highly to marginally relevant for any given query, and there may be disagreement whether any given document is highly or marginally relevant or relevant at all.

That said, researchers seek to identify the effectiveness of various retrieval tools. For example, when searching the Web we have a variety of search strategies we may choose. These range from randomized Web surfing through the application of complex metasearch engines. Many of us limit our searches to a short list of search engines, including Google, AltaVista, Ask, and Yahoo! And most of us limit ourselves to fairly simple search strategies, typically consisting of one or just a few key terms. Although most engines support more complex strategies, these tend not to be used.

There are other commercial database interfaces (like Dialog, Ovid, Lexis-Nexis, and Westlaw) and government services (like THOMAS, EDGAR, and ERIC) that support very sophisticated search strategies. These interfaces are designed to allow the expert searcher to very precisely define search parameters to improve search relevance. Other systems, like LexisNexis's Universe products and Online Computer Library Center's (OCLC) FirstSearch, have been designed to improve relevance for the less than expert searcher.

There has been much research into recall and precision in the information science community. Perhaps TREC (TextREtrieval Conference), sponsored by the National Institute of Standards and Technology (NIST) and the U.S. Department of Defense (DoD), is the best-known example. TREC was begun in 1991 with the objective of providing the information retrieval research community with a large, known database in which to evaluate retrieval strategies. The key to TREC is *known*. The number of records and their content are known. Hence it is possible to devise experiments where the number of relevant and nonrelevant records can be determined for any given search query. TREC goals are defined as

- to encourage research in information retrieval based on large test collections;

- to increase communication among industry, academia, and government by creating an open forum for the exchange of research ideas;
- to speed the transfer of technology from research labs into commercial products by demonstrating substantial improvements in retrieval methodologies on real-world problems;
- to increase the availability of appropriate evaluation techniques for use by industry and academia, including development of new evaluation techniques more applicable to current systems (U.S. National Institute of Standards and Technology, 2004).

CONCLUSION

There is a great deal of uncertainly as to where and how information seeking and information retrieval studies will proceed (see, for example, Wilson, Ellis, and Ford, 2000; Dervin, 2003; and Kuhlthau, 2005b), but there is expectation (and hope) that what we learn about human information behavior can provide direction to design better retrieval systems. Donald Case offers eight "lessons" he has derived from information seeking and retrieval studies:

1. "Formal sources and rationalized searches reflect only one side of human information behavior."
2. "More information is not always better."
3. "Context is central to the transfer of information."
4. "Sometimes information—particularly generalized packages of information—doesn't help."
5. "Sometimes it is not possible to make information available or accessible."
6. "Information seeking is a dynamic process."
7. "Information seeking is not always about a 'problem' or 'problematic situation.'"
8. "Information behavior is not always about 'sense-making' either" (2002: 289–90).

Despite or because of these uncertainties, much effort has and will continue to be expended to understand information seeking behaviors and their importance in a variety of contexts and settings.

The introduction of newer information systems (like the Internet) increases the uncertainty of information seeking theory. However, as the studies of information seeking behavior draw upon theory developed by other disciplines and contribute to those same disciplines, our understanding of the field(s) may improve our information seeking systems and strategies.

QUESTIONS FOR CONSIDERATION

1. If Daniel Boone or Davy Crockett were trying to "kill a b'ar" today, how would their search for information about where and how to find the bear and the best gun to use be different from their actual information seeking behavior at the time they were (at least in legend and song) killing bears? Why would the information seeking behavior be different?
2. Are the "funnies" (or comic strips) in newspapers strictly entertainment or do they include information components?
3. If, as has been argued, information needs are surrogates for other, more basic needs, if all our basic needs were met, would there be any need for information? Why or why not?
4. Is there any instance in which a need for information is not in any way affected by the situation in which the need arises?
5. If an information system (like a library, a bookstore, or a database) were designed to fit your "natural" information seeking behavior, that is, the way you most frequently look for information, how would it be organized?

REFERENCES

Allen, Bryce. 1996. *Information Tasks: Toward a User-Centered Approach to Information Systems.* San Diego: Academic Press.

Atkin, Charles. 1973. "Instrumental Utilities and Information Seeking." In *New Models for Mass Communication Research*, edited by Peter Clarke, 205–242. Beverly Hills, CA: Sage.

Auel, Jean M. 1980. *The Clan of the Cave Bear: A Novel.* New York: Crown.

Bass, William M., and Jon Jefferson. 2003. *Death's Acre: Inside the Legendary Forensic Lab: The Body Farm Where the Dead Do Tell Tales.* New York: G. P. Putnam's Sons.

Belkin, Nicholas J. 1978. "Information Concepts for Information Science." *Journal of Documentation* 34 (March): 55–85.

Belkin, Nicholas J., and Ann Vickery. 1985. *Interaction in Information Systems: A Review of Research from Document Retrieval to Knowledge-Based Systems.* London: British Library.

Bosman, John, and Karsten Renckstorf. 1996. "Information Needs: Problems, Interests, and Consumption." In *Media Use as Social Action: A European Approach to Audience Studies,* edited by Karsten Renckstorf, Denis McQuail, and Nicholas W. Jankowski, 43–52. London: John Libbey.

Case, Donald. 2002. *Looking for Information: A Survey of Research on Information Seeking, Needs, and Behavior.* Amsterdam: Academic Press.

Cuadra, Carlos A., and Robert V. Katter. 1967. "Opening the Black Box of Relevance." *Journal of Documentation* 23 (December): 291–303.

Dervin, Brenda. 1976. "Strategies for Dealing with Human Information Needs: Information or Communication?" *Journal of Broadcasting* 20 (Summer): 324–351.

———. 1989. "Audience as Listener and Learner, Teacher and Confidante: The Sense-Making Approach." In *Public Communication Campaigns*, 2nd ed., edited by Ronald E. Rice and Charles K. Atkin, 67–86. Newbury Park, CA: Sage.

———. 2003. "Human Studies and User Studies: A Call for Methodological Interdisciplinarity." *Information Research* 9 (October). Available: http://informationr.net/ir/9-1/paper166.html (accessed December 2006).

Dozier, David, and Ronald Rice. 1984. "Rival Theories of Electronic Newsreading." In *The New Media: Communication, Research, and Technology*, edited by Ronald E. Rice, 103–128. Beverly Hills, CA: Sage.

Erdelez, Sanda. 1997. "Information Encountering: A Conceptual Framework for Accidental Information Discovery." In *Information Seeking in Context: Proceedings of International Conference on Research in Information Needs, Seeking and Use in Different Contexts*, edited by Pertti Vakkari, Reijo Savolainen, and Brenda Dervin, 412–421. London: Taylor Graham.

———. 2005. "Information Encountering." In *Theories of Information Behavior*, edited by Karen E. Fisher, Sanda Erdelez, and Lynne (E. F.) McKechnie, 179–184. Medford, NJ: Information Today.

Froehlich, Thomas. 1991. "Towards a Better Conceptual Framework in Understanding Relevance for Information Science Research." In *ASIS '91: Proceedings of the 54th ASIS Annual Meeting, Washington, DC, October 27–31, 1991*, edited by Jose Marie Griffiths, 118–125. Medford, NJ: Learned Information.

———. 1994. "Relevance Reconsidered—Towards an Agenda for the 21st Century: Introduction to Special Topic Issue on Relevance Research." *Journal of the American Society for Information Science* 45 (April): 124–134.

Gantz, Walter, Michael Fitzmaurice, and Ed Fink. 1991. "Assessing the Active Component of Information Seeking." *Journalism Quarterly* 68 (Winter): 630–637.

Harter, Stephen P. 1992. "Psychological Relevance and Information Science." *Journal of the American Society for Information Science* 43 (October): 602–615.

Järvelin, Kalervo, and Peter Ingwersen. 2004. "Information Seeking Research Needs Extension towards Tasks and Technology." *Information Research* 10 (October). Available: http://InformationR.net/ir/10-1/paper212.html (accessed December 2006).

Johnson, J. David. 1997. *Cancer-related Information Seeking*. Cresskill, NJ: Hampton Press.

Kenneally, Christine. 2005. "Do They Know Something We Don't: Animals' Senses May Have Helped Them Survive the Tsunami." *Boston Globe* (11 January): C1, C4.

Kuhlthau, Carol. 1993. "A Principle of Uncertainty for Information Seeking." *Journal of Documentation* 49 (December): 339–355.

———. 2005a. "Kuhlthau's Information Search Process." In *Theories of Information Behavior*, edited by Karen E. Fisher, Sanda Erdelez, and Lynne (E. F.) McKechnie, 230–234. Medford, NJ: Information Today.

———. 2005b. "Towards Collaboration between Information Seeking and Information Retrieval." *Information Research* 10 (April). Available: http://informationr.net/ir/10-2/paper225.html (accessed December 2006).

Maslow, Abraham. 1963. "The Need to Know and the Fear of Knowing." *Journal of General Psychology* 68, no. 2: 111–125.

Miller, George. 1983. "Information Theory in Psychology." In *The Study of Information: Interdisciplinary Messages*, edited by Fritz Machlup and Una Mansfield, 493–496. New York: Wiley.

Rees, Alan M., and Tefko Saracevic. 1966. "The Measurability of Relevance." In *Progress in Information Science and Technology, Proceedings of the American Documentation Institute 1966 Annual Meeting, October 3–7, 1966, Santa Monica, California*, 225–234. Woodland Hills, CA: Adrianne Press.

Ritchie, David. 1986. "Shannon and Weaver: Unraveling the Paradox of Information." *Communication Research* 13 (April): 278–298.

Rokeach, Milton. 1960. *The Open and Closed Mind: Investigations into the Nature of Belief Systems and Personality Systems*. New York: Basic Books.

Shepherd, Michael, John F. Duffy, Carolyn Watters, and Nitin Gugle. 2001. "The Role of User Profiles for News Filtering." *Journal of the American Society for Information Science and Technology* 52, no. 2: 149–160.

Taylor, Robert S. 1962. "The Process of Asking Questions." *American Documentation* 13 (October): 391–396.

U.S. National Institute of Standards and Technology. Text Retrieval Conference. 2004. "Overview." Available: http://trec.nist.gov/overview.html (accessed December 2006).

Wilson, Thomas D. 1981. "On User Studies and Information Needs." *Journal of Documentation* 37, no. 1: 3–15.

———. 1997. "Information Behaviour: An Interdisciplinary Perspective." *Information Processing & Management* 33 (July): 551–572.

Wilson, Thomas D., David Ellis, and Nigel Ford. 2000. "Uncertainty in Information Seeking: A Research Project in the Department of Information

Studies." Available: http://informationr.net/tdw/publ/unis/uncerty.html (accessed December 2006).

Zillmann, Dolf, and Jennings Bryant. 1985. *Selective Exposure to Communication*. Hillsdale, NJ: Erlbaum.

ADDITIONAL SOURCE

Fisher, Karen E., Sanda Erdelez, and Lynne (E. F.) McKechnie, eds. 2005. *Theories of Information Behavior*. Medford, NJ: Information Today.

Before beginning the chapter, take a few minutes to list in chronological order the changes you are aware of in the technology used to exchange information. After you have read the chapter, review your list to see what you need to add to it.

Chapter 4

History of Information Technology

Learning Guide

After reading this chapter, you should be able to

- locate the development of communication systems for transmission of information on a historical time line;

- explain how differences in information transmission resulting from the differing characteristics of communication systems have affected use of information in society;

- analyze how characteristics of communication systems affect information transmission;

- analyze the impact of differences in portability through space, variable durability over time, and increased accessibility of specific information on information transmission and use;

- explain the importance of standardization in information communication and transmission;

- assess the impact of increased diffusion of capacity to create, store, retrieve, transmit, and transform information on individual information use;

- discuss how the time required for new communication systems to move from access for a restricted elite to mass access has progressively diminished.

When you have finished the chapter, return to this page to be sure you have learned what you need to know.

INTRODUCTION

The history of information technology goes back much further than most people realize. One could make the argument that it dates to the beginning of human speech, since the human voice is an instrument—a technology if you will—that enables exchange of information. While not all would push the date (a date we do not know) back that far, it is a common misperception that the revolution in digital technology was the first to revolutionize information and the exchange of information. This chapter is concerned with a brief history of the concepts of information and information transmission and their social implications. It addresses the overall evolution of communications systems, which has traversed from the oral tradition to writing, writing technology, printing, publishing, visual and aural communications, telecommunications, and now the Web. This history covers more than 30,000 years. Over this period, we suggest that there has been an increasing complexity of creation, transmission, storage, retrieval, and management of information.

SCIENCE AND TECHNOLOGY DIFFERENTIATED

To examine information technology, its changes, and the impact of technological changes on information exchange, we need first to consider what it is that we mean by *technology*.

Information Technology

Information technology is, in the end, concerned with four processes. The first is *information creation* or capture. This process addresses the initial recording of information. It may include memorization, writing, photographing, audio recording, digitization, and so on.

The second process involves *information transmission*. Certainly, the recording of information is part of this process, but it involves moving information from one point to another. "Information containers" (books, letters, CDs, broadcasts, etc.) can be physically carried (carrier pigeons, your head, the post office, courier services, and so on). They can also be broadcast over the airways and sometimes relayed by satellites (radio, television), via cable (telephony, telegraphy, television, the Internet), and perhaps by some as yet unknown medium. Human beings have used many means to transmit information: voice, signal fires, flags, drums, and electrical and optical signals.

Third, information technology is concerned with *information storage*. How information is stored is primarily dependent on two factors:

- how badly we want the information stored to be retrievable
- how the information was initially packaged

Storage of information went from pigeonholes to bookshelves because books went from scrolls to codices. Scrolls do not store well on shelves; they tend to roll around.

Fourth, information technology is concerned with the *management* and control of information flow and the creation of systems to do just that. This is informatics. As information, information creation, information capture, information transmission, and information storage and retrieval grow more complex, so does informatics.

Science

Science we may consider the discipline that seeks to explain observed phenomena. Scientific theories are explanations put forward that can be tested. Scientists, applying scientific methodologies or protocols, seek to test their theories in order to establish or to change current understanding. Applied science is the discipline that seeks to take new understandings and apply them to address perceived problems. Technology is the application of known and proven tools to respond to those same problems. For example, biologists— beginning with Mendel and his peas—seek to understand and decipher the genetic code and to understand the transmission of traits from parents to offspring. There are, as we know, multitudes of applications for this basic science. Others have taken this knowledge and applied it to specific requirements. Blood transfusion and now organ transplants would be impossible without a thorough understanding of genetics. The research that makes these transfusions and transplants possible is largely applied science. Today, when donor and recipient tissues and blood samples are tested in hospital laboratories, the technologist or physician is utilizing a known process or technology to provide a specific service to a specific patient.

Lest we become too enamored of science and the scientific method, let us remember Soviet agriculture of the 1920s and 1930s. The leading Soviet agronomist, T. D. Lysenko, posited a process he termed "vernalization." Vernalization could, he suggested, change the genetic traits of one species through the process of external manipulations. For example, if one were to cut the tails from all boxer puppies, in time, boxer puppies would be born without tails. Lysenko's theories were to have far more sweeping implications. His work focused on the conversion of winter wheat to spring wheat during a period of famine in the Soviet Union. The Soviet leadership applied (applied science and technology) the Lysenko proposals as agricultural policy with catastrophic results.

Sometimes scientific and technological change comes as a result of tinkering and inventiveness. Industry now seeks to promote technological advances through formal research and development programs (R&D). Perhaps the most dramatic example of the combination of science together with R&D was the development of the first atomic weapons by the Manhattan Project during World War II. When Albert Einstein first proposed to President Franklin Roosevelt in 1939 that the United States undertake the development of nuclear weapons, uranium fission had only been first proven six months earlier. When the Manhattan Project was first initiated in August 1942, the weapons applications of uranium fission ("A-bombs") had yet to be accepted as scientifically demonstrated. It was to take an additional three more years before the Trinity Test in New Mexico in July 1945 first demonstrated the weapon and its first use as "Little Boy" and "Fat Man" against the Japanese cities of Hiroshima and Nagasaki in August 1945.

Technological innovation can result from far less formal processes than industrial or government R&D programs that have large budgets and highly trained personnel. Aaron Segal has described an R&D process he terms "shop floor innovation" (Koehler and Segal, 1987: 56). From smithies to cottage industry to major enterprises, innovation can occur anywhere and everywhere through both formal and informal mechanisms. Segal studied the baseball manufacturers in Haiti and found that significant innovation by otherwise unskilled and uneducated workers was commonplace and frequent.

Segal also argued that the "R&D model" is too restrictive. It is better described as "RDD&D," or research, development, demonstration, and dissemination. Technological innovation cannot have a technical or social impact until it is both proved (demonstration) and known beyond the innovator (dissemination). Moreover, in the RDD&D cycle, there is a final phase of adaptation (RDDD&A). A technology proved in one arena may well be adapted into another. We see many applications of adaptation in the information and communications fields. Consider, for example, the global positioning system or GPS. GPS was developed first by the U.S. Department of Defense as a navigation aid for weapons systems, military aircraft, and naval ships. GPS was quickly adapted for commercial and general aviation and can now be found in private automobiles and cell phones. GPS already has virtually replaced the Long Range Navigation (LORAN) technology used for naval and air navigation, and has become the standard, displacing the VHF Omnidirectional Range (VOR) and other land-based navigation systems for aircraft.

INFORMATION TECHNOLOGY AND THE INFORMATION DISCIPLINES

As we saw with the concept of information itself, information technology is a concern of a number of different disciplines and applications. For example, *librarianship* is primarily concerned with content and with the storage, maintenance, distribution, and retrieval of "information containers." Information containers, of course, are such artifacts as books, journals, tapes, and CDs, as well as less physical containers like Web sites and pages. Digital "containers" cause us a conceptual problem. We are much more able to "get our minds" around the idea of physical objects as containers. It appears to be less easy to conceive of software and digital constructs in the same way.

Informatics addresses the processes for information management and the development of the physical and electronic systems for the performance of those functions. One concern is the transmission of signals or data (or information) over some medium from one point to another without degradation of the signal. Consider the example of telephony. On occasion when one makes a phone call, the conversation that takes place may be unintelligible or misinterpreted because of background noise or insufficient volume. Information theorists are not concerned with the quality or content of the conversation, but rather with quality of the signal carrying the conversation. When Claude Shannon first turned his attention to the problem of communications and noise in the late 1940s for Bell Laboratories (see discussion in chapter 2), he and the rest of the world were not nearly so concerned with "noiseless" communications as we are now. Shannon undertook to reduce the signal to noise ratio in telephony. Today we are interested in the elimination of noise for data transmission across a wide variety of transmission media.

Voice transmission via telephony is not the only way one might carry out a conversation. One might use telegraphy and engage in the same conversation with dots and dashes. Or one might employ radio using those same dots and dashes or using voice transmission. Most recently, one can exchange signal-carrying messages using e-mail or Internet telephony. From the perspective of content, does it matter what the carrier is? From the perspective of the carrier, does it matter what the content of the message is? The answer to both questions is no. However, some discipline has to be concerned with the choice of carrier, the choice of signal type, the choice of signal path, and so on. That discipline is informatics.

To explore this area, let us use a hospital model as an example, especially appropriate since medical informatics is a dynamic field. Consider that you are a patient about to be admitted to your local hospital. What information flows permit that admission and what information flows will be triggered once you walk through those hospital doors? First, an admitting clerk will require you to provide two key pieces of information, your social security number and your insurance coverage, along with other less important data (name, date of birth, next of kin, and so on). These data will be cross-referenced against your physician's admitting orders. You will be assigned a room. Typically a volunteer will escort you there.

Now, you are a walking biological database. At some point someone will likely come along and remove some blood from you. You will no doubt be asked to contribute other bodily fluids as well. What exactly do those tubes of blood represent? That blood is sent to the laboratory (which may or may not be in the same building or, for that matter, the same town). People and machines process the blood and, very often, transmit the results of the various tests automatically back to your nurse, doctor, and chart. At the same time, your account is charged automatically. At some point, that charge, as well as all others, will be transmitted—now primarily electronically—to your insurance carrier. Medical informatics, then, is concerned with the creation and maintenance of the physical and electronic systems that manage these various information flows within the medical setting.

Shift from the medical model to the Internet. The Internet differs from telephony and broadcast technologies (radio and TV) in one fundamental way: Internet messages move in small packets while telephone messages utilize a dedicated line. Internet messages follow multiple paths; a phone link, once made, follows a single path. The manager of Internet networks must be equally concerned with informatics, perhaps in the same way a dispatcher for a trucking company must also decide what box to put on what truck to be taken by some certain time over a variety of routes.

Social informatics, yet another informatics variation, lies at the intersection of information technologies and the social sciences and is a discipline that evolved in the 1990s. Rob Kling (1999) defines social informatics as "a body of research that examines the social aspects of computerization." He has also offered a more formal definition: "the body of research that examines the design, uses, and consequences of information and communication technologies in ways that take into account their interaction with institutional and cultural contexts" (Kling, 2000: 217). Yet another definition is offered in a special issue of the *Journal of the American Society for Information Science* in 1999 on social informatics, edited by Rob Kling, Howard Rosenbaum, and Carol Hert (1998: 1047): "Social informatics (SI) refers to a multidisciplinary research field that examines the design, uses, and implications of information and communication technologies (ICTs) in ways that account for their interactions with institutional and cultural contexts."

The field of social informatics has expanded from one concerned with human-computer interaction, to human-ICT (information communications and technology) interactions, to other perhaps more complex human-machine relationships, such as "human-robot interactions," the focus of a 2004 IEEE meeting. The type of concern addressed in social informatics is illustrated by the work of, for example, Christine Lisetti, Sarah Brown, Kaye Alvarez, and Andreas Marpaung (2004), who in developing an office robot, "Cherry," had as a chief concern the creation of a social interface for Cherry that would be comfortable for Cherry's "users." In a wider application, Microsoft has incorporated an application into its more recent operating systems software to provide access for the visually impaired. One speech-based application allows the user to choose from a number of different "voices."

There are other practical applications for social informatics. In a 1995 article, Harmen Grebel and Jan Steyaert recognize that social informatics has significant applications in social work and in the educational aspects of social work. Terry von Thaden (2000) has examined social informatics applications in accident avoidance in aviation. The cockpit, once inhabited by an altimeter, a wet compass, and an airspeed indicator, has evolved into a complex array of instruments (see www.militaryfactory.com/cockpits/index.asp for an introduction). The new instrumentation includes the GPS (global positioning system) wedded to a moving map, Enhanced Ground Proximity Warning Systems (EGPWS), and collision avoidance systems. Some of these technologies have begun to find their way into ground transportation systems. The design and application of these technologies is of interest to the practitioners of social informatics. Not only must one be concerned with the development of the "gadgets," one must also consider the design of the interface and the training of the end user.

STANDARDIZATION IN INFORMATION TRANSMISSION AND COMMUNICATION

Although it may not be immediately obvious how these discussions relate to the central concern of this chapter, we have used these modern examples to begin an explanation of the history of information technology for a reason. Put very simply, as suggested in the introduction, the history of information technology begins with humans talking to humans. It evolves from humans talking to humans to humans talking to humans and storing that "speech" by using graphic symbols in order to "speak" at a later time to other humans. As humans began storing "speech," an important change occurred: they expanded the sphere for their speech from the immediate here and now to the extended here and now. Much of the history of information technology has to do with the ways humans have found to store information, but it is also concerned with the ways that humans have found to transmit and therefore disseminate information, enabling this trend of expansion of the reach of human "speech." As we will see, information storage and transmission are intimately interrelated. This history "ends" for now (i.e., comes to the present day) with humans talking to humans, humans talking to machines, machines talking to humans, and machines talking to machines.

There is a second trend that we can identify in the history of information technology, one perhaps less obvious. As James O'Donnell explains so well in his book *Avatars of the Word* (1998), we are moving from disorganization toward standardization and have been since we began communicating. Both technology and our desire to communicate effectively in wider and wider circles have forced the need for standardization on us.

Languages

This standardization takes many forms. One of these has been the adoption of one language as a common second language for communication among elites. This common second language has changed over time. In Europe, the first common language was Greek, followed quickly by Latin. In the nineteenth century, French was the language of diplomacy and love, German the language of science and medicine, and Italian the language of music. English has replaced all these languages as the most common second language across almost all fields. An extremely interesting example is aviation English. It is limited to some two thousand words, each with a specific and unique meaning. There is a very good reason for this rigor. Because aviation often requires split-second decisions, there is no room for semantic debate or ambiguous communication. When air traffic control, anywhere any time, instructs a pilot "to turn left on a heading of two five zero, climb and maintain one five thousand and contact Somewhere Center on one three three point two," there are only three things for that pilot to do.

Writing Systems and Symbols

A second response has been to develop different spoken languages but other common communications systems. Chinese is spoken in many, very different dialects, yet it shares a common written language. Chinese pictographs, at least when they were first introduced, were graphic representations or pictures. As language grew more abstract, necessarily so did writing. Japanese writing is based on the written language developed by the Chinese, and both of these languages share a number of similar characters and characteristics. Ancient Egyptian hieroglyphics were based on the same concept but did not survive as successfully as did the Chinese pictographs. Native American sign language was a common means of communication among peoples whose spoken languages were very different.

Many other writing systems were and are based on the representation of the sound of words or phonetics. These languages have the advantage of requiring far fewer symbols to convey meaning than do the pictographic languages. In order to understand these written languages, one must also understand the underlying spoken language:

- "¿Donde está la estación de tren?"
- «Où se trouve la gare?»
- „Wo ist der Bahnhof?"
- "Where is the train station?"

These questions all mean the same thing, and all share a similar symbol set. Despite the fact that all four are European languages with many common roots, there are no other obvious similarities.

Lest we leave this discussion with the idea that the phonetic alphabet languages have replaced or are replacing the pictographic languages, think again. We are surrounded by pictographs, ranging from the oh-so-familiar corporate logos like Disney's mouse ears or McDonald's golden arches to a common set

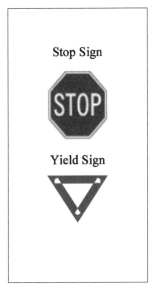

Figure 4-1   Modern Pictographs

Source: U.S. Department of Transportation, Federal Highway Administration. 2006. Manual on Uniform Traffic Control Devices. *Available: http://mutcd.fhwa.dot.gov/Signs/results.cfm?type =all (accessed December 2006).*

of traffic signs. Traffic lights are standardized: red means stop, green means go. Other traffic signs are also standardized. A red, octagonal sign with the letters **STOP** in big letters means "stop" in China, Ukraine, Uganda, and the United States. An inverted red equilateral triangle means "yield." A "female" symbol on a door in a restaurant probably means the same thing everywhere. Sometimes the interpretation of such symbols eludes those from other cultures, however.

Other symbols, if Carl Jung is to be believed, have an almost universal archetypal meaning. There may be an almost universal and inherent interpretation of these symbols. One of the most revered and reviled symbols of the twentieth century is the bent cross or swastika. Until the Nazis arrogated this symbol, it was universally recognized as a positive sign and was found nearly everywhere on the planet (see chapter 13). Beginning in the early 1930s, it came to represent for many of us evil incarnate. In many cultures where the symbol was used, it was erased and replaced.

Standardization of Media and Technologies

Now, let us return to the question of standardization. As communication media and communication technologies become more precise, the interface between media and media and technology and technology must become more standard. This need for standardization is not restricted to machines, hardware and software. There is a story, perhaps apocryphal, that the United States once nearly declared war on France. A French warship, the story has it, sent a note to the Jefferson administration, in French, using the term *demander*. "Demander" translates as "to ask" but was mistranslated as "to demand." In diplomatic parlance to demand anything is language in the extreme. Fortunately the error was caught in time.

The need for standardization has always been with us but has become far more acute in the digital age. This can be illustrated in a number of ways. Consider the "great video machine war" of the 1980s. In the 1980s, there were two competing technologies for the home video audience: VHS and Beta. VHS and Beta are incompatible; one simply cannot put a Beta tape in a VHS machine and vice versa. Beta lost, not because it was an inferior technology; it is not. It lost because it was out-marketed by the VHS proponents. But now videotape is yielding to the DVD (digital versatile disc).

As we develop information technologies to perform more precise functions, the need for standardization will increase. Consider the plethora of operating systems (OS) offered by Microsoft alone. It is possible (is it likely?) that there are non-Windows MSDOS/OS machines running today. Certainly Windows 3.1, 95, 98, ME, 2000, NT, XP, Vista, and so on are currently in use. Some software will run well in one OS environment but crawl in another and fail miserably in a third. Complicate the picture with Apple OS, Unix, Linux, and so on. Software producers must understand and produce software that is compliant with each of the operating systems or they will lose market share.

Standards Organizations

Standards organizations play an important role in keeping all participants in sync. This is particularly useful in fields where there is rapid development, as, for example, in the Internet fields. The ISO (International Organization for Standardization) plays an important role in establishing standards internationally. ISO defines a standard as follows:

> a documented agreement containing technical specifications or other precise criteria to be used consistently as rules, guidelines, or definitions of characteristics to ensure that materials, products, processes and services are fit for their purpose. (International Organization for Standardization, 2005)

There are many standards organizations that play a role in information technology. ISO is among these. Its responsibilities cover all technical fields except electrical and electronic engineering. These fall under the responsibility of the International Engineering Consortium (IEC). Some ISO standards specify abbreviations and codes. For example, ISO 3166 provides two- and three-letter and -number codes for countries and regions around the world. The ISO 9000 series addresses business and accounting practices, including records management.

Many ISO standards originate in national standards bodies (like the American National Standards Institute or ANSI) and industry bodies like the Institute of Electrical and Electronics Engineers (IEEE) and the World Wide Web Consortium (W3C).

The "Internet world of standards" illustrates some of the complexity in standards making. There are several industry focused bodies, like W3C, the Internet Corporation for Assigned Names and Numbers (ICANN), the Internet Engineering Task Force (IETF), and its parent body the Internet Society (ISOC), that promote Internet standardization. Each of these groups tends to set standards for different parts of the process. W3C tends to focus on standards for creation of Web sites, ICANN is concerned with domain name standards, and so on. Many recommendations of these bodies emerge as national and/or international standards in information technology. For example, in 1997 and 1998 two firms competed for the 56k modem market with two different technologies. The matter was resolved by ITU (International Telecommunication Union) Standard V.90. Thus, all V.90 compliant 56K modems are compatible.

WRITING: THE FIRST INFORMATION TECHNOLOGY REVOLUTION

In order to manage information we must first be able to store it. The first step, as we have seen, is the ability to transfer information from one medium to another. Human beings have done this in basically two ways. The first and by far the oldest tradition is the oral tradition, in which the information stored in the memory of one person is transferred to the medium of the voice and then restored in the memory of the hearer. This tradition includes storytelling and the recounting of national and ethnic epics, and there are also strong oral components in theater. Storytelling and theater were, until 100 years ago, the only "multimedia" communications available. There are oral components now in electronic entertainment (radio, TV, recordings), and today's live and unrecorded radio and television broadcasts fall squarely in the oral tradition category.

There are still cultures today that have no written language and that transmit their histories and their knowledge orally. For example, Navajo elders remember rather than transcribe their laws, traditions, and epics. In much of Africa, the radio and the cell phone have become important means for extending the reach of oral traditions. In Uganda, the "ebimeeza" or "round tables" broadcast by radio have become an important means of creating and communicating political and social discourse (Mwesige, 2004). Many of the great epics (the *Kalevala*, *Beowulf*, *Chanson de Roland*, *El cantar de mío Cid*, not to mention the *Iliad* and the *Odyssey*) were first told and retold, then finally written.

The second step in information management is, of course, capturing ideas in some more permanent way. This is often done with writing, which is the second basic means of transferring information and constitutes the first great information technology revolution.

Cave Paintings

The first known recorded information is found in the Paleolithic paintings at the Chauvet-Pont-d'Arc and Lascaux caves and the grotte Cosquer. These paintings date to as early as 30,000–32,000 BCE and represent animals and a nude "venus" or female figure. There are also cave paintings elsewhere in

Europe, in South America, and in Australia. What these paintings represent is a matter of conjecture. They may be magical spells, appeals to the gods, or perhaps merely documentation of a hunt. Certainly they are an effort to communicate information, perhaps to contemporaries, perhaps to the gods, and perhaps to the descendants of those who created them. Whatever they are, they are among the first known attempts to "write." We can speculate that there were other cave paintings that either have yet to be discovered in the modern era or that have disappeared. Therefore, these are the first records successfully archived for very long periods of time. These information records, however, were not sharable over space. Such non-portable forms of information records continued far beyond the early days of cave painting in the symbolism of the architecture of religious buildings, particularly in the architecture of the medieval cathedrals.

Formal Writing Systems

Perhaps the first formal writing system is the Sumerian Cuneiform dating to about 3500 BCE. Cuneiform (wedge-shaped) writing was performed by pressing a stick or stylus into a wet clay tablet. Most Sumerian records were just that, financial records or inventories. Sumerian writing was complex in the beginning: there were more than 2000 symbols, later reduced by more than half.

The Egyptians developed hieroglyphics in about 3000 BCE. Hieroglyphics, or the "Writing of the Gods," consisted of three types of symbols: pictographs (representations of objects), ideographs (representations of ideas), and an alphabet representing phonetics or spoken sounds. As we have seen already, all three of these forms are in current use.

If, indeed, writing began as early as twenty thousand years ago, when did human beings first seek to manage their writing and their knowledge? The Sumerians maintained complex records on their clay tablets and they also preserved mythology. The best known of the Sumerian legends—one preserved on clay tablets—is the Gilgamesh epic. Gilgamesh, a Babylonian tyrant who ruled the city of Uruk, is challenged by Enkidu to relieve Uruk's oppressed citizenry. Another important collection is the compilations of law known as the Code of Hammurabi. Hammurabi ruled Babylon from 1795 to 1750 BCE. At least one copy of the Code was carved into an eight-foot-tall black stone obelisk.

The Egyptian Book of the Dead dates to 1240 BCE. The Book of the Dead is a set of mortuary spells. Some of the contents are found in the Pyramid and Coffin texts that date a millennium earlier. These texts were written either on the walls of the pyramids or on the coffins themselves.

The earliest known Chinese writings date to about 1200 BCE. The best-known example, the Oracle Bone Inscriptions, was discovered in 1899 in

Henan province. Inscriptions in bronze date to about 1000 BCE. The First Emperor of China and founder of the Ch'in dynasty, Shi Huangdi, standardized Chinese script in 221 BCE.

Information Storage

Information storage goes hand in hand with writing. Lionel Casson (2001) demonstrates that there were a number of collections of clay tablets in Sumeria that have been uncovered by archaeologists and that these may be well be the first organized libraries. These collections appear to consist in large part of records of one kind or another.

The Library at Alexandria was among the first research libraries. It was created by one of Alexander's generals and later pharaoh Ptolemy I in 290 BCE. The Ptolemaic dynasty, culminating with Cleopatra, maintained the library as a seat of learning and scholarship. The library fell into decline with the fall of the House of Ptolemy and was ultimately destroyed in 412 CE following religious and secular conflict in Alexandria. As a point of interest, the Library has been reconstructed with support from UNESCO and a number of donor countries. Callimachus, whose *Pinakes* was a chronological subject catalog of the Library at Alexandria collection (Davis and Wiegand, 1994: 5), is alleged to have been very critical of the scroll as an information storage and retrieval device. He is said by many to be the "father of all librarians" and was perhaps the inventor of the library catalog.

Libraries underwent a metamorphosis between the cave paintings and the establishment of the Library at Alexandria. Part of the reason for this was a changed perception in the role of the library and in the form of the "book." Cave paintings (not to mention caves) are fairly awkward to move from one place to another. Recall that Sumerian "books" were in fact clay tablets, also somewhat awkward to move from one place to another, bulky, prone to breaking, and difficult to store.

Frederick Kilgour defines "book"

> as a storehouse of human knowledge intended for dissemination in the form of an artifact that is portable—or at least is transportable—and that contains arrangements of signs that convey information. (Kilgour, 1998: 3)

Certainly material written with a stylus or a stick on clay tablets constitutes a book just as much as another text inscribed on papyrus, parchment, or bond paper. A book may take the form of tablet, scroll, or codex. Books can be handwritten with a brush, a pen, or blown on paper by an ink-jet printer.

Books can also take a digital form. What matters to Kilgour is that it contains intelligible signs and that it can be moved with some minimum of effort.

The book has undergone considerable evolutionary change since it was first introduced in Sumeria. Each change has represented an improvement in the format for the container and in the way in which the intelligible signs are placed upon the book. In very simple terms, these changes have gone from the tablet to the scroll to the codex and now to various electronic storage media. There have also been variations along the way and sometimes specialized "information containers," like microfilm or microfiche, to serve specific purposes. It should be noted as well that as one book form displaces another, the newer form never fully replaces the older. Tombstones and plaques are variations on the stone or wooden tablet. Scrolls are retained for traditional or religious purposes. The codex has been in use for almost two thousand years and shows no signs of obsolescence. The development of a reed paper, papyrus, revolutionized book making, information transfer, and information storage. Papyrus, however, unlike undisturbed clay tablets, was prone to deterioration from aging, insect infestation, fire, and other natural processes. While the invention of printing (use of movable type) changed the processes of book production and the resultant possibility of multiple copies of a work increased the likelihood of survival of an information record, the basic form remained much the same: a linear structure with content that was stable over time and space.

The electronic age has brought with it new formats for the book. These include the hard disk and the handheld book reader. Because of the flexibility of the electronic format, books can and do take a much wider form. Hypertext allows for a wider range of nonlinear structures. Multimedia augments the text as did the illumination of the manuscripts of the middle ages or the etchings and later the photographs that books contained.

Is there a third way? Some have pointed to the Internet and more particularly the World Wide Web (WWW) as perhaps a Kuhnian paradigm shift (Kuhn, 1962) in information management, a change so profound it forces a total break from previous practice and interpretations. One can argue it is much less than that (Koehler, 1999). Because of its ephemeral nature, the WWW resides somewhere between the very impermanent oral tradition and the much more permanent written tradition.

MOVEMENT OF MESSAGES: THE SECOND REVOLUTION

The first information technology revolution provided efficient means of storing information. The second great information technology revolution is concerned with the movement of messages from one place to another. Until very recently, the technology to move messages has involved facilitating or speeding the ability of human beings to carry documents and books from one point to another. And, in fact, much of our efforts remain concerned with that very same function. Consider advances in post office automation or the very real successes of companies like FedEx and UPS that use human beings and machines that carry human beings to move artifacts from one place to another. At the same time, human beings have also employed a wide range of media to speed signals. These have included drums (sound waves), smoke (light waves), signal fires, lighthouses, semaphore flags, cannon fire, and on and on. The problem with all of these systems lay with the facts that

- they could only transmit signals over a relatively short distance;
- complex messages were difficult to send accurately;
- the process was time consuming.

It was not until the nineteenth century that very great increases in speed and accuracy were achieved. Remember that when the nineteenth century opened, there were no railroads, no telephones, no electric utilities, almost no paved roads, and the steamship had just been tested. Goods, services, and people were moved either by horsepower on land or by wind power on water. Or they walked. It was not until 1840 that the first prepaid postage stamp (the Penny Black) came into use in England. It could cost a month's pay to send a letter from New York to California via pony express.

The nineteenth century witnessed a number of major innovations in communications and information technology and in transportation technology that facilitated the physical movement of information containers:

- George Stephenson designed the first steam locomotive in 1814.
- Photography was being developed in the 1820s by innovators like Joseph Nicéphore Niépce and Louis Jacques Mandé Daguerre.
- The first typewriter was introduced by W. A. Burt in 1829, the same year Louis Braille invented Braille printing.
- Samuel Morse invented the telegraph in 1837; Morse code was introduced in 1838.
- Bicycles were introduced by Kirkpatrick Macmillan in 1839.
- The fax machine was invented by Alexander Bain in 1843.
- In 1844, the first commercial telegraph line was established between Baltimore, Maryland, and Washington, D.C.
- In 1854, John Tyndall demonstrated the principles of fiber optics.
- In 1857, George Pullman introduced the Pullman sleeping car for trains.
- Alexander Graham Bell's first patent on the telephone is dated 7 March 1876.

- The fountain pen was first patented by Lewis Edson Waterman in 1884.
- In 1885, George Eastman produced paper-strip photographic film.
- In 1887, Heinrich Hertz discovered the principles of radar.
- In 1892, Rudolf Diesel invented the internal combustion engine.
- Guglielmo Marconi introduced the radio in 1895. His original transmitter had a range of some 100 meters.
- And finally, in 1900, Count Ferdinand von Zeppelin launched the first airship.

The twentieth century was not without its long list of information-related inventions. Radiotelegraphy came into common use:

- The Wright Brothers demonstrated heavier-than-air machine-powered flight in 1903.
- Lee De Forest patented the triode in 1906, first permitting radio voice transmission.
- Color photography was introduced by Auguste and Louis Lumiere in 1907.
- The gyrocompass, critical for air navigation, was invented by Elmer A. Sperry in 1908.
- Thomas Edison demonstrated talking motion pictures in 1910.
- Charles Franklin Kettering helped start the automobile industry with the first electrical ignition system in 1912.
- Radio tuners were introduced in 1916.
- Vladimir Kosma Zworykin invented the precursor to television, the cathode ray tube, in 1929.
- At the same time, John Logie Baird introduced the mechanical television technology, a second precursor to television as we know it.
- The first broadcast of a television program was made by the BBC in 1930.
- In 1926, Robert H. Goddard launched the first liquid-fueled rockets.
- In 1929, Paul Galvin invented the car radio.
- In 1933, Edwin Howard Armstrong invented frequency modulated (FM) radio.
- The first photocopier was invented by Chester F. Carlson in 1937.
- Ladislo Biro gave us the ballpoint pen in 1938.
- The first software controlled computer, the Z3, was booted up by Konrad Zuse in 1941.
- The Z3 was followed in 1942 by John Atanasoff and Clifford Berry's digital computer.
- The cellular phone was first conceived of in 1947 and so too was the transistor, invented by John Bardeen, Walter Brattain, and William Shockley.

- Charles Ginsburg's videotape recorder (VTR) came in 1951.
- The modem and the integrated circuit were introduced in 1958.
- The audiocassette was invented in 1962, followed by the videodisc in 1963.
- ARPANET was introduced in the late 1960s, the Internet in the 1980s, and the World Wide Web in 1991.
- The commercialization of optical fiber was made possible by the innovations of Robert Maurer, Donald Keck, and Peter Schultz in 1970.
- The VCR was introduced in 1970 and the microprocessor in 1971.
- The first word processor was invented in 1971, and WordStar, the first commercial word processing program, was first licensed in 1978.
- Ink-jet and laser printers came out in the mid-1970s.
- MS-DOS and the IBM-PC made their debuts in 1981.
- CDs and CD players began production in 1982.
- DVD players were first marketed in 1996.
- The first MP3 players appeared in 1998.

Based on this list of inventions, several interesting observations can be made. First, initial innovations are frequently made by individuals or a small number of people: Charles Babbage and Ada Byron Lovelace at the beginning of computing, William Gates with operating systems, Steven Wozniak and Steven Jobs with personal computing, Alexander Graham Bell with the telephone, Tim Berners-Lee with the WWW, and so on. It is also worth noting that although an invention or innovation may be credited to a particular individual, there are often competing claimants, such as was the case with radio. Marconi's claim was not only disputed by Nikola Tesla, but in a suit concluded long after the death of both, Marconi's 1904 patent was found invalid by the U.S. Supreme Court, which upheld a Tesla patent from 1900. Once a technology or concept is proven, it often takes an immense investment in human power and money to further innovate. Moreover, often years and much investment are needed to develop a product that can enter a market and have an impact. The cellular phone may have been first conceived of in 1947, but it was not until the mid-1990s that adequate infrastructure existed to make it a commodity.

Ideas and innovation require earlier ideas and innovation. Often ideas and innovation are the result of adapting one concept and introducing it elsewhere. Finally, while there has been a great deal of innovation, adaptation, and inventiveness, there have been few revolutionary ideas in information technology for the past twenty years or so. These technological changes result in an interesting set of phenomena for information.

The overall trend is for an increase in diffusion of information and an increase in the capacity for the creation, transmission, storage, retrieval, and management of information. That in turn increases the possibility of human interaction. A corollary trend has been the increase in speed of transmission of information. From the time when all transmission was oral, when information could only travel at the speed a human could walk, to today's "instant messaging," we have witnessed a total sea change in how quickly information can be shared. This change has had significant impact on every aspect of human life as we know it—our personal lives, our economy, and our political structures. Further, although we have greatly increased our capacity to create more durable information records, we are currently in a period that almost mimics the early days of shared information in the impermanence of much of our recorded communication.

Information Ideas

The Role of Information Technology in Interpreting the Information Record in the Information Technologies of the Past

The so-called Gospel of Judas, an archaeological discovery of the 1970s, has recently been restored, authenticated, and published. The text was included in an information document known as the Codex Tchacos. The process of authentication involved the use of myriad technologies that served to assure today's scholars that the text actually is from the time period in which it was thought to have been created and therefore likely does represent an information record from that time. The process of authentication included not only physical testing of the materials on which the information is recorded but also intellectual testing of the language, script, style, and concepts included in the text, all of which could be thought of as information technologies. This recently discovered text offers a good example of how the information records of the past serve to change thinking in the present, in that the information provided suggests a different view and interpretation of the role of Judas Iscariot from that generally accepted by current mainstream Christianity. Thus the existence of information technologies in prior times (the papyrus on which the text was written, the Coptic language in which the text was recorded, the ink used to inscribe the text) affect our present-day thinking through the transmission of information concepts from those prior times, and the existence of information technologies today make possible the interpretation of the earlier information records.

Discoveries of information from the past—or even the imagined discovery of information from the past, such as that portrayed in *The Da Vinci Code*

(*Continued on p. 78*)

(Brown, 2003)—affect the ways that we interpret information today, and thus for our current understandings it is critical that we be able to access the information technologies of the past, at least the intellectual technologies such as writing and language. The existence of technologies that protect our access to the information of what will be the past, such as the Wayback Machine of Brewster Kahle that provides access to the previous versions of the Web, will help to ensure that we can have ongoing access to the thinking of yesterday that was expressed in the technologies of today, just as we have access to the Gospel of Judas through the papyrus, ink, and Coptic text. The challenge for today is to use information technologies that will provide continuing access to yesterday rather than losing access for hundreds or thousands of years, as happened with the Gospel of Judas, which was lost for approximately 1700 years.

Sources

Brown, Dan. 2003. *The Da Vinci Code*. New York: Doubleday.

Handwerk, Brian. 2006. "Gospel of Judas Pages Endured Long, Strange Journey." *National Geographic News* (6 April). Available: http://news.nationalgeographic.com/news/2006/04/0406_060406_gospel.html (accessed December 2006) .

Internet Archive. 2006. "Wayback Machine." Available: www.archive.org/index.php (accessed December 2006).

Kasser, Rodolphe, Marvin Meyer, and Gregor Wurst, eds. 2006. *The Gospel of Judas: from Codex Tchacos*. Washington, DC: National Geographic Society.

Lovgren, Stefan. 2006. "Lost Gospel Revealed; Says Jesus Asked Judas to Betray Him." *National Geographic News* (6 April). Available: http://news.nationalgeographic.com/news/2006/04/0406_060406_judas.html (accessed December 2006).

National Geographic Society. 2006a. *The Judas Gospel*. NationalGeographic.com. Available: http://www7.nationalgeographic.com/ngm/gospel/index.html (accessed December 2006).

———. 2006b. *The Lost Gospel of Judas*. NationalGeographic.com. Available: www.nationalgeographic.com/lostgospel (accessed December 2006).

SOCIAL IMPLICATIONS OF INFORMATION TECHNOLOGY

As information technologies have been changing over the years, society has been incorporating these technologies and bending them to its needs. At the same time, these technologies have been reshaping the world as we know it.

Nicholas Negroponte has argued, for example, for the withering away of the nation-state as we evolve as digital beings. He finds the state to be too limiting a construct in a world that is too digitally porous (Negroponte, 1995: 230). Perhaps he is correct, but current events lead one to suspect that he is wrong. Back in the 1950s and 1960s some international relations theorists predicted the withering away of the state as well, particularly in Western Europe. European integration may well be moving toward the super-state, while the United States has been extending its extraterritorial powers, and other countries like the Soviet Union and Yugoslavia have disintegrated into smaller nation-states.

Negroponte is right when he points out that "being digital" makes it possible for virtual communities of people sharing similar interests to find one another and interact. The problem is, of course, that these virtual communities may serve socially positive ends, but some may also support socially destructive ends, such as terrorist networks. The "virtual" nature of the digital community makes it possible for individuals to "meet" and interact despite great geographic distances.

We do know that changes in information technology sometimes result in social changes, sometimes social changes may lead to demands for technological changes, and sometimes they go hand in hand. We also know that structural changes are often needed in order for technological innovation to propagate.

One major change observable over the long period of the history of information technology has time and again been the broadening of access to the technology of the time from a restricted elite to a much wider segment of the population. Coupled with this broadening have been concurrent and successive changes in the speed with which each new information technology becomes available for inclusion into the daily life of a broad spectrum of individuals. Today the rapid inclusion of new information technologies occurs most obviously in the developed nations, but that too is changing.

The newer forms of information creation, transfer, and storage will mold and be molded by society. The Internet is a technology with both negative and positive aspects. For example, pornography, hate speech, gambling, and other "social ills" have always been with us. The Internet, however, can break down the traditional barriers because of the ease of access and because of the difficulties in controlling Internet content. The Internet also represents to some the "world brain" as envisaged by H. G. Wells in his collections of essays of the same name in 1938. While Wells's world brain or global encyclopedia would have had extensive quality control that the WWW lacks, and the WWW is far less elitist than world brain would have been, it does offer potential as a very important global information resource and dissemination medium.

There are other information technologies that may have sweeping social impacts. Certainly, the information technologies of the past have changed the *status quo ante*. According to Finigan (1974) early Christians may have contributed to the adaptation and use of the codex as a form of information storage. The codex was seen to be a more efficient means to package and transport the Gospels. It has been argued that early Christians were forced into a distributed publication business because of wide-scale opposition to them and that they adopted a technology from African, primarily Egyptian, use (Frost, 1998). The codex provided a better and more secure means to store information, particularly for persecuted groups. This lesson was not lost on the early Christians. Others have suggested that because the early Christians had adopted an efficient means to store and retrieve religious documents, the use of the codex contributed to the growth and success of the group (Avrin, 1991: 56–60).

The book, the printing press, the telephone, radio, television, and transportation technologies have all had impacts. Old elites always feared the potential impact of these technologies, and with good reason. Each of these technologies, it was predicted, would destroy the moral fiber of the youth and rain destruction on society. It is possible to document these dire predictions from Socrates to the present. Wells, in *World Brain*, in fact, dedicates one of his essays to the decline of the British public school system (which is actually an elite private school system), due in part to new information technology.

CONCLUSION

As ever, it is uncertain where the new technologies will take us. We can observe, almost tritely, that the only constant is change. We know that there are interesting ramifications of instantaneous communications. Until the Israeli government curtailed the reporting, the Iraqi military used CNN reporting for targeting missiles during Desert Storm. Real time e-mail alerted the world as the Soviet Union was collapsing and during the Tiananmen Square protests in China. Very soon game and training technologies will likely "morph" into extremely realistic virtual reality (VR). Karl Marx once claimed that religion was the opiate of the masses. VR may become the new designer drug of choice.

The changes wrought by the new technologies seem likely to continue the trend of increased capacity for information creation, transmission, storage, and retrieval and ever faster speeds for information dissemination. If new technologies also continue the trends of broadening of access to information technologies to a more inclusive population and more rapid diffusion into daily life, the future prospects for the information environment could be considered bright.

QUESTIONS FOR CONSIDERATION

1. What information technology revolutions or changes had to occur before the invention of printing was possible?
2. Transmission of information in some formats is restricted to transmission over time, and the format cannot be used for transmission over space. What are historical examples of this format? What are current examples? Is there any difference in use between the historical and current formats?
3. As communication systems have evolved, one important change has been the increased speed of transmission of information. What is the impact of that change on the way information is used by individuals? By governments?
4. Another change that has occurred with the evolution of communication systems has been increased portability of information through space. How has that increased portability affected individual information use? Information use by business? Information use by governments?
5. Some kinds of information records have the characteristic of being durable over time and not susceptible to undetected change, while other records are impermanent and easily and undetectably altered. What are some advantages and disadvantages of these two types of information records?

REFERENCES

Avrin, Leila. 1991. *Scribes, Script and Books: The Book Arts from Antiquity to the Renaissance.* Chicago: American Library Association; London: The British Library.

Casson, Lionel. 2001. *Libraries in the Ancient World.* New Haven, CT: Yale University Press.

Davis, Donald G., and Wayne A. Wiegand, eds. 1994. *Encyclopedia of Library History.* New York: Garland.

Finegan, Jack. 1974. *Encountering New Testament Manuscripts: A Working Introduction to Textual Criticism.* Grand Rapids, MI: Eerdmans.

Frost, Gary. 1998. "Adoption of the Codex Book: Parable of a New Reading Mode." *The Book and Paper Group Annual* 17. Available: http://aic
.stanford.edu/sg/bpg/annual/v17/bp17-10.html (accessed December 2006).

Grebel, Harmen, and Jan Steyaert. 1995. "Social Informatics: Beyond Technology, A Research Project in Schools of Social Work in the European Community." *International Social Work* 38, no. 2: 151–164.

International Organization for Standardization. 2005. "FAQ 2.10: What Can I Expect to Find in an ISO Standard?" Available: www.iso .org/iso/en/faqs/faq-standards.html (accessed December 2006).

Kilgour, Frederick G. 1998. *The Evolution of the Book*. New York: Oxford University Press.

Kling, Rob. 1999. "What Is Social Informatics and Why Does It Matter?" *D-Lib Magazine* 5 (January). Available: www.dlib.org/dlib/january99/ kling/01kling.html (accessed February 2007).

———. 2000. "Learning about Information Technologies and Social Change: The Contribution of Social Informatics." *The Information Society* 16, no. 3: 217–232.

Kling, Rob, Howard Rosenbaum, and Carol Hert. 1998. "Social Informatics in Information Science: An Introduction." *Journal of the American Society for Information Science* 49, no. 12: 1047–1052.

Koehler, Wallace, 1999. "Digital Libraries and World Wide Web Sites and Page Persistence." *Information Research* 4 (June). Available: http://InformationR .net/ir/4-4/paper60.html (accessed May 2006).

Koehler, Wallace, and Aaron Segal. 1987. "The Caribbean: Can Lilliput Make It?" In *Learning by Doing: Science and Technology in the Developing World*, edited by Aaron Segal, 55–81. Boulder, CO: Westview.

Kuhn, Thomas. 1962. *The Structure of Scientific Revolutions*. Chicago: University of Chicago Press.

Lisetti, Christine L., Sarah Brown, Kaye Alvarez, and Andreas Marpaung. 2004. "A Social Informatics Approach to Human-Robot Interaction with an Office Service Robot." *IEEE Transactions on Systems, Man, and Cybernetics* 34 (May): 195–209. Available: www.eurecom.fr/~lisetti/ ascg/pdf/Lisetti-IEEE-TR-SMC-HRI-SocialInformaticsRobot-2004 .pdf (accessed February 2007).

Mwesige, Peter G. 2004. "'Can You Hear Me Now?': Radio Talk Shows and Political Participation in Uganda." Ph.D. dissertation, Indiana University.

Negroponte, Nicholas. 1995. *Being Digital*. New York: Knopf.

O'Donnell, James J. 1998. *Avatars of the Word: From Papyrus to Cyberspace*. Cambridge, MA: Harvard University Press.

Wells, H. G. 1938. *World Brain*. London: Methuen.

ADDITIONAL SOURCES

About.com. 2006. *Inventors*. Available: http://inventors.about.com (accessed December 2006).

American National Standards Institiute. *ANSI*. Available: www.ansi.org (accessed December 2006).

Basbanes, Nicholas A. 1995. *A Gentle Madness: Bibliophiles, Bibliomanes, and the Eternal Passion for Books.* New York: Henry Holt.

Bibliotheca Alexandrina. Available: www.bibalex.org/English/index.aspx (accessed December 2006).

Ellens, J. Harold. 2002. "You Can Look it Up." In *The Origins of Things, or, How the Hour Got Its Minutes,* edited by Alan L. Boegehold and Jack Meinhardt, 63–67. Washington, DC: Biblical Archaeology Society.

Fang, Irving, and Kristina Ross. 1996. *The Media History Project Timeline.* The Media History Project. Available: www.mediahistory.umn.edu/time/century.html (accessed December 2006).

Febvre, Lucien, and Henri Jean Martin. 1997. *The Coming of the Book: The Impact of Printing 1450–1800.* New York: Verso.

Institute of Electrical and Electronics Engineers. 2006. *IEEE.* Available: www.ieee.org/portal/index.jsp (accessed December 2006).

International Telecommunication Union. 2006. *ITU.* Available: www.itu.int/home/index.html (accessed December 2006).

Internet Corporation for Assigned Names and Numbers. 2006. *ICANN.* Available: www.icann.org (accessed December 2006).

Internet Engineering Task Force. *IETF.* Available: www.ietf.org (accessed December 2006) .

Internet Society. 2006. *Internet Society.* Available: www.isoc.org (accessed December 2006).

Kilgour, Frederick G. 1998. *The Evolution of the Book.* New York: Oxford University Press.

McMurtrie, Douglas C. 1943. *The Book: The Story of Printing and Bookmaking.* New York: Oxford University Press.

Media History Project. 1996. Minneapolis: University of Minnesota School of Journalism and Mass Communication. Available: www.mediahistory.umn.edu (accessed December 2006).

New Voyage Communications. 2000. *Tesla, Master of Lightning.* Public Broadcasting System. Available: www.pbs.org/tesla (accessed December 2006).

Olmert, Michael. 1992. *The Smithsonian Book of Books.* Washington, DC: Smithsonian Books.

Rogers, Timothy. 2002. "A Codex Moment." In *The Origins of Things, or, How the Hour Got Its Minutes,* edited by Alan L. Boegehold and Jack Meinhardt, 105–110. Washington, DC: Biblical Archaeology Society.

Von Thaden, Terry. 2000. "Social Informatics and Aviation Technology." *Bulletin of the American Society for Information Science* 26 (February/

March): 13–14. Available: www.asis.org/Bulletin/Mar-00/von_thaden .html (accessed February 2007).

World Wide Web Consortium. 2006. *W3C.* Available: www.w3.org (accessed December 2006).

Before beginning this chapter, review your list of historical innovations in information technology from chapter 4. Continue to add to your list of information technologies as you read.

Chapter 5

Current Information Technology

Learning Guide

After reading this chapter, you should be able to

- define the following acronyms:
  - POTS
  - OCR
  - ARPANET
  - LAN
  - WAN
  - DLS
  - ISDN
  - GUI
  - OPAC
  - HTML
  - WAIS
  - VR
  - RFID
  - BPL
  - RSS

- identify and describe current information technology used to create, read, store, retrieve, and transmit data and information;
- analyze and describe the differences among information systems that perform similar information functions;
- discuss the most critical current problems with information technology.

  When you have finished the chapter, return to this page to be sure you have learned what you need to know.

INTRODUCTION

As we move from the history of information technology to the consideration of current information technology, it is important to acknowledge that discussion in a printed book of "current" information technology is not a possibility. Change in the technological environment is now occurring at such a rapid pace that any description of "current" technologies will, by the time these words appear in print, be historical. This chapter should perhaps more accurately be titled "More Recent Information Technology."

The previous chapter explored in very broad terms the evolution in the development of information technology and the innovation those technologies bring. We saw that changes in information bring improvements in information dissemination, distribution, storage, collection, and retrieval. We also saw that not only do information technologies affect society, the social ground must be prepared to receive those technologies if society is to benefit from them.

This chapter is a further introduction to the functions and use of technology used to create, read, transmit, store, and retrieve data and information. Remember the "bigger, faster, farther" dynamic we saw as technology develops, and the fourth characteristic posited at the beginning of the previous chapter: more complex. In addition, the new technologies demand new economic thinking. Traditional models may no longer apply. For example, information vendors like journal and book publishers often price their products at a much steeper discount for purchasers in the newly industrializing countries (NIC) (see the digital divide discussion in chapter 13). Commentators refer to the "one legal copy" phenomenon, whereby software and sometimes hardware is purchased and copied without permission from the copyright holder ("pirated") and then distributed locally again at a steep discount in the NICs. Why have not the software and hardware manufacturers gone after these "pirates" with more vigor than they do? Perhaps because there is more profit in selling legal copies in the information economies at a higher price than in lowering the price across the board to a point where it can be afforded by users in the NICs. Or perhaps it is because enforcement and prosecution are simply not worth the cost and ill will.

This chapter's focus is on current (or "more recent") technology rather than on the history of information technology. We will also speculate on prevailing trends and possible future directions in information technology development.

As we explore current technologies and future trends, ask yourself two questions. First,

what are the potential positive and negative implications of this technology as now used and the potential implications of adaptations of this technology?

Second,

do the current and new technologies represent something actually new or are they extensions of older technologies?

For example, Kurzweil technology is software that translates scanned documents into speech. It was developed to assist blind and vision impaired readers. This technology combines scanner technology, optical character recognition (OCR), and computer voice technologies with Microsoft or Apple platforms to produce the spoken word from printed text. Is it a new concept, a new technology? Maybe, but it is also an extension of the idea underlying Braille.

DATA CREATION AND CONVERSION

Information technologies enable a variety of functions related to information, from creation to preservation. There are a number of technologies that can and do generate data on the fly. These are generally classed under the rubric "real-time monitoring." There are numerous applications of real-time monitoring. Some of these systems are interactive; others are not.

Real-time Monitoring Systems

Keep in mind that the idea of real-time monitoring is nothing new. Perhaps the best known such system is the thermostat, a simple closed system used to regulate temperature. When the temperature becomes too high or too low, as measured by a thermometer, the heating or cooling is switched and kept on until the desired status quo is returned. Another example of a real-time monitoring system is the seismograph, used to measure tremors in the earth and maintain a record of those tremors.

There are important medical applications of such systems now in use, with others in the development pipeline. Hospitals employ an extensive array of real-time monitoring systems for their patients. These range from pulse oximetry (measuring oxygen concentration in the blood) to online electrocardiography. These and many other devices provide a constant read-out of patient data and often alert staff when changes occur.

Many military/police/security applications also exist. These include motion detection, the polygraph, and various identification systems. Home alarm systems fall within this category.

Numerous environmental systems employ real-time sensing. Some of these perform their data generation and recording on site; others utilize satellite technology. For example, farmers now use very sophisticated systems to monitor moisture and trigger irrigation systems as needed. Electric utilities monitor the demand for power, map that demand, and bring power plants on- or offline as needed. It is possible to monitor electricity usage at the household (and even sub-house) level to determine usage cycles for billing purposes. Public lavatories use motion detectors to trigger automated flushing.

Retailers may use sophisticated inventory control systems to track product popularity and to ascertain reorder and restocking priorities. Bar codes (recall the trend toward standardization from the previous chapter) can be found on almost any product sold anywhere. The bar code technology and standards were developed in the mid-1970s and are used in a wide range of industries—from libraries managing circulation to food retailers doing price and inventory control. Now replacing bar codes as tracking devices in some industries are the more recently developed Radio Frequency Identification, or RFID, tags, which, as the name implies, use radio frequency signals to identify, locate, and track movement of products.

Artificial Intelligence

Artificial intelligence, or AI, has numerous applications for data creation, conversion, and reading. Much work has been done to provide for machine translations. One of the oldest systems, SYSTRAN, has been adopted by a Web search engine to provide Web translations to and from a relatively small set of languages. The European Union, with some twenty official languages and probably more to come, has an extensive machine language translation initiative and a very large thesaurus of terms. As anyone who experiments with the translators knows, they do not quite get it. But they are doing better.

AI applications for interpreting information have been in the area of expert systems. Expert systems work fairly successfully where there are well-delineated, perhaps binary, decision paths. Many help desks offer a kind of AI:

Your computer won't work?
Check to see, is it plugged in?
Yes, is the switch on?
No, plug it in.

A number of real applications have been made in medical diagnostics, where AI is particularly useful in ruling out potential diseases. It is nowhere nearly sophisticated enough to offer comprehensive treatment programs or to handle the many patient variables that the human practitioner can. AI can offer guidelines. Most AI experts believe that AI systems that truly mimic or replace human decision systems are in the future.

Information Creation and Manipulation Systems

Let us not forget the explosion of technology that allows us to manipulate words, images, and sounds. Word processing and desktop publishing are extensions of the quill pen and the scriptorium of the Middle Ages. Spreadsheet programs allow us to manipulate data. Other computer-based technologies offer a wide set of options for information creation and manipulation. It is likely that these technologies will continue to develop to assist in the information creation process. Already software and hardware are available that offer voice recognition and handwriting conversion.

There have been major advances in document printing, facilitating the dissemination of information. The first color desktop printer became available in the mid-1990s. High-quality color printing was available within just a few years. Several companies make 3D "printers" that produce resin "hard" copies of computer-generated models. These models can then be tested under "real" conditions. For example, aircraft models can be placed in wind tunnels.

Similarly, copying and fax technologies have improved. Xerography was invented by Chester Carlson in 1938, but it did not begin to revolutionize document reproduction until 1958. Prior to photocopying, multiple copies were made on "mimeograph" and "ditto" machines. Single copies of important documents were made using a photographic process or "photostat." Carbon paper was ubiquitous. The fax machine was invented even before xerography, patented in 1843 as a means of scanning images and transmitting them via telegraph, but the fax was not introduced into common use until the mid-1980s, providing the means for almost instantaneous transmission of documents in their original formats over any distance.

INFORMATION TRANSMISSION

Beyond systems for information creation and manipulation, we have systems for information transmission. To recapitulate the discussion in chapter 4, human beings have always transmitted information, if only by screaming at the top of their lungs. Certainly we continue to transmit information over very short distances using light and sound. The telegraph made it possible for us to transmit information over long distances almost instantaneously. And as Tom Standage (1998) has shown us, pneumatic systems were very popular in the mid-nineteenth century to send messages within cities.

We now communicate electromagnetically over the airwaves and optically and electronically over copper wire and fiber optics. The quest is to develop systems to increase transmission volumes, the quality of those transmissions (e.g., noise reduction, signal reproductivity), and the speed at which those signals travel.

Wire transmission is old technology. Analog telephony and telegraphy have been with us for more than 120 years. POTS (plain old telephone service) has improved, costs have been lowered, and the service is rapidly moving away from a solely copper-wire–based technology. Other systems, cable TV for example, have taken greater advantage of fiber optics. This is in part due to the economics of service. Unlike some other utilities, cable has not been subject to universal access requirements; and hence cable has not been strung where it is not profitable to do so. In addition, cable has, by and large, built new infrastructure, which often is less costly than retrofitting that which already exists. POTS, as well, has begun replacing much of its copper wire, but that has not yet fully been achieved for many of the residential customers. Residential customers are often still connected to the system with copper wire—the infamous last mile.

We concern ourselves with POTS, copper wire, and fiber optics because many residential Internet users are connected through their POTS copper-wire service. The Internet, of course, is "old technology." It was developed in the early 1960s, originally as ARPANET (Advanced Research Project Agency Network) as an internet between the U.S. Department of Defense and its contractors, many of them universities. By the early 1980s, ARPANET had migrated to NSFnet (National Science Foundation net). It lost its primary defense function and became a research tool. By the early 1990s, the Department of Commerce and the National Science Foundation undertook to move the system into the private sector, and thus began the commercialization of the Internet. The Internet was recognized as a major new medium; and with the introduction of the World Wide Web in 1991 and the advent of "user friendly" browsers beginning with Mosaic and now multiple versions of Netscape and Internet Explorer plus increasingly popular alternatives such as Firefox, Web surfing is a relatively simple undertaking—that is, if one has fast connectivity and adequate bandwidth to support the volume of information transmitted.

The Internet, intranets, and extranets have spawned interconnectivity needs. These include local area networks (LANs) and their attendant hardware needs and Wide Area Networks (WANs) and their attendant needs. As new hardware and software are developed to support greater bandwidth, new hardware and software are developed to demand greater bandwidth and computing speed. For example, transmission capacity went from 300 baud in the early 1980s to the 56K modem in use today. But 56K is nothing compared to other copper-wire–based technologies like ISDN (integrated services digital network), at four times the capacity of the 56K modem, or DSL (digital subscriber line), reaching 1.5 Mbps (megabytes per second). These pale in comparison to the speeds attainable with T1 and T3 connectivity and from satellite up and down feeds.

We are now moving away from wired systems toward wireless ones. Wireless Internet (Wi-Fi), cell phones, hand-held devices (PDAs), smart houses, are with us and new applications are around the corner. We can expect newer and faster connectivity, as well as new applications for the Internet, Internet-2, and other systems now in planning.

One ongoing concern related to information transmission, regardless of the technology used, has been mechanisms to ensure the information is transmitted only to those for whom it was intended and not to others who might wish to access it and use it, either for ill-gotten gains or for other more threatening harm. Steganography and cryptography are two general approaches for protecting transmission by creating and sending "secret" messages. Steganography is the art of hiding a message, while cryptography encodes the message. The use of invisible ink is a classic example of steganography.

With the advent of digital communications, both steganography and cryptography have become more sophisticated. Steganographic messages can be embedded in various digital streams, including graphic and audio files (Johnson, Duric, and Jajodia, 2000: 58). For an online explanation, see Neil F. Johnson's Web site [1995–2003] at www.jjtc.com/stegdoc/steg1995.html.

The Internet is now recognized as a mechanism through which terrorists and criminals—as well as the rest of us—may communicate. Because it is relatively easy to apply stenographic or cryptographic messages, the Internet is particularly prone to be used for nefarious purposes without detection (Hinnen, 2003). At the same time, use of these types of protections, particularly the use of encrypted files, is necessary to ensure safe transmission of financial information over the Internet and to safeguard against identity theft, which has become a major societal concern.

A recent technological innovation is Internet telephony technology, resulting in Internet competition with POTS. Internet telephony can carry both audio and video signals using TC/IP and SIP (session initiation protocol) technology. In 2003, a number of vendors began offering Internet telephony services and equipment or "voice over IP" (VoIP) service in the United States and Europe. These include such companies as AT&T, Avaya, British Telecom, Cisco Systems, ITXC, Lucent Technologies, Nortel Networks, Qwest Communications International, 3Com, Siemens, Sprint, Time Warner Cable, and Verizon Communications.

The Federal Communications Commission (FCC) in the United States has taken a mixed approach to regulation of Internet telephony, not yet clearly indicating if it will be treated as an information service or as the equivalent of traditional phone service and thus subject to regulations and requirements for traditional service, such as contribution to federal universal service programs. In early 2004, then FCC Chairman Michael Powell indicated that in his opinion Internet telephony differed fundamentally from POTS. This followed a U.S. District Court ruling in October 2003 in Minnesota that Internet technologies were as yet unregulated territory. In November 2004 the FCC ruled that the federal government, not state public utility commissions, had regulatory authority over VoIP (U.S. Federal Communications Commission 2004b). In May 2005 the Commission ruled that Internet phone service providers have to provide 911 emergency service, and in May 2006 the FCC ruled that VoIP providers are subject to the requirements of the Communications Assistance for Law Enforcement Act (U.S. Federal Communications Commission, 2005, 2006).

A second competing technology is Broadband over Power Line (BPL), also called Digital Power Line (DPL) and PLC (Power Line Communications), a broadband technology that can carry signals over low-voltage power lines and that is capable of carrying Internet traffic up to 3 mbps. One advantage that BPL has over other "wired" systems is effective access for rural users, who already have power line access. Both telephony and television can be BPL supported.

One downside to BPL is that it can interfere with radio transmissions. To address the interference issues while at the same time encouraging development of this technology, the Federal Communications Commission issued rules covering BPL equipment and operations that are designed to prevent interference (U.S. Federal Communications Commission, 2004a). The European Commission has also made recommendations to member states in support of development of PLC (what it is called in Europe) technology (European Commission, 2005).

Information Ideas

Understanding the Basics: A Science-Technology Primer

Almost all communications signals are carried over some form of wave, whether they are electromagnetic (including visible light) or sound. Waves vary in size from very long to very short.

These signals are expressed in terms of wavelengths and frequencies. Basically, a wavelength is measured between the wave peaks using the metric scale: kilometers, meters, centimeters, millimeters, etc.

The distance between wave peaks can be quite large and measured in multiple meters or it can be very small (for an interesting and very readable discussion, see NASA's "The Electromagnetic Spectrum" at http://imagers.gsfc.nasa

(*Continued on p. 93*)

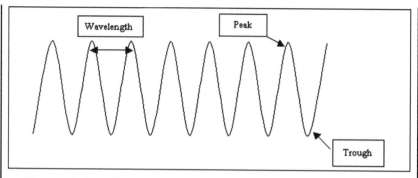

Figure 5-1   Digital Signals

.gov/ems/waves3.html). The visible spectrum, the light and colors we see, lie at about 10E-5 cm wavelength. Radio waves, for the most part, are much longer and have wavelengths of about 10E4 to 10E6 cm. An AM radio wave, then, would be more than two kilometers long. At the very low end of the amateur radio band is VLF/ELF or very low frequency to extremely low frequency long wave radio. The bottom end of ELF is a wavelength of the order of 100,000 km.

Radio frequencies and energies are often expressed not in distances between peaks but rather in cycles. Cycles are measured in iterations per second, or the number of times a wave peak (or trough) passes a certain point in a second. The basic unit of measure is the "hertz," abbreviated hz, and it is usually expressed in orders of magnitude, e.g., kilohertz, gigahertz, etc.

We find expression of this speed in computers and modems. For example, processor speeds and online transmission speeds are expressed as cycles, as some order of magnitude in hertz. The greater the number, the greater is the at-least-theoretical processing or transmission potential of the machine.

The third factor one might consider is "power." Power is a function of the amount of energy used in generating the signal, or watts peak envelope power (PEP). The more power behind a signal, the further it goes and the more clearly it goes. Power, watts, are also expressed in orders of magnitude.

AM and FM

We are used to speaking of radio transmissions as "AM" or "FM" or amplitude modulated or frequency modulated signals. Put very simply, the electromagnetic wave can be modified in several ways to "carry the message." AM or amplitude modulated signals and FM or frequency modulated signals are best known to radio listeners.

Electromagnetic waves in their modulations are "encoded" and "reinterpreted" to produce a variety of visual and aural signals that we can physically

(Continued on p. 94)

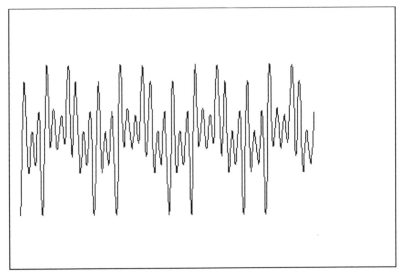

Figure 5-2   Amplitude Modulation Signals

interpret or as electronic signals that other machines—such as computers via modems—can interpret.

AM and FM radio transmissions have different qualitative characteristics. We appreciate that FM carries sound fidelity better than FM but AM travels farther.

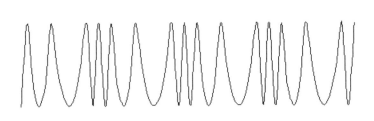

Figure 5-3   Frequency Modulation Signals

Codes

We are probably familiar with the concept behind Morse Code—letters and other characters can and are communicated electronically and through other media. These were often then converted to sound to be interpreted by a human key operator.

The electronic representation of information is by no means a new idea, just as the visual or aural representation of that same information is far older,

(*Continued on p. 95*)

A .-
B-...
C -.-.
D -..
E .
F ..-.
G --.
H ----
I ..
J .---
K -.-
L .-..
M --
N -.
O ---
P .--.
Q --.-
R .-.
S ...
T -
U ..-
V ...-
W .--
X .--.
Y- .--
Z --..

0 -----
1 .----
2 ..---
3 ...--
4 ....-
Etc.

Figure 5-4   International Morse Code

as we have already seen. Morse Code and its variants are too limiting for the kinds and range of communications we wish for and demand today. Note that the code supports a single alphabet, the Latin alphabet, in a single case, without accent or diacritical marks. It is, in sum, an extremely limited code that fulfills an extremely important role.

One reason for keeping Morse Code simple was the limitations of the human sender and receiver. While some expert telegraphers were (and are) magnificent, the typical user can only manage a few characters/words per

(*Continued on p. 96*)

minute with any degree of accuracy. Computers exchanging information, however, are another matter. One more complex answer has been the American Standard Code for Information Interchange, or ASCII. ASCII is a numerical code for various letters and characters written in hexadecimals.

ASCII has been criticized as too limited, as too Eurocentric. Other codes, among them Unicode, have been developed to support non-Latin alphabets. The concepts underlying ASCII and Unicode are the same: each character in each lexicon is represented by a unique number. Although there are many characters and perhaps new characters being developed, there are indeed an infinite number of numbers available that can be assigned to each of the characters. Not only that, these codes must represent the characters correctly in different computer languages on different platforms as well.

Bits and Bytes

Computers, and as we will see much of the rest of the "new" information world, are vested in a binary mathematics—an environment of zeroes and ones. The term "bit" is shorthand for binary digit. Binary numbers, base 2 numbers, are values expressed differently from values we are normally used to seeing in base 10.

Base 2	Base 10
0	0
1	1
10	2
11	3
100	4
101	5
110	6
111	7
1000	8

We use the "natural" digital numbering system, perhaps, because most human beings have ten manual digits. Note, however, that not all human societies at all times have used base 10 counting systems for all things (like twelve inches in a foot, three feet to a yard, 5280 feet to a mile, or until recent memory, British money).

A byte is a set of bits. It usually consists of eight bits, seven significant, that are sufficient to represent one ASCII character, for example. Note that ASCII characters are all one-byte size. In Unicode, Chinese, Japanese, and Korean characters require typically two bytes to represent them.

(*Continued on p. 97*)

Digital Concepts

The binary business is essential to the digital revolution. Note that Base 2 mathematics is a matter of zeroes and ones. Those zeroes and ones can and are represented by electronic or optical pulses switched to "on" or "off." Digital technologies interpret these zeroes and ones, the "on's" and "off's," and provide near-perfect transmission and replication of signal.

STORAGE AND RETRIEVAL: ELECTRONIC DATABASES

Information that has been created may or may not be immediately transmitted; and, even if it is, there must be systems to store the information received and to retrieve it when needed. The first system to retrieve documents in electronic form remotely was developed by the Lockheed Corporation for the U.S. Department of Defense in 1965. At the time, the documents retrieved were bibliographic records, produced in electronic form as a byproduct of the publication of the print format of the records. That bibliographic retrieval system was commercialized as the Dialog Corporation in 1972. Dialog and a number of other online services (Ovid, STN, LexisNexis, WestLaw, First-Search, WilsonWeb, EBSCOhost, ProQuest and so on) provide customized or specialized interface services to a wide range of databases, including access to hundreds of databases created and maintained by other entities. For example, the first database appearing in the Dialog list is ERIC, a product supported by the U.S. Department of Education.

These database retrieval systems were originally linked to their clients by telephone links. Many, like Mead Data Central, the predecessor of Lexis-Nexis, provided clients with rudimentary computers and acoustical couplers running at 300 baud. These systems have since developed sophisticated telnet and now Web GUIs (graphical user interfaces) to facilitate navigation of the database interface.

The Web search engines and Web resident and client resident metasearch engines also offer sophisticated GUI access to search and retrieval services. These systems and the portals that support them have added additional services, such as SDI (selective dissemination of information) services, including push and pull information delivery. Push technologies provide information crafted to the interests and wants of the end user. Most push technologies employ a form of automated "pull." The "pull" is the search and retrieval of new information. The push then is the provision of selected elements of the pull to the end user, based on the user's preferences for information. For example, if you are not interested in newspaper funnies, you might select the

New York Times as your electronic newspaper of choice, and you might limit it to the financial pages. Alternatively, you might also want financial information from various sources, which would be searched and the information relevant to your preferences would be automatically sent to you. For those interested in a continuous push of information in a near real-time mode, the RSS (Really Simple Syndication or Rich Site Summary) feed available from a plethora of information sources provides information retrieved and transmitted from data stores as soon as the storage is accomplished.

Electronic databases have also spawned data mining, data drilling, and knowledge discovery. Data mining has been defined as a methodology to "analyze patterns in data and extract information" (Trybula, 1997: 199). Data mining utilizes various statistical and vector techniques to find otherwise unanticipated relations in the database. Knowledge discovery, "the process of transforming data into previously unknown or unexpected relationships" for the purpose of prediction or other uses (Trybula, 1997: 199), then follows data mining. Data drilling in databases refers to the process of extracting data at increasing levels of detail.

STORAGE AND RETRIEVAL: DIGITAL LIBRARIES

Digital libraries, including Web-based collections, are redefining the role of electronic information storage and retrieval as well as the role of traditional libraries. As Ching-chih Chen has argued, no cohesive or comprehensive theory of digital libraries has yet to be fully developed. Digital libraries include collections of books, journal articles, graphics, newspapers, and other material in digital format; in sum, collections of digitized content. To be a library, that collection should be organized according to some standard (Chen, 1998).

There are many examples of digital libraries. These include Project Gutenberg, the U.S. Library of Congress National Digital Library Program, online journal collections, and so on. The U.S. National Science Foundation is supporting a number of projects to develop and maintain science and technology digital libraries (Zia, 2001). These libraries, like traditional libraries, vary in their collections and their complexity (Bailey, 2006). The Digital Library Federation offers one definition of digital libraries:

> Digital libraries are organizations that provide the resources, including the specialized staff, to select, structure, offer intellectual access to, interpret, distribute, preserve the integrity of, and ensure the persistence over time of collections of digital works so that they are readily and economically available for use by a defined community or set of communities. (Digital Library Federation, 2006)

Michael Lesk (1997) suggests that digital libraries share three common traits: (1) they can all be searched, (2) they can all be accessed from anywhere, and (3) they can all be copied using electronic means without error.

Are digital libraries, then, traditional libraries but more so? Or do they have unique attributes? There are several perspectives. Pinfield et al. (1998) conceive of a combined traditional and digital library, an entity they term "hybrid library." The hybrid library is with us now. Many academic and public libraries have incorporated digital material into their collections if only by incorporating links to that material in their online public access catalogs (OPACs). Libraries might simply "morph" into gigantic and hopefully well-organized portals, or as Lancaster and Warner describe one model, into "switching center[s]" (Lancaster and Warner, 2001: 118). A "switching center" is seen as an information institution that owns none of its resources but serves as a clearinghouse to refer its clients to the desired resource. Switching centers add value by organizing routes of access in more efficient or understandable ways. Atkinson (1993) emphasizes the need for organization, selection, and management of resources in digital libraries just as these resources are managed in traditional libraries.

These tasks may be similar to those provided by traditional libraries, but they require a very different set of tools—technologies if you will—to perform them. The computer science and information science disciplines have been very active in developing digital library technology covering a wide range of commercial, theoretical, and experimental approaches. These technologies include information storage and retrieval technologies, from the Web search engines to development and testing of experimental retrieval engines using Boolean, vector, "fuzzy," probabilistic, and natural language systems. Sometimes these technologies are tested in the real world. Sometimes they are tested using experimental test beds, like the National Institute of Standards and Technology's Text Retrieval Conference database (TREC). For a much more extensive treatment of information storage and retrieval, see Robert Korfhage (1997).

Others are looking at ways to catalog, index, and archive digital documents, including Web pages, using "metadata." The term "metadata" is used to define data about data. For example, when you register for a college class, you are frequently asked to provide an identification code. Your personal code is "data." The instructions on how and where that data will appear in each personal record are "metadata." There are extensive metadata proposals using various markup languages and conventions to provide this service of identifying documents and their information content.

The field of metadata is complex and dynamic. Metadata is being developed to describe all media forms and multimedia, and R&D is being performed to create systems to more efficiently and effectively automate the harvesting of metadata. There are numerous initiatives to develop systems to describe and identify data using special coding, including markup language, that specify the formatting, placement, and processing of the text as well as providing information about the text:

- Dublin Core, the leading Web metadata system, consists of fifteen elements or metadata categories and is an initiative of the U.S. Library of Congress, the Online Computer Library Center (OCLC), and other national libraries worldwide.
- OCLC, originally the Cooperative Online Resource Catalog, is a service developed by OCLC to assist academic libraries and others to catalog digital resources.
- There are a number of SGML/XML–based initiatives, primarily for non-Web, digital resources. These include:
  - the Digital Object Identifier (DOI) used in commercial applications
  - the Government or Global Information Locator Service (GILS) used by the U.S. federal government, some state governments, and a number of other national governments
  - the Platform for Internet Content Selection (PICS) for first- and third-party Web page markup and used, for example, by some filtering software
  - the Resource Description Framework (RDF) used to consolidate metadata into a single system
  - Corpus Encoding Standard (CES), Encoded Archival Description Document Type Definition (EAD DTD), the Model Editions Partnership (MEP), and the Text Encoding Initiative (TEI), all with archival applications
  - Rich Site Summary or Really Simple Syndication (RSS), used for Web syndication

Before leaving these various markup languages, it should be noted that these are all based on HTML, hypertext markup language, first suggested by Vannevar Bush in 1945, conceptualized by Ted Nelson's development of hyperlinks, and first used by Tim Berners-Lee in constructing the WWW. The language of the Web has undergone extensive enhancement since 1991, and changes to each version of HTML emerge almost daily. The changes are guided by strict standards, many of which are administered and vetted by W3C (see discussion of standardization in chapter 4).

INTERACTIVE SYSTEMS: STORAGE, RETRIEVAL, AND CREATION COMBINED

A significant change in our "more recent" information technologies is the development of interactive systems. Over much of the history of recorded information, the systems used to record and provide access to information have been more or less static. That is to say, we could access—usually read—what had been recorded, but we did not actively enter into the system or interact with it to mold the direction taken or the information available. We dealt with what was there, usually in a linear mode. This situation was not always the case, of course, especially in the very earliest times when the storage of the information was in human memory. We could interact with the system (the person) then to shape what we received. But for the most part, we did not have the capacity to tailor what we got. With the development of interactive systems, we now have the capacity to take part in the creation of the record that we access, or at least take part in shaping our experience with it.

As anyone who has played computer games can tell you, interactive systems have a wide variety of applications. They can be used for entertainment—the games. They can be used for training. Airlines, flight schools, and the military use flight simulators to teach people how to fly airplanes.

Interactive systems began as (by today's standards) fairly low-tech boxes that one attached to a television set. At first, black-and-white images chased little pills to eat them or blow them up. Some games have migrated to bigger and faster computers and others are still very sophisticated boxes (again by today's standards) attached to TV sets.

Interactive systems have evolved far beyond a joystick and a TV, and so have their applications. Oil companies use caves or rooms where all surfaces are used to project images to better understand drilling and extraction technologies. Museums have created holographic images of artifacts in their collections or in the collections of other museums. These images permit patrons to examine artifacts much more intimately than could be permitted before. Medical students and physicians practice surgical procedures before encountering live patients. Others use virtual reality to treat anxiety disorders and for pain management (Lear, 1997).

Computer games began as rudimentary virtual reality (VR) experiences. The characters and the settings are now much more realistic, and the day when whole-body participation in the VR experience is commonplace is almost upon us. VR can be used for a wide variety of applications, in education and training and in entertainment. Although we suspect the entertainment component will continue to drive the economics of the technology, at least in the near term, the applications in other settings, such as pain management and phobia therapy, for example, have great promise for improvement of the human condition.

Recent Internet-based additions to information sharing, blogs and wikis, enable us also to take part in the creation of the record, shifting us from being predominantly consumers of information to taking active part in its production. A blog (short for Weblog) is an online journal, which may take the form of a diary or may be more newspaper-like. Blogs are controlled by an individual or group of individuals. In contrast to the interaction possible in some other forms of web-published information, blog readers are most frequently permitted to leave comments and create threads of discussion. According to Wikipedia ("Blog," 2007), Travis Petler coined the term blog in 1997; and the early blogs were often created and managed by college students.

By 2007, Technorati (2007) was tracking more than 70 million blogs, with 175,000 new blogs created daily. This blog growth has occurred in all social sectors, with the blog clearly no longer the exclusive domain of the undergraduate student. Some blogs have taken on the role of journalism, while others provide commentary from the sublime to the ridiculous on any and all human concerns.

Wikis, in comparison, are also interactive online means of communication. The term refers to the online communication format and to the HTML-based "collaborative software" as well ("Wiki," 2007). Unlike blogs, where the "owner" posts commentary and controls the posts of readers, wikis are online interactive vehicles that permit others to create and edit postings. The first real wiki, WikiWikiWeb, was created in 1994 by Howard "Ward" Cunningham. The term "wiki" may have been derived from the Hawaiian for quick or fast.

The best known and perhaps most accessed wiki is *Wikipedia*. Like all wikis, *Wikipedia* permits its "members" and others to post new articles to the online encyclopedia. It also has established a mechanism for editing and proofing entries both by contributors and by its own editors and subject experts.

Facebook, created in 2004, and YouTube, created in 2005, are Web-based social communications and sharing media, part of the burgeoning social networking that has emerged rapidly in the first decade of the twenty-first century. Both Facebook and YouTube are social engines that support the exchange of graphic and video materials. Facebook was created to support social networking among college students (and others possessing .edu e-mail addresses). It has since grown into an interlinking network of different communities.

Interactive technology has been seen as a vehicle to enhance social interactivity as well as a mechanism for better educational delivery. Michael Bugeja has described part of the downside of these interactive vehicles, at least in an educational environment:

Increasingly, however, our networks are being used to entertain members of "the Facebook Generation" who text-message during class, talk on their cellphones during labs, and listen to iPods rather than guest speakers in the wireless lecture hall. (Bugeja, 2006)

Christine Rosen (2004) is critical of Facebook-like technologies, referring to them as "egocasting." Rosen's critique is an elaboration on the work of Cass Sunstein (2001). Sunstein argues that the "channelization" of information, the ability of information consumers to limit the material provided to them through a wide variety of technology—from cable TV, online newspapers, and by extension online social networks—inhibits access to nonselected information. This self-insularity and isolation inhibits learning and may have antidemocratic effects.

It should be noted, however, that all of these interactive, social networking–type media are increasingly significant in the political arena and as part of the democratic election process in the United States. For example, Bill Richardson, a candidate for the Democratic nomination for President of the United States in 2008, linked from his home page to videos of his appearances on YouTube and to his MySpace and Facebook entries. Likewise, Hilary Clinton, another Democratic candidate, posted videos on YouTube, as did Mitt Romney, a candidate for the Republican nomination.

STORAGE AND PRESERVATION

Information containers have had to be stored, preserved, and restored ever since there were information technologies. Regardless of the medium used to record information, there needs to be some means to ensure continued access to that information as the technologies used for recording information change. The digitization of information has created new demands and new challenges for information preservation. Storage and preservation technologies now are being advanced and developed both for the "legacy" (used to refer to older, inherited) information systems and for the new ones.

There are two fundamental approaches to information preservation. The first is

to preserve the original "native" document through the application of some set of technologies.

Rare books, for example, are stored in cold vaults, first to preclude theft but also to slow deterioration. Various document forms are treated to reduce the acid content of paper. As anyone who has stored newspapers knows, they deteriorate very rapidly.

The second approach to preservation is

to make copies, particularly on materials less prone to deterioration than the original.

Many paper documents have been digitized, both to help preserve them and also to help distribute them more widely.

But preservation systems are also needed for digital documents. Web documents offer an even more complex challenge, since by their very nature they are ephemeral. Brewster Kahle, inventor of WAIS (Wide Area Information Server), has developed an Internet archive (see *www.archive.org*) in an attempt to provide long-term access to Web-based information. The Internet Archive is necessarily selective in its collection policies, for if it were to archive every Web page with every change to every page, the archive would quickly be overwhelmed.

How shall we preserve digital materials? Unlike their paper cousins, digital materials require complex hardware and software in order to retrieve and interpret them. The first problem with digital preservation is obsolescence. If one had stored important documents on 5.25-inch floppies, how easy would it be to retrieve that information with the current generation of technology? If one had information in VisiCalc, would present generation spreadsheets and operating systems be able to open and interpret the program? Given the speed of change of storage media, hardware, and software, data retrieval problems for digitized information are here and real. In order to preserve access to the information that has been stored in digital records, we have to plan for its continued migration to the currently operable technology or else revert back to storage media that do not require some kind of equipment interface. And then we have to find ways to ensure preservation of that media.

We do know that the useful lifetime for optical and magnetic media for perfect data retention is on the order of ten to twenty-five years. Microfilm has been shown to be the most stable, with a shelf life estimated at about 500 years. Many firms back up their digitized documents by creating microfilm using very sophisticated equipment. But microfilm has a downside: many of us would prefer not to use it. However, unlike digital documents that require sophisticated equipment in order to read them, microfilm can be read with a magnifying glass and a candle (although that is not the usual approach).

There is a growing industry that provides services, software, and hardware to allow digital archivists to migrate their data collections to new software and hardware. Many digital archivists have established migration schedules and move data to new media on a three- to five-year cycle.

A major resource addressing both information preservation and access concerns is under development sponsored by Google and in cooperation with

Harvard University, the University of Michigan, Oxford University, Stanford University, and the New York Public Library. The University of California system announced its intention to join the project in August 2006, the University of Wisconsin–Madison and the University Complutense of Madrid in October 2006, and the University of Virginia in November 2006. The University of Texas at Austin and the National Library of Catalonia joined in January 2007, followed by Princeton University in February 2007 and the Bavarian State Library in March 2007. The initiative, announced in December 2004 and launched in 2005, is to scan material both in and out of copyright at participating libraries and to provide searchable access to the digitized collection through what is now termed the Google Books Library Project. Under the plan only segments of copyrighted material will be made available directly to the end user without fee. Material out of copyright is to be made available in its entirety.

The Google Books project has the potential to form one of, if not the, largest digital library collection available online through retrospective digitization of existing print materials. A competitor project, the Open Content Alliance, initially sponsored by Yahoo! and the Internet Archive and now supported also by Microsoft and a growing number of libraries, is also scanning full texts of books as well as multimedia content that will be made available online and available for downloading from the Internet Archive. Materials still in copyright are scanned only with permission of the copyright holder (Open Content Alliance, 2005).

There are other such projects, for example the Library of Congress's American Memory collection or the ProQuest project to digitize early English-language texts (out of copyright). Other, more focused digital libraries include digital dissertation and thesis collections including the ETD Digital Thesis and Dissertation Project at Virginia Tech (see http://etd.vt.edu) as well as online thesis and dissertation services in Australia, Africa (abstracts only), most European countries, and the "more traditional" UMI ProQuest service. In addition there are a number of online bibliographic databases that provide access to full-text or abstracted literature, including books and journal articles. Finally, there are also a number of specialized digital libraries such as the National Science Digital Library (www.nsdl.org), JSTOR (which provides access to a select group of dated journal articles), and the International Children's Digital Library.

More than forty European national and other libraries have formed a major digitization project, the European Digital Library (EDL). In 2004, the EDL was formed as a result of an earlier pan-European initiative (TEL). The EDL received further support in August 2006, when the European Commission adopted a resolution recommending that member states undertake to digitize their documents and that National Libraries join together in the EDL project (for additional information, see http://libraries.theeuropeanlibrary .org/aboutus_en.html).

CONCLUSION

About thirty years ago, a leading information "futureolist" predicted a paper-less information system by the new millennium (Lancaster, 1977). Slightly over twenty years later, that futureolist, F. W. Lancaster (1999), recanted. Even Jean-Luc Picard, captain of the Starship Enterprise, likes his tea hot, Earl Grey, and a good book—make that codex—to curl up with.

This chapter has explored some of the new and emerging technologies for creating, transmitting, storing, retrieving, and preserving data and information. As the Picard anecdote suggests, the new does not always replace the old. It often augments it. Moreover, the new often brings with it unanticipated problems. What we do see and continue to see, as observed in the previous chapter, is the expansion of information, the increasing ubiquitousness of access, increased speeds, and new complexities. For the near future, technological change is the watchword. Before long, all the systems discussed in this chapter will qualify as "history" as new technologies come to replace them. Therefore, the information worker of today would be well advised to remain flexible and capable of adapting to new realties. The challenges of current information technology lie in managing the pace of change as new technologies augment older ones, while continuing to ensure access to information regardless of the technology through which it was originally recorded and disseminated.

QUESTIONS FOR CONSIDERATION

1. What are the challenges in preservation of access to digital materials that were not a concern for print materials?
2. Information systems that transmit information now enable "any time, any place" access to information. From the standpoint of the individual, what are some advantages and disadvantages of this type of access?
3. How do interactive information systems differ from static information systems? What are the implications for information preservation of having interactive information systems?
4. What would be the impact on design and use of information technology if there were no standards for development of information technology?

5. As quality and carrying capacity of information systems increase, will information be more or less easily available? What factors must be considered in answering this question?

REFERENCES

Atkinson, Ross. 1993. "Networks, Hypertext, and Academic Information Services: Some Longer-range Implications." *College & Research Libraries* 54 (May): 199–215.

Bailey, Charles W. 2006. *Scholarly Electronic Publishing Bibliography.* Version 65 (2 November). Available: www.digital-scholarship.com/sepb/sepb.html (accessed December 2006).

"Blog." 2007. *Wikipedia.* Available: http://en.wikipedia.org/wiki/Blog (accessed February 2007).

Blumenstyk, Goldie. 2001. "A Project Seeks to Digitize Thousands of Early English Texts." *The Chronicle of Higher Education* (29 June), 47.

Bugeja, Michael J. 2006. "Facing the Facebook." *Chronicle of Higher Education* (23 January). Available: http://chronicle.com/jobs/news/2006/01/2006012301c/careers.html (accessed February 2007).

Bush, Vannevar. 1945. "As We May Think." *The Atlantic Monthly* 176 (July): 101–108.

Carlson, Scott, and Jeffrey Young. 2004. "Google Will Digitize and Search Millions of Books From 5 Leading Research Libraries" *The Chronicle of Higher Education* (14 December). Available: http://chronicle.com/free/2004/12/2004121401n.htm (accessed December 2006).

Chen, Ching-chih. 1998. "Global Digital Library: Can the Technology Havenots Claim a Place in Cyberspace?" In *Proceedings of NIT '98: 10th International Conference on New Information Technology, Hanoi, Vietnam, March 24–26, 1998*, edited by Ching-chih Chen, 9–18. West Newton, MA: MicroUse Information.

Digital Library Federation. 2006. "A Working Definition of Digital Library [1998]." Available: www.diglib.org/about/dldefinition.htm (accessed December 2006).

European Commission. 2005. "High-speed Internet Access via the Electricity Grid: Commission Seeks to Create New Market Opportunities." Press Releases, 8 April. Available: http://europa.eu.int/rapid/pressReleasesAction.do?reference=IP/05/403&format=HTML&aged=0&language=en&guiLanguage=en (accessed December 2006).

Hinnen, Todd M. 2003. "The Cyber-front in the War on Terrorism: Curbing Terrorist Use of the Internet. Abstract." *Columbia Science and Technology*

Law Review 5, no. 5. Available: www.stlr.org/cite.cgi?volume=5&article =5 (accessed December 2006).

Johnson, Neil F. 1995–2003. "Steganography." Available: www.jjtc.com/ stegdoc/steg1995.html (accessed December 2006).

Johnson, Neil F., Zoran Duric, and Sushil Jajodia. 2000. *Information Hiding, Steganography and Watermarking—Attacks and Countermeasures.* Boston: Kluwer Academic Publishers.

Korfhage, Robert R. 1997. *Information Storage and Retrieval.* New York: Wiley Computer.

Lancaster, F. Wilfrid. 1977. *The Dissemination of Scientific and Technical Information: Toward a Paperless System.* Occasional Papers Series, no. 127. Champaign, IL: University of Illinois Graduate School of Library Science.

———. 1999. "Second Thoughts on the Paperless Society." *Library Journal* 124 (15 September): 48–50.

Lancaster, F. Wilfrid, and Amy Warner. 2001. *Intelligent Technologies in Library and Information Service Applications.* Medford, NJ: Information Today.

Lear, Anne C. 1997. "Virtual Reality Provides Real Therapy." *IEEE Computer Graphics and Applications* 17 (July/August): 16–20.

Lesk, Michael. 1997. *Practical Digital Libraries: Books, Bytes, and Bucks.* San Francisco: Morgan Kaufmann.

Markoff, John, and Edward Wyatt. 2004. "Google Is Adding Major Libraries to Its Database." *New York Times* (14 December): A1.

Open Content Alliance. 2005. "Global Consortium Forms Open Content Alliance to Bring Additional Content Online and Make It Searchable." Available: www.opencontentalliance.org/OCARelease.pdf (accessed December 2006).

Pinfield, Stephen, Jonathan Eaton, Catherine Edwards, Rosemary Russell, Astrid Wissenburg, and Peter Wynne. 1998. "Realizing the Hybrid Library." *D-Lib Magazine* 4 (October). Available: www.dlib.org/dlib/ october98/10pinfield.html (accessed December 2006).

Reuters. 2004. "FCC Chief Plans No Internet Phone Regulation." *USA Today* (22 January). Available: www.usatoday.com/tech/news/techpolicy/ 2004-01-22-voip-no-regs_x.htm (accessed December 2006).

Richtel, Matt. 2005. "Internet Phone Services Told to Offer 911 Emergency Calls." *New York Times* (20 May): C8.

Rosen, Christine. 2004/2005. "The Age of Egocasting." *The New Atlantis* no. 7 (Fall/Winter): 51–72. Available: www.thenewatlantis.com/archive/ 7/rosen.htm (accessed February 2007).

Standage, Tom. 1998. *The Victorian Internet: The Remarkable Story of the Telegraph and the Nineteenth Century's On-Line Pioneers.* New York: Walker.

Sunstein, Cass. 2001. *Republic.com*. Princeton, NJ: Princeton University Press.

Technorati. 2007. "About Technorati." Available: www.technorati.com/about (accessed March 2007).

Trybula, Walter J. 1997. "Data Mining and Knowledge Discovery." *Annual Review of Information Science and Technology* 32: 197–229.

U.S. Federal Communications Commission. 2004a. "FCC Adopts Rules for Broadband over Power Lines to Increase Competition and Promote Broadband Service to All Americans." *FCC News* (14 October). Available: http://hraunfoss.fcc.gov/edocs_public/attachmatch/DOC-253125A1 .pdf (accessed December 2006).

———. 2004b. "FCC Finds that Vonage not Subject to Patchwork of State Regulations Governing Telephone Companies." *FCC News* (9 November). Available: http://hraunfoss.fcc.gov/edocs_public/attachmatch/DOC -254112A1.pdf (accessed December 2006).

———. 2005. "Commission Requires Interconnected VoIP Providers to Provide Enhanced 911 Service; Order Ensures VoIP Customers Have Access to Emergency Services." *FCC News* (19 May). Available: http://hraunfoss.fcc.gov/edocs_public/attachmatch/DOC-258818A1 .doc (accessed December 2006).

———. 2006. " FCC Adopts Order to Enable Law Enforcement to Access Certain Broadband and VoIP Providers." *FCC News* (3 May). Available: http://hraunfoss.fcc.gov/edocs_public/attachmatch/DOC-265221A1 .doc (accessed December 2006).

"Wiki." 2007. *Wikipedia*. Available: http://en.wikipedia.org/wiki/Wiki (accessed February 2007).

Zia, Lee L. 2001. "The NSF National Science, Technology, Engineering, and Mathematics Education Digital Library (NSDL) Program: New Projects and a Progress Report." *D-Lib Magazine* 7 (November). Available: www .dlib.org/dlib/november01/zia/11zia.html (accessed December 2006).

ADDITIONAL SOURCES

Blood, Rebecca. 2002. *The Weblog Handbook: Practical Advice on Creating and Maintaining Your Blog*. Cambridge, MA: Perseus Book Group.

Hoffman, Hunter G., Jason N. Doctor, David R. Patterson, Gretchen J. Carrougher, and Thomas A. Furness, III. "Use of Virtual Reality for Adjunctive Treatment of Adolescent Burn Pain during Wound Care: A Case Report. *Pain* 85 (2000): 305–309. See also University of Washington Human Interface Technology Lab. "Virtual Reality Therapy." HITLab Projects. Available: www.hitl.washington.edu/research/vrpain (accessed December 2006).

International Digital Children's Library. Available: www.icdlbooks.org (accessed December 2006).

JSTOR. 2006. *Journal Storage, the Scholarly Journal Archive.* Available: www.jstor.org (accessed December 2006).

Kelly, D., C. Jennings, and L. Dang. 2002. *Practical VoIP Using Vocal.* Sebastopol, CA: O'Reilly.

Labaton, Stephen. 2004. "FCC Clears Internet Access by Power Lines." *New York Times* (15 October): C1.

Lynch, Clifford. 2002. "Digital Collections, Digital Libraries and the Digitization of Cultural Heritage Information." *First Monday* 7 (May). Available: www.firstmonday.org/issues/issue7_5/lynch/index.html (accessed December 2006).

Nardi, Bonnie A., Diane J. Schiano, Michelle Gumbrecht, and Luke Swartz. 2004. "Why We Blog." *Communications of the ACM* 47, no. 12 (December): 41–46.

National Science Digital Library. Available: http://nsdl.org/about/index.php (accessed December 2006).

Project Gutenberg. 2006. Available: www.gutenberg.org (accessed December 2006).

Rogers, Russ, and Matthew G. Devost. 2005. *Hacking a Terror Network: The Silent Threat of Covert Channels.* Rockland, MA: Syngress.

U.S. Library of Congress. n.d. *American Memory.* Available: http://memory.loc.gov/ammem/index.html (accessed December 2006).

Virginia Tech. 2003. *etd.vt.edu.* Available: http://etd.vt.edu/background (accessed December 2006).

Vonage Holdings Corp v. Minnesota Public Utilities Corp., et al. Available: www.nysd.uscourts.gov/courtweb/pdf/D08MNXC/03-08475.PDF

What are the institutions, agencies, or organizations that you know about or have used that either contribute to or facilitate the creation and distribution of information or that manage information or information records? Before you read further, make a list of all that you can think of at this time. For each one on your list, write a brief phrase describing its major function. When you have completed the chapter, check back to see if there are others that you need to add and decide whether you want to revise your descriptions of the functions.

Chapter 6

Societal Institutions for Creation, Distribution, and Management of Information

---

Learning Guide

After reading this chapter, you should be able to

- describe the historical development of societal institutions that create, distribute, and manage information;
- analyze the major functions of those institutions;
- compare and contrast the differences in clientele served;
- assess the impact on information users of current changes in the structure of the institutions.

When you have finished the chapter, return to this page to be sure you have learned what you need to know.

INTRODUCTION

In today's information environment, with the ready ability of anyone with access to a computer and an Internet connection to create and distribute information, not just to friends and acquaintances but throughout the world, and with the ever growing storage capacity for digital information available at ever decreasing costs, one might ask why there are institutions in society that are dedicated to creating, distributing, and managing information. What are the functions of such institutions? Do such institutions still have a viable place in the digital world? To answer such questions it is necessary to review what these organizations have done in the past, analyze how they function now, and consider how they might be changing by examining current trends.

Throughout recorded history (and probably before) there have been individuals, institutions, and agencies that have served to facilitate the process of creating, distributing, and making available to users the information records or "information artifacts" that, in the terms we used in chapter 2, make possible those "informative events" that change the shape of our inward image. These various entities facilitate the information transfer process between the source of the information, be that a person, an organization, or a piece of equipment, and the recipient of the potential information event, or between the sender and the receiver of a message. While we might think of these entities as forming the "bridge" between content and users (Tenopir, 1994: 33), they may also serve to assist in the formulation of the content.

For each information record there may be, and likely will be, several different entities that act on the record in some way in its journey from the creator of the record to the potential user. What is significant is not so much how many different institutions, organizations, or agencies affect the information record (and thereby the potential information event that the user will experience)—although that is not a trivial matter—but what each one does to the record to:

- alter it
- add value to it in some way
- delete portions of it
- change how and by whom it can be accessed and used
- increase the cost to the user

The capacity of the entities to affect and control information records has changed over time with the evolution of new technologies for creating and managing information, as discussed in chapters 4 and 5. What is also changing rapidly now is the degree of separation and independence of the various agencies that function to create, distribute, and manage information. Like the example of the individual person who now is capable of all these functions, so also are the previously separate agencies able to perform them all. As we shall see, this merging of functions was also the case in earlier times.

EARLY INSTITUTIONS AND PROCESSES

Although much of what was preserved and transmitted prior to the use of the printed book depended on the "arts of Memory" (Boorstin, 1983: 480), there were information records created in tangible forms that could be shared over time and space. Some of the physical records were not transportable over space, of course (for example, the information records in the form of cathedrals); and others were not sharable over time (such as smoke signals). But there were information records that constituted some form of stable, transportable communication. And there were societal institutions and agencies that were responsible for the creation, distribution, and management of information.

To recap some of what was discussed in chapter 4, in the ancient world, the medium of the information records of the time and the form they took varied by location. In Sumeria, Babylonia, and Assyria clay tablets, cylinders, and hexagonal prisms inscribed in cuneiform script were stored in earthen jars and baskets. In Egypt papyrus was the medium for information records, and the format was the roll: sheets pasted together to the length needed, secured at one end with a rod, and stored in round cylinders or in cubicles. In the eastern Mediterranean coastal area and islands both clay and papyrus, and leather as well, were used to record information. Other materials used included parchment and wood covered with wax. In the East, in China, information records were made on wood, bamboo, and silk. Although clay and papyrus were the dominant media up until about the fourth century CE, after that time the primary vehicle for stable information records became parchment, and the format became the codex: separate leaves bound together rather than pasted together into one long sheet.

There were libraries (collections of information records) in a variety of societal structures:

- private libraries in the homes of the wealthy
- royal or palace libraries, such as the noted library of Assurbanipal, King of Assyria (669–633 BCE), at Ninevah
- temple libraries and archives
- municipal libraries
- public libraries in both the Greek and Roman world

The greatest library of the ancient world was that in Alexandria, founded in the third century BCE.

Throughout the period of the Middle Ages, in the West, the primary institution that performed the functions of assisting in the creation of information, producing copies of information records that could be distributed, preserving and storing copies of information records, and making such copies available to the very limited audience that was literate was the church. It was within the scriptorium of the monastery that manuscripts were hand copied, illustrated, ornamented, and illuminated, first on vellum and later (from about the second half of the fourteenth century) on paper and assembled into the manuscript books of the time. The monk designated as librarian decided which texts would be copied and assigned the various work involved in preparing the manuscripts to the monks who served as scribes. The texts that were reproduced came from a variety of sources—from other monasteries (although there was some reticence about lending the manuscripts), from travelers who donated manuscripts they had acquired, from bequests of monarchs who sometimes left manuscripts to various monasteries in their wills.

As the Middle Ages progressed, commercial shops with guilds of scribes and illuminators developed as additional places of production of information records. From the church, the center of creation and management of information moved to, or was shared with, the universities, institutions that were established and came into prominence in the twelfth and thirteenth centuries. In the university towns of that period, production of books centered on the stationers' shops, with the actual copying being done through a system of "putting out," where the parts of a book were done by various copyists paid on a piece basis (Eisenstein, 2005: 10–11).

DEVELOPMENT OF THE PUBLISHING INDUSTRY

Although there was woodblock printing in China as early as the ninth century and printing from movable metal type in Korea in the beginning of the thirteenth century, the invention of movable type in Europe did not occur until the middle of the fifteenth century and is generally attributed to Johann Gutenberg. The first European book printed from movable type, thought to have been printed in 1455, was the Mazarin Bible (also known as the Gutenberg Bible), printed in Mainz, Germany. It was the invention of printing in the West, that is, printing from movable metal type on paper, in the 1450s that accelerated the availability of stable information records and eventually led to the growth of the publishing industry, the book trade, and the libraries of modern times, all institutions that facilitate the process of creating, distributing, and making available information records.

From the beginning of printing with movable type in the middle of the fifteenth century, the publishing industry in Europe developed throughout the sixteenth–nineteenth centuries in major cities in Europe and later in the United States. From Germany, printing spread to Italy, France, the Netherlands, England, and Spain before the end of the fifteenth century. By 1539 printing was carried to Spanish America by Juan Pablos, an Italian printer. During the sixteenth century printing was carried around the world by Christian missionaries: to India in 1556; China, 1589; Japan, 1591; and the Philippines, 1593. And in the first half of the seventeenth century, printing spread to the American colonies, where what is considered the first book published in the American colonies, the *Bay Psalm Book*, was printed in 1640.

This printing technology, it has been argued, began the introduction of the general distribution of printed material in Europe. Its consequences were enormous. Books became affordable (relatively). But other changes were necessary. In order for a printing industry to succeed, there was a need for a reasonably literate population. Until the 1300s few in Europe could read. The nobility could not and certainly the peasantry did not. Literacy was limited to the clergy, and even then to a small group. The demand for vulgate Bibles and other works written in local languages created additional demand. Giovanni Boccaccio's *Decameron* (1350) and Geoffrey Chaucer's *Canterbury Tales* (c 1390–1400) were best sellers of their day. But the first modern novel, Miguel de Cervantes' *Don Quixote*, was not to be written until 1605, when distribution and dissemination of works of this kind were made possible by the then well-established publishing industry.

The organized book trade, which predated the invention of printing, expanded with the spread of printing and the growth in publishing. In the early days of printed books, the same person or company might be simultaneously the publisher, the printer, and the bookseller, and perhaps even the author, but these functions soon became separated.

This specialization of function spread, especially in the late nineteenth and the twentieth centuries, to increasing specialization by product and by type. Not only did the different printed products, such as magazines and newspapers, develop into separate publishing establishments, but even within book publishing differentiation by type occurred, with publishers specializing in textbooks, others in professional books, some in religious books, others in scholarly books, and so on.

GROWTH AND CHANGE IN LIBRARIES

The social role of the library has undergone much change since its Sumerian or Alexandrian beginnings. Libraries in Sumeria were established in large part as records repositories. The Library at Alexandria no doubt played that role, but it also served as a research facility. What changed? Certainly the "information containers" did: the books had evolved from clay tablet to papyrus scroll. But social, political, and economic needs had also changed. The quest for knowledge came to be perceived as a social good.

With the fall of the Roman Empire and as a consequence of internal and external religious, social, and political pressures, libraries were eclipsed in the West. Libraries lost their role as research institutions and became archival repositories for the wisdom of ancient sages. As with the production of books, the location of many of these repositories, these "Dark Ages" libraries, were the monasteries (see Staikos, 2000). The Renaissance prompted new interest in knowledge and therefore in the research library. A growing literate middle class created demand for religious and fictional works.

The Renaissance was amplified by the invention of the moveable type printing press (see above). Libraries began to assume a new role. Not only did they maintain their monastic archival function, they once again served as research facilities for the emerging great universities in Europe that replaced the church as the center for creation and distribution of information and the impetus for its collection: La Sorbonne, Heidelberg, Oxford, and Cambridge. Libraries also began to collect the new literature of the day.

By the nineteenth century libraries were well established in Europe and North America. These libraries assumed a new role. The printer Benjamin Franklin, for example, was instrumental in the establishment of a subscription library in 1731, but that library was limited to its wealthy, white male patron members. Public libraries were established with the mission to improve their patrons. These libraries tended to eschew fiction, especially popular fiction.

To meet the need for access to popular fiction and to expand the patron base, circulating libraries were opened in Europe and the United States in the late eighteenth and early nineteenth centuries. These often for-profit enterprises catered to "baser" tastes as well as to women. (There are parallels between the circulating library of its day and the video rental stores of ours.) The circulating libraries, for the most part, yielded to the public library, as the role of public libraries was redefined from "self-improvement" to entertainment center.

By the twentieth century, libraries, like publishing, had become differentiated. For libraries, there were four major variants: the academic, the public, the school, and the special library (Rubin, 2004: ch. 7). Special libraries (corporate, medical, legal) serve very limited and private constituencies. Academic libraries further research but also train students to use libraries. School libraries provide curricular support in primary and secondary schools. And public libraries entertain, improve, and edify.

For more exploration of the details of the historical development of the institutions and agencies that have developed to affect the information record, you may wish to browse the *Media History Project Timeline* (Fang and Ross, 1996).

ESTABLISHMENT OF EDUCATIONAL SYSTEMS

In addition to societal institutions that facilitate the production of information records for distribution and those that collect information records and provide access to them, there is a third set of institutions that must at least be considered briefly in examining development of the structures that affect information and its use in society: the institutions that sponsor creation of new information that can be recorded in stable form and that foster its transfer, especially to succeeding generations, through the function of teaching. The beginnings of one major group within this set have already been discussed above: the universities.

From their beginnings in the twelfth and thirteenth centuries in Europe, the universities (and also colleges) have continued to play a central role in the creation of information. From their early connections to the church, the universities in Europe evolved into separate secular institutions, often with governmental connection or support.

Initially the colleges (the term used for institutions of higher education that grant bachelor's degrees) founded in the American colonies, and later in the United States, focused on the training of ministers and were restricted to men, although the nineteenth century witnessed the establishment of many colleges for women, including those that were "normal schools," the name given to institutions for the education of teachers. In the United States, the major impetus for the establishment of state tax-supported universities was the Morrill Land Grant Act of 1862, which gave federal lands to the states for establishment of colleges that, in addition to traditional academic subjects, provided education in agricultural and technical subjects. It was during the latter part of the nineteenth century that universities in the United States increased their focus on research—and thereby the creation of new information—following the model of the German universities of the time.

Formal education for information professionals also first began in the nineteenth century. For example, the École Nationale des Chartes was established in France in 1821 to train archivists. In 1873, the first formal French professional diploma was established (Accart, 2000). In the United States, Melvil Dewey opened the first American library school at Columbia College (later Columbia University) in 1887.

In the twentieth century, especially after World War II, institutions of higher education proliferated in the United States and around the world. In the United States there was great expansion, not only in number but also in type and function of higher education establishments, with the creation of extended systems of community colleges and vocational and technical schools and the growth of state universities into systems of institutions with campuses at multiple locations within the state.

Not all of these institutions emphasize the creation of new information through research conducted by their faculties, but all play a significant role in facilitating the use of information by and its transfer to successive generations of students. This contribution to the expansion of use of information within a society—as well as the potential for creation of new information that is fostered in the students—should not be underestimated in our examination of societal institutions.

Likewise, the basic transfer of societally valued information, the initial skills in use of information, and the foundation for development of ability to create information takes place in the educational systems that are the precursor institutions to the universities—the elementary and secondary schools, or as they are commonly referred to in the United States, the K–12 system. While there is evidence of formal teaching of young people as early as 3000 BCE in Sumeria and Egypt, the system of formal public education prevalent in the United States today and the universal publicly supported education in other countries is primarily a development stemming from the nineteenth— and in some cases the twentieth—century.

As we observed in the chapter on the history of technology, the overall trend in the history of educational institutions is a broadening of availability from restricted elites to, at least in the case of basic elementary and some form of secondary education, nearly universal education, at least in the Western world. From systems that were restricted to the wealthy, and generally to the wealthy sons, have emerged systems that provide access for all to development of information use skills and transmission to all of a set of basic information.

With this brief review of the historical background of the development of three major categories of societal institutions that assist in the creation, distribution, and management of information and information records, we can now turn to examination of more recent developments and current structures.

MODERN INSTITUTIONS

The major institutions in modern times that have served to affect the information record can be divided into those that focus on

- developing and producing information records for distribution;
- fostering the transmission of information to future generations;
- developing new information;

- distributing information records;
- providing management of and access to information records.

DEVELOPING AND PRODUCING INFORMATION RECORDS FOR DISTRIBUTION

This category encompasses the book publishing industry; the related industries of newspaper publishing, magazine, and journal publishing; the recorded music industry; the film industry; radio and broadcast television; cable and satellite television; and now, Internet or online publishers. The basic functions served by this group of entities, often lumped together in a category called "content providers," are to

- identify information that either has already been created or needs to be created in response to societal need or demand;
- filter that information using measures of quality, accuracy, marketability, or some other standards established by the entity, selecting what should be made publicly available;
- assist the content creator (the author, the composer, the scriptwriter, the reporter, and so on) to shape the "information record" to better meet both identified information needs and those established standards;
- arrange for the production of the information record in a format that can be made available to the targeted individuals who either need it or would be willing to use it (for example, arrange for physical production of the book, the production of the magazine, the CD, etc.);
- participate in the distribution of the information record, either directly or through forwarding it to the appropriate distributing agency, such as, in the case of books, a bookseller, or in the case of films, a movie distributor or a pay cable network.

The financial arrangements through which the activities take place and how they are supported vary widely within this category. Some are supported almost entirely through the prices paid for the information products by the consumer or purchaser of the information record (most books, for example). Some are financed in part or in total through the "selling" of access to the consumers of the information record to advertisers who seek to gain the attention of the consumer through the juxtaposition of special targeted information (a.k.a advertisements) with the information content the consumer selects (newspapers, magazines, radio, and broadcast television). Yet others, like films, depend on very complicated structures of the timing of access to the information record, with varying financial arrangements for each stage: from viewing in theatres, to release of video for DVD viewing, to pay-per-view channels, to pay cable, to network TV, and to syndication (Litman, 2000).

A brief overview of these related industries will provide some sense of the extent of these institutions.

Book Publishers

As indicated above, the book industry has become specialized and differentiated by type or audience. A third category used to distinguish published books is the method of distribution used (Eaglen, 2000: 15). The categories that are usually employed in discussing the book publishing industry, those in use by the Association of American Publishers, are as follows:

* Trade Books

    In this category are those publishers that produce books for the general consumer market, both fiction and nonfiction. Traditionally these books have been sold primarily in bookstores but they are also available in a variety of other merchandising outlets, such as large general retail outlets (like WalMart). In fact, the numbers of books sold in general retail outlets now eclipses those sold in bookstores (Greco, 2000). These books may also be found in libraries and would include both the current best sellers and the backlist titles (books that were published in previous years and are still in print and available for purchase). Think of the books that you see in Borders, Barnes & Noble, Books-A-Million, WHSmith, Waterstone's, or other chain bookstores. Most of these are trade books. Trade books include both adult and juvenile books and may be either in hardcover or paperback editions.
* Mass Market Paperbacks

    This category of publishers produces books that are distinguished from trade books not so much by their subject matter (in fact they often are the very same books) but rather by their size (the familiar approximately $4'' \times 7''$ or "pocket" size), the quality of the physical product (cheaper paper, poorer paper binding) and, initially, the distribution channels through which the books were available. Originally mass market paperbacks were distributed in a manner similar to magazines and newspapers, but today the distribution channels for mass market paperbacks also include those used for trade books, with the exception that libraries usually do not buy mass-market paperbacks for their permanent collections (the bindings do not withstand repeated use). The mass market publishers may be divisions or separate "imprints" of the trade publishing houses, although there are publishers that originated specifically to publish the mass-market paperback book.

- Religious Books

    Publishers in this category issue bibles, testaments, and other religious books, such as books of devotions and prayers, hymnals, inspirational books, and the like. In general, these books are marketed through stores that focus specifically on religious books (sometimes with a denominational affiliation, but not necessarily so), although they may also be found in general bookstores and in the large retail outlets. The publishers may be departments of trade publishers or specific religious groups. This category of book publishing has grown significantly in recent years, with a compound sales growth rate of 14.2 percent in 2002–2005 (Association of American Publishers, n.d.).

- Professional Books

    This area includes book publishers that specialize in books in professional areas, such as law, medicine, business, engineering, and so on and books in science and technology that are aimed to professionals in those areas. (Often in discussions or analyses of the book industry, the areas of science, technology, and medicine are lumped together in what is called STM publishing.) As with religious books, departments of general publishers may publish professional books, but there are publishers that specialize in books for a specific professional area, including professional associations and societies that have a book publishing arm.

- University Presses

    Originally these publishers were subsidized by universities to publish the scholarly work of their own faculty. Today, however, the university presses, while still specializing in scholarly (predominantly but not exclusively nonfiction) works, publish a broader range of books (not just faculty research), market to a wider audience, and generally must be self supporting. The number of university presses has declined in recent years, although the potential for digital publishing could provide an avenue for resurgence in this area (see Rice University, 2006).

- Textbooks

    This category of publishers, which produces textbooks for students, is usually broken down into two subgroups: elementary and high school textbook publishing and college or higher education textbook publishing. As is the case with several of the publishing categories, general trade publishers may have departments that produce textbooks, but most textbooks are produced by publishers specializing in the textbook market. Publishers in the elementary and high school textbook area are subject to more external influence in what is actually included in the content of the books than perhaps in any other publishing category, due to the effect of either textbook adoption or textbook recommendation by state-level review boards. This area of publishing is also distinguished by the fact that it is not the end users of the information record and their needs or demands that the publisher seeks to address, but rather the judgments and preferences of another information institution, the educational system that fosters transmission of information across generations.

- Subscription Reference Books

    These specialized publishers produce the reference books that have been marketed by direct mail or through door-to-door salespeople to individuals or to libraries. The most prominent work in this category is the multivolume encyclopedia, which generally is not available in any of the bookstores or general retail outlets (although some have been available in grocery stores).

- Book Clubs

    This specialized area of publishing is distinguished not by format of the book (it may be hardcover or paperback), content (book clubs cover a broad range of content areas), or audience (book clubs exist for children and adults, for the general reader and for the professional) but rather by the method of distribution and, secondarily, by the quality of the physical product. Individuals belong to the clubs and receive preselected books on a regular schedule, as well as the opportunity to purchase additional books at prices that may be lower than those in the bookstore. Book club books, while generally having the same content as trade books or professional books (published by license arrangement with the original publisher), are not the same physical edition and usually are of lesser quality in terms of paper and binding. Publishers in other categories may have book club divisions or own book club subsidiaries, but there are publishers who specialize in this area.

- Mail-order Books

    This specialized area of publishing has declined significantly, due in part to the alternative availability of books through Internet bookstores such as Amazon.com (Greco, 2000: 5). This category of publishers is distinguished by the distribution method (mass marketing through the mail to the individual consumer) and by its tie to magazine publishers, who dominated the market through their ability to use subscriber lists as their advertising targets.

There are other categories of book publishers not included here, such as vanity publishers (books published and marketed at the author's expense, also called self-published books) and reprint publishers, who specialize in making out-of-print works, particularly classic works, available to consumers. Two other categories tracked as part of book publishing are audiobooks and e-books.

TRENDS

The development of new technologies for distribution of information records (see chapter 5) is having an impact on all segments of the book publishing industry. Perhaps the most evident change is in the area of subscription reference books, which now are more likely to be purchased by the consumer on CD, installed in the consumer-level computer before purchase, or obtained through some online provider. Even in trade publishing, there are significant developments with electronic publishing, either in online form (for example, the experiments of Stephen King in publishing his serial novel, *The Plant*, in 2000–2001 and the serial publication of Walter Kern's novel *The Unbinding* in 2006, prior to 2007 publication in print by Random House) or in the still evolving e-book, used either on a personal computer, PDA, or smart phone through special software or loaded onto a specific e-book reader (a hand-held electronic appliance specifically for reading/viewing content in digital format). Major publishers, such as HarperCollins, Random House, and Simon & Schuster, are involved in e-book production (Hillesund, 2001) and online book retailers like Amazon and Barnes & Noble in the United States as well as book retailers in Europe, such as WHSmith in the U.K., distribute e-books. In the library market, NetLibrary, an arm of OCLC, is one of the major distributors of e-books to libraries. A group of seventy-five university presses plus two scholarly society publishers participated with learned societies of the American Council of Learned Societies in a major five-year (1999–2004) project that published scholarly e-books in history, with 1000 published between 2002 and the beginning of 2006 and 250 to be added each year (American Council of Learned Societies, 2006). Although the elementary and high school textbook publishing area is not considered ready yet for mass shifts to electronic format due to the continuing "digital divide" between those who have access to the necessary equipment and those who do not (Greco, 2000: 7–8), experiments are taking place in college textbook publishing, where there is higher penetration of the necessary equipment infrastructure. Variations in this market include distribution through university bookstores (Borland, 2005) and inclusion of ads in e-textbooks (Stross, 2006).

The other significant trend in the book publishing area, one that goes back to the 1970s, at least, is the merger and acquisition of publishing companies, not only with and by each other to form larger publishing companies, but more strikingly, the formation of the media conglomerates of publishers of all types, film studios, television networks, record companies, cable systems, and Internet service providers. These structural changes and their impact will be discussed later in this chapter.

Newspaper, Magazine, and Journal Publishers

This category of publishers is distinguished by the production of information records that appear in some regular time sequence (for example, daily, weekly, monthly, quarterly), that include collections of different discrete (although possibly related in content) information records (columns, news stories, articles, reviews, short stories, etc.), and that are usually available both through subscription (or maybe registration, in the case of "free" publications) and on an individual purchase basis. Lumped together, these publishers are called "periodical" publishers—their works appear periodically on a continuing basis rather than as a one-time event, as in book publishing.

NEWSPAPERS

The distinctions among these three groups are both glaring and subtle. Everyone knows what a newspaper is:

- It appears daily (or sometimes with less frequency, up to a week).
- It is printed on poor-quality paper, which is in fact called "newsprint," in unbound sheets.
- It can be obtained through subscription or individual copy purchase at newsstands or a variety of other outlets.
- It provides information on the current events of the area covered, be that the world, a particular city, or a particular professional area, such as higher education.
- It may include additional information records aimed to entertain the user.
- It is supported primarily through advertising (the selling of access to readers), not through the price paid by the end user of the information.

Of the entities in this group, the newspaper publisher is more actively involved in directing the creation of content than the other two and is more directly involved with distribution as well.

MAGAZINES

A magazine, in contrast to a newspaper, usually is targeted to a more specific audience, appears less than daily (weekly, monthly, bimonthly, etc.), likely is printed on higher-quality paper (although it does not have to be), and is bound together in some fashion (not just folded sheets as a newspaper is). It too usually is supported primarily through advertising (although this is not universally the case) and generally is available through subscription or individual copy purchase. Daly, Henry, and Ryder (2000) categorize magazines into two major types: consumer magazines and specialized business or trade magazines. The former is targeted to a specific group of readers on the basis of any one or a combination of characteristics of interest or demographics. The latter targets individuals on the basis of their work, may not be supported by advertising, and may not be available on an individual copy basis. The consumer magazine, although not as limited in audience as the other category, today is also a focused publication aimed to a more or less narrowly defined readership, which both influences and is influenced by the advertisers. As mentioned above, what advertisers buy in a magazine is access to potential consumers; and there has to be a match between the readership of the magazine and the advertisers that support it through their ads.

JOURNALS

"Journal" is the term usually associated with periodicals that may have some of the characteristics of magazines: appearing on a regular, less than daily schedule; likely on higher-quality, more permanent paper than a newspaper; and bound in some manner. The chief distinction is in the content, which for the "journal" is more scholarly in nature, regardless of the specific subject coverage. Journals may or may not have advertisements, but the revenue from ads generally does not provide the major support for the journal. In fact, in some disciplines (more frequently in the sciences) the authors are required to pay "page charges" to have their work published. Like the specialized trade magazine, the journal is not likely to be available on the local newsstand, although it may be sold on an individual copy basis from the publisher.

TRENDS

Several trends affecting this general category of content providers are identifiable. As with book publishing, for both newspaper and magazine publishing there have been mergers, consolidations, and acquisitions both within the publishing genre and in the media conglomerate category. For newspaper publishing specifically, the trend has been away from independent, local publishers toward consolidated, national-level conglomerate ownership. Accompanying this trend has been a decline in the number of individual daily newspapers, with an increasingly small number of localities with more than one paper. However, even with these trends, newspapers continue to be less concentrated than other media (Picard, 2004). For magazine publishing, the trend over the last half-century has been increasing specialization, driven primarily by the need to ensure reliable, targeted readership for advertisers (the ads for general audiences having migrated to television). The general interest magazine represented by *Life*, *Look*, and the *Saturday Evening Post* of the

1950s has given way to the niche world of today and publications like *Wine Spectator, Cross Country Skier, and Early Music Today.*

Journal publishing has likewise undergone increasing specialization of focus, driven not by advertisers, however, but by both the increasing level of specialization within academic disciplines and the rise of interdisciplinary studies. The most important trend in journal publishing has been the escalating cost of journals, something that the institutions that facilitate access to information (the libraries) have both bemoaned and berated and now are attempting to circumvent (see the discussion later in this chapter regarding university library initiatives in publishing).

The initiatives promoting a revision of scholarly communication and thereby the infrastructure of journal publication continue to burgeon, particularly in the sciences, through two major avenues: open access journal publication and open access self-archiving, both of which operate in the digital environment. In the former, the peer review process that has been central to scholarly journal publication is continued, but instead of publication by commercial or society publishers of journals that are then sold by subscription to libraries and individuals, the journals are supported through other cost recovery mechanisms and the resulting publications are made available without charge or restriction via the Web. This approach is championed by many who have been concerned over a long period of time about the escalating costs of journal subscriptions and the subsequent restriction of access to research, particularly, but not exclusively, for those in many of the developing countries. Stevan Harnad refers to the current system of publication as one requiring "access tolls," which would be avoided by either of the new avenues (Harnad, 2001). The second avenue, the self-archiving of articles, relies on individuals to make their peer-reviewed work available through deposit in open archives available via the Web, possibly an e-print archive maintained by their university.

Both of these avenues include a number of initiatives in countries around the world. The concept is being promoted through, among other approaches, the Budapest Open Access Initiative generated from a meeting in 2001 of the Open Society Institute (*Budapest Open Access Initiative,* n.d.). In the United States, a key organization promoting the reformation of scholarly communication is the Scholarly Publishing and Academic Resources Coalition (SPARC), formed in 1998 (Scholarly Publishing and Academic Resources Coalition, 2007).

All the content providers in this category are being affected by the availability of electronic publishing, and their participation in new modes of publishing ranges from making the tables of contents of print publications available for examination, to publishing the full text of the daily newspaper, to publishing electronic versions of printed magazines and journals, and beyond to publication in electronic format only. At this point, there is a mix of avenues of availability: some publications are provided with no restrictions, some require registration but no payment, others are subscription-only access. In addition, the distribution channels of some of these publications have added push technologies to their arsenal, using both the older method of announcing new issues and tables of contents to subscribers via e-mail and newer methods such as RSS (Really Simple Syndication or Rich Site Summary) feeds to notify users of new content. What is certain is that change in how newspapers, magazines, and journals are produced and distributed will continue to occur as the technologies evolve. What remains to be seen is whether the more stable functions of identifying, filtering, and assisting the content creator will continue in this segment of the content provider institutions.

Recorded Music Industry

The recorded music industry, which traces its origins back to the invention of the phonograph by Thomas A. Edison in 1877, has migrated through a number of technologies for carrying the information (music) record:

- the cylinder
- the disc record (invented by Emile Berliner)
- the long playing record (LP)
- the stereophonic record
- 8-track tapes
- the audiocassette
- the compact disc (CD)
- MP3 files

During almost all of its history, from the earliest days, the recorded music industry has been dominated by a few firms, a market condition that is defined as a "tight oligopoly" (Hull, 2004: 121, 123). This condition changed in the mid-1950s and 1960s; but beginning in the 1970s, through consolidation of the distribution mechanisms and through mergers, the number of content providers has steadily declined to a position where now four media conglomerates control over 75 percent of the industry worldwide (Hull, 2004; Bishop, 2005). The costs that have been associated with the basic functions of this area of the content providers are

- identifying information (music) that has already been created or needs to be created (identifying artists and signing them to exclusive contracts);

- filtering the information on the basis of quality, marketability (generally the major concern), or other standards;
- assisting the content creator (the artist) to shape the information record (the musical performance that is recorded) to better meet information needs and identified standards;
- arranging for production of the information record (music) in a usable, marketable format (recording the music and making multiple copies);
- participating in the distribution of the record.

These costs have been such that proliferation of this category of content providers has occurred only when costs associated with one or more of these functions has declined. The industry is currently characterized by consolidation and a high degree of vertical integration but a continued presence of diversity in the actual recordings available (Hull, 2000). As Bishop observes (2005), the dominance of the "Big Four" has led to an oligonomy, a situation in which the companies are in an oligopoly to music consumers and an oligopsony (only a few buyers for many sellers) for those creating the music.

TRENDS

As noted, the trend in the recorded music industry has been toward increased consolidation. Even while the number of individual labels may not decline, the ownership and distribution has become concentrated in four firms: Universal Music Group (owned by Vivendi), Warner Music Group (previously owned by AOL Time Warner but now a separate company), SONY BMG Music Entertainment (owned 50 percent by SONY and 50 percent by Bertelsmann), and EMI Group. The 2004 merger of previously separate SONY Music and BMG has been annulled by the European Union Court of First Instance; and, as of this writing, it is not clear whether the merger will survive (European Union, 2006).

The other major trend is the migration to distribution—and, the industry hopes, sales of licensed online subscriptions or of legal single copies—for recorded music digitally, over the Internet, rather than in a physical medium. This movement has been escalated and complicated by the distribution and sharing of MP3 music files via the Internet without payment, using the peer-to-peer technology that was the basis of the original Napster and similar software programs (such as Gnutella) that facilitate such exchange. The Recording Industry Association of America (which represents the interests of the recording industry) first attacked the challenge through lawsuits against alleged copyright violators who downloaded music files. More recently, solutions have emerged in the music services, such as iTunes, which provide low-cost but legal downloading, that protect both copyright interests and market interests of the companies and the artists and make music available online. An alternative solution being tried is the provision of free, legal downloading that is supported by advertising (Pfanner, 2006).

The distribution of music online raises the possibility of movement away from the oligopolistic (and oligonomic) characteristic of the industry, in that the costs of functions of production and distribution can be substantially reduced. The support by independent music producers, including independent artists who market their own label, of the peer-to-peer approach that first surfaced during the Napster controversy suggests that such change may be possible. In addition, distribution of music online provides the alternative of access (for limited periods) through a monthly subscription fee to a collection of music products rather than downloads on a per-song basis. The shift away from any physical container for music is leading to changes in the functions identified above as part of this area as well as shifts in performance of the functions from content providers to content creators, resulting in changes in the structure of the industry (Bockstedt, Kauffman, and Riggins, 2006).

Film Industry

The film industry, like the recorded music industry, can be traced back to the nineteenth century and Thomas A. Edison, whose Kinetograph, Kinetoscope, and related inventions were the basis for development of motion pictures. Also like the recorded music industry, the costs involved in carrying out the basic functions of content providers in this category are substantial. The coordination of the various components of creation and production, the up-front funding that film production requires, and the complicated mechanisms for distribution in various markets (theaters, pay-per-view, cable TV, network TV) and in several formats (film, DVD) make this industry one that is also subject to oligopoly, or domination by a small number of companies.

This domination has been a characteristic of the film industry from the 1930s and 1940s, when five corporations held sway in all aspects— production, distribution, and exhibition (the companies also owned the first-run movie theaters)—in a strongly vertically integrated industry. In the 1950s and 1960s the number of companies was eight and then by 1975 fell to six (Compaine and Gomery, 2000). Today, six continue to dominate production and especially distribution; and because of the sales and mergers that occurred in the 1980s and 1990s, two of those six overlap in ownership with the media conglomerates in the recorded music industry: Sony Pictures (owned by Sony) and Universal Pictures (owned by Vivendi). The other four are Disney (owned by Disney/ABC), Warner (owned by Time Warner), Paramount (owned by Viacom), and Twentieth Century Fox (owned by News Corporation) (see Compaine and Gomery, 2000: 360).

TRENDS

The film industry depends for its financial success on the variety of downstream opportunities for a film to return a profit beyond the theatrical exhibition, including the venues of pay TV, video sales and rental, and cable and broadcast TV in both domestic and international markets. Because of this situation and in keeping with the mergers in all aspects of the media industry, the film industry in the 1990s became increasingly horizontally and vertically integrated, with the mergers of giants like AOL and Time Warner bringing increased horizontal integration as well as vertical integration that could facilitate access of film companies to the downstream venues (Compaine and Gomery, 2000).

The reconfiguration of media conglomerates continues with the merger of the Vivendi Universal entertainment holdings with those of NBC, which is owned by General Electric. The Vivendi movie studios, TV studios, cable networks, and theme parks have been transferred to the new NBC Universal in a deal approved in April 2004 by the U.S. Federal Trade Commission (Ahrens, 2004).

AOL Time Warner, the media conglomerate whose AOL holdings have not performed as well as expected after the merger, has changed its name back to Time Warner and has sold its Warner Music division to an investor group headed by Edgar Bronfman, Jr. Bronfman at one time controlled the Universal studios that just moved from Vivendi to GE/NBC (Kirkpatrick and Sorkin, 2003), illustrating the complicated and almost Byzantine transitions that occur within these industries.

Also like the recorded music industry, the film industry is facing major changes in the medium through which the information record is distributed. Not only has the video cassette market migrated to the digital versatile disc (DVD), but the delivery of films in digital format through the Web is developing along several lines: subscription, rental (downloaded file usable for a limited time) and purchase. The industry faces some of the same concerns about delivery and file sharing without payment to the film companies with which the recorded music industry has been coping, and copy protection or viewing restrictions embedded in the files will be part of the formula for success in this delivery channel (see Quain, 2006, for discussion of challenges in Web delivery).

Radio

Radio as an industry is a twentieth-century institution, beginning with the first commercial radio station, KDKA, in 1920 in Pittsburgh. However, like recorded music and film, the inventions on which the industry was based occurred in the late nineteenth century, with the work of Guglielmo Marconi and Nikola Tesla and the later work in the early twentieth century of Reginald Fessenden, Edwin H. Armstrong, and Lee de Forest.

The radio broadcasting industry today is characterized by market specialization, similar to what has occurred with magazine publishing. The all-purpose radio station that provided a range of news, sports, music, and entertainment programming (from soap operas to detective stories to westerns to comedies) that dominated the heyday of radio in the 1930s and 1940s began to give way in the 1950s and migrated to the station targeted to a particular market segment, again as was the case with magazines, as a means of ensuring delivery of an audience for advertisers. The networks that had provided common programming also declined, as stations focused on either delivery of particular music genres (with small bits of news, weather, and traffic reports), which dominates today's radio; talk shows or news/talk combinations (often, although not exclusively, at the local station level); or sports. The functions of the content provider have diminished significantly in radio, with the major functions for many radio stations now being selection and distribution of already produced information records, either musical recordings or some kind of syndicated programming such as the political commentary of a Bill O'Reilly.

As noted earlier, the financial support for radio comes through the juxtaposition of special targeted information, a.k.a advertisements, with the information content that a consumer will select, and that information content is not paid for directly by the user. The niche market format of radio today makes it a very effective vehicle for advertising. The most popular radio format currently is country, followed by news/talk, although the latter format reaches a higher percentage of listeners over twelve (Radio Advertising Bureau, 2004). In contrast to the other content providers discussed in this chapter, radio is today much more of a local medium in terms of revenues (advertising) and the market served (Albarran, 2004).

TRENDS

As a result of the further loosening of restrictions on ownership of multiple radio stations in the 1996 Telecommunications Act (prior to this legislation there had been strict limits, which were gradually expanded in the 1980s and 1990s), the radio industry, like the others discussed above, saw a trend toward merger and concentration of ownership (Hull, Greco, and Martin, 2000) but not to the extent of the recorded music and film industries. Interestingly, two of the top radio groups (in terms of revenue) are part of the media conglomerates seen in the film industry: CBS Radio-Infinity Broadcasting (owned by

Viacom) and ABC Radio (owned by Disney/ABC). Other recent trends include a shift in dominance from AM to FM stations. The largest radio group, in terms of both number of stations owned and revenue, Clear Channel Communication, is an advertising conglomerate, with ownership of advertising venues, including billboards, in 63 countries.

As with other media, radio is also finding new ways to deliver its information content. The streaming of radio stations over the Internet adds another means of distribution to the broadcast, one that does not have the geographical limitations imposed by the broadcasting power of the station. The addition of podcasting as a delivery mechanism for radio programs has likewise overcome the synchronous time limitation of traditional radio delivery, making information selected for this venue available without regard to time or space. A third delivery alteration is subscription radio, a digital audio radio service delivered to listeners who pay a monthly fee for access, similar to the access structure for cable television. This innovation has broadened choice of information content available to listeners as well as provided a new revenue stream—beyond advertising—for the industry.

Broadcast Television

Broadcast television is a twentieth-century development, its beginnings resting primarily on the work of Philo Taylor Farnsworth and Vladimir Kosma Zworykin. Although television as an industry did not develop until the 1940s, the first scheduled broadcast station was founded in 1928 in Schenectady, New York. The early history of television as an industry includes the expansion of the previously founded radio networks into television, as well as in the 1950s and 1960s, the development of a broad range of program content. In addition to news and sports, the information records delivered via television included the types of shows that had earlier found a home in radio: variety shows, comedies, soap operas, westerns, detective stories, dramas, quiz shows, and the early versions of the television news magazine.

Like radio, the financial support for the information provided via television comes from the advertisers, not directly from the consumers of the information. However, unlike radio, where niche marketing occurs through establishment of a station format, the delivery of audience to the advertiser in broadcast television has depended on the shaping and timing of delivery of the information record to the target audience. Although targeted audience stations have developed, primarily based on language, the aim of broadcast television as a content provider has continued to be, in the aggregate, a more general audience than that of radio.

In the early days of television, the basic functions of content providers were carried out to a large extent by the networks; but in a manner similar to radio, these functions became limited to selection and distribution of already produced information records. This change was brought about, not just by industry developments, but also by federal regulation through the Federal Communications Commission (FCC) and federal antitrust suits resulting from concern about the power of the networks to control programming (Compaine and Gomery, 2000). Following the deregulation that occurred in the latter 1990s and beyond, the major production of prime-time programming shifted back to the networks (Ferguson, 2004). The other major areas in which the full range of functions is carried out either by the local television station or the network with which it is affiliated are news (and related soft news categories, such as the currently popular news magazines) and sports. Due to the mergers and growth of media conglomerates, the entities that provide other packaged program content from which the networks and stations select are also likely to be part of the same media company, evidencing a high degree of vertical integration in the television industry.

TRENDS

Partly as a result of the removal by the Telecommunications Act of 1996 of restrictions on multiple ownership and ownership in different media markets, the trend toward consolidation observed in other content providing industry segments also dominates broadcast television. The major broadcast networks are all part of a larger conglomerate: NBC is owned by General Electric, ABC by Disney/ABC, CBS by Viacom, and Fox by News Corporation.

One major technological change occurring in the television industry relates to the switch to high definition television (HDTV), which is digitally based. The FCC is regulating the process of transition to digital TV from analog broadcasting, which will cease after 17 February 2009 (U.S. Federal Communications Commission, 2006). Another technologically related change, currently in what could be characterized as an experimentation phase, is the delivery of popular broadcast TV programming via the Web, either on a time-delayed or real-time basis. Combined with the proliferation of interface devices for such delivery (personal computers, PDAs, smart phones, etc.), this placement facilitates both time and location shifting for access to the information content, going beyond the time shifting afforded initially by videocassette recorders and now primarily by digital video recorders (DVRs).

Cable and Satellite Television

Cable television began in 1948 as a way of extending access to broadcast television content for areas where the broadcast signal could not reach, either because of distance or topography. It was initially called community antenna television (CATV), with the name derived from the community antenna that received the broadcast signal and then retransmitted it over cable. In the early history of cable television, there was considerable concern about the effect that cable could have on broadcast TV, and there were significant controls placed on cable television by the Federal Communications Commission, the federal agency that regulates and controls both radio and television (and other communications industry segments).

Use of satellites for television delivery was also originally an enhancement of the delivery capability of broadcast and cable TV and a means to deliver program content to both systems. As a separate delivery system going directly to the home television (requiring a receiving dish), DBS (direct broadcast satellite) did not become a viable part of the scene until the mid-1990s, although in rural areas individuals had used large satellite dishes to bring down signals that were being sent for broadcast network and cable use. Both cable and DBS have multiple channel delivery capacity, which provides a means to distribute additional information content far beyond that of just extending the broadcast television stations.

The cable television industry has developed as an information content provider in a manner similar to that of radio: market specialization and segmentation. The financial support of cable television is mixed: the consumer pays for delivery of the information content (based on the mix of channels delivered), for access to certain kinds of information content (usually the so-called premium channels), and advertisers continue to pay for access to the delivered audience. The multiple channel delivery capacity made possible the niche formatting that has become the characteristic of much of cable television, which in turn provides increased precision in the delivery of the audience to advertisers. As would be expected given the richer capacity of television with its visual component, the range of formats is broader than that of radio, ranging from the news, sports, and music formats of radio through such diverse topics as history, cooking, weather, children's programming, and movies.

The actual delivery portion of the cable television industry, the cable system operators, which function as monopoly franchises in delivery of cable programming at the local level, are likely to be owned by the same parent company as the cable programming network, another example of vertical integration in the industries that we have examined.

TRENDS

Cable and satellite television follow the general trend of the other content providers in becoming part of media conglomerates. All of the top five cable networks in number of subscribers (National Cable and Telecommunications Association, 2006) are part of conglomerates, most of which have appeared in other industry segments: Discovery Channel (partially owned by Cox Enterprises), ESPN (owned by Disney/ABC), CNN and TNT (owned by Time Warner) and USA Network (owned by NBC Universal). News Corporation owns the major satellite company, DirectTV.

Two technological trends in regard to cable relate to the delivery portion of the industry rather than the content provider portion: the provision of Internet access via the cable systems that deliver cable programming and the expansion into provision of telephone service, making cable a telecommunications service provider, not just a content provider (Bates and Chambers, 2004). Related to this technological capacity is a possible growth area in content: the provision of interactive programming that is technically possible. This capability has been available now for some time without any significant growth in popularity, but it is an area that will bear watching.

Internet/Online/Web Publishers

Content providers on the Internet range so broadly as to be almost impossible to describe accurately, from any individual with Internet access to nearly all of the content providers covered in the other sections on this topic. From the book publishers who are expanding into e-book delivery via the Internet; to the newspaper, magazine, and journal publishers who are using the Web as a delivery mechanism; to the recorded music companies that are trying to provide legal distribution of their wares via the Internet; to the radio and broadcast TV stations, which maintain and actively promote their Web sites; to the cable networks, which also have a Web presence. Beyond these entities are the many other categories of institutions that publish information on the Web as a means of enhancing their primary mission (or perhaps even shifting the venue of their primary mission), be that selling products or services (either on the Web or in a face-to-face environment), providing information to users (like libraries), or the conduct of government (e.g., the many sites at all levels of government).

The financial structure of information records provided online is mixed. While the commonly held belief is that everything on the Web is free, such is not the case:

- For some information content, the structure is similar to that of broadcast television, with advertisers supporting the information provision in exchange for ads placed on the Web pages and no direct cost to the user.
- In a similar situation, the information is provided without cost to the user, either because it is being provided as part of the services of the

providing entity (such as information at a government Web site) or because the provider company is trying to sell goods or services, or goodwill, to the user (the information at a car manufacturer's Web site, for example).

- A third structure is one in which the user pays for the information. The restricted access online databases (e.g., LexisNexis) are examples of this arrangement.
- In the fourth structure, the user pays, generally on a subscription basis, but the site also carries advertising.

There are several important characteristics that distinguish Internet provided content from that content provided by the other content providers discussed thus far:

1. the instantaneous nature of global availability
2. the high potential for and ease of interactivity
3. the cross-medium, cross-provider searchability and findability of the information
4. the inherent multimedia format potential

None of the other categories has even one of these characteristics, much less all four. For this reason, online/Internet/Web content provision could be assessed as having the greatest long-term promise for all information users. However, there are still significant disadvantages in this category that equate to advantages for some of the others:

- Online content requires more sophisticated interface devices as well as a higher degree of technological literacy to access the content than any of the other categories.
- The installed base of interface devices is still lower worldwide than for such devices for content in any other provider category.
- Even with the increasing (although far from ubiquitous) availability of wireless networks, the portability of access to information content remains lower than most other categories, particularly books, magazines, newspapers, and recorded music.

TRENDS

For a segment where the most prevalent distribution system (the Web) is still less than two decades old, identifying trends in terms of information content provision is difficult, in part due to the very rapid changes that occur. Major intellectual property issues continue to play out in this area (for example, see discussion above concerning recorded music), and digital rights management is a far from settled issue. What is certain is that the basic functions of the content provider for information distributed via the Web are easier to perform than for any other category examined, which suggests a continued proliferation of content provision in this area. The expanded provision of personal information content via social networking sites, the addition or migration of content from other media (see earlier discussions of podcasting and Web-based delivery of TV programs), and the expansion of available interface devices for use of online content all argue for such a conclusion. And, as observed in the previous chapter, the changes in technology that are enabling the ease of content provision continue to blur the boundaries between the content provider and the content user, shifting from a society of high consumers of information to one where the individual is simultaneously both a consumer and a producer, capturing content via the devices that are converging the information production and use functions and reformulating existing information in "mashups."

FOSTERING THE TRANSMISSION OF INFORMATION TO FUTURE GENERATIONS AND DEVELOPING NEW INFORMATION

The primary societal institutions that accomplish the functions of both fostering transmission of information to future generations and developing new information are those falling within the general category of educational institutions:

- elementary, primary, and secondary schools (or the K–12 system in the United States)
- institutions of higher education
  - colleges and universities
  - vocational and technical schools

As entities that deal with information records, both in the transmission mode and in the act of recording new information, these societal institutions differ in the way that they affect the record and in how they facilitate the "information events" that occur for the individuals served by the institutions. In general, there is a curve of increasing choice by the user in what information records he or she will be connected to, and what information events may occur, as the user proceeds through what is a sequential system. The kindergarten child, for example, has very little choice about what information he or she will experience, while the Ph.D. student, at the other end of the educational institution spectrum, has a very high degree of choice, at least within the general limits established for accepted scholarship. The determination of what information is to be transmitted at each level of the system is societally constructed, based on what the particular society deems appropriate for "educated" or "trained" (in the case of vocational and technical schools) persons to know; and the actual content has differed over time and may differ from one culture to another.

The financial structures for support of these institutions likewise differ across countries. Within the United States at all levels there are two basic systems, one in the public sector and one in the private sector. In the public sector, participation in the information transmission that occurs is paid for by government, via tax support, through the K–12 structure. Beyond that, the information user pays for part of the costs of the information transmission activity, although it continues to be heavily subsidized by governmental (tax) support. In the private sector, the user pays the primary portion of the costs throughout, although there may be subsidization through private support, or in the case of schools with religious connections, through underwriting by religious bodies. Even in the private sector, however, there is public subsidization of the information transmission activity through favorable tax laws exempting educational institutions from various kinds of taxes and eligibility for certain governmentally supported funding programs.

The development of new information occurs primarily in the higher education institutions portion of the category. One of the primary purposes of universities is the generation of new information. Both students and faculty are encouraged, supported, and required (at least in the case of faculty and some graduate students) to produce new information. The support and fostering of research that will result in new information that can then be distributed in some form by the appropriate content providers discussed above is a key component of the university mission. By providing this structured means by which new information can be developed, society has established a mechanism to ensure that this information activity will occur.

That is not to say that all new information is created solely in universities—far from it. The research and development divisions of many companies and the research arms of agencies of government (such as the National Science Foundation) develop new information that is related to the missions of their institutions. Collectively, the new information generated in these other areas is greater than that produced in the educational establishments. However, it is only within the educational institutions that there is, at least theoretically, total freedom of choice of what research avenues to pursue and what new information to try to develop.

TRENDS

The most significant current trends among educational institutions at all levels are the increasing uses of the various information technologies for both transmitting the information record and teaching the successive generations how to use information. The use of technology for instruction is not new: the slate board and the quill pen were technology. However, the creative ways in which technology is being used to extend access to education and to enhance learning is a change of exponential magnitude. Within higher education, in addition to the use of technology, a growing trend is the increased availability and delivery of very targeted educational opportunities: programs designed for and delivered to the workplace, education available wherever the potential learner may be.

Information Ideas

The Role of the Museum

The museum plays a unique role as a societal institution in that while it primarily has been constructed as an institution to preserve the tangible physical artifacts of a culture, it has a significant, although in earlier times not acknowledged, role in the creation of information by the ways in which the artifacts are displayed and the connections formed by the placing of items together. Traditionally, the museum removed items from their contexts and reassembled them in ways that fit the information expectations of the society in which the museum was situated, not necessarily in ways that fit the understandings of the culture from which they came (see Stam, 2005: 57). This repositioning of the objects creates information that previously did not exist, giving the museum a unique role as creator of information.

Another somewhat unheralded role of museums has been in the distribution of information. This role is one that has played out via the acquisition of artifacts by museums, taking the cultural information objects from their origin and placing them in physical locations often at great distances from their initial context. While this practice is currently considered both legally and ethically questionable (see Corsane, 2005: 6–7), a raping, as it were, of the cultural heritage of a country, one does have to acknowledge that such removals acted to distribute information about the cultural achievements or natural history of a country to distant locations and to peoples who would otherwise know nothing of them. The current debates about and efforts toward restitution of cultural artifacts to their original homes is in part a debate about a redistribution of information, a return of information to its origin.

(*Continued on p. 140*)

Such a return likely will, in fact, result in the creation of additional information through the interpretation of the meanings of the artifacts in their original contexts.

Museums manage information through the management of the physical manifestations of a culture, the information records of the society in nontextual and nonauditory form. In doing so, the museum acts as do the other institutions discussed in this chapter to alter the record (often by cleaning it and restoring it to closer to its original form), to add value to it (by preserving it and making it available for future generations), to delete portions of it (by removing it from its original context), and to change how and by whom it can be accessed and used (by placing it in a location far distant from its origin). As an information institution, the museum could be said to fall partially into each of the categories examined in this chapter. Certainly the museum has and continues to play an important—and distinct—role as a societal institution dealing with information.

Sources

Corsane, Gerard. 2005. "Issues in Heritage, Museums, and Galleries: A Brief Introduction." In *Heritage, Museums and Galleries, an Introductory Reader*, 1–12. London: Routledge.

Stam, Deirdre C. 2005. "The Informed Muse: The Implications of 'The New Museology' for Museum Practice." In *Heritage, Museums and Galleries, an Introductory Reader*, ed. Gerard Corsane, 54–70. London: Routledge.

DISTRIBUTING INFORMATION RECORDS AND PROVIDING MANAGEMENT OF AND ACCESS TO INFORMATION RECORDS

The function of distributing information records, that is, the physical distribution, is carried out by some of the segments of the information arena that have been discussed previously, both in chapter 5 on information technology and in this chapter: cable system operators, DBS, the various distribution channels for films, the varying distribution channels for portions of the book publishing industry, and the distribution of information records via the Web. However, there are two additional entities that need to be briefly mentioned. One is the Internet Service Provider or ISP, which facilitates Internet access for the individual. Another is the Internet portal, which facilitates access to resources and services available on the Web.

The major cross-cultural societal institution that provides management and access to information records, as well as serving to physically distribute information records, is the library. As the discussion in chapter 5 indicated, the institution is in a transitional phase, moving into a blended structure that is simultaneously both physical, rooted in time and space, and digital, accessible anywhere anytime. This hybrid institution, as it has been called, performs the same basic societal functions in relation to information that the library has traditionally carried out: the identification, selection, acquisition, organization and description, storage and retrieval, preservation, analysis, interpretation, evaluation, synthesis, dissemination, and management of information records. In addition, the library as an institution is, in some cases, returning to its earlier function of an active role in developing and producing information records for distribution. In the academic library arena, there is an active movement, SPARC (Scholarly Publishing and Academic Resources Coalition), which supports alternative means of scholarly communication and publication.

The library as an institution does act on the information record, be it physical or digital, to affect how and by whom it can be accessed. The library adds value to the record by the metainformation about the record that it creates in the processes of organization and storage. It affects who may access the record, at least a particular physical or digital manifestation, by establishing rules that govern what users in what circumstances may use what records. In the long term, through the collective preservation efforts of the institution, it helps to ensure continued accessibility to the record.

TRENDS

The functions of management of and access to information records as well as the earlier functions of developing and producing information records in the areas of scholarly records are in what could be characterized as the early stages of the transformation of scholarly communication. The changes are a result of pressures from increasing costs for these activities, particularly the functions traditionally carried out by scholarly publishers, as well as the increasing interest in making not only conclusions of research available but also the raw data sets available for verification and reuse. Instead of these information records going through the traditional publishing process, there are several alternative avenues for their development, production, management, and long-term access. Two of the most promising are the institutional repository and the open access journal. In the case of the repository, items produced by an institution's personnel (most often a university) are digitally stored and made available via the Web. The open access journal, generally following the academic peer review process similar to that of traditional journal publishing but with an economic structure that makes the information records available at no cost to users and available via the Web, is the other developing new structure. Other

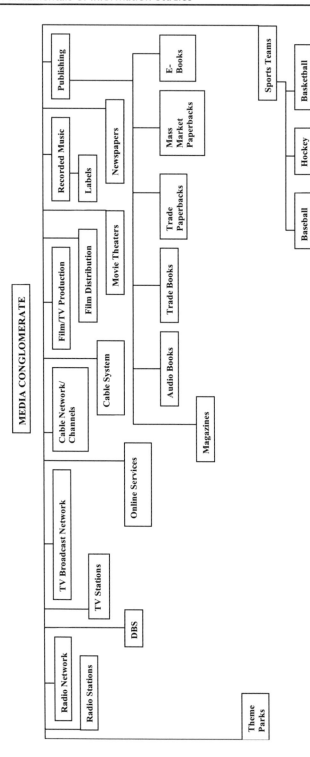

Figure 6-1   Structure of Sample Media Conglomerate

alternatives under discussion and development are self-archiving (the researcher provides access) and disciplinary repositories. While the long-term viability (and the final economic structures) of these various alternatives are unknown, all are trends that bear attention and monitoring.

A companion transformation, again in fairly early stages, is the broadening of the concept of the library's function beyond providing access to and managing information to enabling the creation, use, and production of information in the broadest array of formats by all members of society, paralleling the shift from the consumer society to the producer society in relationship to information that is mentioned above in the previous chapter.

CONCLUSION

As we have seen in the previous discussions, the major trend occurring in the societal institutions that create and distribute information is increasing concentration of ownership across all segments of the categories that have been examined and across categories as well. Both horizontal and vertical integration of the production and distribution industries have increased. Those who create and produce the content and those that deliver the content are concentrated in a small number of media conglomerates (see figure 6-1). Whether this concentration will work to the detriment of information availability, as many have feared, is not clear; but current predictions are less dire than earlier ones, in part because of continuing shifts in the exact configurations of the conglomerates as well as the partial dissolution through sell-offs of some of the concentrated segments.

To some extent, it will be the responsibility of those institutions that teach future generations to use information and that foster development of new information, as well as those that have a major responsibility for management of and access to information records, to work to ensure that whatever structure of the production and distribution functions evolves, information availability will be preserved.

QUESTIONS FOR CONSIDERATION

1. How do the functions performed by information content providers change from one format to another? Is the value to society different depending on the medium? For example, is what book publishers add to the value of an information record worth more than what a Web content provider adds?
2. Is there any value to society in having a category of institutions that devotes a substantial portion of its resources to development of new

information? Would information get developed anyway? What might be different if this function were eliminated?

3. Some critics of mergers that have formed media conglomerates charge that such mergers are detrimental to society and result in less information being available. What do you think is different in terms of society's access to information if one company controls what were previously separate publishing companies, cable systems, film studios, television networks, record companies, and Internet service providers?

4. There are agencies and agents that assist in connecting users with information they need (like libraries) or information that society thinks everyone should have (like schools). Are such agencies and agents needed if access to information is readily available on a 24/7 basis via the Web? Why or why not?

5. Do individuals who create and distribute information via the Web have any obligation to society to perform the same functions for quality assurance that traditionally have been performed by publishers?

REFERENCES

Accart, Jean-Philippe. 2000. "Bibliothécaire, Documentaliste: Même Métier?" *Bulletin des Bibliothèques de France* 45, no. 1: 88–93.

Ahrens, Frank. 2004. "FTC Approves NBC's Vivendi Universal Deal." *Washington Post* (21 April), E03. Previously available: www.washingtonpost.com/wp-dyn/articles/A28880-2004Apr20.html (accessed June 2004).

Albarran, Alan B. 2004. "The Economics of the Contemporary Radio Industry." In *Media Economics: Theory and Practice*, 3rd ed., edited by Alison Alexander, James Owers, Rod Carveth, C. Ann Hollifield, and Albert N. Greco, 207–220. Mahwah, NJ: Lawrence Erlbaum.

American Council of Learned Societies. 2006. "About the Project." *History E-Book Project*. Available: www.historyebook.org/intro.html (accessed December 2006).

Association of American Publishers. "Table S-1—Estimated Book Publishing Industry Net Sales 2002–2005." *Industry Statistics*. Available: www.publishers.org/industry/2005_S1FINAL.pdf (accessed December 2006).

Bates, Benjamin J., and Todd Chambers. 2004. "The Economics of the Cable Industry." In *Media Economics: Theory and Practice,* 3rd ed., edited by Alison Alexander, James Owers, Rod Carveth, C. Ann Hollifield, and Albert N. Greco, 173–192. Mahwah, NJ: Lawrence Erlbaum.

Bishop, Jack. 2005. "Building International Empires of Sound: Concentrations of Power and Property in the 'Global' Music Market." *Popular Music and Society* 28 (October): 443–471.

Bockstedt, Jesse C., Robert J. Kauffman, and Frederick J. Riggins. 2006. "The Move to Artist-Led On-line Music Distribution: A Theory-Based Assessment and Prospects for Structural Changes in the Digital Music Market." *International Journal of Electronic Commerce* 10 (Spring): 7–38.

Boorstin, Daniel J. 1983. "The Lost Arts of Memory." In *The Discoverers*, 480–488. New York: Random House.

Borland, John. 2005. "Publishers Loosen Rules on e-Textbooks." CNET News.com (12 August). Available: http://news.com.com/Publishers+loosen+rules+on+e-textbooks/2100-1025_3-5830640.html (accessed December 2006).

Budapest Open Access Initiative. Available: www.soros.org/openaccess/read.shtml (accessed December 2006).

Compaine, Benjamin M., and Douglas Gomery. 2000. *Who Owns the Media? Competition and Concentration in the Mass Media Industry.* 3rd ed. Mahwah, NJ: Lawrence Erlbaum.

Daly, Charles, Patrick Henry, and Ellen Ryder. 2000. "The Structure of the Magazine Industry." In *The Media and Entertainment Industries: Readings in Mass Communications*, edited by Albert N. Greco, 26–45. Boston, MA: Allyn and Bacon.

Eaglen, Audrey. 2000. *Buying Books.* 2nd ed. New York: Neal-Schuman.

Eisenstein, Elizabeth L. 2005. *The Printing Revolution in Early Modern Europe*, 2nd ed. Cambridge, UK: Cambridge University Press.

Eprints.org. 2002. "Self-Archiving FAQ." Available: www.eprints.org/self-faq (accessed December 2006).

European Union. Court of First Instance. 2006. "Judgment of the Court of First Instance in Case T-464/04: Independent Music Publishers and Labels Association (Impala) v. Commission of the European Communities." Press Release no. 60/06 (13 July). Available: http://curia.europa.eu/en/actu/communiques/cp06/aff/cp060060en.pdf (accessed December 2006).

Ferguson, Douglas A. 2004. "The Broadcast Television Networks." In *Media Economics: Theory and Practice,* 3rd ed., edited by Alison Alexander, James Owers, Rod Carveth, C. Ann Hollifield, and Albert N. Greco, 149–171. Mahwah, NJ: Lawrence Erlbaum.

Greco, Albert N. 2000. "The Structure of the Book Publishing Industry." In *The Media and Entertainment Industries: Readings in Mass Communications*, edited by Albert N. Greco, 1–25. Boston, MA: Allyn and Bacon.

Harnad, Stevan. 2001. "The Self-Archiving Initiative." *Nature Web Debates* (26 April). Available: www.nature.com/nature/debates/e-access/Articles/harnad.html (accessed December 2006).

Hillesund, Terje. 2001. "Will E-books Change the World?" *First Monday* 6 (October). Available: http://firstmonday.org/issues/issue6_10/hillesund/index.html (accessed December 2006).

Hull, Geoffrey P. 2000. "The Structure of the Recorded Music Industry." In *The Media and Entertainment Industries: Readings in Mass Communications*, edited by Albert N. Greco, 76–98. Boston, MA: Allyn and Bacon.

———. 2004. *The Recording Industry*. 2nd ed. London: Routledge.

Hull, Geoffrey P., Albert N. Greco, and Stan Martin. 2000. "The Structure of the Radio Industry." In *The Media and Entertainment Industries: Readings in Mass Communications*, edited by Albert N. Greco, 122–156. Boston, MA: Allyn and Bacon.

Kirkpatrick, David D., and Andrew Ross Sorkin. 2003. "Bronfman Starts Comeback with Warner Music Deal." *New York Times* (24 November): A1.

Litman, Barry R. 2000. "The Structure of the Film Industry: Windows of Exhibition." In *The Media and Entertainment Industries: Readings in Mass Communications*, edited by Albert N. Greco, 99–121. Boston, MA: Allyn and Bacon.

National Cable and Telecommunications Association. 2006. "Top 20 Cable Program Networks—As of September 2006." *Cable Industry Statistics*. Available: www.ncta.com/ContentView.aspx?contentId=74 (accessed December 2006).

Pfanner, Eric. 2006. "Universal Music Group and an Online Site Plan a Joint Venture to Challenge iTunes." *New York Times* (30 August), Technology Sec.

Picard, Robert G. 2004. "The Economics of the Daily Newspaper Industry." In *Media Economics: Theory and Practice*, 3rd ed., edited by Alison Alexander, James Owers, Rod Carveth, C. Ann Hollifield, and Albert N. Greco, 109–125. Mahwah, NJ: Lawrence Erlbaum.

Quain, John R. 2006. "Films that Come over the Net Don't Come Easy." *New York Times* (31 August).

Radio Advertising Bureau. 2004. *Radio Marketing Guide & Fact Book for Advertisers, 2004–2005 Edition*. New York: Radio Advertising Bureau. Available: www.rab.com/station/marketing_guide/2004rmg&fblow.pdf (accessed December 2006).

Rice University. Public Affairs. 2006. "Rice University Press Reborn as Nation's First Digital Academic Press." Houston: Rice University News & Media Relations. Available: http://media.rice.edu/media/NewsBot.asp?MODE=VIEW&ID=8654 (accessed December 2006).

Rubin, Richard E. 2004. *Foundations of Library and Information Science*. 2nd ed. New York: Neal-Schuman.

Scholarly Publishing and Academic Resources Coalition. 2007. "About SPARC." Available: www.arl.org/sparc/about/index.html (accessed 8 May 2007).

Staikos, Konstantinos Sp. 2000. *The Great Libraries: From Antiquity to the Renaissance (3000 B.C. to A.D. 1600)*. Translated by Timothy Cullen. New Castle, DE: Oak Knoll Press and The British Library.

Stross, Randall. 2006. "Words of Wisdom vs. Words from Our Sponsor." *New York Times* (27 August, final edition), sec. 3: 3.

Tenopir, Carol. 1994. "Quality in Distribution Channels." *Library Journal* 119 (1 February): 33–34.

U.S. Federal Communications Commission. 2006. "Digital Television (DTV): FCC Consumer Facts." 12 April. Available: www.fcc.gov/cgb/consumerfacts/digitaltv.html (accessed December 2006).

ADDITIONAL SOURCES

Alexander, Alison, James Owers, Rod Carveth, C. Ann Hollifield, and Albert N. Greco. 2004. *Media Economics: Theory and Practice*. 3rd ed. Mahwah, NJ: Lawrence Erlbaum.

BBC News. 2004. "Brussels Objects to Sony-BMG Deal." 25 May. Available: http://news.bbc.co.uk/1/hi/business/3744825.stm (accessed December 2006).

Bertelsmann Media Worldwide. Available: www.Bertelsmann.com (accessed December 2006).

Columbia Journalism Review. 2006. "Who Owns What?" Available: www.cjr.org/tools/owners (accessed December 2006).

Eisenstein, Elizabeth L. 1983. *The Printing Revolution in Early Modern Europe*. Cambridge, UK: Cambridge University Press.

EMI. 2005. Available: www.emigroup.com (accessed December 2006).

Fang, Irving, and Kristina Ross. 1996. *The Media History Project Timeline*. The Media History Project. Available: www.mediahistory.umn.edu/time/century.html (accessed December 2006).

Helm, Burt. 2006. "Curling up with a Good E-Book." *Business Week* 9, no. 3966 (January): 30–32.

King, Stephen. 2006. *Stephen King.com: The Official Web Site*. Available: www.stephenking.com (accessed December 2006).

Lankes, R. David, Joanne Silverstein, Scott Nicholson. n.d. *Participatory Networks: The Library as Conversation*. Syracuse, NY: Syracuse University School of Information Studies, Information Institute of Syracuse. Available: http://iis.syr.edu/projects/PNOpen/ParticiaptoryNetworks.pdf (accessed March 2007).

Lynch, Clifford. 2001. "The Battle to Define the Future of the Book in the Digital World." *First Monday* 6 (June). Available: www.firstmonday.org/issues/issue6_6/lynch/index.html (accessed December 2006).

Randle, Quint. 2001. "A Historical Overview of the Effects of New Mass Media Introductions on Magazine Publishing During the 20th Century." *First Monday* 6 (September). Available: www.firstmonday.org/issues/issue6_9/randle/index.html (accessed December 2006).

Recording Industry Association of America. 2003. *RIAA*. Available: www.riaa.com/default.asp (accessed December 2006).

Schoenherr, Steven E. 2005. "Recording Technology History." Notes revised 6 July 2005. Available: http://history.sandiego.edu/gen/recording/notes.html (accessed December 2006).

Sony Corporation. 2006. *Sony Global.* Available: www.sony.net (accessed December 2006).

Time Warner. 2006. Available: www.timewarner.com/corp (accessed December 2006).

Viacom. 2005. Available: www.viacom.com (accessed December 2006).

Vivendi. 2006. Available: www.vivendi.com (accessed December 2006).

Wyatt, Edward. 2006. "The Bottom Line on E-Textbooks." *New York Times* (23 April), Final ed., sec. 4A: 10.

How many information professions are there? You probably have interacted with members of one or more of the information professions. Before you read this chapter, see how many information jobs you can list. Make note of what these jobs have in common and how they are different. When you have finished the chapter, see if you have changed your mind about the similarities and the differences. This chapter will introduce you to some of the information professions. However, keep in mind that while those described are representative of the field, the list presented here is not by any means comprehensive.

Chapter 7

The Information Professions

Learning Guide

After reading this chapter, you should be able to

- explain the major differences among the disciplines of computer science, management information systems, library science, and information science;
- identify and describe changes in the roles of information professionals that have occurred in response to changes in communication systems and information technologies;
- analyze the different functions performed by information professionals working in various sectors of the economy;
- assess the impact of the work environment on the roles and functions of an information professional.

When you have finished the chapter, return to this page to be sure you have learned what you need to know.

INTRODUCTION

Defining what constitutes an information profession is a less straightforward task than one might think. While generating a list of information jobs is a fairly easy assignment, determining what characteristics make a position, or a category of positions, part of the information professions calls for analysis of what and how many information components are included in the position.

It could be argued that every human endeavor involves some form of information transfer, exchange, creation, reduction, component, and so on. The surgeon uses knowledge and skills acquired from education and training (information transfer), an examination of the patient (information creation), and information generated at the time of surgery. A similar model can be developed for football quarterbacks, police detectives, hunter/gatherers during the ice ages, explorers then and now, or even university professors.

For some professions, the information component is more obvious than for others. Journalists by definition seek to discover information and to report that information back to a larger or different audience. Intelligence agents also seek to uncover information but generally report their findings to a much smaller audience. Researchers in the natural or social sciences seek to explain natural or human phenomena. Attorneys, accountants, and physicians all seek to apply a general body of knowledge to specific individuals or cases. Any farmer who disregards information on planting/harvesting cycles, pest control, or market dynamics does not remain a farmer for very long.

The information professions are extremely diverse and are becoming more so. The field includes storytellers and shamans; librarians and computer scientists; information managers in education, business, competitive and military intelligence, and entertainment; information architects, CIOs (chief information officers), CKOs (chief knowledge officers), and information brokers.

The more diversified information technology becomes, the more diversified the information professions become. But, however diversified the information professions have become, they continue to share a number of characteristics. Harold Borko's definition of information science could be adapted to serve as a definition of the characteristics of an information profession as one

> that investigates the properties and behavior of information, the forces governing the flow of information, and the means of processing information for optimum accessibility and usability. It is concerned with that body of knowledge relating to the origination, collection, organization, storage, retrieval, interpretation, transmission, transformation, and utilization of information. (Borko, 1968: 3)

The number and diversity of information professionals change just as surely as the information environment and information technologies change. For example, before the mid-1990s there were no Webmasters (with perhaps the exception of spiders). Computer science as a discipline did not exist before the 1950s. European and American universities offered very limited curricula before the mid-nineteenth century: theology, logic, rhetoric, Greek and Latin, and maybe mathematics and astronomy.

The number and kinds of information professionals continues to increase. There are several factors that help drive that trend. These include an increased understanding of

- the immediacy and time value of information
- quality control and information management
- the evaluation of quality and utility of specific technologies
- the need to mediate between decision makers, information gatherers, and information processors
- information flow control and management

This chapter is concerned with the role and impact of various information systems and technologies on the information professions and on society, and vice versa. As information increases in reach, complexity, and speed, the number, complexity, and differences among the information professions increase as well. The growing complexity of technology; the increased differentiation of creators, managers, transmitters, and interpreters; and the greater dependence on technology complicate our understanding of the information environment and the people who populate it.

CATEGORIES OF THE INFORMATION PROFESSIONS

As a means of assisting the understanding of the information professions, identification of a structural framework in which to think about them is helpful. We have already alluded to the three traditions that make up the information environment: the oral tradition, the written or print tradition, and the electronic tradition. With each of these, there are associated specific categories of information professionals:

- *oral tradition*—storytellers, shamans, actors, singers, consumers
- *written or print tradition*—authors, publishers, distributors, managers (libraries), evaluators
- *electronic tradition*—information architects, network managers, software/ hardware engineers, broadcasters

In the succeeding traditions (those that develop later in time), some of the categories from the previous traditions continue, making the transition to the new format (see figure 7-1).

Emerging traditions do not ever completely replace the traditions that precede them, but they may displace them. For example, the theater is alive and well despite the ubiquity of the cinema, radio, and television. Town criers no longer scream out the news in the streets. They were displaced first by newspapers and later by network anchors. In a way, in fact, information technology has served to legitimate some professions and to raise their status in society. For example, prior to the advent of television, actors, professional athletes, and other entertainers were frequently seen as somewhat unruly, uncouth, and certainly out of the mainstream. Professional "wrestlers" may be unruly, but are they out of the mainstream today? The entertainers of our day are showered with wealth and acclaim and have come to represent a new elite.

Figure 7-1 charts a progression through the oral, written, and electronic traditions. It also charts a progression from information creation through storage. It should be noted that there are feedback loops from creation, transmission, management, and storage. New information can be, and often is, created from information management or interpretation.

The arrows shown in figure 7-1 indicate that, for example, the role of storyteller migrates from one tradition to another. Moreover, storytellers can be and often are involved in the creation, transmission, management, and storage of their tales. On the other hand, while a librarian may also be a storyteller, storytelling is not inherent in the function "librarian." What we are suggesting is that the inherent definition of "researcher" does not preclude "publisher," but the inherent definition of "publisher" precludes "author." In other cases, the difference between Webmaster and publisher may be a matter of medium rather than inherent definitional differences.

	ORAL	WRITTEN/PRINT	ELECTRONIC
CREATION	Storyteller↓→	Author, Researcher, Journalist, Inventor↓→	Programmer, Database Compiler↓
TRANSMISSION	Driver, Messenger, Troubadour, Signalman↓→	Scribe, Amanuensis, Courier, Entertainer, Publisher↓→	Lineman, Network Manager ↓
MANAGEMENT, MANIPULATION, AND INTERPRETATION	Shaman↓→	Editor, Librarian, Dispatcher, Archivist↓→	CIO, CKO, Systems Librarian, Webmaster, Information Architect↓
STORAGE	Storyteller, Shaman→	Librarian, Archivist, Records Manager→	Network Manager, Database Maintainer

Figure 7-1   Information Profession Relationships

A final note: it is something of a misnomer to label the present environment "electronic." First, it is not just electronic; it is also "light-based." Perhaps "subatomic" would be a better label. Second, electrons and photons are used to write and transmit binary, digital representations of information. Thus the "subatomic" environment has more to do with more efficient, more universal, and far quicker means for information transmission and storage than with information creation. That said, the subatomic environment allows our storytellers to tell their stories using far more realistic props than ever before. Contrast, if you will, the 1960s *Star Trek* of Captain James T. Kirk and the twenty-first-century *Star Trek* of Captain Jonathan Archer. Ironically, the latter predates the former in the chronology of the tale but postdates it in production.

Where does this leave us? If we accept the notion that all human activity has an information component, then all human professions are information professions. That is not a very useful definition. Recall the last half of our adaptation of Harold Borko's definition to the information profession: "It is concerned with that body of knowledge relating to the origination, collection, organization, storage, retrieval, interpretation, transmission, transformation, and utilization of information" (Borko, 1968: 3).

In the discussion that follows we will limit ourselves to some of the information professions that meet Borko's test. We explore both "old" professions like librarian and some of the newer ones like "information architect." Many of the newer information professions have a great deal in common with their predecessors but with a layer of technology imposed on the definition. As we will see, however, the older professions have adapted and acquired the technical knowledge as well.

Differentiating the information professions by creation, transmission, management, and storage is not a particularly easy task. All of the information professions share all of the listed characteristics. We can, however, attempt to distinguish the "dominant trait." Before addressing these categories, we need to clarify four major fields that contribute to the information professions.

Computer Science

Computer science is an extremely broad field that covers everything from computer languages to game playing through the development of search and retrieval systems for digital libraries. Computer scientists can be divided (but not very well) by their areas of interest. One computer science bibliography has grouped the fields as shown in figure 7-2. These fields are all related to information management, manipulation, and/or transmission. The skills these disciplines represent overlap into library science and information science and the specific professions that grow out of them.

- Artificial Intelligence
- Compiler Technology, Programming Languages, and Type Theory
- Database Research
- Distributed Systems, Networking, and Telecommunications
- Computer Graphics and Vision
- Logic Programming
- (Computational) Mathematics
- Neural Networks
- Object-Oriented Programming and Systems
- Operating Systems
- Parallel Processing
- Software Engineering and Formal Methods
- Theory/Foundations of Computer Science
- Typesetting

Figure 7-2 Computer Science Disciplines

Source: Achilles, Alf-Christian. 2006. The Collection of Computer Science Bibliographies. Universität Karlsruhe, Lehrstuhl Informatik für Ingenieure und Naturwissenschaftler. Available: http://liinwww.ira.uka.de/bibliography/index.html#browse (accessed December 2006.)

Management Information Systems (MIS)

Management information systems (MIS) is a discipline oriented toward business management in an information-rich and global environment. Many universities have MIS programs, sometimes at the master's and doctoral degree levels, in their colleges of business. The curricula include computer science and technology and systems management, as well as the business management courses. The degree supports those seeking expertise in electronic commerce and e-government, and various informatics applications.

Library Science

The ODLIS Online Dictionary (Reitz, 2006) defines library science as "The professional knowledge and skill with which recorded information is selected, acquired, organized, stored, maintained, retrieved, and disseminated to meet the needs of a specific clientele."

Information Science

The same source defines information science as "The systematic study and analysis of the sources, development, collection, organization, dissemination, evaluation, use, and management of information in all its forms."

Both library science and information science are very complex fields. It is arguable that all disciplines discussed in this chapter fall within the definition of information science, including the computer and library sciences. Indeed, there is a great deal of overlap among these professional areas. With the advent of advanced information technologies, it is perhaps arguable that there has been considerable blurring among the fields. And it has been argued that information science is growing in complexity as its underlying parts converge and as the questions it seeks to address grow more complicated (Koehler, 2001).

INFORMATION CREATION/DISCOVERY PROFESSIONS

The information creation professions are those that generate new information from observation, imagination, intuition, analysis, redefinition, and research. These include but, of course, are not limited to authors, artists, researchers, and intelligence agents. These are the content originators. Often, content originators produce content from existing content. The new content represents a reinterpretation of the "old" based on new information or the skills, experience, and knowledge the information creator brings to the process.

Authors and Artists

Authors and artists can be classed as those who work in fiction and those in nonfiction. Artistic works, whether written, aural, visual, or multimedia, are cultural icons as well as emotive expression. While they may not describe in precise terms "reality," they are nevertheless expressions of culture and convey information from the artist to the viewer.

Journalists

Journalists engage both in information creation and in information transmission. The journalism profession is concerned with the gathering, sorting, interpreting, and "repackaging" of information. Repackaging prepares information for transmission through the various news media—now often shortened to just "the media." The media, of course, are newspapers, newsletters, radio, television, and most recently the World Wide Web. Messages can now be forwarded to consumers via pagers and other hand-held electronic devices. The most recent innovation in the news stream is the incorporation of the end user with the marriage of traditional news agencies, with the Web permitting selective news or push/pull services.

Researchers

Researchers in the natural sciences, social sciences, the humanities, and the professions observe the corpus of knowledge within their expertise, bring to bear analytic tools, and explore and test hypotheses based on their knowledge, skills, and expertise. Researchers in the natural sciences seek to understand physical, chemical, and biological phenomena. In the social sciences, researchers seek to explain human behaviors at a variety of different levels and in different contexts. Those in the humanities seek to interpret the meaning of various human artifacts or cultural mores and folkways. This book, for example, is in many ways an expression of research findings of its authors as well as their "secondary research." It is also a product of the authors' interpretation of the work of others. In many cases, that work is recognized by the references we make.

There are a number of professions that fall under the rubric of applied science and technology. These include the engineering, medical, legal, marketing, and financial/accounting professions as well as the fields of corporate, political, and military intelligence. These professions seek to discover, analyze, and manipulate information to meet a specific need or application. For example, an attorney may search legal precedent in order to resolve a legal issue. For the attorney's purpose, for matters of law, he or she will explore both statutory and judicial resources. What is "fair game" for the lawyer depends in large part on the arena and the rules for that arena. What distinguishes the legal and quasi-legal professions (like accounting and regulation) from others is the source of the rules or norms "consulted." Lawyers are concerned with human-made rules (statutes, regulations, and judicial rulings) rather than "natural" norms. The social scientist is concerned with both human-made and natural norms.

Intelligence Agents

The intelligence agent in the broadest sense of the word is concerned with gathering and analyzing information for the immediate or near-term benefit of others. These agents often focus on primary sources, but also may rely on secondary sources. There is a wide array of tools available to the intelligence agent. The Central Intelligence Agency (CIA), for example, a major home to the intelligence agents of the U.S. government, relies on both overt and covert resources. These resources vary widely. During the Cold War, Sovietologists developed a technique termed "kremlinology." The Kremlin is the set of buildings where the Czarist, Communist, and currently republican governments of what is now Russia sit. Put simply, kremlinologists examined open information to try to tease out information about the Soviet government. For example, during the May Day Parade in Moscow and at other major public events, the members of the Politburo (highest policy-making body of the Communist Party) would stand together on the viewing stand. Who stood next to whom, and particularly next to the General Secretary, was considered a significant indicator of whose star was rising and whose was falling.

There are many other open source resources. These include newspapers, television, programs, speeches, the 10K reports of publicly traded companies, patent filings, journal articles, Web sites, and so on. An open source resource is any information piece freely accessible in the public domain. Libraries are, of course, an excellent resource for anyone interested in accessing public information; and since the advent of the World Wide Web, there is another easily accessible resource. It goes without saying that the intelligence and police agencies around the world are keenly interested not only in the kinds of information that can be retrieved from libraries and the Web but also in who is retrieving that information. It has been demonstrated more than once that very sensitive information can be derived from open sources. For example, about twenty-five years ago a Princeton University student drew "workable" plans for an atomic weapon based on open source information he found in the university's library. Others have used the library and/or the Web to learn how to make drugs or make fertilizer bombs. Intelligence agents in business, operating in the area known as competitive intelligence, use primarily open sources. However, through special techniques of analysis they discover information that was previously unknown.

There are also "less open" or covert information sources used by intelligence agents, governmental and otherwise, and others from which to gather information. Both the Americans and Russians have "bugged" each other's embassies. Air France was involved in a scandal when it was discovered that the seats on transatlantic flights had been bugged so as to eavesdrop on the conversations of business travelers (Waller and Sancton, 1995). Someone—the United States was accused—bugged the Boeing 767 that was to be the official plane of Chinese President Jiang Zemin (Pomfret, 2002). The Allies during World War II broke the top secret codes of both Germany and Japan, enabling access to an immense volume of military intelligence. It is now possible to read license plates from space.

We quite correctly tend to think of libraries, archives, and database services as information storage, management, and transmission enterprises, but these institutions also have an information creation function, especially "information about information." Thus, some professionals who work in these institutions could also be included in the information creation category of professionals, although we have placed these professional groups elsewhere since their dominant characteristic is not information creation.

The point we are trying to make is that there are many professions involved in information creation and, if you will, re-creation. There is complex interplay among the information creation, transmission, management, and storage professions. But without information creation, there would be little use for all the others.

INFORMATION TRANSMISSION PROFESSIONS

The information transmission professions are also legend. Put very simply, the information transmission professions are concerned with moving data from point A to point B. In a very real sense, the information transmission professions have very little interest in the content of the transmission but a great deal of interest in the reproducibility, reliability, and speed of that transmission.

The information transmission professions can take many forms. It is arguable that a transportation infrastructure qualifies as part of information transmission, thus those who work in this infrastructure might be included in the information transmission category. Airlines, trains, buses, automobiles, and donkey carts all carry people, goods, and messages. One system may be inherently faster or more reliable than another, but they serve the same end. An airline or a bus company may carry you or a message. It does not concern itself with what is in your head—at least not usually—or in the content of the message. It concerns itself with getting the container from place to place. Some transmission mechanisms offer different service guarantees, and it is for the consumer to determine which to use. For example, the U.S. Postal Service will reliably carry a letter from one place to the next through its regular delivery mechanisms, but in order to ensure delivery within a tight and specific frame one might elect to use Express Mail or FedEx or another courier service.

This type of physical message transmission is inherently slow, although speed is a relative thing. In the seventeenth century it often took three months or more for a message to physically travel from Europe to North America. In the late nineteenth century, transatlantic and transcontinental messages could be sent instantaneously, but at great cost, by telegraph. In the late twentieth century messages could be transmitted through a variety of media rapidly with great complexity at relatively little cost. For example, in 1960 a three-minute telephone call from Europe to the United States cost about $25 in 1960 dollars. That is on the order of $160 in 2005 dollars. That same phone call, depending on your calling plan, could cost as little as $ 0.20 in 2006 dollars (or even at no cost if using VoIP). In 1960, the call was transmitted in analog format via undersea cable. There was a great deal of noise inherently a part of the call. In 2006, the telephone message would be transmitted digitally via satellite or cable, and it would be virtually noiseless.

Let us remember that information transmission professionals have been transmitting information through a number of media for a very long time. Signal drums, flags, smoke, and lights were once commonplace. Even today, navies still use semaphore, a method of visual communication using hand-held flags to represent letters and concepts, for ship-to-ship communications. Traffic lights communicate information. That blue light in your rearview mirror says "pull over; you have a ticket." In the mid-nineteenth century, a complex system of pneumatic tubes was laid under the streets of London, Paris, and other cities (Standage, 1998). "Physical" messages were moved rapidly within the cities. These systems were interlinked through telegraphy, creating a rapid and efficient information transmission system. Telegraphers, postmen, runners, linemen, signalmen, and many others operated these systems.

In the twentieth century, the costs and time needed to transmit messages were greatly reduced through a growing complexity of transmission technologies. This growing number of technologies simultaneously increased the number of information transmission professionals, both in number and in kind. By the 1930s, it became theoretically possible and feasible to send a letter by airmail across the country or across the world almost overnight. By the 1980s, it did become possible to send that letter almost anywhere in the country overnight and by the late 1990s almost anywhere in the world. This capability has been made possible by the growth of a major transportation infrastructure.

The telephone system revolutionized information transfer. It also created a new class of information worker. Certainly, telegraphy created a need for telegraphers, linemen, a telegram delivery (courier) system, and so on. The telephone created a need for "online" customer service and call placing personnel—the operator and later directory assistance. A successful telephone system bred the need for telephone books and for someone to compile and distribute them. In addition, the telephone revolution generated a need for system/service maintenance and improvement. Recall the Claude Shannon discussion from chapter 4. AT&T (American Telephone and Telegraph) and the successor Baby Bells after the breakup of the AT&T system were always concerned with reducing line noise, improved switching technologies, new transmission technologies (from strung line to microwave), and better call placement (from requesting a connection from a human operator to dials to tones).

With the advent of long distance point-to-point data transmission, a number of other companies began to offer services. These included not only AT&T but also companies like Sprint and MCI. Their concern in the beginning was with data transmission, not voice. Telnet systems, for example, accessed with a dial-up number and carried over the last mile by POTS, connected the user to the service provider. Many of these service providers were database companies, providing access to information they created or to information created by others through an interface they created.

The Internet was the great information transmission innovation of the late twentieth century. Beginning as ARPANET, designed to interlink defense contractors with the Department of Defense, the Internet expanded rapidly through the 1980s and beyond. ARPANET, sponsored by the U.S. Defense Department's Advanced Research Projects Agency (ARPA), was one of many responses to the Soviet launch of Sputnik I in 1957. ARPA, under the leadership of men like J. C. R. Licklider, Robert Taylor, and Lawrence Roberts, perceived the need for a distributed network and therefore less vulnerable communications in the event of a Soviet nuclear attack against the United States. Like many other innovative communications technologies, the Internet grew out of a national defense concern and defense funding.

The first Internet transmission professionals were men like Paul Baran, Vinton Cerf, and Jon Postel. Baran, called "grandfather of the Internet," first conceived of the "packet switching" concept that underlies signal transmission on the Internet. He also first conceived of the idea of a distributed network. Donald Davies, the second Internet grandfather, developed similar ideas and first employed the term "packet" for Internet messages. Uncles of the Internet include Leonard Kleinrock and Lawrence G. Roberts, each of whom made significant contributions to packet switching technology and theory. Cerf, said to be the "father of the Internet," and Postel, charged with managing the Internet numbers assignment system, and many others facilitated the growth of the system from five or six nodes in 1962 to approaching a billion in 2006. The "invention" of the World Wide Web by Tim Berners-Lee in 1991 revolutionized and popularized the Internet.

The growth of the Internet and particularly of the Web has created a number of new information transmission professions. These include information architect, network manager, HTML/Java/applet programmer, and so on. However, again because of the dominant characteristic of the professional group, information architects are discussed in the next category.

MANAGEMENT-RELATED PROFESSIONS

The information management professions focus on the design and maintenance of systems that organize and manage information for use, sometimes in specific contexts or formats, sometimes for specific user groups. Some of the information professional areas, such as librarians and archivists, fall almost equally into the management and storage categories. Those discussed in this section focus more predominantly on management for immediate use and less on longer-term management and storage. The examples included here also focus on the newer and emerging information management professionals.

Information Architect

Information architects are themselves not agreed on what one is (IAwiki, 2006). The Argus Center for Information Architecture offered the following early definition for information architecture: "The art and science of organizing information to help people effectively fulfill their information needs" (Hagedorn, 2000). This definition applies equally well to any information professional, perhaps because information architecture is a relatively new and as yet not fully defined field. There are some who very narrowly define the information architect as Webmaster with additional Web-based information management responsibilities. By this definition, an architect is essentially a very well qualified Web site designer and maintainer.

Rosenfeld and Morville (2002) suggest a slightly less broad definition. Information architecture is the art and science of design and implementation for complex Web sites with complex information content.

Information architecture has also been more broadly defined as the system by which information is presented to the end user in an effective and efficient manner. Neither the technology nor the information format is specified, although Web delivery is strongly implied. Another definition is that "information architecture (IA) is the art, science, and business of organizing information so that it makes sense to people who use it." With this as definition of the field, then, "information architects are the members of the team who choreograph the complex relationships among all the elements that make up an information space," regardless of what constitutes that information space—a Web page, a CD-ROM, or other technology (American Society for Information Science and Technology, 2001).

Education programs for information architects are very recent in appearance and have yet to stabilize in terms of curricula and expected outcomes, as could be expected in a field that is newly emergent.

IT (Information Technology) Manager

IT manager is a generic job title. Until recently, an IT manager was someone who took care of specific technological concerns, for example, technical writing and computer programs. IT managers are now expected to have Internet, intranet, and extranet skills as well as database and information classification skills. The IT manager should also be conversant with programming skills and network hardware and software issues. Information technology includes computers, telecommunications, software systems, transmission, storage, and utilization of information.

The IT manager is likely to develop informatics systems for his or her enterprise. As we have already seen in chapter 4, informatics is concerned with the management and movement of information and the creation of systems to do just that.

IT management includes network management. A network manager is responsible for maintaining a computer network. This can include a local area network (LAN) or connections to an external network. It may also include Internet service providers (ISPs) and the maintenance of the integrity of the node and customer access to the system.

The IT manager is likely to answer to the CKO, CIO (see below), or equivalent corporate officer.

A management information systems degree, either at bachelor's or master's level, is typically an education path followed by those seeking positions as IT managers in the business environment. Other education paths would be degrees in computer science, telecommunications, or information management and technology. Although the IT manager is not so recently developed a position as the information architect, there is still not a standard path for those who would be IT managers, but rather multiple avenues of education and career development can be followed.

Chief Knowledge Officer (CKO)

The chief knowledge officer (CKO) is closely related to the IT professional and is particularly akin to the chief information officer (CIO). What differentiates the CKO and the CIO is the line responsibility for networking and other hardware and software decisions. The CKO has less direct responsibility than the CIO, which in part explains why most chief IT professionals are CIOs rather than CKOs.

The CKO is typically a ranking member of corporate decision making. The position is a relatively new one, created to help businesses integrate technology and human resources. It has been argued that CKOs have three critical responsibilities: creating a knowledge management infrastructure, building a knowledge culture, and making these structures pay off economically. Thus the mission of the CKO is to provide vision and leadership for creating and sustaining a culture of knowledge sharing in the company to strengthen key business processes in a continually changing and competitive industry.

CKOs are frequently promoted out of corporate libraries and information management and informatics centers. CKO positions in the public sector are rarer but do exist (Duffy, 1998). The CKO is not a position that has as yet a

- As the Chief Knowledge Officer for the agency, the incumbent is responsible for ensuring that GSA employees have the right information at the right time in the right place. Knowledge lives in people, while data and information reside in computers. The CKO provides the leadership required to successfully transform GSA into a learning organization that is flexible, agile and open to change.
- Working cooperatively with GSA's CFO, CPO and CIO, the CKO builds collaborative work environments, infrastructure, resources and skills to provide the necessary enterprise architecture for knowledge management within GSA.
- The CKO serves as chief advisor to the Administrator, Deputy Administrator and Chief of Staff on all matters pertaining to knowledge management, including the identification of goals, strategy, tools, measurements, targets and project management.
- Develops program management structure to support GSA's major business lines and regional offices in selective pilot and demonstration projects related to knowledge management. Encourages, coaches, steers and directs, where necessary, these GSA initiatives to deliver positive and measurable results to the organization.
- Serves as primary spokesperson, both within and outside of the agency for GSA's knowledge management program. Represents GSA at conferences, forums, consortia and academic seminars, as well as, to the print media, and serves as the chief GSA expert on knowledge management.
- Develops knowledge and skills of GSA audiences at all levels, including the leadership, SES, middle management, knowledge workers and entry level workers in the full range of knowledge management and development.
- Identifies highly knowledgeable and skilled employees, and ensures that they maximize these skills in their jobs and in their careers. Provides guidance and encouragement to these valuable employees.
- Working cooperatively with the CPO, redirects training to more actively support the knowledge management agenda; for example, expanding GSA's distance learning capabilities, reinventing GSA's library as a knowledge management center, etc.
- Working cooperatively with the CIO, ensures an adequate electronic knowledge environment at the enterprise and organizational level.
- Working cooperatively with the CFO, identifies resources to support knowledge management efforts.
- Provides predictive KM strategy based upon research of state-of-the-art business practices in the private and public sectors. Benchmarks with both private and public sector entities to ensure that GSA stays on the cutting edge.
- Develops and maintains a knowledge management portal for GSA, including WEB interface, interactive Lotus Notes applications, databases, data warehouses, and educational links.
- Facilitates the growth of communities of practice, and identifies knowledge sharing needs throughout the agency. Fosters learning and knowledge creation.
- Provides access to knowledge-sharing tools; evaluates their effectiveness and recommends leading-edge tools as standards for the agency.
- Represents GSA at the Council of Knowledge Management Officers, sharing best practices, new techniques, technologies and information, and working collaboratively with colleagues in similar positions throughout government.
- Identifies skill and knowledge gaps in the GSA workforce, and working collaboratively with GSA's CPO, develops strategies to enhance GSA's skill set.
- Visions the future, and articulates strategies for GSA to meet its goals in a rapidly changing environment. Develops measures of effectiveness and results.
- Maintains working relationships with senior GSA officials, and officials at other agencies to keep abreast of KM developments. Exchanges information with the GSA leadership, and fosters an atmosphere of growth and openness for the agency.
- Communicates GSA's commitment to knowledge management and leads by example.
- Serves as a member of the GSA Leadership Council, and as a member of the GSA Deputies Council.
- Responsible for fostering the EEO program within GSA by assuring equal opportunity in recruitment, selection, promotion, training, awards, assignments and special program objects to effectively use the strength of a diverse work force.

Figure 7-3   Example of Duties of a CKO

Source: U.S. General Services Administration. Office of Knowledge Management. 2003. "Chief Knowledge Officer." Previously available: http://ioa-qpnet-co.gsa.gov/QuickPlace/km/PageLibrary85256C6B005EDD06.nsf/h_7A67D139B238F48C85256C7E006AA3AF/AA565305CD6E4A9385256D5000521948/?OpenDocument (accessed May 2006).

clearly defined set of education requirements or a standardized career path, except that the position requires considerable expertise and experience in knowledge management.

Chief Information Officer (CIO)

The CIO is defined as the corporate officer responsible for the management and maintenance of the information technology of an enterprise. This responsibility includes the ability to anticipate technological changes and therefore to maintain currency and corporate competitive advantage. It can include oversight for technology acquisitions (both hardware and software) and for information acquisition and distribution within the enterprise. The CIO typically has management responsibility for "information" workers in the company.

Because the CIO position, like the CKO, is relatively new, the definition of the profession is not yet fully developed. However, there are examples. The U.S. Department of Labor provides the following mission statement for the CIO:

> To provide leadership, policy guidance and assistance to Departmental agencies in all aspects of using information technology to implement and manage those programs within the Department. (U.S. Department of Labor, Office of the Chief Information Officer, n.d.)

To meet that mission, the CIO will do the duties similar to those listed in figure 7-4.

There is a Web site for U.S. federal government CIOs (www.cio.gov).

In addition to corporate and government environments, the CIO has become a fairly standard position in higher education, although the exact title in that environment varies widely. As with the CKO, there is no standard educational or career path that leads to a CIO position.

Chief Privacy Officer (CPO)

The chief privacy officer (CPO) is defined as a high-level management position. The CPO concept is a new one that grew out of privacy concerns created by the new information and communications technologies. The CPO is charged with developing privacy/technology guidelines within an organization and between the organization and its clients. He or she must be familiar with laws and regulations that guide privacy issues as well as organizational policy and contractual obligations. In addition, the CPO may develop privacy policy and perform a major function in identifying and implementing sensitive information policies. Thus the role of the CPO incorporates both legal and technical concerns to help meet organizational goals.

Enable efficient and effective communications and information sharing through interoperability and interconnectivity. This includes:

- determining necessary DOL Information Technology commonality and compatibility needs to develop requisite Information Technology architecture strategy, and providing resources to finance innovative cross-cutting Information Technology initiatives; and
- promoting DOL information exchange/accessibility of internal and external DOL customers through the Internet and Intranet.

Manage DOL information collections. Limit the amount of information required from the public and report progress in restricting paperwork to that required by law or other essential need.

Promote and facilitate learning opportunities that ensure DOL's workforce is adequately trained and experienced in Information Technology.

Assure that all Information Technology investments are effective and efficient in accordance with Federal and Departmental guidance to execute sound capital planning and investment strategies.

Provide guidance to agencies in execution of their Information Technology investments for consistency with departmental strategic and capital plans, and Information Technology architecture.

Develop and manage Information Technology policies to ensure departmental compliance with regulations in addition to providing assistance and guidance to agencies in their dealings with Information Technology issues and initiatives.

Plan on a strategic basis for and coordinate the management of the Department's information technology and information systems.

Prepare an annual budget report on information technology for inclusion in the Department's budget submission to Congress, describing the progress in achieving goals.

Ensure that an adequate level of security exists for all agency automated information systems, whether maintained in-house or commercially. Also, ensure that all DOL employees and contractors are adequately trained in security information technology issues.

Enter into contracts that provide for multi-agency acquisitions of information technology in accordance with guidance issued by the Director, OMB.

Provide oversight and maintenance to ensure and maximize the quality, objectivity, utility, and integrity of information, including statistical information, disseminated by the Department.

Ensure that an index of information disseminated to the public is included in the Government Information Locator Systems (GILS) created pursuant to section 4101 of Title 44, U.S.C.

Figure 7-4 Example of Duties of a CIO

Source: U.S. Department of Labor. Office of the Chief Information Officer. 2006. "CIO Mission." Available: www.dol.gov/cio/about_cio/cmission.htm (accessed December 2006).

The CPO position first came to the fore in the corporate world but has since spread into governmental, higher educational, and health care arenas. In all of these areas the position is relatively new. For example, IBM appointed its first CPO in November 2000; the U.S. Postal Service named its first CPO in March 2001; and in higher education, the University of Pennsylvania named a CPO in March 2002, the first in the Ivy League schools. However, recent federal privacy regulations, such as the Health Insurance

Portability and Accountability Act, which requires privacy officers in health-care–related entities, has spurred attention to this area of information positions (Ulfelder, 2004). Of the three positions, CKO, CIO, and CPO, the CPO is the most recent to emerge; and the long-term viability of such positions is not yet clear.

STORAGE-RELATED PROFESSIONS

This group of information professionals includes many who incorporate other information aspects, particularly management. They are categorized here as storage-related due to the emphasis in each on either the long-term storage for retrieval as needed of information in various kinds of containers or the extraction from stores of information needed by users.

Archivist

Archivists are professionals who are responsible for the management of important historical records. Professional archivists combine the talents and abilities of information specialists, librarians, editors, record managers, conservators, researchers, and historians.

The archivist should have specific experience related to the institution's concerns.

An archivist's primary responsibilities are to

- select or acquire
- arrange
- describe
- preserve records

A record, we should point out, is any "knowledge container" that contains "recorded" information. He or she may also perform archival reference services, direct exhibitions, and plan outreach and fund-raising activities. Archivists often specialize in an area of history so they can better determine the records in that area that qualify for retention and should become part of the archives.

Since there are both public and private archives, archivists work in both the public and the private sectors. Public archives are archives that are associated with public institutions (national archives, state archives, archives of state agencies, like universities). Private archives include those in corporations wishing to preserve their historical record. Coca-Cola, for example, maintains both an archive and a museum (The World of Coca-Cola) in Atlanta, Georgia. It also provides an online history of the drink and the company at http://heritage.coca-cola.com. Thus, not only do archives help maintain the historical record; they may also have marketing applications.

As noted in chapter 5, there have been efforts to archive the Web. These efforts include development of markup and naming technologies that provide some stability to Web page and site location: URI (Universal or Uniform Resource Indicator), URN (Uniform Resource Name), URC (Uniform Resource Classification), as well as OCLC's PURLs (Persistent Uniform Resource Locator). These are not archival technologies per se; they provide a more permanent address for the elusive URL. As has already been discussed, there have been a number of proposals to actually save "snapshots" of the Web, including the Internet archive created by Brewster Kahle (www .archive.org). For archivists whose information to be preserved is contained in Web sites, the development of means to preserve the historical Web sites is a pressing current issue.

By virtue of their function, archivists are concerned with record preservation. Unlike records managers (discussed later in this chapter), archivists have very long time horizons and must have expert knowledge of the preservation technologies and practices appropriate to their collections. (See Banks and Pilette, 2000; U.S. Library of Congress, 2006; U.S. National Archives and Records Administration, 2006; Stanford University Libraries, 2006, for additional information on preservation.)

Although not all archivists have the same educational preparation, the two main disciplinary areas that have provided education programs for archivists have been history and library science, both at the master's degree level. As with others in the storage category, both the educational requirements and the career paths for archivists have a greater degree of standardization than the professionals discussed in the management category.

Records Manager

The profession of records management is relatively new, although the function records managers perform is an ancient one. The position has become highly professionalized in recent years, in part because technology used to support it has become far more sophisticated, but also because society has placed greater demands on its institutions for the maintenance and protection of a wide variety of records.

Both communications (information transmission) technologies and the development of storage and retrieval systems that can manage large amounts of information have fed the demand for records maintenance. In addition, modern society is very much records based. Records follow us through our lives—birth certificates, school transcripts, tax records, business documents, and so on. It is the responsibility of the records manager to maintain the integrity of those records.

Records managers can be found in a variety of venues. They work for public and private institutions, including departments of vital statistics, universities, police departments, and corporations. There is also a growing entrepreneurial sector: there are companies in most communities that offer records management on contract. Companies, governments, and individuals may store documents with firms that specialize in document management.

The records manager receives a record, catalogs it in a way it can be easily accessed, and stores the record so it can be retrieved on demand. Records managers are responsible not only for active records, but also for inactive ones, and for regular appraisal of records for their usefulness and validity.

The records management profession has grown more complex over time. There are often legal requirements for corporations, governments, or individuals to maintain certain types of documents for some specific period of time. For example, the Internal Revenue Service (IRS) requires individuals to retain tax records for three years. In addition, companies may require that certain document streams—say, purchase orders—be kept for some defined number of years. Governments and universities are expected to maintain a wide range of records, including such documents as birth and death certificates and transcripts, for many years. The records manager must be aware of both institutional and legal retention policies for the retention and disposition of various records.

These duties of the records manager may appear to overlap with those of the archivist. There is, however, a fine distinction. The archivist maintains documents that have an inherent historical value, while the records manager maintains records that have personal or institutional value. Once the personal or institutional value of a document disappears, the records manager should dispose of it. Thus the records manager maintains records on a specified schedule; the archivist maintains them for posterity.

In the performance of their duties, records managers carry out many of the same tasks as librarians and archivists. They receive, catalog, store, and retrieve documents. They employ sophisticated computerized document management systems and maintain high storage and protection standards for their materials. They perform these tasks, however, for different reasons. Records are maintained for the benefit of their owners rather than for society or for posterity. Once records cease to be of value to their owners they are to be destroyed. From a business perspective, the maintenance of records can be costly. Physical records take up space. Office and storage space is expensive. If records are to be used, they must be retrievable. That too is expensive. Once records are no longer of value to decision making, the burden of maintaining them cannot be justified.

The professionalization of the records manager position has fostered some change in the education of the records manager, although the inclusion of records management as a bachelor's level program or as a separate master's level program in colleges and universities has generally not occurred (Pemberton, 1994). At the master's level, records management is often included in the same program as archival education. Alternatively, some universities offer a certificate program in records management.

Curator

A career as a curator is an option for an information professional who has expertise in the field of the information collection, such as science, art, or history. Curators, archivists, museum and archives technicians, and conservators all have similar job descriptions. They

> acquire and preserve important documents and other valuable items for permanent storage or display. They work for museums, governments, zoos, colleges and universities, corporations, and other institutions that require experts to preserve important records. They also describe, catalogue, analyze, exhibit, and maintain valuable objects and collections for the benefit of researchers and the public. (U.S. Department of Labor, Bureau of Labor Statistics, 2006)

In addition, they may help coordinate educational outreach programs, such as tours and workshops. Often they conduct research on subjects relevant to their collections.

As with other information professionals in this category, the duties and roles associated with curatorship can be broad and varied. In smaller facilities a single curator may perform all the functions; in larger facilities a curator is more likely to specialize in a particular segment of the collection and perhaps even a specific duty of curatorship within that segment. Curators

- initiate and/or supervise collection development and research by studying the subject area(s) of the museum's collection and locating suitable objects within the community, through fieldwork (e.g., archaeological excavations), or through other museums, private collectors, artists, dealers, and potential donors
- conduct or supervise an acquisitions program in which objects are selected or collected, researched, documented, and cataloged
- provide storage and ensure that acceptable environmental conditions are maintained and that collections are preserved (or delegate this work to conservators)

- plan and assume a major role in organizing exhibitions by conducting research, determining themes, selecting materials, and acting as consultants regarding overall design
- establish specifications criteria for reproductions and oversee their manufacture or select items from commercially available replica sources
- prepare catalogs, grant applications, articles, texts, scripts, and promotional publications related to exhibitions and the museum's general collections
- promote knowledge and study of the collection through lectures, tours, workshops, exhibitions, and Web sites
- train, supervise, and coordinate the work of junior staff and volunteers

The curator most often works in a public or a not-for-profit setting, although museums of corporations (such as the previously mentioned World of Coca-Cola) would also have curators. Educational requirements for curators are determined by the nature of the collection but would nearly always include expertise both in information and in the particular subject field of the collection, generally at the master's level.

Cataloger

Catalogers are the organizers of information in the information professions and therefore play an essential and valuable role in the identification, location, and access of information that has been or is to be stored. They play a pivotal role in libraries, whether traditional, hybrid, or digital, by describing and organizing the individual items that make up a collection. (We are using the term "library" and "item" very liberally.) Catalogers create and maintain bibliographic records, i.e., the information needed to identify information and information containers, or the metadata for each item. They prepare bibliographic records by creating them, by copying the record from another source, or by using records from a bibliographic utility. They assign appropriate subject headings, search terms, and classifications based on the intellectual content and use of information items. In addition, they develop control procedures that ensure consistency in the terms used to describe and identify the information containers.

Catalogers are found in many places. They are not limited to libraries. The online search service Yahoo! employs catalogers, for example, to develop and maintain their colon-classified, faceted, chain-indexed catalog or search engine. Catalogers together with computer scientists are involved in development of automated and semi-automated cataloging systems (like DOI®, Digital Object Identifier) for digital collections.

- The incumbent is responsible for identifying, evaluating, selecting, and cataloging online, paper, and microfiche resources published by U.S. Government agencies and for related support activities.

- Performs original descriptive and subject cataloging of Federal documents in accordance with Anglo-American Cataloging Rules Second Edition (AACR2), Library of Congress Rule Interpretations, and other authorities consistent with GPO's participation in national cooperative cataloging programs. Publications to be cataloged include serials, monographs, or maps published online and in other media.

- Consults a variety of sources and analyzes data in order to create appropriate bibliographic access.

- Performs subject analysis of all material cataloged.

- Creates new bibliographic records or adapts existing records available in OCLC (Online Computer Library Center).

- Creates national-level quality bibliographic records for serials, monographs, or maps for the OCLC database.

- Utilizes MARC (Machine-Readable Cataloging) tagging for appropriate data file formats.

Figure 7-5   Summary of Duties and Responsibilities of a Cataloger

Source: U.S. Government Printing Office. 2002. "Merit Promotion Vacancy Announcement, Announcement Number 02-073, Position Librarian (Cataloger)." Issue Date 03/06/02. Previously available: www.access.gpo.gov/employment/02073.pdf (accessed October 2002).

In addition to subject area knowledge, skills requirements for catalogers now include:

- knowledge of MARC (Machine Readable Cataloging) formats
- experience with a bibliographic utility
- experience with an integrated online library system
- Internet experience and knowledge of HTML
- knowledge of trends in access to digital information
- knowledge of metadata standards (for example, XML)

In general, catalogers are educated in programs in schools of library and information science and have master's degrees.

School Library Media Specialist

Once called school librarian, the school library media specialist (SLMS) is employed by most public and private K–12 schools. School media specialists are generally expected to hold teacher certification as well as to have educational preparation at the master's level in library and information science (LIS). There is, however, some variation in the rules from state to state: In some states an LIS master's degree may not be required for certification as an SLMS (required for employment in all public and many private schools) but in its place courses in LIS may be required.

The school library media specialist serves

- as the lead professional for development of students' information literacy
- as a partner with teachers in development and implementation of the curriculum of the school
- as the key resource for identifying, evaluating, providing, and accessing information needed by the members of the school community

The SLMS is expected to have a high level of expertise in information technologies and often serves as the key information technology expert in the school.

Since in most instances the SLMS will be the only identified information professional in the organization (teachers could certainly be included as information professionals), the duties performed are broad and extend to all of the technical aspects of organizing information for use and providing information services to the entire learning community of the school: students, teachers, administrators, and, to some degree, parents and others in the local community.

Special Librarian

According to the Special Libraries Association, "Special librarians are information resource experts who collect, analyze, evaluate, package, and disseminate information to facilitate accurate decision-making in corporate, academic, and government settings" (Special Libraries Association, 2006). Their organizations include corporations, private businesses, government agencies, museums, hospitals, associations, and information management consulting firms. The special librarian differs from the public librarian in that he or she provides service not for the general public but for his or her employer and differs from the academic librarian and the school library media specialist in that the focus is on immediate provision of the information needed, not on educating the user to be self-sufficient in information needs. Moreover, the special librarian most likely will concentrate on and develop collections and services specific to the needs and interests of the employer or client.

The services provided by special librarians will vary depending on the library and its users. The special librarian must develop the same set of collection development, information classification, retrieval, and patron services required of other librarians (Christianson, King, and Ahrensfeld, 1991). In addition, the special librarian may also be expected to have subject-related knowledge beyond that of a generalist. They may also be expected to have technical and management skills (Tchobanoff and Price, 1993).

It is difficult to generalize about special libraries and librarians. There are numerous such libraries with a wide variety of specializations and interests. These include law, medical, corporate, scientific, and associational libraries. Moreover, special libraries, for example, law libraries, might be found in individual practices, law schools, courts, or bar associations, each serving a different part of the discipline. Law librarians would be expected to have specific skills related to the information structures of that field that perhaps a medical librarian might not. For example, the law librarian would be expected to have expert Westlaw or LexisNexis skill while the medical librarian should be Medline proficient.

The educational requirement for the special librarian is usually, although not universally, a master's degree in LIS. In addition, and often of greater significance, however, is a requirement for subject expertise in the field of the employing enterprise, whether acquired by formal education or through some other means.

Systems Librarian

Systems librarians are library employees who provide planning, development, management, and broad oversight of all library computer systems and networks, including both hardware and software. The systems librarian has responsibility for

- maintenance of the library's computer-based infrastructure systems, including the OPAC (online public access catalog)
- the circulation system
- the library intranet and Internet connectivity
- hardware and software maintenance and upgrades
- other library computing and network requirements

The systems librarian also may have responsibility for maintaining the library's Web presence.

This person is responsible for incorporating the principles and practices of librarianship into the principles and practices of systems administration. In addition, the systems librarian may provide support for patrons with the use of computer systems. Systems librarians have automation duties and responsibility for management of the library's integrated system, technical responsibilities of computer systems, and interpersonal duties of service and liaison with other technology departments, vendors, and community resources (Xu and Chen,

1999). According to Susan Thompson, when correctly designed and implemented, computer systems can provide library services for staff and patron (Thompson, 1999). Therefore it is the function of the systems librarian to ensure that computer systems are not an end in themselves but a means to an end. They also have responsibility for facilitating technological change in libraries and in assisting other staff to adjust (Gordon, 2003).

As with other information professional positions that are "librarian" positions, the standard educational requirement is generally a master's degree in LIS. However, systems librarians also must have computer systems hardware and software expertise and may follow a career path into systems librarian from a computer science educational background.

Information Broker

An information broker is someone who provides an information service to a client on a contract basis for a fee. The scope and terms of the service are defined by the contract and may range from answering a reference question or document delivery to conduct of extensive research or organization of the total information files of a company.

O'Leary says of information brokering: "Whether done by an individual or a large firm, whether online or conventional, it is a for-profit version of traditional library reference service" (O'Leary, 1987: 25).

The information broker might then be defined as a "librarian for hire." Most information brokers are single proprietorship or small partnership entrepreneurial private-sector enterprises. There are, however, a number of larger information brokerages that hire some number of employees. These too are typically small businesses (Rugge and Glossbrenner, 1997). Most information brokers must have the skills of a reference librarian. They often have subject expertise in the market niche they seek to occupy (Bates, 1999). Those who are single proprietors or in small partnerships often prefer to be known as "independent information professionals" rather than information brokers (Bates Information Services, 2006).

The last *Burwell World Directory of Information Brokers* listed approximately 1,800 companies in 51 countries that are focused on providing information whether by retrieving it, organizing and analyzing it, or consulting regarding information use and management. Independent information professionals, or information brokers, depending on individual preference, provide information services to organizations of all sizes and types, either in conjunction with existing company staff or by contract, to all areas of paying individuals and public and private-sector organizations. Although document delivery, literature surveys, and data gathering are still the mainstay of some information brokerages' work, other companies gather data, analyze it, and provide comprehensive high-quality substantive reports that play a key role in their client's decision-making process.

Information brokers frequently engage in "competitive intelligence" for corporate and private clients. Typical clients range from small business owners to Fortune 500 companies, insurance and investment firms, advertising and public relations agencies, and manufacturing and service industry entities. Some provide assistance to the legal profession through legal research and support services. Other independent information professionals perform public record research—civil and criminal court proceedings, bankruptcy filings, vital statistics, professional licensing, property ownership, tax liens, vehicle registrations, and Security and Exchange Commission filings such as the 10K or 10Q reports required of publicly held corporations. They provide expertise in data mining or warehousing and information for merger and acquisition efforts. Independent information professionals also serve clients in the science and technology fields, often specializing in patent searching, engineering, chemistry, or computer programming and software design.

Although many information brokers have a master's level education (usually in LIS), as is typically the case with entrepreneurial endeavors, there are no standardized educational requirements. Likewise, although many information brokers began their careers as librarians, there is no standard career path that leads to this information professional position.

CHANGES IN THE INFORMATION PROFESSIONS

As is clearly discerned from the descriptions of selected positions in the information professions in the preceding pages, titles and positions in the information field, as in many other fields, are in a state of growth and change. New titles arise

- sometimes as a result of changing philosophy within the environmental context
- sometimes with duties remarkably similar to those of earlier or currently established position
- sometimes with changes that reflect an expansion of scope

New positions also grow out of changing circumstances and needs that demand a new skill set different in both breadth and depth from any previously required. A few examples will help to illustrate some of these differing ways in which titles and positions arise—and sometimes fade away.

A good example of the change in title growing out of changing philosophy in the environmental context is the already discussed school library media specialist. Starting off life in the information professions under the title "school librarian," as the concept of the school library and its role in K-12 education evolved, so also did the title change to such variations as "learning resource specialist," "school media specialist," and "school library media specialist." In the early days of the school library in the United States, those who were part-time librarians in the schools were referred to as "teacher-librarians" (Lester and Latrobe, 1998: 5). This title is still used in the Canadian context.

The newly styled "metadata specialist," when one examines closely the duties and responsibilities involved, looks remarkably similar to the older position of "cataloger," albeit within a primarily digital environment. Depending on the specific situation, the position may have a scope broader than the cataloger has—going beyond or sometimes entirely outside the traditional library—but the fundamental intellectual scope and intellectual processes involved are the same, differing in application setting and in tools used to accomplish the work.

Another relatively new title, one that either reflects an expansion of scope or a new skill set sufficiently different to require additional education (depending on when and to whom one listens), is "knowledge manager." In the early use of this title, there was considerable similarity with the duties of the "special librarian" but with expansion of scope to include responsibility for managing knowledge resources both internally generated and externally acquired (see Flynn, 1995, for example). As the practice and techniques of knowledge management have developed and grown into a nascent field of study, the use of the title as well as the duties and qualifications of the position have changed. A recently posted job ad for a knowledge manager at a large, prominent, international practice law firm included the following description of the position:

> The purpose of the Knowledge Manager position is first, to ensure that the knowledge systems needs of working lawyers are represented in all production domain decision-making, and that the systems purchased or developed to support knowledge initiatives at the Firm provide the best tools possible for our lawyers and secondly, to ensure that knowledge systems purchased or developed by the Firm are effectively deployed and supported for the lawyers in the Firm.
>
> It is expected that the Knowledge Manager, as part of the Knowledge Team, will actively provide guidance and consultation in all areas of the knowledge management approach, including process, content planning, policy and standards. The Knowledge Manager ensures that our projects and systems are meeting the needs of our lawyers.

> Specific duties & responsibilities will include: defining and managing business-level systems requirements for knowledge (production domain) systems, actively working with lawyers throughout the Firm to better understand and document the needs of practice groups, offices and the general marketplace, evaluating options and recommending solutions to help improve productivity. (Baker and McKenzie, 2004)

A title that is currently emerging on the scene, so new that the terminology is as yet unsettled, is that of "informationist," or, possibly, "information specialist in context" (Medical Library Association, 2006). This new information position, blending the knowledge and skills set from both information specialists and clinical staff in the health care environment, would be part of the health care team in the clinical setting. While the idea is not one that is totally new—a similar concept emerged in the 1970s for information workers called "clinical medical librarians"—it goes beyond any previous positions in both the breadth and depth of knowledge and skills required. One of the earliest (perhaps the first) papers proposing the position called for training programs that would include "basic medical concepts, principles of clinical epidemiology, biostatistics, critical appraisal, and information management" as well as "the practical, working skills of retrieving, synthesizing, and presenting medical information and the skills of functioning in a clinical care team" (Davidoff and Florance, 2000). Although the position is not yet one likely found in the local hospital, it has developed sufficiently to have been supported by a National Library of Medicine Senior Fellowship for Informationist Training (U.S. National Library of Medicine, 2006) as well as an Individual Fellowship for Informationist Training (U.S. National Library of Medicine, 2003), to be an established position in the Eskind Biomedical Library's (EBL) Clinical Informatics Consult Service of Vanderbilt University (Mizzy, 2003), and to have been the subject of conferences and meetings in both health science library and clinical medical arenas.

As these brief examples suggest, new positions, changes in positions, and changes in titles can be expected as a way of life in the information professions. The pace of change is related in part to the rate of change in information technology, but it is also connected to growing societal awareness of the centrality of information in all spheres of life.

As the positions and titles change, so too does the education required for entry into the field. As a new position arises and stabilizes, the emergence of educational preparation for that position is not far behind. Formal programs of study for knowledge management, virtually unknown a decade ago, now exist at undergraduate, graduate, and doctoral levels (Sutton, n.d.). The information architect, another position that has emerged in the past decade (although the term was coined in 1975 [Morville, 2004: xiii]), now has a number of formal degree programs grounded in various disciplines from which to choose (see www.asis.org/educationprograms.html for a list). Even the video gamer now has access to formal graduate degree preparation: in 2002 Southern Methodist University inaugurated a graduate certificate program in video-game design and there are now others available at bachelor's and graduate levels (Mangan, 2005). Heretofore the video-gaming profession consisted primarily of self-starting on-the-job learners without formal academic credentials in the field.

Information Ideas

Our Unknown Predecessors: Johann David Köhler

Johann David Köhler might be considered a great-grandfather of information science and a grandfather of library science. Köhler (usually transliterated into English as Koehler and not a known progenitor of one the authors of this work) was born in Colditz in 1684 and died in Göttingen, Germany in 1755. He was a professor of logic and history at universities in Altdorf and later Göttingen and served briefly as university librarian at Altdorf. His academic interests focused on Roman coins as historical artifacts, ancient weapons, and genealogy.

Köhler's credentials as library and information scientist are based upon three of his monographs: *Syllogie aliquot Scriptorum de bene ordinanda et ornanda Bibliotheca* in 1728; *Hochverdiente und aus bewährten Urkunden wohlbeglaubte Ehren-Rettung Johann Guttenbergs, eingebohrnen Bürgers in Mayntz . . .* in 1741; and *Anweisung für reisende Gelerte, Bibliothecken, Münz-Cabinette, Antiquitäten-Zimmer, Bilder-Sale, Naturalien- und Kunst-Kammern, u.m.b. mit Ruken zu befeben* in 1762. The 1728 *Syllogie . . .* is a bibliographic examination of major history texts of the day and is in keeping with the role of historians then and now.

The 1741 *Hochverdiente . . .* is an examination of the assertion that Johannes Gutenberg was indeed the inventor of movable print—the printing press—against competing claims. Bernhard von Mallinckrodt (1591–1664) is credited with writing the first defense of Gutenberg as the inventor of the printing press in 1639 (Schmidmaier, 2001), but Köhler is said to have authored a second and definitive defense (Eck in Köhler reprint, 2000: 109).

Johann David's third and most important work within this context is the 1792 *Anweisung für reisende Gelerte. . . .* It opens with *"Bücher zu kennen ist allen Gelehrten unentberlich"* (Köhler, 1762: 5); or roughly that the knowledge of

(*Continued on p. 179*)

books is vitally important for all learned people. This work is essentially a travelogue. In its first 60 pages, Köhler describes the major European libraries of his day from Berlin to Rome and London. He discusses major theories of classification and cataloging by several authors, usually based on subject cataloging. He also explores what has now come to be known as descriptive bibliography: how books are produced, the types of inks and papers used, the quality and type of binding, printed and copied documents, illustrations and colors, and so on. He also distinguishes between public and closed libraries as well as open and private libraries. Private libraries, he argues, were biased according to the interests of individual collectors while open libraries sought a broader representation of thought on given subjects. Some libraries were public in that all learned persons might use them; others were closed to the general public.

Köhler urges users to familiarize themselves with individual library catalogs before searching for materials in those libraries. He also argues that library catalogs should be organized along subject lines.

Finally, Köhler published a scholarly journal on Roman coins and numismatics in general. His son Johann Tobias Köhler continued that interest.

Sources

Köhler, Johann David. 1741, reprint 2000. *Hochverdiente und aus bewährten Urkunden wohlbeglaubte Ehren-Rettung Johann Guttenbergs, eingebohrnen Bürgers in Mayntz . . .* with afterword by Reimer Eck. Munich: Saur.

————. 1762, partial reprint 1973. *Anweisung für reisende Gelerte, Bibliothecken, Münz-Cabinette, Antiquitäten-Zimmer, Bilder-Sale, Naturalien- und Kunst-Kammern, u.m.b. mit Ruken zu befeben* with afterword by Erika Wenig. Bonn: Bouvier Verlag Herbert Grundmann. [Only the first section, "Bibliothecken," is reprinted.]

Schmidmaier, Dieter. 2001. "Johann David Köhlers Verdienst." *Bibliothek Forschung und Praxis* 25, no. 2: 253–255.

(Our thanks to Vera Blair, wife of one of the authors, for translations of the German-language materials.)

CONCLUSION

There is an old aphorism that the only constant is change. In the information environment, the corollary to that law (also an old saw) is that the more things change, the more they stay the same (or *plus ça change plus c'est la même chose*).

Many of the skills, responsibilities, and duties of some of the newer information professions are very similar to those of the more established; they differ in part in the vocabulary used to describe their responsibilities and in part in the technical sophistication required to carry out their base level duties. It is arguable that there is little difference between a systems librarian and an information architect. Indeed there has already been a differentiation in terminology for the new information professions between "Webmaster" and "information architect." An information architect is a Webmaster, only more so.

By noting the similarities among the information professions, we are not depreciating their differences. Each requires a number of different and often unique skills.

We would also point out a misconception: that some of the newer professions require less formal preparation than do the older ones. First, any new profession or skill area lacks a training infrastructure. The Wright brothers did not nor were they required to take formal flight training. One hundred years ago, prospective physicians and attorneys could "read" medicine or law with a practitioner in journeyman style. The law, medicine, and aviation not only grew more complex over time, but the formal body of knowledge in those fields also grew larger. As a consequence, a more formal training system (college and professional education, flight school) together with appropriate apprenticeships (clerking, internship, building hours) became the norm.

The same is true of the information professions. The first formal library school in the United States was established at Columbia College (later to be Columbia University) under the leadership of Melvil Dewey in 1887. Libraries have been with us for millennia. Why was the first school in the United States opened less than 125 years ago? We suggest two reasons: increased demand for librarians and a need for librarians with a standard set of skills and knowledge. Bill Gates dropped out of Harvard. How can a college dropout have been so successful? The reason, we postulate, is that Mr. Gates pioneered a new field where an existing body of knowledge did not then exist. (He is, of course, also very bright.) Once a body of knowledge is developed, some form of formal training is needed to certify the practitioner, to introduce the neophyte to the standards and practices of the profession, and to ensure that all that has come before need not again be learned the hard way. No software programmer/entrepreneur can enter the field in the same way Gates did unless and until he or she brings a radical and fundamental new contribution to the table. As the new information professions stabilize, so too will the educational preparation required for their practice. However, as with all things related to information, stability is a relative term. Continuing evolution of education for the information professions can be expected to be the norm.

QUESTIONS FOR CONSIDERATION

1. Information professionals work in the public sector, the not-for-profit sector, and the private for-profit sector. How does the sector in which information professionals work affect their roles and functions?
2. Information professionals are found in different places in the organizational structure of the companies, agencies, and institutions in which they work. How does the place on the organization chart affect the role of the information professional?
3. Information is considered a form of valuable intellectual capital in for-profit sector companies. How would this perception of what information is change the role of information professionals in such companies?
4. As communication systems for transmission of information have expanded from oral to print to electronic, have the fundamental roles of information professionals changed and if so, in what ways? For example, are there more commonalities or differences among storytellers, librarians, and information architects? Have the roles been changed by changes in the technologies for creating, managing, transmitting, and interpreting information?
5. The various categories of information professions, while perhaps having commonalities in what they do, may differ substantially in their value systems. Why would this be the case? For example, why would an information architect in a for-profit company have different values related to information from an archivist working in a university?

REFERENCES

Achilles, Alf-Christian. 2006. *The Collection of Computer Science Bibliographies.* Universität Karlsruhe, Lehrstuhl Informatik für Ingenieure und Naturwissenschaftler. Available: http://liinwww.ira.uka.de/bibliography (accessed December 2006).

American Society for Information Science and Technology. Special Interest Group: Information Architecture. 2001. "Information Architecture and Architects Defined." Available: www.asis.org/SIG/SIGIA/definition .html (accessed December 2006).

Baker and McKenzie. 2004. "Knowledge Manager." Available Positions. LawNet (23 July). Previously available: www.peertopeer.org/prodev/position_detail.aspx?nvID=000000011605&h4ID=000000276605 (accessed September 2004).

Banks, Paul N., and Roberta Pilette. 2000. *Preservation: Issues and Planning.* Chicago: American Library Association.

Bates, Mary Ellen. 1999. "Shopping for an Information Broker: 'Please Don't Squeeze the Charmin.'" *Searcher* 7 (September): 52–56.

Bates Information Services. 2006. "FAQs about the Independent Info Pro Business." Available: www.batesinfo.com/faq.html (accessed December 2006).

Borko, Harold. 1968. "Information Science: What Is It?" *American Documentation* 19 (January): 3–5.

*Burwell World Directory of Information Brokers.*1998. 13th ed. Houston: Burwell Enterprises.

Christianson, Elin B., David E. King, and Janet Ahrensfeld. 1991. *Special Libraries: A Guide for Management.* 3rd ed. Washington, DC: Special Libraries Association.

Davidoff, Frank, and Valerie Florance. 2000. "The Informationist: A New Health Profession?" *Annals of Internal Medicine* 132 (20 June): 996–998. Available to subscribers: www.annals.org/cgi/content/full/-132/12/996 (accessed December 2006).

Duffy, Daintry. 1998. "Knowledge Champions." *CIO Enterprise Magazine* (15 November). Available: www.cio.com/archive/enterprise/111598_ic.html (accessed December 2006).

Feldman, Susan E. 1988. "The Entrepreneurial Librarian." *The Reference Librarian* 22: 161–171.

Flynn, Kathleen M. 1995. "The Knowledge Manager as a Digital Librarian: An Overview of the Knowledge Management Pilot Program at the MITRE Corporation." In [Proceedings of] *Digital Libraries '95: The Second Annual Conference on the Theory and Practice of Digital Libraries* (11–13 June), Austin, TX. Available: www.csdl.tamu.edu/DL95/papers/flynn/flynn.html (accessed December 2006).

Gordon, Rachel Singer. 2003. *The Accidental Systems Librarian.* Medford, NJ: Information Today.

Hagedorn, Kat. 2000. *The Information Architecture Glossary.* Argus Center for Information Architecture. Argus Associates (March). Available: http://argus-acia.com/white_papers/ia_glossary.pdf (accessed December 2006).

IAwiki. 2006. "Defining the Damn Thing." Available: www.iawiki.net/DefiningTheDamnThing (accessed December 2006).

Koehler, Wallace. 2001. "Information Science as 'Little Science': The Implications of a Bibliometric Analysis of the Journal of the American Society for Information Science." *Scientometrics* 51, no. 1: 117–132.

Lester, June, and Kathy Latrobe. 1998. "The Education of School Librarians." In *The Emerging School Library Media Center: Historical Issues and Perspectives*, edited by Kathy Howard Latrobe, 1–15. Englewood, CO: Libraries Unlimited.

Maher, William J. 1992. *The Management of College and University Archives.* Metuchen, NJ: Society of American Archivists and Scarecrow Press.

Mangan, Katherine. 2005. "Joysticks in the Classroom: Game-Design Programs Take Off." *The Chronicle of Higher Education* 51, no. 22 (4 February): 29–31.

Medical Library Association. 2006. "Information Specialist in Context." *MLANET* (14 August). Available: www.mlanet.org/research/ informationist (accessed December 2006).

Mizzy, Danianne. 2003. "Job of a Lifetime: Informationist: Making Rounds Makes a Difference." *C&RL News* 64 (March). Available: www.ala .org/ala/acrl/acrlpubs/crlnews/backissues2003/march2/informationists .htm (accessed December 2006).

Morville, Peter. 2004. "A Brief History of Information Architecture." In *Information Architecture: Designing Information Environments for Purpose*, edited by Alan Gilchrist and Barry Mahon, xii-xvi. London: Facet. Available: http://semanticstudios.com/publications/historia.pdf (accessed December 2006).

O'Leary, Mick. 1987. "The Information Broker: A Modern Profile." *Online* 11 (November): 24–30.

Pemberton, Michael J. 1994. "Records Management Education: In Pursuit of Standards." *Records Management Quarterly* 28 (July): 58–61.

Pomfret, John. 2002. "China Finds Bugs on Jet Equipped in U.S." *Washington Post* (19 January): A1.

Reitz, Joan M. 2006. *ODLIS: Online Dictionary for Library and Information Science.* Westport, CT: Libraries Unlimited. Available: http://lu.com/- odlis (accessed December 2006).

Rosenfeld, Louis, and Peter Morville. 2002. *Information Architecture for the World Wide Web.* 2nd ed. Cambridge, MA: O'Reilly.

Rugge, Sue, and Albert Glossbrenner. 1997. *The Information Broker's Handbook.* 3rd ed. New York: McGraw-Hill.

Special Libraries Association. 2006. "Association Profile." Available: www .sla.org/content/SLA/assnProfile/index.cfm (accessed December 2006).

Standage, Tom. 1998. *The Victorian Internet: The Remarkable Story of the Telegraph and the Nineteenth Century's On-Line Pioneers.* New York: Walker.

Stanford University Libraries. 2006. *CoOL, Conservation OnLine.* Available: http://palimpsest.stanford.edu (accessed December 2006).

Sutton, Michael J. D. "A Topical Review of Knowledge Management Curriculum Programs in University Graduate Schools: Library and Information Science, Business, Cognitive Science, Information Systems and Computer Systems Schools." Available: http://web.archive.org/web/

20051113222248/http://www.pitt.edu/~pgray/TopicalReview.pdf (accessed December 2006).

Tchobanoff, James B., and Jack A. Price. 1993. "Industrial Information Service Managers: Expectations of, and Support of, the Educational Process." *Library Trends* 42 (Fall): 249–256.

Thompson, Susan. 1999. "Riding into Uncharted Territory: The New Systems Librarian." *Computers in Libraries* 19 (March): 14–20.

Ulfelder, Steve. 2004. "CPOs: Hot or Not?" *Computerworld* 38 (15 March): 40.

U.S. Department of Labor. Bureau of Labor Statistics. 2006. "Archivists, Curators, and Museum Technicians." In *Occupational Outlook Handbook*, 2006–2007 ed. Available: www.bls.gov/oco/ocos065.htm (accessed December 2006).

———. Office of the Chief Information Officer. n.d. "CIO Mission." Available: www.dol.gov/cio/about_cio/cmission.htm (accessed December 2006).

U.S. Library of Congress. 2006. *The Library of Congress Preservation*. Washington, DC: Library of Congress Preservation Directorate. Available: www.loc.gov/preserv (accessed December 2006).

U.S. National Archives and Records Administration. "Preservation and Archives Professionals." Available: www.archives.gov/preservation (accessed December 2006).

U.S. National Library of Medicine. 2003. "NLM Senior Fellowship for Informationist Training (F38)" (21 October). Available: http://grants.nih.gov/grants/guide/pa-files/PAR-04-014.html (accessed September 2004).

———. 2006. "NLM Individual Fellowship for Informationist Training" (4 August). Available: http://grants.nih.gov/grants/guide/pa-files/PAR-04-013.html (accessed December 2006).

Waller, Douglas, and Thomas Sancton. 1995. "Halt! Friend or Foe?" *Time* (6 March): 50.

Wilson, Thomas C. 1998. *The Systems Librarian: Designing Roles and Defining Skills*. Chicago: American Library Association.

Xu, Hong, and Hsin-liang Chen. 1999. "What Do Employers Expect? The Educating Systems Librarian Research Project 1." *The Electronic Library* 17 (June): 171–179.

ADDITIONAL SOURCES

American Association of School Librarians and Association for Educational Communications and Technology. 1998. *Information Power: Building Partnerships for Learning*. Chicago: American Library Association.

American Library Association. 2006. Available: www.ala.org (accessed December 2006).

ARMA International, the Association for Information Management Professionals. 2006. Available: www.arma.org (accessed December 2006).

Association for Computing Machinery. n.d. Available: www.acm.org (accessed December 2006).

Association of Independent Information Professionals. 2006. Available: www.acm.org (accessed December 2006).

——— Public Relations Committee. 2003. "The Independent Information Professional." Baton Rouge, LA: Association of Independent Information Professionals. Available: www.aiip.org/Resources/IIPWhitePaper .html (accessed December 2006).

Chief Information Officers Council. 2006. Available: www.cio.gov/index .cfm (accessed December 2006).

Information Architecture Institute. 2006. "Schools Teaching IA." Available: http://iainstitute.org/pg/schools_teaching_ia.php (accessed December 2006).

International Association of Privacy Professionals. 2005. Available: www .privacyassociation.org (accessed December 2006).

International Storytelling Center. 2006. Available: www.storytellingcenter .com/index.htm (accessed December 2006).

Kessler, Michelle. 2000. "Position of 'Privacy Officer' Coming into Public Eye; More Firms Are Hiring CPOs to Protect Their Companies, Customers." *USA Today* (30 November): 1B.

Mendels, Pamela. 2000. The Rise of the Chief Privacy Officer." *Business* Week *Online* (14 December). Available: www.businessweek.com/careers/ content/dec2000/ca20001214_253.htm (accessed December 2006).

National Writers Union. 2006. Available: www.nwu.org (accessed December 2006).

Pemberton, Michael J. 2002. "Chief Privacy Officer: Your Next Career?" *Information Management Journal* 36 (May/June): 57–58.

Rosof, Libby. 2002. "First Chief Privacy Officer Named." *The Penn Current* (28 March). Available: www.upenn.edu/pennnews/current/2002/032802/ feature3.html (accessed December 2006).

Society for Information Management. 2006. Available: www.simnet.org (accessed December 2006).

Society of American Archivists. 2003. Available: www.archivists.org (accessed December 2006).

Society of Competitive Intelligence Professionals. *SCIP.ORG.* Available: www.scip.org (accessed December 2006).

Society of Professional Journalists. 2006. Available: www.spj.org (accessed December 2006).

Special Libraries Association. 2006. Available: www.sla.org (accessed December 2006).

U.S. Postal Service. 2001. "Postal Service Names First Chief Privacy Officer." Release no. 01-017 (7 March). Available: www.usps.com/news/2001/press/pr01_017.htm (accessed December 2006).

Does information and the way that information is created, transmitted, stored, and used affect the way that a society functions and how it views itself in relation both to its own history and to contemporary societies? From your reading of previous chapters, think back to the society of the time when information records were in the form of manuscripts, or even earlier, to when the majority of information transmitted was in oral form. Did people of that period define their reality any differently from the way we define ours? Before you read further, try to imagine what your life would have been like in that earlier time. What information activities would not have been available to you? Would not having those change how you perceived the world? Try writing a description of what your day would have been like in that time. Then read on, to find out some possible ways in which your world might have been different and how information changes society.

Chapter 8

The Impact of Information on Cultures and Societies

Learning Guide

After reading this chapter, you should be able to

- analyze a society or culture to determine if it could be classified as an "information society";

- assess the ways in which changes in information technologies may alter perceptions or constructions of reality;

- explain the impact or potential impact of information and information technologies on political structures in a society;

- determine ways in which particular information technologies may empower or disempower individuals and/or political groups.

When you have finished the chapter, return to this page to be sure you have learned what you need to know.

INTRODUCTION

In chapter 1, we considered how information, or the lack of information, affects one's daily life and activities and the impact that information has on the way a society functions on a day-to-day basis. In this chapter we will look in depth at the issue of how information affects society and culture. To begin, we will consider what makes a society an "information society," as one so frequently hears as the characterization of society today, contrasting this with the societies of earlier times, which have been labeled agricultural societies and then industrial societies. In order to answer questions such as the following:

> *What does it mean to be an information society and how do we know if we are in one?*

we will need to consider whether all nations today are part of the information society or just certain ones. If so, then which ones, and how do we decide that?

IDENTIFYING AN INFORMATION SOCIETY

A useful approach to defining information societies has been suggested by Frank Webster, who proposes examining a society on the basis of economic, occupational, spatial, technological, and cultural criteria to determine the extent to which an information society exists (Webster, 2002). Although Webster says there are problems with each of these definitions (Webster, 2002), employing this framework is a useful approach to thinking about the varied aspects of an information society and what possible measures we might use to define one. To his list we can add a governmental criterion.

Measuring the Impact of Information on the Economy

The earliest study that attempted to measure information in the economy, in this case the U.S. economy, was that done by Fritz Machlup in his landmark 1962 work, *The Production and Distribution of Knowledge in the United States*. This study, and others that followed it, measured information-related activities as components of national production. Although Machlup used the term knowledge, what he essentially was measuring was what we would consider information industry production. What he found was that in 1958, knowledge production accounted for 29 percent of the U.S. GNP (gross national product). Machlup's purpose was both to define and to measure the knowledge, or information, economy.

The next major study was that completed by Marc Uri Porat, a nine-volume work that was supported in part by the National Science Foundation and published by the U.S. Department of Commerce. Using the National Income and Product Accounts, Porat asked the question, *"What share of our national wealth originates with the production, processing and distribution of information goods and services?* Or, what is the extent of the information activity, (as opposed to agriculture, services or industry), as a portion of the total U.S. economic activity?" (Porat, 1977: 1–2). He found that for 1967, 46 percent of the GNP was attributable to information activity, which he defined as including *"all the resources consumed in producing, processing and distributing information goods and services"* (Porat, 1977: 2). In constructing his analysis, Porat examined and measured information activity that occurred in the market and that which did not, looking at what he called the primary information sector, *"firms which supply the bundle of information goods and services exchanged in a market context"* and the secondary information sector, *"all the information services produced for internal consumption by government and non-information firms"* (Porat, 1977: 4). (All emphasis in the original.)

In a 1986 update of Machlup's work, Michael Rogers Rubin and Mary Taylor Huber found that knowledge production accounted for 34.3 percent of GNP in 1980 (Rubin and Huber, 1986). Other figures range much higher in the measurement of the information sector of the economy.

Regardless of what current percentage of GNP is accounted for by information activities, and these measurements will vary depending on how the information activity components are defined, we are left with the question

When, that is at what percentage level, is a society an "information society" in economic terms?

Critics point out that taking this approach is misleading, since it does not distinguish among types of information activity, counting them all as equal in contribution to the definition of an information society, when in fact some information activities have more impact than others in changing the nature of the society (for example, see Webster, 2002).

Another economic approach to determining the "information society-ness" of a society is based on consumption, measuring the ratio of household expenditures for information-related activities to total household expenditures. Research in this vein has been undertaken in Japan by the Research Institute for Telecommunications and Economics (Steinfeld and Salvaggio, 1989). Another possible related economic measure is a comparative one: how much is spent for information compared to other household or individual expenditures (Schement and Curtis, 1995). But we are left with a question similar to the one above:

What ratio of household expenditures for information-related activities to total household expenditures must be present in order for a society to be an information society?

Are we there when the percentage of household expenditure, or the actual dollar amount, on information is higher than any other good or service?

Considering the Society from an Occupational Perspective

We can use occupation as a measure of an information society in two different ways. The first is related to the economic measures of percentage of GNP and considers what percentage of the workforce is engaged in information work and what percentage of labor income information workers earn, as compared to those who work in other sectors. In his 1977 study, Porat measured these dimensions, finding that in 1967, 45 percent of the workforce was in the information sector and earned 53 percent of all labor income (Porat, 1977). In a later update of his work, Porat found that in 1983, the information workforce constituted 56 percent of the total workforce and earned greater than 75 percent of all wages (Porat, 1984). In Porat's studies, information workers passed industrial workers as a percentage of the workforce in the 1950s, having exceeded those in agriculture and service in the 1920s (Porat, 1977).

Critics have argued over how Porat assigned the percentages of various jobs as "information work," and one reanalysis finds the changeover to dominance by information workers occurring in the 1920–1940 period (Schement and Curtis, 1995: 83). This same work found information workers to be 50 percent of the workforce in 1980, 52.6 percent in 1986 (Schement and Curtis, 1995). There is also some disagreement as to whether the information sector of the workforce is continuing to grow and, if so, how fast, relative to other sectors, and in which areas, which makes a difference in the impact on society. For example, growth in information occupations that are nonroutinized in their work and that require higher levels of training make a greater impact on change in society than growth in lesser trained jobs that are more routinized in information handling. There is at least some evidence that while the latter have been declining (jobs like file clerks, bank tellers, data entry operators), the former are increasing (Martin, 1998).

While these studies have all focused on the workforce in the United States, similar studies have been made for other countries, especially for the European countries and Japan, and show similar increases in the share that information occupations have of the total workforce, although in general the United States leads in this societal change. The extent to which the information sector is growing as a part of the workforce, as well as the growth in contribution to GNP, is related to the level of development of the country (Dordick and Wang, 1993); and there is wide variation among nations. In general, a lower percentage of the workforce is engaged in information work and a lower percentage of GNP is attributable to information activities in lower income (usually less developed, or in current parlance, newly industrializing) countries.

As with the GNP economic measurement, considering the percentage of information workers in the labor force can be misleading as a primary indicator of an information society. Not all information work is of the same value or impact, and the practice of exporting some lower-valued information activities (such as data entry) complicates the picture. Further, the export of higher-level information activities as well as the import of highly skilled information workers, both of which are occurring in developed countries, makes the situation even more complex.

The second approach to using occupation as a measure of an information society is to consider the extent to which the use of information and information activities, particularly the use of information technology, has affected the structure and conduct of work. Arguments are made that information technology has changed the way that people work, causing a reorganization of the basis of work away from the characteristics of industrial society. Other observers, rather than seeing a distinct break, find continuity, with the information society being a new type of industrial society brought about in part by the need of industrialism for information with which to make decisions and by which to exercise control (Schement and Curtis, 1995).

Examples of using changes in the structure and conduct of work would include consideration of the degree of teleworking within a society. In the United States, a 2005 teleworking survey found an increase of 30 percent of employee teleworkers over the previous year, with an increase of working not only from home but also from outdoor locations, on planes, in cars, and in the locations of those who were clients or customers (International Telework Association and Council, 2005). In the U.K. in spring 2005, 8 percent of the workforce were teleworking, double the percentage in 1997 (Ruiz and Walling, 2005). Another change in the structure of work brought about by information intensity and the ability to disperse work activities due to the availability of information technology is the practice of "hoteling," an arrangement whereby employees have no permanent office but have access to office space available on a reservation basis, similar to reserving hotel rooms. Yet another is the practice by some physicians to use e-mail as the mode for house calls.

In colleges and universities, the structure of work is also shifting due to the infusion of information technology. In 2005, 78.7 percent of college courses used e-mail, 58.6 percent used Internet-based resources, 43.4 percent had a Web site, and 45.9 percent used course management tools (Green, 2006). Applications for admission are routinely being completed and submitted online: in 2005, 96.4 percent had undergraduate applications available at their Web site (Green, 2006). In fall 2000, West Virginia Wesleyan became the first university to require online application by undergraduates (Dean, 2000), although MIT's Sloan School of Management instituted that requirement for their business school applicants in August 1998.

Again we are left with a question:

When do we reach the information society, using restructuring and change in the conduct of work as a measure?

Diffusion of Information Technology as an Indicator

In part, the consideration of restructure and change in the conduct of work is dependent on the extent to which information technology has been diffused throughout a society and is thus available as the underpinning for change. It is a common practice to consider the extent of diffusion of information technology into all areas of society as one potential defining principle of an information society. Broadly defined, we could say we have always been—or have been almost throughout recorded history—an information society, in that technologies for recording and distribution information have been diffused throughout society for a long period of time, particularly if we think of paper, pen, slate tablets, or even church bells as forms of information technology. However, what is usually considered in this approach is the diffusion of computer and telecommunications technologies.

Studies along the technological diffusion dimension look at such measurements as television sets, computers, and phones per hundred people; Internet access; and access to broadband. At a more precise level, consideration is made of the use of specific genres of a technology, such as the penetration of mobile phones or the extent of use of PDAs. Another granular approach is to make these kinds of measurements for subsets of the society, such as populations identified by factors like race and ethnicity, education level, geographical location, family structure, age, gender, and physical ability. Place of access (home or work) may also be examined. These measurements sometimes reveal that, although a nation as a whole might be characterized as an "information society" using a technological diffusion approach, there may be differing degrees of attainment of that level within the subpopulations, giving a possible false impression of the "information society-ness." We considered this within-society divergence in our initial discussion of information in society (see chapter 1).

No matter what measures are used, again we have a question:

> *When is technological diffusion sufficient to declare a country an information society?*

Do we use access by a given percentage of households or individuals as a cutoff? Which technologies must be thus diffused—and do we continue to reassess as information technologies change?

At present, no matter what information and communication technologies are considered, by measures of technological diffusion, in general, the most "informationist" of societies are found in the Western developed nations, with nations of Oceania and Africa showing the least development in information society terms, especially when considered in terms of percentage of access by the population. The nations occupying the top of the list change positions depending on what specific technology is considered. For example, broadband penetration is highest in Iceland, whereas cellular phone penetration is highest in Luxembourg (International Telecommunication Union, 2006a, 2006b). However, as noted in chapter 1 (see chapter 1 Information Idea), the Digital Opportunity Index constructed by a group led by the International Telecommunication Union ranks both Asian and European countries in the top five (Korea, Japan, Denmark, Iceland, Hong Kong), with the bottom five of 180 world economies located in Africa (International Telecommunication Union, 2006a).

The widely varying degrees of "information society" observed in different nations are clearly illustrated by differences in the metaphors used to describe the access to the technology. At the time the phrase "information highway" was being popularized in the United States, the Education and Research Network (Ernet) of India talked in its mission of providing an "information footpath" (Holderness, 1998: 43, quoting Ernet home page, 1997). Some of the variation occurs as a result of infrastructure problems, but there are also political and ideological factors at work. Access to information technology and to information may be restricted by dictator governments or deployed toward communal needs rather than for individual use.

The diffusion of information technology and its pervasive use, while generally considered a positive sign for a nation, may have individual negative impact. The blurring of boundaries between work and home and between work and leisure (Schement and Curtis, 1995) that can result from the diffusion of information technology has potential for negative impact on personal life, particularly the functioning of the family. However, recent studies indicate that positive impact is also occurring, for example, in improving connections with family members (Horrigan and Rainie, 2004). At work, the bombardment of constant interruptions from information devices can threaten productivity. According to a recent study, interruptions cause U.S. workers loss of 2.1 hours of productivity daily (Spira, 2005), for a total cost of $588 billion a year (Spira and Feintuch, 2005). According to 1999 studies by the Institute of the Future and the Gallup Organization, U.S. workers at that time were interrupted by phone, fax, or e-mail every ten minutes and received an average of 200 e-mail messages a day (BBC News, 1999).

Changes in the Impact of Space

In chapter 1 we considered the impact of the loss of what McHale refers to as the information float, or the "time cushion" that used to exist because of the physical distances that information had to travel when it was transported from one place to the other by whatever transportation mode was available at the time. As Webster notes, the effect of space—and therefore time—has been substantially altered by the development of information networks that transport information across vast distances almost instantaneously (Webster, 1996). As was discussed earlier, this change undermines power relationships that were based on controlling information and has changed the relationship between an event and its consequences. The ability to gain instant access to information without needing either to be in the presence of the information holder, or even to have access to means of physical transportation, means that information activities are not dependent on geographic placement.

What this diminution of the power of space and time has occasioned, or at the very least made possible, is the development of global commerce, global money markets, and a global media environment. While these developments may have their negatives in loss of national identity and loosening of national control, that this change has made a dramatic impact on the nature of society, on the ways that we conceptually frame our relationships to other nations, and on the way we conduct business on both governmental and personal levels would seem to be indisputable. It has potential for significant impact on political organization, as a result of the growing disjuncture between the spatial basis of political organization, including the funding of government, and the increasingly nonspatial environment of e-commerce.

And once more we return to a question:

To what degree does the time/space constraint on information have to be eliminated in order for a country to be labeled an information society?

How "wired" do we have to be?

Information as a Key Component of Governmental Decision Making and Politics

Another way to consider the extent to which a society is influenced by and dependent on information and information activities is to examine the role these play in government. The section above suggests that the control of information has changed as a result of the change in the space/time dimension of information. A closer examination of this area can add to our understanding of an "information society."

Information has perhaps always been the currency of administration and organization, the oil that lubricates the wheels of government and of enterprise. The role of information in government has been the subject of numerous studies. There are several theories that incorporate information as a primary variable, which we could take as supporting the concept that information as a key factor in government may be an indicator of an information society. These theories are:

- the "rational actor model"
- "incrementalism"
- the "bureaucratic politics model"
- the "organizational process model"

The *rational actor model* is based on the notion that a single actor or group of actors, having perfect access to all pertinent information, makes "rational" decisions. We have come to recognize that there are no actors with perfect access to all pertinent information. Herbert Simon (1997) was to argue that decision makers often opt for the first "reasonable" option provided to them rather than exploring and weighing all possible options as the rational actor would. Decision makers "satisfice" rather than maximize decision outcomes because they lack the time, resources, and complete information to do so. Moreover, decision makers are constrained by a range of phenomena that limit their access to perfect information and informed options.

Incrementalism (see Lindblom, 1959 and 1979) holds that there are many actors in any decision process. Because there are many actors, there are many potential desired outcomes. The actors will negotiate amongst themselves to reach an outcome, usually at the "lowest common denominator." Decision makers reach an incrementalist decision through bargaining and manipulating possible outcomes. Incrementalism also assumes a "feedback loop." No decision, once reached, is immutable; it is constantly subject to renegotiation among the parties.

The *bureaucratic politics model* concerns itself with the various bureaucratic interests and how these interests affect the policy outcomes (Allison and

Halperin, 1972). This model assumes that the various actors involved in the negotiation of a policy outcome do so for personal or institutional aggrandizement or benefit: bigger budgets, more staff, enhanced access, etc. Negotiation positions are predicated on the role or position represented by the players. The Secretary of State, for example, will represent the interests of his or her office and the Department; and these may be different from the institutional interests of, say, the Attorney General.

The *organizational process model* holds that decision outcomes are at least in part a product of the organization through which they flow and the rules that shape the debate. In the end, standard operating procedures guide and perhaps dictate policy outcomes. Foundations, for example, are often constrained in grant making by the "rules of the game" (Diaz, 1999).

These various alternative models to rational decision making suggest the importance of information, different paths of information access, and different modes of information control in the decision process. Lee Strickland (2002) provides an interesting application of both the bureaucratic politics and the organizational process models. He notes that there are a variety of different information constructs: chains, star or hub, and the multichannel. How information flows through these channels, or can be disrupted, is in part a function of the information construct itself. The multichannel model is analogous to the Internet. Information (packets) can travel many different pathways to the same end. Break a node in a chain—like Christmas lights strung in series—and the chain fails.

The media as an information source and its influence on government has also been the subject of a number of studies. George Quester (1990), for example, sees the introduction of television into previously relatively "television-less" societies as potentially destabilizing. He finds that it has influenced domestic policy in the People's Republic of China. On the other hand, the Chinese government has demonstrated a willingness to limit Internet access through a variety of means, including license and access costs. The Canadian federal government has regulated television and radio broadcasts for the past thirty years. They do so by insisting on a minimum of Canadian content for all broadcast media in order to blunt the "cultural imperialism" of the United States. In France, the Académie Française attempts to limit the introduction of non-French words into the language (e.g., le weekend, le sandwich). The famous and first ever televised debates between presidential candidates (Kennedy and Nixon) in 1959 proved the power of the medium in elections. This was further reinforced by the immediacy of error shown in the Ford-Carter debate in 1975 (when President Ford stated that Poland was not behind the "Iron Curtain," as it most certainly was in 1975).

Television and particularly the news media have taken on new salience. If

Ammon (2001) is correct in his assessment of CNN and other networks, these networks have come to replace more traditional and formal mechanisms for the performance and management of foreign policy and diplomacy. Television news networks have displaced many traditional diplomatic communications channels and are frequently far more rapid in disseminating information to elites as well as non elites. Ammon (2001) argues that diplomatic history can be divided into several paradigms, each identified with a dominant communications medium. Recall that diplomatic (and other) communications between countries and continents once required months for messages to pass from one capital to another. The advent of the steamship and the telegraph significantly reduced transmission times in the nineteenth century, and these were further shortened in the twentieth by telephone, the airplane, and then the Internet. Ammon (2001) identifies CNN as the primary network telediplomacy actor. Since 2001, and Ammon's analysis, CNN's ratings may have slipped a little with the introduction of other 24-7-365 global networks like Fox News Network and MS-NBC.

In the telediplomacy era, the current era, television can make an indirect and direct impact on diplomacy (Ammon, 2001) and implicitly on the conduct of other government functions. It is the immediacy of these networks and not necessarily their accuracy that influences decisions and therefore outcomes. As a consequence, government decision processes have been reshaped somewhat by informal transnational actors that have come to replace some of the functions of more formal state organs.

The Internet, in particular e-mail and the World Wide Web, may have further punctured the veil of government supremacy by forcing a global pluralism on the nation-state. This brings us back full circle to the politics of incrementalism. New information sources may muddy the decision process rather than make it more rational. It opens more channels for competing information sources, information sources that may or may not be completely accurate.

The Internet and its ability to create virtual communities of interest may also contribute to the formation of government domestic and foreign policy. Blogs may be particularly effective in creating communities of interest at the extremes of opinion, and homogeneous opinion groups tend more to extremist opinion than heterogeneous ones (Sunstein, 2004). Perhaps, therefore, blogs and other insulating Internet communications media tend to create more polarized communities that lead to more polarized thinking, thinking that may be translated into government and private-sector policy initiatives.

Information sources may also not be favorable to governments in power. Governments have often sought to limit the publication of information deemed harmful to it or information that may compromise national security. The First Amendment to the U.S. Constitution holds that

> Congress shall make no law respecting an establishment of religion, or prohibiting the free exercise thereof; or abridging the freedom of speech, or of the press; or the right of the people peaceably to assemble, and to petition the Government for a redress of grievances.

Yet certain limits have been placed on freedom of speech and of the press. These include prohibitions on incitement to riot, limits on the right of one person to libel another, and the right of government to classify some information to protect the national security. Oliver Wendell Holmes (*United States v. Shenck*, 1918) distinguished another limit: "No one has the right to cry fire in a crowded theater."

In the United States, the limitation on some forms of pornography has also been upheld. There has been a particular focus on child pornography to the point that "virtual child pornography" was prohibited even if it featured adults or computer-generated images that portrayed children until the 1996 Child Pornography Prevention Act was struck down by the U.S. Supreme Court in April 2002.

There are also limits placed on "hate literature." The classic example was the pamphlet that circulated in Russia prior to World War I, *The Protocols of the Learned Elders of Zion*. This document, shown to be a forgery, alleged a Jewish plot for world enslavement. Although the *Protocols* had very limited distribution, it gained prominence through Adolf Hitler's *Mein Kampf* as a justification for anti-Semitism.

Disinformation is also used by governments. Perhaps the best known example was the sham army commanded by General George Patton prior to the Normandy Invasion during World War II. The Germans were prompted to believe the invasion would come at the Pas de Calais rather than Normandy.

Propaganda is frequently used to influence policy. The term "propaganda" is often misconstrued to mean false information, when in fact propaganda can be either true or false. Propaganda is information mobilized toward a certain end. Marketing and advertising are propaganda. Political campaigns are full of propaganda. So is political debate. For example: cut taxes or lower the national debt. These are both noble goals but carry political overtones.

As these examples have illustrated, the influence of information as a factor—the key factor in government and decision making—is not a recent phenomenon, which might lead us to conclude that in this sphere any organized and governed society, by virtue of its existence, is necessarily an information society. But we come to another question:

Are there perhaps degrees of being an information society insofar as government and politics are concerned?

There may be an answer to this question in the considerations of the next section, the extent to which the awareness of information as a factor pervades the culture of a society.

Infusion of Information into the Culture

The degree to which awareness of information and its role in shaping society is infused throughout the culture of a given society is another possible way to assess the "information-ness" of that society. How consciously is information recognized? How much information is flowing through the society?

Although we can—and shortly will—point to many examples of heightened awareness, what is not readily available is any form of actual measurement of the movement of information in a given society. There has been some work done in this direction. The previously mentioned Japanese Research Institute for Telecommunications and Economics has attempted to measure consumption of information as perception of information, examining total information flow at the unit of the word, with formulas for converting media into word units, as an alternative to measuring consumption based on purchase. There has also been some work done in the United States in this vein, but this direction has not been in the mainstream of measurement of the information society (Steinfeld and Salvaggio, 1989).

What is readily apparent, at least in the United States, is the intellectual acceptance of information as a major societal flow. As a beginning point, one can cite the existence of studies such as those of Machlup, Porat, and Rubin and Huber. Attention to the study of information flourishes in the academy, with departments as widely varied as English and computer science, economics and visual arts, and psychology and film and video studies all claiming the study of information as their own. The study of information and its role in society has, in fact, become arguably the most valuable intellectual turf within the university.

Another clear sign of the infusion of the notion of information as a major societal force is the attention given to it by government. Attention to information policy in all of its forms has escalated both in the United States and throughout the world. From Newt Gingrich, former U.S. Speaker of the House, we had a proposal to provide a tax credit "for the poorest Americans to buy a laptop." In Oakland, California, the city council adopted a policy requiring computer equipment and Internet access for future public housing projects as a means of providing welfare and low-income residents with a means to acquire job skills, followed by a pilot project with IBM to put computers and a local area network in public housing units. In his 1996 State of the Union address, President Bill Clinton decreed that "Every classroom in

America must be connected to the information superhighway, with computers, good software and well-trained teachers. We are working with the telecommunications industry, educators and parents to connect . . . every classroom and library in America by the year 2000" (Clinton, 1996). In the post-9/11 era, policies regarding what information about citizens and others can be gathered and in what manner that gathering may be done by the U.S. government have been key areas of controversy and deliberation by all three branches of the federal government.

Government attention to information in society has not been limited to the United States. In fact, one of the earliest documents focusing on this topic was the 1978 Nora and Minc report, *L'informatisation de la Société*, which was written for the president of France.

Many U.S. national controversies over the last twenty to thirty years have, in fact, been controversies about information—who had it, when, and what did they do with it. Such information issues have played out in the Pentagon Papers matter, in Watergate, in the Whitewater debacle, in the Enron affair, in the Valerie Plame leak case, and in the Mark Foley page scandal.

Attention to and interest in government information policy has never been higher, and we will discuss this aspect later, in chapters 11 and 12.

Schement and Curtis note the incorporation of "the idea of information" into our daily lives (Schement and Curtis, 1995: 220), and indeed information has been popularized in all aspects of our day-to-day affairs. Newspapers feature information sections. Movies use e-mail as central elements of the plot (*Mission Impossible*) and even in the title (*You've Got Mail*). "Information" as a word and as an idea pervades television commercials. Information technologies are the infrastructure for our shopping, as we buy goods and services online. Even the Boy Scouts integrated this information idea into their handbook, with advice on Internet use. In our language we have incorporated the terms related to information and information technology, not just as the nouns they began as, but turning them into verbs like "faxed," "e-mailed," "spammed," and "phished."

Information has become part of our humor structure, from Peter Steiner's *New Yorker* cartoon "On the Internet, nobody knows you're a dog" to Mike Keefe's *USA Today* editorial cartoon of the street beggar whose sign reads "No home page on the Web." Along with the pervasiveness that makes the humor possible, however, has come a pathology: Information Fatigue Syndrome, with accompanying research on its impact and how to manage it (Akin, 1998).

With this approach, we again come back to our central question:

How pervasive must information be in the society, in the cultural awareness of it as a force and as a daily idea, for a society to be an "information society"?

Information Ideas

Identifying an Information Society: Secret Information as the Basis of a Society

Although we are dealing in this chapter with ways in which the incursion of information and information technology into a society can be used to determine whether or not the society would qualify as an information society, there have been societies throughout history (using the definition of society that denotes a group of people who join together in support of a common interest) that have been based on secret information. That is, the basis of inclusion in the society is that the individual has been made privy to information that is closely guarded and not shared with those who are not members. Some of these societies have a religious basis, but others are social or civic institutions that function to provide access to power or to contribute, often in a secret manner, to the common good.

Historically, one of the most well-known such societies is the Rosicrucians, which began in the early 1400s but for which written documentation is available only from the early seventeenth century. Not only did the society have secret knowledge, but the membership in the society was secret as well. Variations of the society continue to the present day.

A secret society that has garnered much attention in the past few years as a result of its being featured in Dan Brown's blockbuster bestselling novel, *The Da Vinci Code*, is the Priory of Sion. This group supposedly was founded in the eleventh century, but the bulk of evidence is that it never existed at all. Nonetheless, it holds a place as an example of such a society, even if it operated only in the minds of those who originated or perpetuated the hoax.

Another such society, a real one that continues today in the United States primarily as a society to contribute to the common good, is the freemasons. The exact origin of the freemasons is not known (and may be related to the Rosicrucians), but there is evidence of freemasons as early as the fourteenth century. Others in this vein are the Elks, the Odd Fellows, and the Order of the Eastern Star.

In colleges and universities, social sororities and fraternities, which have secret information shared in initiation rites, are modern-day descendants of these societies based on information known only to the members. The sororities and fraternities, while carrying out projects that contribute to society, are primarily social institutions that provide access to social activities and give support to members through a variety of structures available exclusively to the members.

The tradition of the totally secret society, that is, that membership in it as

(*Continued on p. 202*)

well as the information held by members is secret, also continues today at some universities. Examples are the Skull and Bones Society at Yale University and the Seven Society at the University of Virginia, membership in which is only revealed after the death of a member.

Source
Fogarty, Harry. 2005. "Rosicrucians." In *Encyclopedia of Religion,* ed. Lindsay Jones. Vol. 12. 2nd ed. 7929–7931. Detroit, MI: Macmillan Reference USA.

CONSIDERING THE IMPACT OF INFORMATION AND INFORMATION TECHNOLOGIES ON SOCIETIES

Regardless of whether a society is currently an "information society" or not, it is possible to consider how changes in the way information is recorded, stored, and accessed affect the perception and use of that information and how it thereby affects the society, how information changes the experience of what is real and the mental constructs that interpret experience. But first, in order to do that, we must consider the nature of reality.

Within the context of this discussion, the approach is taken that reality does not exist, but that it is constructed. Moreover, the way reality is constructed changes, resulting in different constructions at different times in the past. For example, at one time the world was flat. Although we know that not to be the case now, that was reality across societies at an earlier time. Earth and man (and at that point it was "man," with no consideration of "woman") were the center of the universe. We now have a different construction of the universe, but that reality existed prior to the ideas of Copernicus in the early sixteenth century.

As James Burke points out, we also have different constructions of reality in different societies existing at the same time, different explanations of phenomena, different perceptions of what is going on (Burke, 1985: 307). We construct different stories to explain our perceptions. In the movie, *The Gods Must Be Crazy*, Xi, the African bushman who finds the Coke bottle that has fallen from the sky, constructs a quite different reality of where the bottle came from and what eventually must be done with it than the reality of the pilot who had tossed the bottle from a plane. Proponents of creationism or intelligent design explain the origin of the earth and of humans in a quite different manner from that of their contemporaries whose reality is derived from Charles Darwin's concept of evolution or from physicists who advance the big-bang theory.

Burke further notes that reality is different for each person, that we each have a different frame of reference, a unique mental structure of the world into which we place our experiences and observations, and that that structure enables the creation of our reality. Without it, there is no reality. We experience the external world through a structure of what reality is supposed to be, dismissing what does not fit into our structure. The structures do change over time and are replaced, when observations occur that cannot be fit into the version of reality that prevails. Given this approach, objectivity is impossible, because the structure—our perception of reality—defines what we look for, what we see, what questions we ask. We create knowledge within this structure of the individually and societally constructed reality (Burke, 1985).

The belief and value systems of the society shape what we add to our information and knowledge base. Theodore Roszak comments on this phenomenon:

> When was the Declaration of Independence signed and who signed it? Facts. But behind those facts there lies a major cultural paradigm. We date the past (not all societies do) because we inherit a Judeo-Christian view of the world which tells us that the world was created in time and that it is getting somewhere in the process of history. We commemorate the names of people who "made history" because (along other lines) we inherit a dynamic, human-centered vision of life which convinces us that the efforts of people are important, and this leads us to believe that worthwhile things can be accomplished by human action. (Roszak, 1986: 106)

With this framework as backdrop, we can consider the ways in which information and the way information is recorded, stored, and used has affected our changing concepts of reality.

Oral Society

Prior to Gutenberg and the invention of the printing press in the West, which led to a major revolution in reality, society was quite different. Although it is sometimes dangerous to deal with generalizations, we can describe in general terms what society was like in medieval times, prior to Gutenberg. For most people, reality and life was local. They knew very little about other places, other people, and other societies. Society and societal institutions were oral. Information was stored in human memory, and memory was the major way of transporting information across time and space. The capacity of memory was much greater and elaborate systems were developed for this storage and transportation. The societal institutions were preserved through memory and oral transmission: the laws, the ritual and liturgy of the church, and the literature of the time (see Boorstin, 1985). The sources of information and authority were old people, those who had more information stored in memory. Information from outside the local area came from troubadours, who passed on information about the outside world in their songs—information stored in rhyme. The church was the dominant influence and the source of information, both oral and visual, in the icons, paintings, and physical structure of the cathedrals (based on Burke, 1985: 91–123, who provides a full description of this time).

The influence of information on this society and the character of information were very different from what we experience today. First of all, information that was transportable or reproducible was quite malleable in this world, not fixed as it is in a print society. It was subject to errors in transmission: the embellishments and errors that occurred in the oral telling of information, the errors in copying that occurred in manuscripts. For most people, information was accessible only by being in the physical presence of someone who knew it. Very little information was transported across time and space, and since most people were not literate, unless that information was in oral form, it remained inaccessible. The way that information was recorded and stored thus influenced the perception of reality of the time; and the inaccessibility of information from other societies, either those of a distant time or those physically distant, provided for a degree of stability in reality. Information that did not fit the structure seldom intruded.

Print Society

The invention of the printing press is interpreted by many scholars, with Elizabeth Eisenstein as the lead interpreter of its impact, as introducing a major change agent into society, which brought change in the nature of information. First, it provided an accessible way to store information (Boorstin, 1985) and took away the reliance on memory. It led, over a period of time, to the development of standardized texts with a common, predictable organizational structure: the printed book with a title page that provides credit for the intellectual content and for the publication of the work; sequential, linear organization; numbered pages; and other devices that assist in the access and use of the information, such as the index and the table of contents. Through the enhanced capacity for replication of information, or at least of the standardized information container, it gave access to information to a much larger body of people. This capability of producing a fixed text that is reliable and unchanged across time and space changed the nature of the information transmitted, in that it brought a sense of closure or completion to the information, which did not continue to interact with the environment to the extent that occurred in the oral culture and even with manuscripts (Ong, 1991). Although this "fixity" is challenged by some (see Johns, 1998), long term it did make possible a higher likelihood that multiple individuals would have the potential for a similar "informative event" by accessing the same "informative artifact," to return to the terms of chapter 2. It also made it possible for more people to know something without being in the physical presence of the holder of the information. The printing press is also generally credited with making possible the enlargement of the base of knowledge, in that it brought an increased ability to generate more information because it was possible to build on what was already known.

This increase in mutual access to information, the sharing of information and ideas, changed the reality of society by introducing information that did not fit the prevailing structure, making possible—in fact, driving—more rapid alterations of reality, while at the same time making possible a greater shared reality. Some scholars credit this increased change with fostering our notion of progress and perhaps also our view of history as being connected in time (see, for example, Burke, 1985: 123).

The availability of information in a recorded, transmittable medium made possible changes in how learning could occur: One could learn by reading a text. It was no longer required to sit at the feet of a master and hear from him. Self-taught individuals became a possibility. We could have an Abraham Lincoln who taught himself. Another change in learning that was fostered in the development of the book (which was an outcome of the invention of printing) was a linear approach to the organization of knowledge.

In the realm of government, printing made it possible to disseminate opinion and to influence others beyond the reach of the human voice (Burke, 1985). It facilitated enforcement of laws by having printed copies so that all could know what they were, an important step toward using information as a means of power and control. The ability to have standardized documents (like the printed laws) that could be mass produced and distributed is credited with providing the means for the development of the centralized nation-state (see Deibert, 1997: chapter 3, for example). A corollary development supporting the establishing of national boundaries, one that also is related to the availability of printing, was the stabilization of language, especially the local language.

Printing is credited with changing the structure of the church by making it possible for the Protestant Reformation to occur as it did through the ability to share Martin Luther's theses across space in simultaneous time (Deibert, 1997; Burke, 1985). Although printing did not cause the Protestant Reformation (just as it did not cause the development of the nation-state), printing provided an environment in which these developments could occur, in ways and at rates of change that would not have been possible without it.

Fundamentally, printing made an enlarged sense of the world possible through providing access to information about society beyond the local. At the same time, print changed the way thought and consciousness were constructed, moving from a sound-dominated construction to a sight-dominated construction (Marvin, 1979, quoted in Dewar, 1998: 23; Ong, 1991: 104). This change in how consciousness (or, our reality) is constructed, resulting from the medium through which information is recorded, transmitted, and used, illustrates the pervasiveness and depth of the impact of information and its associated technologies on society and culture.

Beyond Print to the Electronic Society

Subsequent information and communication technologies have continued expansion of access to information across time and space and, like print, have affected our perceptions of reality. These changes wrought in our perceptions of reality change our sense of community and impact our value systems.

In our discussion of "beyond print to the electronic society," we need to recognize that these media are in many ways extensions of earlier forms. The telephone does not make verbal communication possible nor does the telegraph make written communication possible. Their contribution is to reduce the time-space limitations of the spoken and written word and to give near immediacy to communications on a global scale. The Internet, and more particularly the World Wide Web, have added a dimension of community to communications. Information technologies, whether we are talking about oral communications and memory, the book, or the Internet, redefine and sometimes replace the *context* in which the information they carry is interpreted. This context change is spatial, temporal, semiotic, and semantic.

TELEGRAPH AND TELEPHONE

The telegraph made possible the instantaneous transmission of messages across space and time from one individual to another, making it possible to share information in written form (although the transmission was encoded in electric signals) on an individual level without the delay inherent in the physical transportation of letters and without being in the physical presence of the other person. This individual sharing of information was further extended with the telephone, which provided individual interactive oral communication across space in real time—the first medium to provide synchronous interactive information exchange beyond a shared physical presence.

RADIO

It was the radio, making possible oral communication across space simultaneously to large numbers, that was a major extension of the possibility of sharing of information across a society, with similarities to the impact of printing. Radio had the potential for expanding public collective reality on a scale similar to that occurring with printing and, in fact, did have that effect during the 1930s and 1940s. Witness, for example, the reality created by the 1938 Orson Welles broadcast of *War of the Worlds*, when panicked listeners who missed the opening explanation that the broadcast was a dramatization of the H. G. Wells novel believed there actually was a Martian invasion.

TELEVISION

Television, even more vividly than radio (due to the visual element), provides instantaneous information of what is happening in the rest of the world, expanding individual reality structures across space and giving access to the individual realities of others. It is television, more than any preceding medium of recording, transmitting, and delivering information, that fostered the development of the "global village." Television changes the sense of community through provision of information, extending the community of the individual beyond the physical location. In so doing, television influences values of a society by exposing it to the values and expectations of other societies, and, especially, to other lifestyles. With this information medium, we see in real time the lives—or the invented lives—of others.

Originally television as a means of sharing information had the potential to enhance the sharing of a common reality, due to the mass nature of the medium providing mass access to the same information at the same time, not only within one society but also in societies across the world. This potential was realized during the heyday of network broadcast television, particularly in the events of high drama that were shared around the globe: the 1963 shooting and funeral of President John F. Kennedy; the 1968 funeral of Martin Luther King; and the 1981 wedding and then the 1997 funeral of Princess Diana. With the increased specialization and balkanization that has occurred as a result of the proliferation of information providers in the cable delivery version of television, the impact on society is reversing: a decreasing commonality of information and a balkanization of realities.

Even though television provides access to multiple realities outside of one's own existence, it can have an isolating impact in that it is noninteractive on the individual level. There is no connection with others who view the same television program. Instead of spending time with friends, people watched *Friends*. In contrast to print, television is still a one-to-many information medium, whereas print is experienced more as a one-to-one (one mind to another) sharing of information. The videocassette recorder accelerated the decline in "same time" access for the television medium, and the decline continues to accelerate with the DVD recorder and the availability of TV episodes via the Internet.

COMPUTERS, THE INTERNET, THE WEB, AND THE DIGITAL BEYOND

The recording, storage, and distribution of information in digital format, using a combination of the networked digital infrastructure that makes distribution possible and the variety of devices now available for data capture, manipulation, and display, are making an impact on societies and cultures that many liken to the extensive impact of the invention of the printing press. Regardless of whether one agrees on the exact interpretation of how important it was to have the information production and distribution capabilities that the printing press enabled, there are few that would argue that it did not play a significant role in the way that society accesses and uses information. The extent of the impact of digitized information is likewise still under debate, but we can make some observations and suggestions of what that impact is and likely will be.

First, the current information technology has the potential to move the recording of information back from a fixed medium to one that is highly malleable, somewhat akin to the oral tradition. With the ability to change text or visual displays in ways that are imperceptible to all but the technical expert (and such changes are being made regardless of current legal and ethical prohibitions), the preservation of information in the form intended by the creator of the information is at risk. There are technological solutions to this concern, ways to prevent such change and to retain "fixity" in the digital medium, but these solutions carry with them negative aspects that impede information use and access.

This threat to the preservation of access to information is compounded by rapid changes in the technology used to record and store information and even more by the changes in the interface devices that are needed to access digital information. The potential to lose information—to deprive future societies of the knowledge that we have produced—is high. In the print society, the existence of multiple copies that needed no interface device acted as a natural protective covering for the survival of the recorded information; but in the digital society, earlier versions of documents are routinely discarded and planned migration across platforms is not yet a common feature of the digital environment.

Another significant change, also reminiscent of the oral (and manuscript) society, is the potential change in the concept of authorship and the relationship of an individual to a created work. The crediting of intellectual labor to an individual, the concept of individual authorship, emerged with the change from oral to print culture (Birkerts, 1994). Eisenstein refers to this concept as "print-made immortality" (Eisenstein, 1979: 121), which has become a central idea in the creation and use of information in society, expanding into legal realms with the development of the concept of copyright and ownership of intellectual property and embedded in national and international law and treaties. Thus the authorship concept is a significant one in today's construction of reality, particularly as regards the production and management of information. In the digital environment that concept is subject to change, perhaps even under attack, as the ability to share information in real time without regard to location and the ability for creators of information to interact with each other is driving new ways of information generation. The twenty-first-century "collaboratory" of interactive information creation in which information initiators, reactors, and users all function together to craft new knowledge has the potential to alter this concept of single responsibility for information generation.

A closely related concept to this possible collaborative approach is the increasing fluidity of knowledge in the digital society. The technology makes possible greatly enhanced speed of information change. Dewar (1998) notes that the feedback cycle for information has changed by orders of magnitude; and the currently dominant delivery platform, the Web, only exacerbates the situation with the frequent, unpredictable, and undetectable (until one looks) comings and goings of the information available there.

As knowledge becomes more fluid, our ways of accessing it in the digital environment of the Web change dramatically from the linearity of print. The "basic movement is laterally associative rather than vertically cumulative" (Birkerts, 1994: 122); movement is across pages and ideas rather than a cumulation of ideas and thoughts that move sequentially, which may lead to change in the linear narrative form that dominates print. In print it is the author or provider of the content who determines the sequencing of information. In the Web world, control goes to the individual user, who then can create realities in the information that are unique and entirely different from the views of reality of the author. The reader becomes a cocreator, once the concept of the "single narrative line" (Pavlik, 1998: 310) is removed.

Beyond these immediate and direct impacts on information and information records, the realm of digital information and associated technologies is changing perceptions of reality and the mental constructs that we employ to structure our observations and experiences. The loss of linearity in information form may change our notion of progress. Whereas television allowed us access to view multiple realities, the Internet and online interaction structures provide means to exist simultaneously in personally constructed multiple realities. The creation of virtual communities makes everything both local and global simultaneously, both intimate and distant. The "localness" of the oral society is achievable on a global scale, changing the concept of community.

This change in the concept of community, to one based on commonality of interest rather than geography or place, has the potential to affect governance structures, which are still based primarily on physically contiguous spaces. Some argue that the digital environment is providing the means to bring an end to the nation-state, with "*Nationalism*, the visceral underpinning of modern world order . . . giving way to *nichelism*—a polytheistic universe of multiple and overlapping fragmented communities above and below the sovereign nation-state" (Deibert, 1997: 198). The porousness of national borders, which may be easily penetrated by other ideas, can be viewed as a potential force for change in that the ability of a government to control information is removed (Pavlik, 1998). At the same time, the digital environment fosters support for resurgent nationalism by providing a means of communication regardless of the physical dispersal of those who would rebuild their separate nation-state.

Another potential for impact on society that the digital environment for information is engendering is the empowerment of previously disempowered and disenfranchised individuals and groups. The broadening of communication and information sharing across socioeconomic barriers in the more egalitarian atmosphere of the Internet may assist in providing access to participation in society, as well as giving a ready means of information sharing—and thus power building—among political, social, or other minorities. As the previously mentioned *New Yorker* cartoon implies, the gender, racial, and disability barriers that impede access to full participation in a face-to-face environment do not have the same impact in the digital world; however, if use of digital video cameras becomes part of the standard digital communication structure, that advantage will be diminished.

Perhaps we should consider some of the things that the digital environment may not have brought to us but may enhance for us. The Internet did not create instantaneous communications on a global scale. In the nineteenth century, the telegraph and later the telephone did that for us. Likewise the Internet did not bring us immediate entertainment. In the late nineteenth and throughout the twentieth century, cinema, photography, audio and later video recordings, radio, and television—all analog technologies—brought nearly all forms of entertainment to our living rooms. And all these information formats were preceded by that yet to be eclipsed information carrier, the printed word. The Internet has facilitated the transmission and creation of new content and the transformation of old content into a medium more efficiently and cheaply broadcast to a general audience or narrowcast to a specific audience than ever before. The revolutionary nature of the Internet is not its digital character, but its potential ubiquity and individuality.

The digital character of the Internet permits its content to be created easily but also to be reproduced easily. The digital character of the Internet and of other databases also allows those contents to be more easily indexed using machine-based technologies and makes it possible for the information contained in those indexed databases to be more easily retrieved using machine-based technologies. This change has the effect of rendering what was an art a technology. But this, too, is not new to human society. The Luddites of the early nineteenth century who protested the replacement of human energy in the craft cottage industries by the machine and steam power or the neo-Luddites of the late nineteenth century, and even into our own time, who decried the loss of jobs to technology and electricity fought what some saw as a dehumanizing replacement of humans by machines, but what others would argue is the liberation of humankind from drudgery.

Technology has also meant that the social and economic roles of human beings can expand beyond the limits of a hunter-gatherer society. It has already been suggested that the Internet and before it the vast array of technological innovation have diminished (but not eliminated) various ethnic, racial, gender, and disability barriers. The Internet is bringing with it social change, just as the telephone, telegraph, cinema, radio, recordings, and all other technologies did. We can speculate on what the future may bring in terms of social restructure, but the escalation of the rate of technological change makes prediction more hazardous than ever.

Finally, there are the potentials for strongly negative impact on society that information created, stored, and used in digital format brings. These will be more fully discussed in chapter 13, but for now, a brief mention of several possible negative changes is appropriate:

- The possibility of a "Big Brother" surveillance society is stark reality in the transition from the print to the electronic world. The ability to unobtrusively monitor and capture information about individuals and to use that information in ways the individual is unaware of is great.
- The potential for further balkanization and fragmentation of society is also inherent in the increased ability to tailor information to the individual, thus diminishing the commonality of shared information that the invention of printing made possible and that was fostered through the generation of multiple copies of the same information made available across time and space.
- Increasing destabilization of society is possible as a result of the instantaneous detailed information about world events, both through

the loss of the time cushion for governments and in the impact on world markets.

CONCLUSION

The overall impact on society of this last phase of information technology can be summarized as enhancing the individuality of reality. While the construction of reality is still strongly shaped by what is commonly accepted in the society of the time and place, the extension of access to information about the multiple realities around the globe provides a much broader base from which to construct our individual understanding. What becomes real is not what one can see or touch, but what the mind can connect with, and that has become broader and more diverse than ever before. Whether that individualization will lead ultimately to structural demise of society as we have known it is a story this chapter cannot tell.

QUESTIONS FOR CONSIDERATION

1. In what ways can one measure the "information society-ness" of a nation? Should the same definition and measurements be applied to all nations?
2. If access to information and information technologies empowers both individuals and political minorities, what are some of the consequences of such empowerment for society?
3. Has the effect on society of the Internet, and particularly the Web, been greater or less than the effect of the invention of printing? What evidence supports your answer?
4. Information technologies have been credited both with helping to foster a common knowledge base and a common set of values in a country and with leading toward diminution of shared knowledge and values. Which do you think is the more valid assessment? Why?
5. If the construction of reality by individuals is based on the information and information technologies of the time, would differential access to information and information technologies among nations create different perceptions of reality at national levels? What impact might such differing perceptions have on relations among nations?

REFERENCES

Akin, Lynn. 1998. "Information Fatigue Syndrome: Malady or Marketing?" *Texas Library Journal* 74 (Winter). Available: www.txla.org/pubs/tlj74_4/akin.html (accessed December 2006).

Allison, Graham T., and Morton H. Halperin. 1972. "Bureaucratic Politics: A Paradigm and Some Policy Implications." In *Theory and Policy in International Relations*, edited by Raymond Tanter and Richard H. Ullman, 40–78. Princeton, NJ: Princeton University Press.

Ammon, Royce J. 2001. *Global Television and the Shaping of World Politics: CNN, Telediplomacy, and Foreign Policy.* Jefferson, NC: McFarland.

Birkerts, Sven. 1994. *The Gutenberg Elegies: The Fate of Reading in an Electronic Age.* Boston, MA: Faber and Faber.

Boorstin, Daniel J. 1985. "The Lost Arts of Memory." In *The Discoverers*, 480–488. New York: Random House.

Boy Scouts of America. 1998. *The Boy Scout Handbook.* 11th ed. Irving, TX: Boy Scouts of America.

Burke, James. 1985. *The Day the Universe Changed.* Boston, MA: Little, Brown.

Clinton, William Jefferson. 1996. "State of the Union Address." 23 January. Available: http://clinton2.nara.gov/WH/New/other/sotu.html (accessed December 2006).

Dean, Katie. 2000. "College Requires Online App." *Wired News* (17 May). Available: www.wired.com/news/culture/0,1284,36378,00.html (accessed December 2006).

Deibert, Ronald J. 1997. *Parchment, Printing, and Hypermedia: Communication in World Order Transformation.* New York: Columbia University Press.

Dewar, James A. 1998. *The Information Age and the Printing Press: Looking Back to See Ahead.* Santa Monica, CA: RAND.

Diaz, William A. 1999. "The Behavior of Grantmaking Foundations: Toward a New Theoretical Frame." In *Private Funds, Public Purpose: Philanthropic Foundations in an International Perspective*, edited by Helmut K. Anheier and Stefan Toepler, 141–153. New York: Kluwer Academic/Plenum.

Dordick, Herbert S., and Georgette Wang. 1993. *The Information Society: A Retrospective View.* Newbury Park, CA: Sage.

Eisenstein, Elizabeth L. 1979. *The Printing Press as an Agent of Change: Communications and Cultural Transformations in Early-Modern Europe.* Vol. 1. Cambridge, UK: Cambridge University Press.

———. 2005. *The Printing Revolution in Early Modern Europe.* 2nd ed. Cambridge, UK: Cambridge University Press.

Green, Kenneth C. 2006. *Campus Computing 2005: The 16th National Survey of Computing and Information Technology in American Higher Education.* Encino, CA: The Campus Computing Project.

Holderness, Mike. 1998. "Who Are the World's Information Poor?" In *Cyberspace Divide: Equality, Agency and Policy in the Information Society*, edited by Brian D. Loader, 35–56. London: Routledge.

Horrigan, John B., and Lee Rainie. 2004. "The Broadband Difference: How Online Americans' Behavior Changes with High-speed Internet Connections at Home." Washington, DC: Pew Internet & American Lift Project. Available: www.pewinternet.org/pdfs/PIP_Broadband_Report.pdf (accessed December 2006).

International Telecommunication Union. 2005. "Economies by Broadband Penetration, 2005." Available: www.itu.int/ITU-D/ict/statistics/at_glance/top20_broad_2005.html (accessed December 2006).

———. 2006a. "Digital Opportunity Index, 2005." 29 September. Available: www.itu.int/osg/spu/statistics/DOI/ranking2005.html (accessed December 2006).

———. 2006b. "Mobile Cellular, Subscribers per 100 People." Available: www.itu.int/ITU-D/icteye/Reporting/ShowReportFrame.aspx?Report Name=/WTI/CellularSubscribersPublic&RP_intYear=2005&RP_int-LanguageID=1 (accessed December 2006).

International Telework Association and Council. 2005. "Annual Survey Shows Americans Are Working from Many Different Locations Outside Their Employer's Office." Press Release, 4 October. Available at: www.working fromanywhere.org/news/pr100405.htm (accessed December 2006).

Johns, Adrian. 1998. *The Nature of the Book: Print and Knowledge in the Making.* Chicago: University of Chicago Press.

"Let 'Em Have Laptops." 1995. Summary of *New York Times*, 6 January, A11, quoting Speaker of the House Newt Gingrich in *Edupage* (8 January). Available: www.ee.surrey.ac.uk/Contrib/Edupage/1995/01/08-01-1995.html (accessed December 2006).

Lindblom, Charles. 1959. "The Science of Muddling Through." *Public Administration Review* 19 (Spring): 79–88.

———. 1979. "Still Muddling, Not Yet Through." *Public Administration Review* 39 (November/December): 517–526.

Machlup, Fritz. 1962. *The Production and Distribution of Knowledge in the United States.* Princeton, NJ: Princeton University Press.

Martin, Stana B. 1998. "Information Technology, Employment, and the Information Sector: Trends in Information Employment 1970–1995." *Journal of the American Society for Information Science* 49 (October): 1053–1069.

Marvin, Carolyn. 1979. "Book Review." *Technology and Culture* 20 (1979): 793–794. Quoted in James A. Dewar, *The Information Age and the Printing Press: Looking Back to See Ahead* (Santa Monica, CA: RAND, 1998), 23.

McHale, John. 1976. *The Changing Information Environment.* Boulder, CO: Westview Press.

"MIT's Management School Says No More Paper Applications." 1998. *Investor's Business Daily* (4 August). Summarized in *Edupage* (4 August). Available: www.ee.surrey.ac.uk/Contrib/Edupage/1998/08/04-08-1998 .html (accessed December 2006).

Nora, Simon, and Alain Minc. 1980. *The Computerization of Society: A Report to the President of France.* Cambridge, MA: MIT Press.

"Oakland and IBM Ready to Bridge 'Digital Divide'; New Learning Center Marks Start of Model Computer Training Program for Public Housing Residents." 1999. *Business Wire* (29 July). Available: www.findarticles .com/p/articles/mi_m0EIN/is_1999_July_29/ai_55290703 (accessed December 2006).

Ong, Walter J. 1991. "Print, Space, and Closure." In *Communication in History: Technology, Culture, Society,* edited by David Crowley and Paul Heyer, 102–113. New York: Longman.

Pavlik, John V. 1998. *New Media Technology: Cultural and Commercial Perspectives.* 2nd ed. Boston, MA: Allyn and Bacon.

Porat, Marc Uri. 1977. *The Information Economy: Definition and Measurement.* Washington, DC: U.S. Department of Commerce.

———. 1984. "Information Workers within Bureaucracies." *Bulletin of the American Society for Information Science* 10 (February): 15–17.

Quester, George H. 1990. *The International Politics of Television.* Lexington, MA: Lexington Books.

Roszak, Theodore. 1986. *The Cult of Information: The Folklore of Computers and the True Art of Thinking.* New York: Pantheon.

Rubin, Michael Rogers, and Mary Taylor Huber. 1986. *The Knowledge Industry in the United States, 1960–1980.* Princeton, NJ: Princeton University Press.

Ruiz, Yolanda, and Annette Walling. 2005. "Home-based Working Using Communication Technologies." In U.K. Office for National Statistics, *Labour Market Trends* (October): 417–426.

Schement, Jorge Reina, and Terry Curtis. 1995. *Tendencies and Tensions of the Information Age: The Production and Distribution of Information in the United States.* New Brunswick, NJ: Transaction Publishers.

Simon, Herbert. 1997. *Administrative Behavior: A Study of Decision-Making Processes in Administrative Organizations.* 4th ed. New York: Free Press.

Spira, Jonathan B. 2005. "We Interrupt Your Regularly Scheduled E-Mail." *Blogs-Jonathan Spira* (11 November). *Collaboration Loop.* Available: www.collaborationloop.com/blogs/we-interrupt-your-email.htm (accessed December 2006).

Spira, Jonathan B., and Joshua B. Feintuch. 2005. *The Cost of Not Paying Attention: How Interruptions Impact Knowledge Worker Productivity:*

Executive Summary. New York: Basex. Available: http://lib.store.yahoo .net/lib/bsx/interruptes.pdf#search=%22Basex%20interrupt%20work %20September%202005%22 (accessed December 2006).

Steiner, Peter. 1993. "On the Internet, Nobody Knows You're a Dog" [cartoon]. *The New Yorker* 69 (5 July): 61.

Steinfeld, Charles, and Jerry L. Salvaggio. 1989. "Toward a Definition of the Information Society." In *The Information Society: Economic, Social and Structural Issues,* edited by Jerry L. Salvaggio, 1–14. Hillsdale, NJ: Lawrence Erlbaum.

Strickland, Lee. 2002. "Information and the War Against Terrorism." *Bulletin of the American Society for Information Science and Technology* 28 (December/January): 12–17.

Sunstein, Cass. 2004. "Democracy and Filtering." *Communications of the ACM* 47, no. 12: 57–59.

Webster, Frank. 1996. "The Information Society: Conceptions and Critique." *Encyclopedia of Library and Information Science* 58: 74–112. New York: Marcel Dekker.

———. 2002. *Theories of the Information Society.* 2nd ed. London: Routledge.

ADDITIONAL SOURCES

BBC News. 1999. "New Technology Makes Work Harder." 1 June. BBC Online Network. Available: http://news.bbc.co.uk/hi/english/sci/ tech/newsid_357000/357993.stm (accessed December 2006).

"The Blogosphere." 2004. Special Issue, *Communications of the ACM* 47, no. 12 (December) [dedicated to the analysis of the "Blogosphere"].

Davis, Donald D., and Karen A. Polonko. 2001. *Telework in the United States: Telework America 2001 Survey.* Washington, DC: International Telework Association and Council.

Johnson, Amy Helen. 2000. "Touch Down." *Computerworld* 34, no. 12: 77–79.

Neuman, Johanna. 1996. *Lights, Camera, War: Is Media Technology Driving International Politics?* New York: St. Martin's Press.

Taylor, Philip M. 1997. *Global Communications, International Affairs, and the Media since 1945.* London: Routledge.

University of Western Ontario. Business Library. 2001. "Hoteling or Hot Desking" (19 December). Available: www.lib.uwo.ca/business/hoteling .html (accessed December 2006).

World Times. 1997. "The Information Society Index: Measuring Social, Information, and Computer Infrastructures." *World Paper* (June 1996). Reproduced in Wilson Dizard, Jr., *Meganet: How the Global Communications Network Will Connect Everyone on Earth*, 4–5. Boulder, CO: Westview.

Information as a commodity poses difficulties in traditional economics in that it has characteristics that are not like other goods. Before you begin reading this chapter, see if you can list some of the ways in which information as a commodity, that is an item that can be bought and sold, may be different from other commodities. How might these differences affect such issues as cost, price, supply, and demand?

Chapter 9

Economics of Information

Learning Guide

After reading this chapter, you should be able to

- define the following terms:
  - public good
  - private good
  - merit good
  - externality
  - experience good
- analyze whether in a given situation information and information records would be defined as a public good, a private good, or a merit good;
- identify the various ways in which the value of information is determined;
- assess the factors considered in pricing of information and information goods;
- evaluate the roles of governments in information and the provision of information goods and services and relate the role of a specific government to the prevailing political structure in the nation.

When you have finished the chapter, return to this page to be sure you have learned what you need to know.

INTRODUCTION

Information and economics have a number of different, but related, connections. One can consider the role of information in economic decision making, that is, what information is needed and when to make informed decisions that affect the economy, such as buy and sell decisions in the stock market. Another connection one can consider is how information activities contribute to the economy. In the previous chapter, we took this approach. We examined the role of information activities in the economy, considering what percentage of the gross national product was attributable to information production and use. We also looked at the percentage of the workforce engaged in information work as an indicator of an information society. Another approach is to consider information itself as an economic actor, which is what we will do in this chapter. We will look specifically at information as an economic good, that is, one that can be bought and sold in the marketplace. Information has characteristics that cause it to behave differently, from an economic perspective, from other goods and services. These characteristics and their impact will be discussed. We will also review some of the aspects of cost, pricing, and value of information and information goods. Then we will consider the conditions in which there is likely to be subsidization of provision of information. Finally, we will look into the role of government in the economics of information, discussing options for that role.

Before any of these matters can be discussed, there are a few basic definitions and concepts that must be introduced.

KEY DEFINITIONS AND CONCEPTS

There are three closely related definitions that need to be understood connected to information as an economic good: private good, public good, and merit good. Additional concepts that need to be understood for this discussion are externalities and ancillary values.

Private Good

A private good is a good consumed by one person, the primary benefit of which accrues to that person. It is acquired to maximize personal satisfaction, and only those who buy it will benefit from it. It also has the characteristic of "excludability," that is, if the good is used by one person or group it is not available for use simultaneously by another and those others may be easily excluded from use of the good. Examples would be a coat, a candy bar, a computer keyboard.

Public Good

A public good can be used simultaneously by many, that is, consumption can be shared. It is also not depleted by use; use by one person does not decrease the amount available to others. A public good is "nonrival." It may or may not have the property of being "nonexcludable," that is, it may or may not be very difficult to exclude others or nonpayers from the benefit of the good. Although a good with these characteristics may be provided privately, for those which are nonexcludable, the difficulty of exclusion means the good is not voluntarily paid for; and the level of provision of the good is determined in the political process, not via a market mechanism. The typical example of a public good is national defense. The protection afforded one person in a country by the national defense system in no way diminishes the value to the next person. Nor can individuals in a country be excluded from the benefits of national defense. The level of provision of national defense is decided by political means, not in the marketplace.

This concept of public good was developed by economist Paul Samuelson in the mid-1950s (Samuelson, 1954). His definition of a public good is one "which all enjoy in common in the sense that each individual's consumption of such a good leads to no subtraction from any other individual's consumption of that good" (Samuelson, 1954: 387). The concept is also called "social good" and "collective good."

Merit Good

A merit good is a private good that society thinks is important enough to supply publicly or to interfere with individual preference as expressed through the marketplace. That is, a merit good is a good considered beneficial to society regardless of consumer preference. Therefore, society interferes with the market mechanism and regulates the use (supplies with public funds) because the good might not be consumed to the socially desirable level if left to the consumer. A merit good has benefits that accrue to society beyond that gained by the individual who is consuming the good. An example of a merit good is education. It can be supplied privately (in the marketplace), it has benefits to society that are in addition to the individual benefit of the person receiving the education, and it is supplied publicly. The level of provision of merit goods, like public goods, is determined in the political process. This concept is associated with economist Richard Musgrave (1959).

Externalities

An externality is a spillover effect, a result that occurs when action by one party has an effect on one or more other parties not involved in the action.

For example, smoking has negative externalities. In the case of a good, an externality occurs where benefits or costs accrue to those other than the direct producers or consumers of a good. These benefits and costs are not taken into account in decision making regarding the provision of a good, since the cost is borne by or the benefit received by individuals other than those who are making the provision decision. The extent of externalities in provision of a good influences both the amount supplied and by whom it is supplied. The good may have both positive and negative externalities. Kingma (2001) offers junk mail as an example: it is considered a negative by some, a positive by others. Externality in relation to a good is the same as the concept of ancillary value. If the ancillary value of provision of a good is positive, it is considered a benefit. If it is negative, it is a cost. Such ancillary values may be either private or social or both. For example, education has private ancillary value to employers in that it reduces training costs and value to society in that it enhances the ability of the individual to function as a citizen (Bates, 1988).

INFORMATION AS AN ECONOMIC GOOD

Information as a commodity has interesting characteristics that make it difficult to address in economic terms. It is

- not depleted by use. Using information has no diminishing effects on the amount or quality of information available to others. In fact, since information is used to create more information, rather than diminishing the amount, use has at least the potential for making the volume of information increase;
- nonrival, in that there may be multiple simultaneous users of the same information. If someone else is reading this chapter at the same time that you are, you are making simultaneous use of the same information without influencing each other's access to the ideas contained in it;
- difficult to exclude individuals from the benefits of use, at least in part.

However, in tangible, expressed form, it is possible to exclude individuals from access to information. For the purposes of economic analysis, it is critical to separate the concept of "information" from "information good," that is, to distinguish the information product or carrier of information from the information itself, as we did in chapter 2 in distinguishing between "information" and the "information record." Taylor (1986) discusses this as the difference between the information content of messages and the information resources that store, package, and carry the messages. Or, to use another approach, the information must be separated from the "object potentially conveying information" (Saracevic and Kantor, 1997: 529) in order to discuss the economic character of information and the information container.

The information container or information record would appear to have some characteristics that are different from that of information per se. The information record has the following attributes:

- Individuals may be excluded from use of it.
- In some manifestations (e.g., printed documents), only one person may use it at a time.
- Multiple uses diminish the value of the item. The information carrier (again, at least in some information technologies, such as the book) wears out.

Given the attributes identified above, information can be viewed as falling into the public good category:

- Use of it benefits society as a whole.
- Simultaneous use without any infringement on availability for other users is possible.
- It can be shared without diminution of the utility to the original holder.
- Use does not diminish value, but rather may enhance value.

On the other hand, information provision, access to information and its dissemination, and particularly access to information carriers, can be viewed as meeting private good characteristics:

- It is possible to exclude individuals from access to the expressed form of information. To a degree that is what is done, or attempted, through copyright, which protects the expression of the information, not the information itself, and provides exclusionary rights in that expression.
- It is possible to provide access to information and its dissemination as a good that is bought and sold in the marketplace, following the preferences of the individual consumers.

While information can perhaps most easily be categorized as a public good and the information container can be categorized as a private good, the economic model that is used for information provision, access to information, and its dissemination in the United States has in part been the model of the merit good. Even information, in terms of its supply, has also been treated as a merit good. These are concepts that need further exploration.

At some minimal level, access to information may be a merit good, in that there is a need to have societal provision of information to a certain level, which is established through the political process. At more specialized, advanced, and individualized levels, access to information should perhaps be considered a private good. In instances in which the public cannot really participate in assimilation of or benefit individually from access to specific information, where information is highly specialized, for example, or where the information is highly user specific and where costs related to provision of that information can be isolated from generalized costs, access to information may be more appropriately modeled as a private good. To determine where that boundary is, between the access to information that should be treated as a private good and access to information that should be a merit good, involves the concept of externalities.

As a general rule, where there are positive externalities for society as a whole, where there are benefits to society beyond the benefits to the individual, it is more likely that a good will be provided as a merit good. The difficulty inherent in the information provision decision is that it is not always clear whether positive externalities will occur. Potential positive externalities exist in information provision, that is that the access to the information will create value not just for the user but for others as well, but realization of that potential may be unpredictable and dependent on the individual case of the user to whom the information access is provided.

The position that there is a threshold level of provision of access to information that should be considered a merit good is the policy that lies behind the provision of public education with public funding through the secondary school level. It is entirely possible for education to operate totally as a private good, with consumption left to the preferences of the consumer. However, the ancillary social value, that is, the positive externalities, is considered to be sufficient to warrant the public support.

There is also a similar position that undergirds the provision of public libraries: there is a minimum level of access to information that is necessary to function as an informed citizen in a democracy. Hence, access to information will be provided through a publicly funded institution, rather than being left entirely to the choices made by individuals.

The threshold levels for both public education and public libraries are defined in the political process. To accurately determine the line between the merit good level and the private good level of provision of access to information we need to be able to determine the point at which the societal benefit of such provision is greater than or equal to the societal cost, for it is at that point that information provision arguably should follow the merit good approach. Such measurement, however, is very difficult.

COST, PRICING, AND VALUE OF INFORMATION

In addition to the economic model for information, other economic aspects of information that bear examination are cost, pricing, and value of information and information provision and their interrelationships. A basic question for any society is on what basis and by whom should access to information be paid. To some extent, this is the same question as what should be the economic model for information, but it allows us to pursue the issue from several perspectives.

Costs

If we treat information provision as a private good, as the preceding section suggests is a possible approach, we can assume that the user or consumer of the information will pay full costs for the information. Such costs would include the total cost for production and use of the information, as well as access to it. In general, there are high fixed costs for production of information (that is, generation and initial production in shareable form) and low variable costs for reproduction of the information carrier, including costs of reproduction in various formats. The actual costs of sharing the information, the marginal cost beyond the initial fixed cost of production, may actually be zero (Bates, 1988); but there are costs for the carrier. The fixed costs of generation are sunk costs, nonrecoverable if production for further sharing with multiple users is cancelled (Shapiro and Varian, 1999).

It is hard to accurately cost information, especially to determine the appropriate allocation of overhead costs. The total cost of development of new information is often not included in the cost assessment because it has been produced with public funds, through governmental funding of research or through some other means of public subsidization, such as the employment of the generator of the new information in a university or other public institution that supports information creation or through support from a private foundation. The costs of production often reflect only the cost of the information good or information carrier, not the cost of the information itself.

What also are not generally taken into account are the societal costs, the negative externalities that may be related to the information. Where societal costs of a good are not accounted for, the tendency is to produce and consume more of the good than would otherwise be the case. For example, to use the example provided by Kingma, the societal costs of junk mail are not incorporated into costs of generation and provision of access to the information that such mail affords. In this case, societal costs would include the environmental impact of the need to produce additional paper, the increased load on the postal system, the additional burden on collection and disposal of trash, and the cost of the time of the recipient of the junk mail.

This last unaccounted-for cost is illustrative of another cost related to information and information provision that is generally not considered, the cost in terms of time and effort to use the information container or record, to extract and process that potential for an "informative event" that the record contains. In many cases, a significant cost of information is in its use, at least as that is cumulated over multiple users. However, this cost factor is even more difficult to measure than others that are not considered and likewise difficult to impact or control.

What we are often left with in assessing the cost of information are the costs related to the production, distribution, storage, and management of the information good, not the information itself. Even within that more limited approach, there are ways beyond full user payment that costs of information can be supported.

Pricing

The setting of prices for information goods and services is likewise a complicated matter. Pricing does, of course, take costs into account, although as we have just seen, the true costs are not usually part of the equation. One assumes that the price of information goods or services supplied in the market, that is those that follow the private good model, will include production costs plus overhead plus some profit to provide return on investment. But, as the discussion of cost issues illustrates, this matter is complex. Recall also the discussion in chapter 6 of the successive revenue streams that are needed in some parts of the information industry, such as the film industry, to provide opportunity for cost recovery and eventual profit. The production and marketing of information at different times in different formats to different users in different markets for different prices, which Shapiro and Varian call "versioning" (Shapiro and Varian, 1999: 53–81), further illustrate the very complicated factors that must be taken into account in setting prices for information.

Beyond the function of price as a means of recouping cost and providing profit, there is the additional function served by price as a means of allocating goods and services. Individuals who assess that their potential benefit from the good or service will be greater than the price will purchase it, therefore the good or service will go to those who will benefit most from its consumption (Kingma, 2001). However, with information, this assessment of potential benefit, which is related to value, is a difficult task.

Value

The valuing of information is complicated by the fact that information is an "experience good," that is, in order to assess the value one has to experience the good, a concept developed by Phillip Nelson (see also Shapiro and Varian, 1999: 5). There are a number of ways in which value of information can be defined. One is the *exchange value*: how much someone is willing to pay in the market for the information. This is the traditional way that the economist measures value. However, often what is measured is the market value of the information systems and products, not the information itself, because in the market context, the two are difficult to separate. This concept is also a limited one for some purposes of valuing information goods and services, in that there are significant providers of information goods and services that do not operate in the market setting, such as libraries and public education.

Another concept of value is *apparent value*. This concept is explained by Taylor as encompassing not only the exchange value but also the investment that the user of information is willing to make in terms of energy and time as well as the user's opportunity costs (Taylor, 1986). This measure is akin to the user cost discussed previously, but as an aspect of value, suggests an active, deliberative role on the part of the information user. While this concept is useful in constructing a more complete measure of the value of information, it is not generally incorporated in any way into information pricing. However, there are situations in which the higher the investment the user is willing to make, the higher the possibility that the information good or service can be obtained at a lesser price in terms of dollars expended.

Another approach to value of information is the concept of *value in use*, which measures the actual value of the information in the situation in which it is used by the individual. This is a value that is determined totally situationally and cannot be known until the use has occurred, when one can measure the benefit of the use. This concept of value differs not only from person to person but changes for the individual depending on circumstances. It is an outcome of the fact that information is an experience good. Braman calls this the "hetereogeneity of value" and notes that the value in use may have no relationship to the exchange value of the information good or service (Braman, 1995: 105–6). This value concept, while not necessarily related to the exchange value, has some utility for setting price, in that the anticipated value in use will be a factor in the range of prices that a consumer is willing to pay for an information good or service.

Other concepts that assist in understanding the value of information include three different ways of approaching the issue: the *normative value* approach, the *realistic value* approach, and the *perceived value* approach. The normative value approach ascribes the value of information as the difference between the expected utility of a decision made without the information and the utility of the same decision made with the information. The realistic value approach measures the effect of information on the actual outcomes of use, and the perceived value is that value ascribed to the information by the user (Saracevic and Kantor, 1997). It is only this last approach that may be useful in determining an acceptable price. Normative value and realistic value are concepts that may assist in determining value after use, but the price of information or information goods and services must be set prior to use.

And finally, we have the *ancillary value* of information or information goods and services, a concept that was discussed above. In pricing, the ancillary value is generally not included, since it is not received by the consumer, but it plays a role in the determination of whether there will be some measure of subsidy that is provided for the information or access to the information, which will be discussed in the next section.

The price of an information good or service, which in the terminology we are using will mean provision of access to a potential information experience, incorporates recovery of cost as an intent and is likely related to the predicted value in use as perceived by the consumer. Since the value of the information experience cannot be known until it occurs and varies across individuals, the actual pricing of the information good or service generally does not operate in ways similar to the pricing of other tangible goods and services.

SUBSIDIZATION OF INFORMATION PROVISION

If information and provision of access to it has positive externalities, there may be subsidization of the information and provision by government, either totally or with some measure of user fees. The extent of user charges for publicly subsidized information or access to information may be based on a variety of different factors:

- The extent to which the charges support provision of the information access service or extend the service.
- The use patterns of the information or information access. There may be an attempt to shift use patterns from high use information or services to lesser used services by the charges attached to the preferred information or services. This approach also serves as a means of subsidizing less valued resources that may be valuable from a societal point of view but under-used or in lesser demand based solely on user preference.
- The total volume of use. One way to ration access to or control use of information is through the user charges, raising charges when demand exceeds capacity.

There are other means of subsidizing information and information services beyond governmental subsidy. One example is advertising, which subsidizes the information provided through the mass media, or in the case of broadcast television, radio, and some Web pages, totally supports the provision of information access. Kingma (2001) notes that information goods that are nonexclusionary in nature, such as those just mentioned, are typically paid for by advertising.

Another example of subsidization of information services used to occur with the structure of telephone rates, in which individual and rural phone service prices were heavily subsidized by business and urban phone users. Currently, there are "e-rate" subsidies that provide support for discounted telecommunication rates for public libraries, public schools, and rural health care providers in order to provide universal access to Internet delivered information, with the costs supported through a universal service fund to which the telecommunications carriers make payments, an arrangement that was enacted into law as part of the 1996 Telecommunications Act. In practice, these costs are shared collectively across consumers of telephone services, inasmuch as the universal service costs are passed through to consumers on their phone bills.

Another example of cross-user subsidization of information provision is the special pricing (or, in some cases, no-charge access) for educational institutions from database vendors. For example, the charge to law schools for Lexis access is at a lower rate than that charged to law firms, and schools of library and information science have access to LexisNexis and select Thomson databases at no cost. This kind of provision of access to information for educational purposes is subsidized by the other consumers of the information.

In the societal institutions that have been established to provide access to information as a merit good, libraries and schools, there may also be the imposition of user charges that incorporate considerations of the factors listed above. For these societal institutions, assessing user fees serves one of the purposes of pricing, that of allocation (Kingma, 2001). There are other considerations that come into play:

- the cost of assessing the user charge (for a clear discussion of this aspect see Kingma, 2001: 117–21)
- the policy implications of instituting direct user charges on top of the indirect charges made through taxation that supports the institution
- potential inability of users who are expected to use and thereby contribute to societal benefit (the ancillary value) to pay the additional charges, which raises issues of equity and exclusion from access
- the added value of the information service for which the charge is made, which assumes that this value can be determined
- the added cost of the information service for which the charge is made, which assumes that it is possible to isolate and quantify that cost

- the potential for improving access to the services provided without a charge by reducing the number competing for that service
- the potential for subsidizing other services that will not have a charge, thereby increasing the overall societal benefit of the institution

ROLE OF GOVERNMENT IN THE ECONOMICS OF INFORMATION

The role of government in the economics of information varies, depending on the political structure of the country and on the prevailing political climate. Two major potential roles of government are to foster the development of information and to equalize access to information. In terms of approach, the government may serve in two different modes: as facilitator of information creation and provision of access or as regulator of activities related to information and its provision.

Government Role in Development of Information

There are several ways that government can assist in the development of information.

CREATION, GENERATION, PRODUCTION, DISSEMINATION OF INFORMATION

One way, obviously, is to serve as creator, generator, producer, and disseminator of information. All governments act in this way, producing voluminous amounts of information in the conduct of and about the conduct of the various functions of government. The costs of this information production are borne centrally, at whatever level of government is acting, and distributed over the base of taxpayers as part of their support of the functions of government. Costs of access to this governmentally produced information may also be distributed across the taxpayer base. For example, consider the many government Web sites that provide access to information at no direct cost to the user. To explore some of these, go to FirstGov (United States) and Directgov (United Kingdom). In other cases, the costs of access to the information are charged to the information user, but only at the level of the marginal cost of production of the information carrier.

GRANTS OR OTHER SUPPORT

Governments may also create, generate, produce, and disseminate information in areas that are not in any way related to the function of government, although in the United States, the general policy of government is not to compete with private-sector activities, so that there are large categories of information in which the government would not act in this role. However, in order to foster information creation and production and to foster development of new distribution mechanisms and new information systems, even governments that eschew direct production participate in information development through provision of grants or other support mechanisms. In the United States, for example, federal grants that support information creation and development of distribution mechanisms are offered through a variety of agencies, including the National Endowment for the Humanities, the National Science Foundation, the National Institutes of Health, and the Institute of Museum and Library Services.

If a government takes this approach, subsidizing information activity through grants rather than or in addition to direct involvement, the questions arise of which information activities should be fostered and how would this support for development be best accomplished. There are various points in the creation, production, dissemination, management, and use of information that are possible points of governmental intervention through grant support. Which of these are appropriate for government support? Is the appropriate role of government to provide funding support at all points?

When that question is answered, the next question appears: What is the most efficient and effective means of government intervention? Should, for example, the government conduct research and development or contract for such R&D, and then turn over the results to the private sector? This approach was taken in the early development of systems for online retrieval of databases. The National Aeronautics and Space Administration contracted with Roger K. Summit and Lockheed to develop a system to retrieve their aerospace research documents, which over time and with subsequent development under government contracts, became the basis for what is now Dialog, the online information service owned by Thomson Corporation.

INFRASTRUCTURE DEVELOPMENT

Another way in which government can act to foster information activity is to create, or support the creation of, the necessary infrastructures for information. The activity of the U.S. government in the forerunner networks to the Internet, such as ARPANET and NSFNet, provide an example of governmental involvement in information infrastructure construction.

REGULATION

Additionally, government may foster information activity through regulation, particularly regulation that protects markets so that the private sector can develop information, information goods, and information services. The role of government in regulation was discussed briefly in chapter 6, in regard to concern for the impact of cable television on the broadcast television industry and the restrictions on cross-ownership. In addition to actions that regulate internal information activities, governments may impose tariffs on information goods and services imported from other countries as a means of fostering the development of the local (i.e., in that country) information industry activities, including all aspects of information creation, production, dissemination, management, and use.

Government may also inhibit the development and/or the transfer of information. For example, government has played an important role in the development of nuclear technology but tries to limit very carefully the spread of the fruit of that research. Government may also seek to prohibit or discourage certain lines of investigation while fostering others. In recent years, the U.S. federal government has sought to limit research into fetal tissue and stem cells or human cloning. But, at the same time, government has promoted research into the human genome.

Role of Government in Equalization of Access to Information

The role of government in equalization of access to information and information goods and services is related to the perspective of information access as a merit good. The consumption of information by individuals is taken to produce ancillary social value above that accruing to the individual consumer, and thus government intervenes to increase consumption beyond what would occur if individuals were left to make their own decisions. Added to this concept is the notion that there is some kind of "right" to information and that society has a responsibility to guarantee some minimal level of access, both for the individual's benefit and for the overall societal good.

The questions that arise, however, are not easily addressed:

- To what level should equity of access be assured?
- What is the threshold level of information that should be provided by society so that the marginal benefit to society is greater than or equal to the marginal cost of providing the information?
- How should such access to information be provided?
    - through publicly supported information agencies, such as schools or libraries?
    - by direct payment or voucher to the individual, for use in purchasing information access in the market?

In the United States, government continues to make efforts at equalizing access through such avenues as the agencies of formal education, through public libraries, through access to government information via depository libraries, and via the World Wide Web. At this time, the debate rages over whether direct payment (via voucher) to the individual for information activities is an appropriate approach to equalization. This approach has been judged constitutional, at least for access to K–12 education. The Clinton administration supported federal governmental effort at equalizing access to information within the private sector via programs aimed at the well-publicized "Digital Divide," including the Technologies Opportunities Program and the Community Technology Centers program. The Bush administration veered away from this kind of governmental intervention (Krim, 2002), while supporting the voucher approach for schools.

The question that must continually be addressed is, to what degree does government interfere with market mechanisms, or, what is the appropriate level of government incursion into the information marketplace? Considerations that influence the answer to the question include the following:

- What is the social value of information, beyond private benefit?
- What is the audience to whom the information is directed? In the United States, the wider the audience, the more likely it will be for government to provide.
- To what extent is the information or access to it available in the private sector? Again, in the United States, if the information good or information service is not available, it is more likely to be acceptable for government to provide it.
- What mix of public and private provision of information best protects the unrestricted flow of information?

In summary, the explanations of Moore (1998) help to delineate the role of government in the economics of information. His analysis is that the role of government may be that of facilitator, establishing the conditions for information activity, but leaving information development and provision to the private sector. Alternatively, the government may play the role of interventionist (what Moore labels the *dirigiste* approach), playing a key and active role in information development and provision. Within these two models, the choice of which is integrally related to the political economy of the nation, government may affect the economics of information within a country. In general, the United States, Great Britain, Canada, Australia, and members of the European Union follow the first model, while countries of East Asia, Latin America, and newly industrialized countries follow the latter (Moore, 1998).

Information Ideas

Control of Information through Economic Intervention

As discussed in this chapter, the role of the governments of the United States, Great Britain, Canada, Australia, and members of the European Union are perceived as following the general model of government as facilitator, establishing the conditions for information activity and leaving information development and provision to the private sector. One might question the extent to which this behavior is observed throughout the various areas related to development and provision of information, particularly in the United States. The influence of economic intervention—or more precisely, the threat of withholding or not providing economic support—is used in the United States in a number of information arenas.

A key approach to control of information activities in the United States occurs in the relationship between federal funding and information activities. The federal government, in its role as dispenser of financial support to information institutions such as schools and libraries, regulates what types of information can be provided in those institutions. This regulation has occurred most recently in the requirement that schools and libraries that apply for e-rate funding to support Internet access (see page 354 for further discussion) install filters on Internet access computers to control the types of information that the clients of those institutions can retrieve. Further controls of this type—requiring information control as a condition of funding—are proposed in the Deleting Online Predators Act (H.R. 5319, still under consideration in August 2006), which would prohibit access to both specific types of information content and information technology (social networking Web sites and chat rooms).

Another avenue of control of information activity via economic intervention occurs in the grant funding process of U.S. federal agencies, particularly the National Science Foundation, but also through others, such as the National Institutes of Health, the Institute for Museum and Library Services, and the National Endowment for the Arts. These grant-making agencies affect both the direction and type of information developed and the ways in which information is distributed and made accessible, establishing, as it were, what information is considered important and what audiences for the information are the most deserving. While this influence perhaps could be interpreted as "facilitation," a more cynical view might be that it is information control through economic intervention.

The government also intervenes through controls on how—what technologies will be used—to develop information through the granting or withholding of funding. A current obvious case in point is the U.S. presidential veto of the Stem Cell Research Enhancement Act of 2005 (H.R. 810), which would have

(Continued on p. 235)

made federal funds available for embryonic stem cell research using donated embryos from in vitro fertilization. In contrast, the European Union voted to fund such research, again offering an example of how economic intervention by governments directs—one could say controls—development of information.

Other countries, not characterized as "facilitators," have been even more direct in their control of information. The Soviet Union sought to control the dissemination of information from its birth in 1917 to its collapse in 1991 by regulating access to information through the licensing of presses, mimeograph machines, and later photocopiers. Both Cuba and the People's Republic of China place strict limitations on access to the Internet and the use of e-mail. In 2002, China blocked both Google and AltaVista because the two search systems provided access to prohibited sites. Yet according to the BBC (2006), in 2006, Google.cn was created to comply with Chinese information regulations, a form of self-censorship.

In many other countries, access to information—whether in traditional formats or electronic—is limited for economic reasons. Information resources are too scarce or are inequitably distributed in many developing countries. In these countries, access to electronic information is severely curtailed because of lack of infrastructure, the dearth of Internet-ready computers, information illiteracy, and the high cost of use. According to the International Telecommunications Union (Gray, 2006), while wired and especially mobile telephone usage is increasing in Africa, it is well below global averages. In Sub-Saharan Africa, fewer than ten percent of the population are mobile or wired telephone subscribers. Cost is seen as a major barrier.

Sources

Bilefsky, Dan. 2006. "EU to Finance Stem Cell Research." *International Herald Tribune* (25 July). Available: www.iht.com/articles/2006/07/25/news/union.php (accessed December 2006).

British Broadcasting Corporation. 2006. "Google Censors Itself for China." *BBC News* (25 January). Available: http://news.bbc.co.uk/1/hi/technology/4645596.stm (accessed December 2006).

Bush, George W. 2006. "President Discusses Stem Cell Research Policy." U.S. White House, *Presidential News and Speeches* (19 July). Available: www.whitehouse.gov/news/releases/2006/07/20060719-3.html (accessed December 2006).

Gray, Vanessa. 2006. "The Unwired Continent: Africa's Mobile Success Story [África, el continente móvil]." *Economía Exterior* no. 36 (Spring): 82–90. Available: www.itu.int/ITU-D/ict/statistics/at_glance/Africa_EE2006_e.pdf #search=%22UN%20telephone%20usage%20statistics%20Africa%22 (accessed December 2006).

TRENDS IN INFORMATION ECONOMICS

One significant current trend affecting the economics of information, influenced particularly by the role that government takes in facilitating and regulating activities that may impact information activities, is the out-migration of employment from the postindustrialized information economies to the industrializing information economies. We can witness the shift occurring as a result of the overall status and characteristics of the economies of the various countries.

Before the advent of the "information revolution," we could witness two types of immigrations: economic immigrations and political immigrations. Political immigrations usually resulted during and after a political upheaval in a country—a revolution, a coup d'etat, or the like. The typical immigrant was often well trained, a member of the local elite, and one who brought useful skills and sometimes significant wealth to his or her new homeland. Economic immigrants, on the other hand, often left their home countries to escape economic hardships and sometimes worse—famine, war, or environmental disaster. These immigrants often came with little wealth and few high-value skills.

These economic immigrants, sometimes legal and sometimes not, are often welcome in their new host countries in good times but are not so welcome during economic downturns. The United States has witnessed numerous periods of immigration for economic reasons, then reaction and contraction, as have other countries. These U.S. immigration waves include Chinese and Japanese laborers brought in to build the railroads and work in the mines in the second half of nineteenth century, Irish immigration to escape the Potato Famine in the mid-nineteenth century, and Eastern Europeans arriving in the late nineteenth and early twentieth centuries. Today there is significant Mexican and Central American immigration into the United States, Turkish immigration into Germany, and Moroccan and Algerian immigration into France, to give but three examples.

We are witnessing another form of economic movement as well. Rather than individuals coming to jobs (the economic immigrant), jobs are going to individuals. This movement is by no means only a recent phenomenon. In the United States, manufacturers began by shifting plants (jobs) from high wage areas (the North) to low wage areas (the South) as early as the 1920s. The textile industry that emerged in north Georgia and the furniture industry of North Carolina, for example, are the result in large part of relative differences in wages between the North and the South.

With the globalization of the economy, these trends have been magnified. The North American Free Trade Agreement (NAFTA) facilitates trade among Canada, Mexico, and the United States. It has also resulted in some degree of manufacturing employment being shifted into lower wage areas.

We also see this phenomenon in the European Union. Important parts of the "Irish miracle" of the late twentieth century, for example, were the relatively low wages and low taxes in Ireland relative to the rest of Europe. Other "low wage, low tax" countries have also benefited, while countries without these tax and wage advantages, the Nordic countries, for example, have suffered.

There is now a new phenomenon. Service employment, much of it in information and information technology, is now being exported. Perhaps the first manifestation of the trend began when telephone call centers were shifted offshore. With improved satellite digital telephony and computerized reservations and other systems, many companies could and did shift their customer telephone services to countries like Barbados and India, where labor costs were substantially lower than in North America or Western Europe.

We are now seeing that many companies are beginning to shift various computing requirements to lower wage areas, often to India. (See Edward Yourdon, who predicted the trend in his 1992 *Decline & Fall of the American Programmer*, recanted in his 1996 *Rise and Resurrection of the American Programmer*, but seems to have been proven right after all.)

The trend appears to be clear. Given the range of information technologies available to us, the speed at which they operate, and the ever decreasing cost at which they operate, we can expect to see more higher-skill service sector employment move from the information economy countries to lower wage but high skill countries like China, India, Brazil, and the countries of Eastern Europe. Thomas Friedman's (2006) analysis of global economics brings him to conclude that the "world is flat." By that he means that technology and human ingenuity have overcome the barriers of distance and national boundaries to create global supply and distribution systems and thereby greater economic efficiencies. This globalization, while not altering the basic concepts of the economics of information, is affecting where and how the concepts interact with other aspects of the world economy.

CONCLUSION

The economics of information are complicated and challenging, due in large part to the characteristics of information that differ from that of most tangible goods. The economic analysis of information needs to be considered both distinct from and in concert with the economic analysis of the carrier of the information, but this also makes the matter more complex. Information per se can most accurately be described as a public good, while information goods and services may either be private goods or merit goods.

Determining the cost of and appropriate prices for information and associated information goods or products is also difficult, particularly given the presence of subsidies in the creation of information, possible subsidies in the various activities related to information goods and services, and the challenge of determining value in what is an experience good.

The role of government in the economics of information may be as facilitator or interventionist, and the functions that government performs in relation to information and information goods vary with the specific type of information as well as the political structure of the country. Changes in information technology are redistributing the location and thus the functioning of information activities in the global economy. As we have seen in this chapter, the economic aspect of information is inseparable from information policies at national and international levels, which will be addressed in later chapters.

QUESTIONS FOR CONSIDERATION

1. Should information or information provision be considered a public good, a private good, or a merit good? Would changing circumstances or contexts cause your answer to change?
2. How is the value of information determined? If you received a specific piece of information today and the same piece of information tomorrow, would it have the same value on both days? If you and your best friend both received the same piece of information at the same time, would the value of the information each of you received be the same or not? Why?
3. If you have information that you wish to sell, what factors should you consider in setting a selling price? Why would the factors you identify be appropriate to include in setting a price?
4. Information and information services are said to be different in terms of economic behavior from other goods and services that are exchanged in the marketplace. What characteristics of information and information services cause the difference?
5. What are possible roles for government in the economics of information? How might one assess what role(s) are more likely to be taken up by a specific government? Why do roles taken by governments differ from country to country?

REFERENCES

Bates, Benjamin J. 1988. "Information as an Economic Good: Sources of Individual and Social Value." In *The Political Economy of Information*, edited by Vincent Mosco and Janet Wasko, 76–94. Madison, WI: University of Wisconsin Press.

Braman, Sandra. 1995. "Alternative Conceptualizations of the Information Economy." *Advances in Librarianship* 19: 99–116. New York: Academic Press.

Friedman, Thomas. 2006. *The World is Flat: A Brief History of the Twenty-first Century.* 1st updated and expanded ed. New York: Farrar, Straus & Giroux.

Kingma, Bruce R. 2001. *The Economics of Information: A Guide to Economic and Cost-Benefit Analysis for Information Professionals.* 2nd ed. Englewood, CO: Libraries Unlimited.

Krim, Jonathan. 2002. "Two Tech Programs For Poor Would Die." *Washington Post* (5 February): E1.

Moore, Nick. 1998. "Policies for an Information Society." *Aslib Proceedings* 50 (January): 20–24.

Musgrave, Richard A. 1959. *The Theory of Public Finance: A Study in Public Economy.* New York: McGraw Hill.

Samuelson, Paul A. 1954. "The Pure Theory of Public Expenditure." *Review of Economics and Statistics* 36: 387–389.

Saracevic, Tefko, and Paul B. Kantor. 1997. "Studying the Value of Library and Information Services, Part I. Establishing a Theoretical Framework." *Journal of the American Society for Information Science* 48 (June): 527–542.

Shapiro, Carl R., and Hal R. Varian. 1999. *Information Rules: A Strategic Guide to the Network Economy.* Boston: Harvard Business School Press.

Taylor, Robert S. 1986. *Value-Added Processes in Information Systems.* Norwood, NJ: Ablex.

Yourdon, Edward. 1992. *Decline & Fall of the American Programmer.* Englewood Cliffs, NJ: Yourdon Press.

———. 1996. *Rise & Resurrection of the American Programmer.* Upper Saddle River, NJ: Yourdon Press.

ADDITIONAL SOURCES

Cooper, Michael D. 1978. "Charging Users for Library Services." *Information Processing & Management* 14: 419–427.

Directgov. 2006. Available: www.direct.gov.uk (accessed December 2006).

Musgrave, Richard A. 1959. "On Merit Goods (1959)." In *Public Finance in a Democratic Society, Vol I: Social Goods, Taxation and Fiscal Policy,* 34–40. New York: New York University Press, 1986.

Musgrave, Richard A., and Peggy B. Musgrave. 1980. *Public Finance in Theory and Practice,* 3rd ed. New York: McGraw-Hill.

Nelson, Phillip. 1970. "Information and Consumer Behavior." *Journal of Political Economy* 78 (March–April): 311–329.

Repo, Aatto J. 1989. "The Value of Information: Approaches in Economics, Accounting, and Management Science." *Journal of the American Society for Information Science* 40: 68–85.

U.S. General Services Administration. Office of Citizen Services and Communications. *FirstGov*. Available: www.firstgov.gov (accessed December 2006).

U.S. Institute of Museum and Library Services. Available: www.imls.gov (accessed December 2006).

U.S. National Endowment for the Humanities. Available: www.neh.gov (accessed December 2006).

U.S. National Institutes of Health. Available: www.nih.gov (accessed December 2006).

U.S. National Science Foundation. 2006. Available: www.nsf.gov (accessed December 2006).

In chapters 1 and 8 we have referenced the use of information as a source of power in society and briefly mentioned how control of information and its use are employed by those who seek power. Chapter 1 specifically discussed information as "an instrument of influence and control in the lives of individual citizens, in the political structure of the country, and in the relationships among nations." But what does "information as power" mean? Does the power derive from the content? Or is the power inherent in the control of information more than in the actual meaning? Does information always empower those who have it? List the ways in which you have seen information used as an instrument of power in your daily affairs, by government, and in commerce. Then reflect on these questions before you read on about some of the answers that others have given to such questions.

Chapter 10

Information, Power, and Society

Learning Guide

After reading this chapter, you should be able to

- identify and explain key concepts related to information, power, and society from the following theorists and writers:

  - Bertrand de Jouvenel
  - Karl Marx
  - Max Weber
  - Hans Kelsen

  - Niccolò Machiavelli
  - Alexis de Tocqueville
  - Michel Foucault
  - Michael Harris

- discuss ways in which information and power are related, including how information may affect access to and use of power in society;

- describe ways in which use of power of the state to control information affects society;

- discuss how changes in information technology may change the relationship between power and information.

  When you have finished the chapter, return to this page to be sure you have learned what you need to know.

INTRODUCTION

What is power? Power has been defined in many different ways. We will not presume to exhaust the literature. Instead we will touch lightly on several major thinkers, particularly those who have concerned themselves with the interrelationship between power and information. Occasionally we will seek to draw other, less obvious candidates into the argument. Finally, we will not attempt to develop our own theory to explain the interrelationship between power and information; nor will we seek to suggest that one school of thought offers a better explanation (or has greater power) than another. In the review of the first edition of this book that prompted this chapter, Douglas Raber (2004) suggests that we have taken something of a Foucauldian structuralist approach. Perhaps we do favor a structuralist analysis, but that should in no way inhibit others from seeking other theoretical explanations.

THOUGHTS ON POWER

Different disciplines approach the definition and impacts of power in very different ways. For example, philosophers and political theorists have sought to understand power, information, and information in context with power. Sociologists address power relationships among individuals and between individuals (or groups of individuals) and institutions. Political scientists often, but not always, focus their attention on government, groups competing for power, and the state. They are also interested in the phenomena that enhance or inhibit the power of the state or various aspects of the state. (The definition of the word "State" is usually "country" or "nation-state," rather than the major political subdivisions [cantons, Länder, provinces, and states] found in federal countries like Australia, Brazil, Canada, Germany, Mexico, the United States, Venezuela, or others.)

Economists generally focus on a limited range of institutions, those with economic and financial influence. Others are concerned with the flow of goods and services, exchange rates, markets, value, and regulation. Much has been written in recent years on the commodification of information and the economic role information has—the economic power of information, so to speak.

Can we suggest that there are power-information interrelationships that transcend a traditional, modern, or postmodern power-information society? It is easy to say that philosophers have grappled with these and other kinds of questions since philosophy began. It is more difficult to provide a coherent theory that addresses all possible permutations of the relationship between power and information. According to one leading theoretician, "By power is meant that opportunity existing within a social relationship which permits one to carry out one's own will even against resistance and regardless of the basis on which this opportunity rests" (Weber, 1962: 117).

We point out the obvious because how one perceives power and how one perceives information very much depends on the perspective one takes. We will begin by using Max Weber's definition of power as given above. We will explore other definitions and other theories. Finally, we will relate definitions of power to our discussions of information and informing.

On Theory

Bertrand de Jouvenel (1962) and Max Weber argue (1921) that power is the exercise of the "legitimate monopoly" of violence by the state or what Hans Kelsen (1967: 7) has called the "force monopoly of the state." Jouvenel, Weber, and Kelsen recognize that the use of force has always been a component of human interaction. A part of the civilizing impulse has been the redirection of the legitimate use of force away from the individual and the vesting of that use in an abstraction—the clan, the group, an institution, the state. For Jouvenel, individuals subject themselves "voluntarily" to central authority, from which they receive benefits. The greater the need for the surrender of power to central authority, the greater is the reciprocal allocation of benefits. Jouvenel's position is reminiscent of social contract theories, perhaps best represented by Thomas Hobbes (*Leviathan*, 1651) and Jean-Jacques Rousseau (*The Social Contract, or Principles of Political Right*, 1762). According to Hobbes, people grouped together for self-protection. In so doing, they surrendered their individual autonomy to a central power. Rousseau opens his first of four books with what is perhaps his best known aphorism: "Man is born free; and everywhere he is in chains." (Rousseau, 1762) But why? Rousseau tells us that the social contract was necessary as society grew more complex. The social contract according to Rousseau is a contract with the general will. That contract protects the group while at the same time preserving individual liberties in the civil society.

Economic and political theorists have incorporated power and information, sometimes implicitly, sometimes explicitly, into their analyses. Karl Marx, it is argued, was an early contributor to the debate on the relationships among power, economics, and morality (Miller, 1984). Marx described class dynamics driven by economic engines as the basis of power in society. Power has its basis in the ruling class (Miller, 1984: Part 2). Marx's two best-known works are *Das Kapital* (2000), first published in 1867, and *The Communist Manifesto* (2005), first published in 1848, which he coauthored with Friedrich Engels.

The Communist Manifesto opens with its now famous, perhaps infamous, line "A spectre is haunting Europe—the spectre of Communism" (2005). The communist proletarian movement is in struggle for survival with the bourgeoisie and the upper classes. Marx and Engels concern themselves with the powers of production and class struggle. If information was not an important productive power in 1848, it most certainly is one today. These works elaborate Marx's labor theory of value as the determinant of capitalism as it emerged through the process of dialectical materialism. One end, according to Marx and Engels, was made explicit in *The Communist Manifesto* (2005):

> The immediate aim of the Communist is the same as that of all the other proletarian parties: formation of the proletariat into a class, overthrow of the bourgeois supremacy, conquest of political power by the proletariat.

If the role of information is less clear in the founding documents of Communism, its application as a vehicle of power and persuasion were well understood by the architects of Russian Communism, Marxism applied, if you will. V. I. Lenin, Leon Trotsky, and other Bolsheviks were very adept in the uses of propaganda to promote their ideology and as a mechanism to inculcate socialism in the Soviet Union (Theen, 1972).

Max Weber is considered one of the founders of modern sociology and public administration. Perhaps his most famous work is *The Protestant Ethic and the Spirit of Capitalism* (1930) written in 1905–1906, in which he argued that Protestantism contributed to the development of capitalism in Europe and North America. One of his major contributions to social science analysis was his development of *Ideal Types*. For Weber, ideal types are an abstraction of how institutions might be construed. The social scientist could make comparisons between the ideal type and what was actually observed in the field. Weber did not mean that the ideal type was a pure or perfect concept, but rather an idea that defines the most appropriate attributes of the type. One might, for example, ask, what is an ideal university? One might then compare Harvard or the University of Oklahoma not with one another but against the ideal. If the ideal university is one where research and scholarship are appreciated above all else, Harvard and the University of Oklahoma might compare differently to the ideal. If the ideal university is one with a winning football team, the outcome of the comparison would likely be even more different.

Weber also distinguished between power and authority. Authority implies the ability to cause others to act in a certain way based upon some legitimizing force. Power is more broadly the ability to induce behavior through legitimate or illegitimate means. Weber held that there are three forms of authority: legal authority, traditional authority, and charismatic authority. One problem with the distinction between power and authority is the ability to distinguish between the legitimate and illegitimate exercise of power. When, we might ask, did the exercise of power by the American Revolutionaries in 1776 cease to be an illegitimate challenge to the British Crown and become the legitimate action of a sovereign state? Hans Kelsen's (1967) answer to this question would have been, once the new government was able to displace the former government in its exercise of the force monopoly of the state.

Hans Kelsen (1881–1973) was one of the leading legal positivists. His concerns were not with fundamental institutional building blocks of society, but rather with jurisprudence and the theoretical basis of law. He was primarily concerned with the "ought" of the law. Law, in its purest sense, is not based in a moral code nor is it a derivative of the natural or social sciences. It has its basis in what he labeled "the Basic Norm." Norms are structured as "ought" statements. They are an expression of human will. Laws are reflections of higher norms filtered through human interpretation. Laws define behaviors that "ought" to be followed. They also define sanctions that "ought" to be brought when a law is disregarded. Although Kelsen does not explicitly acknowledge the role of information, information plays an important, if not essential, role in determining the "oughts."

INFORMATION AS POWER

If money is the currency of economics, power is the currency of politics. Our concepts of "money" have grown beyond precious metals, stone rings, seashells, or whatever else human beings have valued as a medium of exchange to an abstracted use of tokens ("money") that represent value. If "money" is an abstraction, "power" is an order of magnitude more abstract. If information equals power ($i = p$), does it necessarily hold that power equals information ($p = i$)? Perhaps the associative laws of algebra would hold were we able to sufficiently quantify "p" and "i." But as we have suggested throughout this text, there are many definitions of "information." There are more still for "power." We can speak of political, economic, cultural, sexual, and personal power. Power concepts have been addressed by philosophers since the time of the early Greeks. Let us examine a few of these.

Plato, in *The Republic*, provided a guide to utopian society based upon power vested in aristocratic or oligarchic governance. Society would be best guided and ruled by a wise, hereditary Guardian class, which would exercise power legitimately.

Aristotle provides us with a highly personalized use of power:

> Now if it is in our power to do noble or base acts, and likewise in our power not to do them, and this was what being good or bad meant, then it is in our power to be virtuous or vicious. (*Nicomachean Ethics*, Book III, Chapter 5)

To attain and maintain power by controlling information flows, Niccolò Machiavelli offered in the early sixteenth century the following decision-making theory in *The Prince*, first published in 1513:

> Because there is no other way of guarding oneself from flatterers except letting men understand that to tell you the truth does not offend you; but when every one may tell you the truth, respect for you abates.
>
> Therefore a wise prince ought to hold a third course by choosing the wise men in his state, and giving to them only the liberty of speaking the truth to him, and then only of those things of which he inquires, and of none others; but he ought to question them upon everything, and listen to their opinions, and afterwards form his own conclusions. (Machiavelli, *The Prince*, Chapter 25)

Machiavelli's advice can be read to imply several different "information as power" dynamics. The decision maker, here the prince, determines to whom he or she will listen as well as the context in which he or she listens. Advisors to the prince also have power, albeit a more limited power. They first must consent to advise the prince. They also control to some degree the "what" and the "how" of the advice they do consent to impart if and when they are consulted by the prince. It remains to the prince, however, to act, to exert power based on that advice. Hence both the advisers and the prince hold power through the holding and use of information.

Machiavelli provided divine right monarchs with advice on how to maintain power through use and control of information. In a different approach, Alexis de Tocqueville provided analysis on how to moderate power. One can read Tocqueville's *Democracy in America,* written in the 1830s, to mean that multiple information channels (books, newspapers) as well as inter-layered social institutions (schools, church, family), some of which are information institutions, protect democracy and limit the abilities of a tyrant to emerge and act. Thus dispersion of information can be seen to disperse the holding and exercise of power.

Contrast Tocqueville's analysis of the foundations of democracy with Hannah Arendt's (1951) analysis of the foundations of totalitarianism. Totalitarianism's chief characteristic is the use of terror to achieve political ends. Incorporated into that use of terror is the systematic destruction of independent social institutions (schools, family, the church, the press, the academy, etc.) that might compete with the state for social and political power. The grip of totalitarianism is so pervasive that the act of thinking "wrong thoughts" is subversive. Thus to nurture democracy, competing information sources are needed to moderate power. To sustain totalitarianism, rigid central state control over information and ultimately over the thought processes of the citizenry is essential. As an afterthought, the collapse of the Soviet Union in 1991 suggests one of two possibilities. Either independent social institutions were too strong and ingrained, in the final analysis, to ultimately submit to state power; or the Communist Party of the Soviet Union did not, in the end, exert sufficient force to overcome those institutions and to prevent access to alternative sources of information.

R. J. Rummel (1976: 2, 19) offers a complex definition of power:

> First, power is the linkage between different states of being; between potentialities and actualities, between dispositions and manifestations, and between determinables and determinants (specifics).
>
> Second, that linkage is a strength-of-becoming, an active will-to-completeness. It is a push from the level of pure potentiality, of mere possibility, to ever greater levels of clarity and definiteness.
>
> Third, it is an imminent energy, an inherent force-towards-identity of all beings.
>
> Fourth, it is a *vector* whose *direction* is towards greater specificity, determinateness, completeness, identity, and whose *magnitude* is the strength-of-becoming, will-to-completeness, and force-towards-identity of a being. This is saying that power has a direction—it is "pointed" at something—and strength to actualize a potential of some kind. Thus, the use of the concept "vector." Power itself is a basic ontological concept and, like being, indefinable. However, we can bracket its qualities to provide meaning and understanding of its nature, and thus power functions as "linkage," as "will-to-completeness," as imminent "energy," as "strength-of-becoming," and as "force-towards-identity."
>
> Finally, in essence, power is a *vector-towards-manifestation*.

We began with a definition of power as the ability to make things happen and end with one that describes power as a vector. These definitions have one thread in common. Power is to be applied with purpose, a "force-towards-identity." The exercise of power is in itself an informing function.

As seen through these various definitions, the exercise of power does not necessarily require the use of violent force. Vested authority may exercise power by virtue of position. We come to understand that our actions carry consequences related to the power relationships in the societies in which we live. Authority and the exercise of authority through action are transmitted as a function of social information. The transmission of information provides both force and vector in the application of power and responses to that application of power.

Occam's Razor

Mathematicians like to speak of "elegant solutions" to their problems. The simpler theorem is the better theorem. "Occam's razor," simply put, is that the simpler proof, the one that requires the fewest elements, is preferable to and probably more "true" than the more complex.

> We could still imagine that there is a set of laws that determines events completely for some supernatural being, who could observe the present state of the universe without disturbing it. However, such models of the universe are not of much interest to us mortals. It seems better to employ the principle known as Occam's razor and cut out all the features of the theory that cannot be observed. (Hawking, 1998: 71)

The sociologist Claude Lévi-Strauss (1958: 57) introduced Occam's razor to the study of structuralism (more on structuralism below). He held that

> it is obvious that the best model will always be that which is *true*, that is, the simplest possible model which, while being derived exclusively from the facts under consideration, also makes it possible to account for all of them. Therefore, the first task is to ascertain what those facts are.

Applying Lévi-Strauss's and Hawking's arguments to matters more mundane than astrophysics and myth, we might suggest that the simpler any argument is, the less information it demands to be valid, the more powerful it is. "Power" in this context has to do with the explanatory ability of an argument. This view of the relationship between power and information appears at first glance to be inverse to what one would expect. Here "less information" leads to "more power"—a reminder that the equation $i = p$ does not imply that the variables necessarily have equal coefficients.

From Heraclitus to Hawking

Both power and information vary and change. They vary and change both in terms of their inherent quality and in terms of their relevance and impact. The fifth century BCE Greek philosopher Heraclitus is credited with the aphorism here paraphrased as "you cannot step into the same river twice" (see, for example, Kahn, 1979). In essence, Heraclitus believed that there was no constant save change. Information changes; power changes. Information changes us and changes power relationships. Power changes information and it changes us. As we have seen throughout this work there are multiple definitions of information and its use, development, and application. There are an equally diverse number of definitions of power.

We can take a cosmic view of power and information. The universe is in flux, whether it was created by a Big Bang or by Intelligent Design. As Heraclitus did indeed observe, the one observable constant is change, which is, of course, an apparent contradiction.

Quantum mechanics tells us that we cannot achieve absolute predictive ability over any given particle's position or velocity in a complex system. Known as the uncertainty principle, that particle's actions cannot be known until they are observed. How that particle may subsequently act cannot be known with absolute certainty. Absolute predictability at the subatomic level as well as at the human systems level or, for that matter, at any level of abstraction is impossible. While we cannot do a particularly good job predicting the actions of a single particle, we can approach but never quite achieve absolute predictability of aggregates within a system. These may include voting behavior of particular groups in a society or the movement of molecules in an experiment. Instead of particles, let us consider voters. Given certain demographics, a political pollster can predict within a certain error range the number of votes that will be cast for one candidate over another. That same pollster can also predict the probability that any given voter will vote (or not vote) for any given candidate or at all. The pollster cannot know with absolute certainty how that individual voter will behave, very much in the same way the physicist cannot predict the path and the speed of any given subatomic particle. Hence, in this analysis, access to information about an event, prior to the event, which would give power to the holder of the information, is not possible.

Existentialism and Structuralism

Existentialism at its root is concerned with individual rationality in an irrational universe. Human beings are essentially powerless no matter the degree to which we experience and understand the "reality" outside of ourselves. While we experience "the world," the conclusions we may derive based on those experiences are as absurd as the information upon which they are based. In his novel *La Nausée*, published in 1938, Jean-Paul Sartre (1972a) was to argue that our ideas are derived from our experiences. Perhaps so, but our attempt to anthropomorphize that externality is meaningless. Indeed inani-

mate objects, inanimate as they are, are inherently indifferent to human beings. In *Le Mur*, published in 1939, and set during the Spanish Civil War,
Sartre (1972b) painted word pictures of the impossibility of people trying to
act rationally in response to the irrational. Albert Camus (1985) was to emphasize the absurdity and meaningless of life (*Le Mythe de Sisyphe*, first published in 1942). For Camus, science was a futile exercise in an equally futile
effort to seek the truth. Sisyphus was the antiheroic figure of Greek mythology
forever condemned to roll a rock up a hill to have the rock roll back before
reaching the top. The myth is a metaphor for futility. For the existentialist, science imitates art imitates life. Our sources of information are varied, and all
are equally incomprehensible despite our best efforts to comprehend them.

If existentialism is about the powerlessness of the individual in the face
of irrationalism, structuralism is about the power of institutions in the face
of rationalism. Structuralism contradicts the basic existentialist assumptions of
human freedom and looks to the cultural determinates (structures) that dictate human behavior (e.g., Lévi-Strauss, 1969). Structuralism grew out of
Ferdinand de Saussure's *Cours de linguistique générale* (1972), first published
in 1916, and the work of subsequent scholars in the structures of linguistic
analysis. Structuralists and linguistic structuralists seek to understand the
symbolic and semiotic impact on human action by defined structures.
Among these cultural structures are information, information packages, and
the means by which information is communicated within a society. Structures, because they influence or direct human behavior, empower and are
empowered by that behavior. Claude Lévi-Strauss (1969) was to argue that
language and myth are the primary "carriers" of the collective conscience, the
underlying structure of human behavior. If language and myth are among
the determinants of human behavior, then information serves to fuel those
determinants. Lévi-Strauss would argue later that "[a]lthough they belong
to *another order of reality*, kinship phenomena are *of the same type* as linguistic phenomena" (1958: 34). Recall that Alexis de Tocqueville argued that
family (a kinship phenomenon) was one of several social institutions that
intermediate between the individual and the state, thereby buffering the
power of the state. At the same time, the press, books, and other information sources (linguistic phenomena, perhaps) are strong intermediaries as
well. If, however, the state can replace intermediating social structures with
itself, the relationship between self and state is redefined in the worst case to
totalitarianism. The state, where it is predisposed and permitted to do so,
manipulates information to overcome the power of intermediating social
structures.

Michel Foucault (1926–1984) might be described as a historian of the science of thought. We have Foucault classed as a structuralist and postmodernist. He described himself as a post-structuralist and later rejected that label as well (Raulet, 1983). Information and knowledge, the "statement" as seen by Foucault, have a more heterogeneous function, in opposition to the more homogenous interpretation of his European colleagues. It is this difference that set him apart from the structuralists. However, as we describe Foucault and his work, he has very much set the stage for discourse on power, information, and knowledge in the late twentieth and early twenty-first centuries.

Above all else, Foucault (1966) is concerned with power. Power, for Foucault, is manifested in how society is structured. Power also lies in having knowledge because that knowledge imparts authority in both senses of the word to the holder of knowledge. If power is, as Foucault (Foucault, Ewald, Fontana, and Senellart, 2004: 355) has defined it, *"une action sur des actions"* (an action on actions), it provides structure to the discourse and behaviors of others.

Foucault (1969) was particularly interested in the power of discourse, of the statement (*énoncé*). It is the "statement, the "*énoncé*," that gives meaning to speech, to discourse. Statements are precursors to rules. For Foucault, then, the *énoncé* is an important function of information that sets the stage, in the end, for political action. Finally, it should be noted that Foucault (1976) was interested in the *science of sexuality* and its impact on politics.

Michael Harris provides another way of conceptualizing the connection between information and power, although he uses the institution of the library as the means through which information enables the exercise of control. Harris (1995) posits that there are three societal factors that influenced the kinds of libraries found in the "ancient world." These are social conditions, economic conditions, and political conditions. He argues that on the whole "libraries will flourish generally in those societies where economic prosperity reigns, where the population is literate and stable, where the government supports library growth, where large urban areas exist, and where book trade is well established" (Harris, 1995: 5).

Harris further argues that a positive ideology supporting a book culture is critical. These ideologies can be addressed "under three broad headings: control, memory, and commodity" (1995: 6–7). By control, Harris means that social elites utilize books (and other media) to control and form public opinion. Libraries are a necessary adjunct to that control. Libraries serve the memory function by contributing to the preservation of national identities, perhaps collection development with a purpose. They are also a mechanism through which researchers may clarify and sometimes redefine that national identity. The commodity value of libraries lies in their inherent ability to make markets for intellectual material. Libraries create a subsidy for "cultural commodities" by helping to underwrite scholarly enquiry as well as more pedestrian interests.

Harris bases his argument on the work of the sociologist Claude Lévi-Strauss. Lévi-Strauss was to argue that there is an inherent relationship between power and information, just as Tocqueville did a century before. For Tocqueville, one of the strengths of the American system of governance was the existence of competing mechanisms, including information channels, between the individual and government. Those mechanisms served to moderate the impact of state power on the individual.

Information Ideas

Information as Power in Religion and Mythology

One of the earliest examples of information as power with all of the complex issues related to this dynamic is in the biblical (*Genesis* 2 and 3) story of Adam and Eve, who were forbidden to eat the fruit of the tree of knowledge of good and evil. Such prohibition is certainly one of the earliest uses of control of information, since, according to the biblical story, if Adam and Eve ate the fruit they would have the same knowledge (information) of good and evil as the Hebrew god. Gaining access to the knowledge by violating the prohibition (or breaking the rules, as discussed in this chapter) had dire consequences, although the transgressors did not die, as was threatened. In this case, in contrast to what is usually expected, having information worsened the plight of the individuals who had it.

Another mythological story that suggests harm done by seeking information is the Greek myth of Pandora and her box. The story is generally couched in terms of curiosity—but what is that but the seeking of information? In this case, negative power is released by the action of seeking information: Pandora opening the box and releasing all the harmful elements placed there by the gods. As in many present-day situations, the relationship between information and power in this story is shaped by the context, rather than by the inherent characteristics, of information itself.

Athena, the Greek goddess of wisdom, is usually portrayed with a helmet and a spear, suggesting again a strong connection between wisdom (a more evolved form of information) and power. Of course, Athena was also goddess of war.

INFORMATION AND POWER

Throughout this book we have explored social, political, and economic processes and institutions that are interrelated with information and the informing process. In this chapter, we seek to explain information and its relationship to power. Notions of power and information have been explored from a variety of theoretical perspectives. Let us now turn to a consideration of power in its various manifestations and the various aspects of informing we have presented.

If we were to sum up the definitions of power, we would suggest that power is about the ability to compel. Those who exercise power may do so legitimately or illegitimately, and power may be exercised on a grand scale or on a very small scale.

Let us consider the relationship between power and compelling. Power might better be understood in degrees of the ability to compel. First, if indeed we are invested with free will, we can decline to be compelled. When we decline to be compelled, we ought to consider the consequences of that action. For there to be consequences, someone with the authority to determine that a delict has been committed must so determine. Authority must then impose the sanction. Following Kelsen's arguments discussed earlier in this chapter, this process is fraught with a series of "oughts." The "malefactor" ought to have obeyed (or ought not to have disobeyed), the digression ought to have been detected, and appropriate sanctions ought to be brought against the malefactor. The equation is never absolute; there is always uncertainty involved.

The degree to which any institution can compel human behavior varies widely. Recall the social contract theories. Our relationship with the state, with government, is of a higher order than our ties to many other social institutions. The social contract between the state and the individual is assumed to be implicit. In other circumstances it is more explicit. When a group of children band together to play a game, they agree to abide by the rules of the game. Or when an adult joins a social organization or decides to play chess with a friend, that adult is bound by a certain set of rules. What are the consequences of changing the rules or deciding not to belong or to play? One consequence is a new game. In 1925, Harold Vanderbilt revised the rules of auction bridge (a game that evolved from whist) to create a new variation, contract bridge. The three-point shot in basketball was introduced in 1961. Basketball itself did not exist until 1891. Both contract bridge and basketball have millions of adherents, all dependent to some degree on rules and rules changes.

In other settings, the consequences of changing the rules or not obeying the rules may be more serious. One need not follow the rules established by an employer, but if the employee does transgress those rules he or she may lose his or her employment. Except in very exceptional cases, that individual is unlikely to incarcerated, fined, or executed. Hence, the individual may choose to opt out of some social arrangements with minimal sanctions, from others with significant consequences, and from a few with truly catastrophic implications. Break the rules of society and the legal system may impose fines, prison sentences, or worse. Break the rules of international behavior and war may result.

Information is very intimately related with the ability to compel. Indeed, it is the information concerning consequences of failure to follow the rules that gives those rules power. Further, it is the information about the rules that ensures attention to them in the first place. Beyond these inherent relationships there are further issues of control related to information and the power of the institutions that exercise control.

Exercise of Power over Information

One first formal application of state power to the control of information came in the form of license and censorship. A further refinement, the British Statute of Anne of 1710, was the first to formally define copyright. The Statute of Anne extended copyright of then contemporary works to authors or those to whom copyright was transferred for a period of twenty-one years, with a fourteen-year extension if the author(s) were still living. As John Feather (1994) demonstrates, before 1710, books were published under license to the Crown. The license served to effect two ends. The first was to protect the monopoly held by the licensed publisher. The second was to ensure that only those materials that had been approved by censors, the licensing agency, could be legally published. Other European countries followed similar licensing functions.

Today, under the Berne Convention and other copyright acts, copyright does not provide a vetting function. It is only in most recent years that the liberal democratic governments of western Europe and North America have not attempted to exercise some large degree of censorship. In the late 1920s, James Joyce's *Ulysses* was challenged as obscene in the United States. In his 1930 opinion, Judge Augustus Noble Hand of the Second U.S. Circuit Court of Appeals set the standard for obscene works in his decision in favor of the book. The standard he proposed was that a work had to be evaluated on the whole rather than on isolated passages (*United States v. One Book Entitled Ulysses by James Joyce*, 72 F.(2d)705). Based on that standard, *Ulysses* was not obscene. As late as 1960, books like Henry Miller's *Tropic of Cancer* could not be legally imported into the United States. In 1959, the U.S. Post Office sought to prohibit the delivery of postcards mailed from Spain with stamps on which Goya's *Nude Maja* painting was reproduced as obscene (U.S. Postal Service, 1959).

To this day, the U.S. government continues to regulate nudity and profanity over the airwaves; witness recent Federal Communications Commission decisions against Howard Stern and Janet Jackson and the networks that carried them. European countries have more liberal stands. "Wardrobe" mishaps are not of so great a consequence in Western Europe, where advertising often incorporates female upper torso frontal nudity as an acceptable marketing tool.

However, symbols are powerful, and the symbolism conveyed in information products can represent as well as perpetuate the power relationships within society. Catharine MacKinnon (1989) posits that state power and male power are one and the same thing. Sexual harassment through rape is manifestation of the exercise of male power over females reified in law. Pornography and other sexual communication might equally serve as a cultural phenomenon for one segment of society to dominate another (MacKinnon and Dworkin, 1998). Similarly, behaviors that denigrate racial, ethnic, and religious differences would also represent the social dominance of one group over others. We play lip service to "political correctness," but it is too often observed in its breach.

The clash of one culture with another can be destabilizing. Catharine MacKinnon and Andrea Dworkin (1998) militate for the rights of the sexually oppressed over those of the pornographer. Few of us would argue within the cultural context of the United States in the third millennium that pornography is a social good. Attacks on pornography are at the same time attacks on the freedom of expression. For the time being, the line has been drawn against pornography that incorporates children or representations of children. Whether the line has been drawn correctly is a cultural and political question for societies to address.

In general, censorship has usually taken a more political than moral direction. Authoritarian and totalitarian governments have been particularly vigilant to control political speech. As we discuss in other chapters, even liberal democratic governments may exercise some control over certain classes of materials. The French and German governments, for example, prohibit anti-Semitic and pro-Nazi materials.

Interpersonal communications present us with an interesting case study. For most of their history, telephony, telegraphy, and the mail were either highly regulated monopolies or they were controlled directly by government. The trend over the last quarter of the twentieth century in many countries was to either deregulate these industries or, where they were government entities, to spin them off into the private sector. Postal services are the exception that makes the rule. Many postal systems, the U.S. Postal Service among them, may still be government owned. They are, however, now expected to compete in the marketplace and to act like private entities.

The television and radio industries were once very stringently regulated, and aside from the United States, most countries retained ownership of some portion of their domestic broadcast industries. Like the telephone company and the post office, broadcasting has been deregulated in some parts of the world and the airwaves have been relaxed to permit private-sector broadcasters to compete with government-owned stations. In certain sectors, because of social concerns, some governments have begun to more closely regulate the broadcast industry. For example, the U.S. Federal Communications Commission began tightening and enforcing its obscenity rules in the early 2000s by restricting the use of the "seven bad words" and by taking a dim view of "wardrobe malfunctions." Often social needs and concerns are used as justification to implement these programs—social morals, community standards, and most recently the protection of minors. At other times or in other places a different set of criteria are used to regulate the various media. These have ranged from a sense of good or bad taste to defamation of political symbols or the state. The penalties imposed have ranged from monetary fines or license forfeiture to imprisonment and execution. Theocracies have been particularly harsh in controlling speech—consider the Inquisition, the Reformation, and the Counter-Reformation in the west or the interpretation of Islam in the twentieth-century Middle East.

Another area in which the state seeks to exercise control over information is in the cultural content of information distributed or used within the country. For example, the Canadian Broadcasting Act of 1991 stipulates:

> the Canadian broadcasting system should encourage the development of Canadian expression by providing a wide range of programming that reflects Canadian attitudes, opinions, ideas, values and artistic creativity, by displaying Canadian talent in entertainment programming and by offering information and analysis concerning Canada and other countries from a Canadian point of view . . . the programming originated by broadcasting undertakings should be of high standard. (Section 3.(1)(d)(ii) and (g))

Why does Canada need legislation to "encourage the development of Canadian expression"? Perhaps it is because Canadian culture was once so dominated by the United Kingdom and is now heavily influenced by the United States. How are "Canadian attitudes, opinions, ideas, values and artistic creativity" determined? What is Canadian talent? What is meant by "high standard"? These questions, implementation, and enforcement are left to the Canadian Radio-Television and Telecommunications Commission to determine.

Canada is a complex country. Like the United States, it has a federal structure. And like the United States, Canada is the result of European colonization where the British were, in the end, the dominant imperial power. Unlike the United States, Canadian independence from British political control was not the result of violent revolution but through more of a peaceful evolution. The seat of the federal government is Ottawa. The country is divided into provinces and territories. Quebec is largely French speaking; the other provinces are largely English speaking. In addition, there are significant native populations. The federal and provincial governments are parliamentary in form rather than presidential.

Canada has had its share of regional cultural, political, and economic stresses and disequilibria. And it has often found itself in the shadows of its southern neighbor, the United States. That said, however, the country has a strong tradition of respecting civil liberties.

Why, then, does Canada feel the need for legislation to require Canadian content in its commercial broadcast mix? There are several answers to this question. First, most Canadians live well within the television broadcast reach of the border. The United States is the preeminent producer of entertainment programming. That programming reaches both Canadian and U.S. markets with no heed to boundaries. Simply because of the economies of scale, the Canadian broadcast entertainment industry does not have the same effect as the U.S. industry. Recall too that the implementing legislation stipulates a requirement of high broadcast standards. "High standards" are difficult to define. The U.S. entertainment industry is not generally perceived to produce a relatively high proportion of "high standard" output. Is *I Love Lucy* or Garth Brooks' music "high standard" material? The actor Lorne Greene (1915–1987), well known for his iconic roles in the television series *Bonanza* and *Battlestar Galactica* as well as other major roles, was Canadian born. When Canadian content regulations were first implemented in the 1970s, programming that featured Canadian-born actors, like Lorne Greene, met the test for Canadian content, wherever it was produced.

To put this discussion in the context of this chapter, the U.S. industry is significantly more powerful than is the Canadian simply as a result of relative size. To counter that power, the Canadian federal government may believe that one way to redress that imbalance is to require some degree of Canadian content in the broadcast mix. This represents the use of political power to offset economic power, the use of control of information to bolster cultural power.

France is another example of a country seeking to protect its cultural heritage by formally seeking to limit the effects of foreign influences. The

Académie française, founded in 1635, has as part of its mandate to protect and maintain the purity of the French language. The *Conseil supérieur de la langue française* establishes usage and ratifies orthographic changes. In 1990, for example, the *Conseil supérieur* revised its rules for compound words, standardized plurals for certain words, and the introduction of words of foreign origin. It also modified the use of accent marks. The *Académie française* has been wrongfully accused of prohibiting absolutely the introduction of foreign words into the French language. It has, however, sought to closely regulate and limit those terms sometimes by seeking French terms to fulfill language needs in transition. The *Académie française* Web site provides examples of unacceptable terms and their acceptable French: "On ne dit plus *tie-break* mais *jeu décisif, baladeur* replace *walkman, logiciel* se substitue à *software,* etc." This translates into English as "One no longer says *tie-break,* but *jeu décisif, baladeur* replaces *walkman, logiciel* is substituted for *software,* etc." (*Académie française*).

Is society restructured by imposing broadcast quotas or by vetting vocabulary? How important is it to favor k. d. lang (a Canadian) over Loretta Lynn (an American) in broadcast play or to insist on *fin-de-semaine* rather than *le weekend?* Are these efforts, found in Canada, France, and elsewhere in the world, more symbolic than substantive?

Government efforts to maintain the status quo are efforts to restrain structural changes in society and therefore implicitly in government. These policies are mechanisms to underpin and maintain the fundamental concepts that cement a society as defined by its culture and its language.

The degree to which free speech and intellectual freedoms are abridged varies from place to place and time to time. Recall Michael Harris's argument (1995: 4–5) that the three societal factors—social conditions, economic conditions, and political conditions—influenced the kinds of libraries found in the "ancient world." These same factors influence not only libraries but all other information entities in our postmodern postindustrial contemporary world.

It has already been suggested that government policies are undergoing change. Government has also been challenged by new technology. There are demands placed on government to more closely guard digital rights by the producers of entertainment and to protect traditional free access standards on the other.

POWER AND TECHNOLOGY

The introduction of new technology has information consequences. As we have seen, there have been several watershed changes, beginning with the invention of writing, paper, the codex, the press, the steam engine, the telegraph, the telephone, the internal combustion gasoline engine, radio, television, and now the

Internet. Each of these new technologies has had consequences for society and the way in which power is used and distributed in society. Generally speaking, those elites and other segments of society that have been able to adapt new technologies to promote their interests have been more able to maintain or improve status, while those who have not been so successful have declined. We do not suggest that successful technological adaptation is the sine qua non for other successes, but it is most certainly a major aid.

Several examples of successful adaptation have been given in earlier chapters. Among these are the contribution of the codex and the printing press to competing religious groups. The ability to maintain records permits societies to grow more complex. The ability to communicate instantaneously at a distance allows the exercise of power by traditional as well as new segments of society in ways not before imagined. New technologies have bred new industries and have permitted existing enterprises to create and amass wealth again in ways not before imagined.

These new technologies have created social webs interlinking human beings and societies beyond the traditional "here and now" to a much wider interrelationship based upon those communications links. The greater and more efficient the technology, the greater is the expanse of the social web. Writing in 1893, Émile Durkheim (1984) argued that society is not a disintegrated set of atomized units, but rather it is made up of individual members linked together with ties that supersede immediate interactions. These ties lead to functioning communities. The more expansive and efficient the communications mechanisms that link the ties, the larger a society can become.

Moreover, those nonelites who are successful in adapting and manipulating information technologies may displace, replace, or compete with old elites. In so doing, they become new elites. As a result, social structures must be adapted, enhanced, or changed to respond to new realities. In recent years we have witnessed significant changes in the information economy and its regulation. International institutions have either been strengthened or created to respond to broader regulatory needs. These include the World Intellectual Property Organization (WIPO) and the World Trade Organization (WTO). The Internet Corporation for Assigned Names and Numbers (ICANN) is one of the more recent additions, established to assist in the globalization of and exponential increase in Internet use. (See discussion of these organizations in the next chapter.)

A second but equally important trend has been the vertical and horizontal consolidation of more traditional information elites. As shown in several chapters, there have been key consolidations in the publishing, newspaper, broadcast, and entertainment industries. There have been similar, if less spectacular, concentrations in the computer hardware and software industries.

At the same time, there has been a strong trend toward deregulation of various information industries by government. This trend, often credited to U.S. President Ronald Reagan and U.K. Prime Minister Margaret Thatcher, began during the presidency of Jimmy Carter. The Carter administration undertook the deregulation of the U.S. airline industry, a process still playing out. The deregulatory urge removed structural impediments to the consolidations witnessed in the information industries while punishing those firms that had successfully adapted to the status quo ante.

As a result of changes in technology and the regulatory environment, old elites found themselves competing with successful upstarts—AT&T with Sprint, Eastern Airlines et al. with Southwest et al.—or with completely new industries: Amazon.com, eBay, Dell Computers, Microsoft, America Online, and so on. These new firms rank among the new elite. Not only are some of them inordinately wealthy; they are also powerful.

Social Capital

Social capital consists of the sum of at least semi-institutionalized social networks that the parties to an exchange recognize. Pierre Bourdieu (1986) posits three types of capital: economic, cultural, and social. Economic capital concepts are too limited, he argues, to account for the sum of all exchanges. Others apply a wider definition. Francis Fukuyama (1999a) speaks in terms of trust. John Field (2003) suggests that social networks create social cohesion, which in turn creates social capital.

Social capital has value. The networks that permit social cohesion are anchored by various institutional nodes. These nodes gain or lose importance as society and technology change. Robert Damien (1995) and Dorit Raines (1996) each suggest, for example, that the library was the primary information node in seventeenth-century Europe. Libraries continue to exist into the twenty-first century and continue to serve as information nodes, but they are by no means primary.

Francis Fukuyama (1995a, 1999a) has extensively explored social value and the networks upon which it is established. Social capital consists of "an instantiated informal norm that promotes cooperation between two or more individuals" (Fukuyama 1999b: 25). Social capital can have positive values between individuals and yet have negative general social values. Issues of trust are inherently intertwined throughout the networks. Societies that promote trust beyond smaller units have positive and negative advantages over those that have smaller trust arenas.

Fukuyama (2004) extends his analysis of social capital to the international stage in his *State-Building: Governance and World Order in the 21st Century*. He concerns himself with definitions of "stateness" and the implications of weak states and their impacts on international structures. Weak states contribute to the instability of the international order. To undergird weak states and reduce international instabilities, strong states may find it necessary to intervene. Stateness, stability, and trust are inherently intertwined (Fukuyama, 1995b).

Trust, we suggest, has a strong informing component and eases cooperative behavior among participants who not only trust one another, but are also able to communicate that trust to the group. Thus a final element of power may lie in the ability to enhance or diminish the sense of trust and to communicate those changes. We would suggest that as technological aspects of the informing function expand so can the radius of the trust arenas.

CONCLUSION

This chapter has as its focus the relationship between power and information. As we have seen, both power and information are defined in very different ways. The purpose of a book such as this one is not to argue for one set of explanations over another or even to provide a holistic definition of the interrelationship between power and information. Our purpose has been to introduce the reader to the wide variety of different definitions and interpretations.

If, in its final analysis, power is the ability to compel through either positive or negative means (carrots and sticks), information in some of its manifestations is the mechanism used to inform such compelling. Yet, threats and inducements may not only prove to be empty in some cases; their impotence may also be known. What, then, is the "power" of a known empty threat?

In *Our Posthuman Future*, Francis Fukuyama (2002) raises some very interesting questions concerning the effects of nanotechnology, genetic engineering, and new pharmaceuticals and their abilities to control human behavior. We could add innovations in the information technologies to that list. These technologies might be employed by governments to promote democratic or antidemocratic ends. They might also be employed by corporations to promote competitive or anticompetitive motives.

One response to these perceived technological threats to our definitions of self and our definitions of humanness might be to increase national and necessarily international regulation of these emerging technologies. There are already debates surrounding the appropriateness of human stem cell research and human cloning. In the United States there is some significant resistance to both. But in other jurisdictions, there is greater acceptance.

The purpose of this chapter is not to explain power in terms of information or information in terms of power. Instead, we have touched—often too briefly—on major social and economic theories that explain both power and information in common terms. We recognize that because both power and information are abstractions, it is possible to expand the definitions of both to the point that the one can be substituted for the other. Once that happens, any explanatory power the one has for the other becomes lost.

That said, the two are intimately interrelated. To understand power we must understand information. The exercise of power limits the exercise of information, yet without information there would be no power.

We should end with these words from Shakespeare: *"There are more things in heaven and earth, Horatio, Than are dreamt of in your philosophy"* (Hamlet I, v, 166–67).

QUESTIONS FOR CONSIDERATION

1. Consider the various information sources the typical citizen encounters on a daily basis. Who controls those sources? How effective is that control? What is the context of the control?
2. What kind of power do the creators of information have? Are there controls on that power?
3. The famous quotation from Lord Acton says, "Power corrupts, and absolute power corrupts absolutely." If information = power, does information corrupt? How so? Is there such a thing as "absolute information"?
4. If controls on information by the government are one form of maintaining the power of government, does it necessarily follow that loss of control of information leads to loss of power of government?
5. In what ways does technology alter the relationship between information and power?

REFERENCES

Académie française. Available: www.academie-francaise.fr (accessed June 2006).

Arendt, Hannah. 1951. *The Origins of Totalitarianism.* New York: Harcourt, Brace and World.

Aristotle. 350 BCE. *Nicomachean Ethics.* Translated by W. D. Ross. Cambridge, MA: The Internet Classics Archive. Available: http://classics.mit.edu/Aristotle/nicomachaen.html (accessed December 2006).

Bourdieu, Pierre. 1986. "The Forms of Capital." In *Handbook of Theory and Research for the Sociology of Education*, edited by John Richardson, 241–258. New York: Greenwood Press.

Camus, Albert. 1985. *Le Mythe de Sisyphe.* Paris: Gallimard. First published 1942.

Canada. Department of Justice. 2003. "Broadcasting Act, 1991, c. 11." Available: http://laws.justice.gc.ca/en/b-9.01/text.html (accessed December 2006).

Damien, Robert. 1995. *Bibliothèque et État: Naissance d'une Raison Politique dans la France du VXIIe Siècle*. Paris: Presses Universitaires de France.

Durkheim, Émile. 1984. *The Division of Labor in Society*. Translated by W. D. Halls. New York: Free Press. Originally published 1893 as *De la division du travail social: étude sur l'organisation des sociétés supérieures*.

Feather, John. 1994. *Publishing, Piracy, and Politics: An Historical Study of Copyright in Britain*. London: Mansell.

Field, John. 2003. *Social Capital*. London: Routledge.

Foucault, Michel. 1966. *Les Mots et les Choses: Un Archéologie des Sciences Humaines*. Paris: Gallimard.

———. 1969. *L'Archéologie du Savoir*. Paris: Gallimard.

———. 1976. *Histoire de la Sexualité*. Vol. 1, *La Volonté de Savoir*. Paris: Gallimard.

Foucault, Michel, Francois Ewald, Alessandro Fontana, and Michel Senellart. 2004. *Naissance de la Biopolitique: Cours au Collège de France (1978–1979)*. Paris: Gallimard.

Fukuyama, Francis. 1992. *The End of History and the Last Man*. New York: Free Press.

———. 1995a. *Trust: The Social Virtues and the Creation of Prosperity*. New York: Free Press.

———. 1995b. "Social Capital and the Global Economy." *Foreign Affairs* 74 (September/October): 89–103.

———. 1999a. *The Great Disruption: Human Nature and the Reconstitution of Social Order*. New York: Free Press.

———. 1999b. "Social Order and Civil Society." *IMF Conference on Second Generation Reforms*, 8–9 November, Washington, DC. Available: www.imf.org/external/pubs/ft/seminar/1999/reforms/fukuyama.htm#I (accessed December 2006).

———. 2002. *Our Posthuman Future: Consequences of the Biotechnology Revolution*. New York: Farrar, Straus & Giroux.

———. 2004. *State-Building: Governance and World Order in the 21st Century*. Ithaca, NY: Cornell University Press.

Harris, Michael H. 1995. *History of Libraries in the Western World*. 4th ed. Metuchen, NJ: Scarecrow.

Hawking, Stephen W. 1998. *A Brief History of Time*. Updated and expanded tenth anniversary edition. New York: Bantam.

Hobbes, Thomas. 1651 [2002]. *Leviathan, or The Matter, Forme, & Power of a Common-Wealth Ecclesiastical and Civill*. Project Gutenberg e-book

3207. Available: www.gutenberg.org/dirs/etext02/lvthn10.txt. Originally published London: Andrew Crooke, at the Green Dragon (accessed December 2006).

Jouvenel, Bertrand de. 1962. *On Power: Its Nature and the History of Its Growth*. Boston, MA: Beacon Press.

Kahn, Charles. 1979. *The Art and Thought of Heraclitus: Fragments with Translation and Commentary*. London: Cambridge University Press.

Kelsen, Hans. 1967. *Pure Theory of Law*. Translated from the 2nd rev. and enlarged German edition by Max Knight. Berkeley, CA: University of California Press. Originally published 1934.

Lévi-Strauss, Claude. 1958. *Structural Anthropology*. Translated by Claire Jacobson and Brooke Grundfest Schoepf. London: Allen Lane. Originally published as *Anthropologie structurale*.

————. 1966. *The Savage Mind*. Chicago: University of Chicago Press.

————. 1969. *Elementary Structures of Kinship*. Rev. ed. Translated by James Harle Bell, John Richard von Sturmer, and Rodney Needham, editor. Boston, MA: Beacon Press. Originally published 1949 as *Les Structures élémentaires de la parenté*.

Machiavelli, Niccolò. 1513 [2006]. *The Prince*. Translated by William K. Marriott. Project Gutenberg e-book 1232. Available: www.gutenberg .org/files/1232/1232-h/1232-h.htm (accessed December 2006).

MacKinnon, Catharine A. 1989. *Toward a Feminist Theory of the State*. Cambridge, MA: Harvard University Press.

MacKinnon, Catharine A., and Andrea Dworkin, eds. 1998. *In Harm's Way: The Pornography Civil Rights Hearings*. Cambridge, MA: Harvard University Press.

Marx, Karl. 2000. *Das Kapital*. Washington, DC: Regnery Publishing. First volume published 1867; volumes 2 and 3 edited by Friedrich Engels and published in 1865 and 1894.

Marx, Karl, and Friedrich Engels. 2005. *The Communist Manifesto*. Project Gutenberg e-book 61. Available: www.gutenberg.org/etext/61 (accessed December 2006).

Miller, Richard W. 1984. *Analyzing Marx: Morality, Power and History*. Princeton, NJ: Princeton University Press.

Plato. 360 BCE [1994]. *The Republic*. Translated by Benjamin Jowett. Project Gutenberg e-book 150. Available: www.gutenberg.org/dirs/etext94/repub13.txt (accessed December 2006).

Raber, Douglas. 2004. "Fundamentals of Information Studies: Understanding Information and Its Environment." *Library Quarterly* 74 (October): 486–488.

Raines, Dorit. 1996. "La Biblioteca-Museo Patrizia e il 'capitale sociale'—modelli illuministici e l'imitazione dei nouvi aggregati." In *Arte, Storia, Cultura, e Musica in Friuli nell'età del Tiepolo, Proceedings Forum Udine* (19–20 December): 63–84.

Raulet, Gérard. 1983. "Structuralism and Post-Structuralism: An Interview with Michel Foucault." *Telos* 55 (Spring): 195–211.

Rousseau, Jean-Jacques. 1762 [n.d.]. "Subject of the First Book." In *The Social Contract, or Principles of Political Right*. Translated by G. D. H. Cole. Available: www.constitution.org/jjr/socon_01.htm#001 (accessed June 2006).

Rummel, R. J. 1976. *Understanding Conflict and War, Vol. 2: The Conflict Helix*. Beverly Hills, CA: Sage. Available: www.hawaii.edu/powerkills/NOTE11.HTM (accessed December 2006).

Sartre, Jean-Paul. 1972a. *La Nausée*. Paris: Gallimard. First published 1938.

———. 1972b. *Le Mur*. Paris: Gallimard. First published 1939.

Saussure, Ferdinand de. 1972. *Cours de linguistique générale*. Edited by Tullio De Mauro. Paris: Payot. Originally published 1916.

Theen, Rolf H. W. 1972. "The Idea of the Revolutionary State: Tkachev, Trotsky, and Lenin." *Russian Review* 31, no. 4: 383–397.

Tocqueville, Alexis de. 1836–1839 [2002]. *Democracy in America*. Available: http://xroads.virginia.edu/~HYPER/DETOC/toc_indx.html (accessed December 2006).

U.S. Postal Service. 1959. "In the Matter of the Mailing of Approximately 2,000 Postal Cards by United Artists, Inc. Initial Decision of Hearing Examiner." Available: www.usps.com/judicial/1959deci/m-15.htm (accessed December 2006).

Weber, Max. 1921. "Politik als Beruf." In *Gesammelte Politische Schriften*, 396–450. Munich: Drei Masken Verlag.

———. 1930. *The Protestant Ethic and the Spirit of Capitalism*. Translated by Talcott Parsons and Anthony Giddens. London: Unwin Hyman. Available: http://xroads.virginia.edu/~HYPER/WEBER/cover.html (accessed December 2006).

Weber, Max. 1962. *Basic Concepts in Sociology*. Translated and with an introduction by H. P. Secher. New York: Citadel Press.

ADDITIONAL SOURCES

Braman, Sandra. 2006. *Change of State: Information, Policy, and Power*. Cambridge, MA: MIT Press.

Foucault, Michel. 1970. *The Order of Things: An Archaeology of the Human*

Sciences. Translated from *Les Mots et les choses: un archeologie des sciences humaines.* Paris: Gallimard.

Hearn, Jeffrey. 2000. "The Bibliography Project: Michel Foucault." *The Untimely Past.* Available: www.untimelypast.org/bibfou.html (accessed December 2006).

Huntington, Samuel P. 1996. *The Clash of Civilizations and the Remaking of World Order.* New York: Simon & Schuster.

What organizations and agencies, governmental or otherwise, do you know of that have responsibility for regulating information? Before you begin reading this chapter, make a list of all that you can think of. Indicate for each one whether the agency is a governmental agency or not. If it is a governmental agency, make a note of whether it is a local, state, national, or international agency. When you have finished reading this chapter, compare your list to those that are discussed.

Chapter 11

The Regulation and Politics of Information

Learning Guide

After reading this chapter, you should be able to

- understand and define the following terms:
  - regulation
  - deregulation
  - privatization
  - multinational enterprise (MNE)
  - intergovernmental organization (IGO)
  - nongovernmental organization (NGO)
  - state public service commission
  - universal service
  - sunshine laws

- identify the organizations represented by the acronyms in the following list and explain the significance of each organization to the regulation of information:

ANSI	IFLA	OMB
CIA	IMF	UNESCO
FOIA	ISO	USAID
FCC	ITU	USPTO
FTC	NIST	W3C
ICANN	NSA	WIPO
ICSU	NTIA	WTO
IEC	OECD	

- describe the issues involved in regulation of information;
- identify key aspects in access to and ownership of government information.

When you have finished the chapter, return to this page to be sure you have learned what you need to know.

INTRODUCTION

Information policy, as discussed in this and the next chapter, is a part of public policy, like defense policy, health policy, immigration policy, welfare policy, and so on. Although we will be considering information policy from a governmental, largely national or international perspective, it is possible to consider it from other perspectives, such as the information policy of a corporation, a university, a law firm, a synagogue, or any other societal entity, even a family. While considering information from these multiple perspectives would be both interesting and informative, we do not do so for two primary reasons. First, such extended discussion is beyond the scope of this book. Second, and more important, information policy of any of the entities occurs within the framework of the larger public policy perspective, operating within the constraints of information policy at international, national, and sometimes state levels. Hence to understand information policy at these more granular levels one must first understand this larger context.

This chapter touches on some of the key governmental and nongovernmental players in the information environment. Its focus is primarily on U.S. and international actors. It is important to keep in mind, however, that almost all countries have analogous institutions to regulate and police information purveyors, sometimes far more rigorously than is done in the United States.

Before beginning examination of these regulatory bodies, we might first ask if such regulation is necessary. Can the entities of the information environment self-regulate or is government intervention not only desirable but also required? Larry Downes (2004) of the University of California–Berkeley School of Information Management and Systems argues, for example, that the Internet can be largely self-regulated. Regulation, according to Downes, is in large part a function of the ability of a system to employ and apply technology to secure certain ends. In the absence of effective technology, regulation is doomed. Moreover, Downes argues, governments do not respond to any system's regulatory needs until there is sufficient clamor amongst stakeholders to force a response. Technological, nongovernmental regulation does not require the same level of discontent that does governmental. To support his argument, Downes references e-mail spam and Web pop-up advertisements. Effective 1 January 2004, U.S. federal law has sought to prohibit unsolicited spam (the Controlling the Assault of Non-Solicited Pornography and Marketing Act of 2003 [PL108-187] or Can-Spam Act) and the Federal Trade Commission has sought to limit pop-up ads.

Both Japan and the European Union seek to regulate Internet spam—termed digital privacy rules. The Japanese law came into force in July 2002.

European legislation was passed in October 2003 to be implemented by the member nations to limit spam and to regulate tracking of individuals through their cell phone signatures. But this gets us ahead of our story.

We suggest in this chapter that private-sector regulation can be an effective tool where issues are largely technical. As we show, the regulation of the Internet was for many years effectively managed by a small group of private-sector technocrats. Once, however, a previously technical domain expands into the political and economic arenas, technical-level regulation is no longer sufficient. Government regulation is then inevitable. It is equally true, as Downes argues, that technical solutions must exist before regulations based on political and economic concerns can be effective.

REGULATION OF COMMUNICATION

Governments have long regulated or participated in the information environment. All governments have established postal services to move the mail—communications—from one point to another. Governments have joined together in the Universal Postal Union to facilitate the movement of mail across national boundaries. Many governments have extended their reach to ownership and management of the telephone and telegraph services and included all under a single umbrella ministry (the post, telegraph, and telephone or PTT ministries). In the United States, direct government ownership of the means of moving messages was limited to the postal service, but until relatively recently, the federal government very closely regulated the other services.

In the United States, there are limitations placed on the government's ability to regulate or inhibit information. The most important of these limitations is the First Amendment to the Constitution of the United States. It holds that

> Congress shall make no law respecting an establishment of religion, or prohibiting the free exercise thereof; *or abridging the freedom of speech, or of the press*; or the right of the people peaceably to assemble, and to petition the government for a redress of grievances. (Italics added)

Although the First Amendment prohibits abridgment of freedom of speech and press, it does not prohibit government regulation of a wide range of communications issues (see, for example, the discussion in Benjamin, Lichtman, and Shelanski, 2001) and more recently of communication in cyberspace (Edwards and Waelde, 1997; Wallace and Mangan, 1996).

Deregulation and Convergence

In the past thirty years, the United States and, for that matter, a large number of other governments have sought to either deregulate or divest themselves of the communications industries. Many governments have sold off their ownership (called privatization) of the telephone and telegraph services and have undertaken to deregulate those industries. In the United States, as a consequence of deregulation in 1984, the regulated monopoly American Telephone and Telegraph (AT&T) was broken into AT&T and seven "Baby Bells," regional telephone companies originally limited to the offer of local telephone service. Long distance service was opened to competition with AT&T by other telephone companies (like MCI and Sprint). In a further move, the Telecommunications Act of 1996 opened local telephone service to competition as well. The deregulation of telephony continues. As we saw in chapter 5, regulatory bodies, such as the U.S. Federal Communications Commission (FCC) are struggling with decisions about whether or how to regulate VoIP. Interestingly, AT&T has been absorbed by one of its Baby Bells, SBC Communications (originally Southwestern Bell), although the company has chosen to call itself by the original parent name. This merger, plus others (Bell Atlantic and NYNEX merged prior to becoming Verizon through a further merger with GTE; Pacific Telesis, Southwestern Bell, and AmeriTech merged to form SBC) partially reversed the 1984 deregulation.

Similarly, postal services have undergone significant change in recent years. The first Postmaster General was Benjamin Franklin, appointed to the post in 1775. In 1789, the Post Office Department was created. From that time forward, the Post Office Department supported, employed, improved, and developed new technologies to move the mail: better roads, fleets of wagons to move the mail, Pony Express to speed the mail, adoption of railroads and later air transport to carry the mail, and so on. In 1896, a precursor to universal electric and telephone service, rural free delivery (RFD), was implemented to carry the mail to rural customers, rather than requiring them to go into town to pick up their mail. In 1963, the ZIP code system was introduced to facilitate mail sorting, distribution, and delivery.

In 1970, the Postal Reorganization Act (PL 91-375) established the United States Postal Service (USPS) as an independent agency of government, with the Postmaster General no longer serving as a member of the president's cabinet. The USPS has sought to provide service without deficit. It has done so in two ways: (1) It has increased rates to match costs. (2) It has implemented a comprehensive automation program to facilitate mail handling and delivery. In recent years, competition to the USPS has grown. This competition includes companies like FedEx, UPS, DHL, and other couriers. These courier services offer express delivery, at a price. The USPS in turn has implemented similar tracked, express services and, in 2001, entered into agreement with FedEx to offer complementary services (U.S. Postal Service, 2001).

The history of postal, telegraph, and telephone services, their deregulation and privatization, and subsequent cooperation point to one form of convergence among communications systems and social institutions. Both government and private institutions are offering similar information products.

A second convergence is the blurring of lines among the telephone, cable, and Internet systems. For example, cable and telephone systems provide Internet connectivity as Internet service providers (ISPs). Some telephone companies have entered the cable market and some cable companies offer telephony. The Internet can and does carry both two-way voice and one-way entertainment. Delivery of television programs via the Internet is rapidly emerging as an alternative to broadcast and cable. The differences among communication systems, both technically and regulatorily, are disappearing.

A third convergence is the vertical and horizontal consolidation of the means of information production, dissemination, and consumption, as previously discussed in chapter 6. The AOL-Time Warner marriage, acquisition of Netscape, and before that the consolidation of Turner Broadcasting with Time-Life illustrate the concentration of the means of production and distribution in fewer hands. As technical convergence continues, it makes ownership convergence easier.

INFORMATION CONTROL

As information sources and resources grow more complex, so do the mechanisms created by governments and by some intergovernmental and nongovernmental organizations to control them. As we will see, this growing complexity applies not only to information content but also to information transmission and therefore consumption as well. One part of this information control process is standardization, which was initially discussed in chapter 4. As the need for standardization has increased, a function of increases in information and of the means of transmission, so has the need for standards organizations. The development of standards requires social institutions to create and enforce them. There is another factor pressing for information control: the desire on the part of the creators and disseminators of information to protect their product, balanced by the individual and social rights of access and use (fair use) of that information. We will suggest that these developments are of long standing and have well-established historical antecedents.

Institutions of Information Control

Two forms of social institutions have responded to these needs for standardization, protection, and rights of access: governments and nongovernmental organizations. Speaking very broadly, nongovernmental organizations are extremely effective when the issues they are charged to resolve are of a largely technical nature and when there are relatively few stakeholders involved. When these largely technical matters begin to take on larger political and economic meaning and/or when the number of stakeholders expands, or when there are inherent political and/or economic overtones, technical bodies are incapable of resolving the issues. It is incumbent, then, on the governmental regulatory structure to participate. A good example of what was once a largely technical issue is the Internet and the assignment of Internet names and numbers. In the beginning, one man, Jon Postel, together with a small staff, was able to manage Internet names and numbers in his spare time. By the mid-1990s that was no longer possible. Moreover, many had begun to recognize the numerous uses to which the Internet could be put, particularly the World Wide Web. The number of interested parties and stakeholders exploded, and so did the technical workload. As we will see later, Postel's IANA (Internet Assigned Numbers Authority) was metamorphosed into ICANN (Internet Corporation for Assigned Names and Numbers). ICANN as originally designed perhaps lacked adequate stakeholder representation, something the organization later sought to remedy and has again revisited.

There is a very long history of information politics and regulation. The old saying that information is power has much truth to it if the efforts to control the spread of information tell us anything. It is also said that he or she who controls information controls power. This saying has two related meanings: the creator of information has power and the information gatekeeper has power. The information creator influences outcomes and decision making through new information. The one who decides what the decision maker sees likewise shapes the outcome of decisions.

Let us also recognize that no one ever has full access to all information about anything. As discussed in chapter 8, decision theorists have posited several models to explain the decision process. The rational actor model, the organizational process model, and the bureaucratic politics model (Allison, 1969) suggest how decision makers choose among possible alternatives. If information access can be controlled by "sub-elite" information gatekeepers, decision makers may in fact not have access to perfect and complete information. Indeed, parties seeking to influence decisions may use a number of strategies, including the provision of imperfect, incomplete information and, at times, patently false information to decision makers.

Information control almost certainly began the very first time anyone spoke up to challenge the authority of the clan chieftain. Today there is an extensive system to regulate and control information, the transmission of information, its ownership, and its consumption. Indeed, as the information environment grows more complex, so does the network of regulation.

Levels of Regulation and Control

The network of regulation extends from the local level to international organizations. For example, until recently local governments in the United States franchised and regulated cable television companies, licensing them and approving cable rates. Local governments implicitly or explicitly censor films, books, and other entertainment media in the name of community standards. Or they may zone "adult" entertainment outlets into specific areas of town or into extinction.

State governments in the United States have broad regulatory powers, particularly over the information transmission industries. This regulatory control generally is exercised through a state utility or public service commission, although the names of these regulatory bodies vary (see list at www.dps.state.ny.us/stateweb.htm). The regulatory commissions may set standards for telephone systems, particularly in intrastate commerce. The states may also establish traffic laws and, to a degree, regulate transportation by, for example, setting weight and length limits for trucks.

The U.S. federal government plays the most prominent role in information management and regulation. The Federal Communications Commission (FCC) licenses broadcast companies. The Federal Trade Commission (FTC) oversees mergers and expansions. These are but a sampling of the federal presence. The Patent and Trademark Office (USPTO) maintains a registry of patents, trademarks, and service marks to provide protection to the owners of intellectual property. We will explore these further below.

The fourth and final level involves a number of often interlocking and overlapping international organizations. These range from the World Intellectual Property Organization (WIPO) and the World Trade Organization (WTO) to the United Nations Educational, Scientific, and Cultural Organisation (UNESCO). Again, we will explore the functions of these organizations later in this chapter.

Finally, it must be stressed that there are parallel regulatory bodies in the some two hundred other countries that populate political space. The European Union and Japanese patent offices are responsible for the protection of technological innovation rights in their respective spheres, just as the USPTO is in its sphere. Other national governments have similar regulatory agencies, although configurations and regulatory coverage by specific agencies vary from country to country, depending on historical development, level of economic prowess, political structure, and cultural values. Anyone seeking to do business on a global scale (and who does not now so wish) must be cognizant of and respond to the regulatory authority of these bodies. National and local governments in these many countries have greater or lesser authority than their U.S. counterparts and, in some cases, participate as owners of some of the means of communication or transportation. As noted earlier, many governments own or once owned the telephone and telegraph systems, as well as the postal services (the PTT Ministries). Recall that the U.S. federal government owns the U.S. Postal Service and once upon a time managed it as an office of government (when it was the Post Office). Others own and operate (or have owned and operated) national airlines and railway systems. Although many national governments have privatized the PTTs and their airlines and railways, many others have either renationalized them or have never sought to privatize them.

As the information mosaic grows more complex and becomes ever more internationalized, just so does the network of information regulation. We will also see that the range of players and stakeholders has grown.

FORMS OF INFORMATION REGULATION

Governments and other social organizations have always sought to control the flow and types of information to which their citizens can have access. One early example was the publication of prohibited books, the *Index*, by the Roman Catholic Church shortly after the onset of the Protestant Reformation in Europe. Authoritarian and totalitarian states in the twentieth century prohibited a large range of literature. There are periodic efforts in the United States to shelter children from the likes of *Huckleberry Finn, In the Night Kitchen, Catcher in the Rye*, or the Harry Potter series because of racial, sexual, or heretical content.

These efforts to control content or access have, in the end, often failed. The Catholic *Index* was used as a marketing device by Protestant booksellers and publishers. Soviet censorship was undercut by the underground publishing medium, known as *samizdat*. The closing scene of Ray Bradbury's *Fahrenheit 451*, in which individuals are seen walking around in circles reciting books, illustrates an important point: in a society where most books are prohibited, in order to protect their culture, people will memorize the literature to preserve it.

Governments to one degree or another have sought to limit information access by prohibiting access to specific classes of the population. The prohibition may be broadly defined or it may be limited to specific groups—and these days that special class is often children. In the name of protecting children by denying access to certain information, governments sometimes deny access to everyone. For example, local, state, and the U.S. federal government have sought to impose limits on Internet access to block obscene or gratuitously violent material. Legislation has sought to require public libraries and schools to install filtering software on some or all of their public access computers with an end to deny access to certain Web material. These policies have worked with varying degrees of success and have been challenged as ineffective and cumbersome. Other governments have sought to limit hate speech. The German government threatened action against CompuServe unless it restricted access for its nationals to Nazi Web sites. The French government threatened eBay and other online vendors offering Nazi memorabilia for sale.

CONTROL AND USE OF GOVERNMENT INFORMATION

Government information is information produced or gathered in the process of or in support of the conduct of the responsibilities of government as well as information produced by government when private-sector entities fail to do so. There are as many approaches to the access and use of government information as there are governments. We can distinguish at least two major dimensions: (1) access and (2) ownership.

Access to Information Held by Government

Speaking very broadly, government information can be described as open, privileged, or sensitive. Open information is just that. There are no controls on its distribution, and under the prevailing rules of the government that has it, anyone can see it.

Privileged information is personal information. It includes tax returns, medical records, and other personal information. In principle, the governments that collect such information are not to divulge it to anyone except those who have a need to know. There is sometimes a fine line between open or public information and privileged or private information. Thus, property transfers, marriages, births, deaths, and divorces, various licenses (including driver's license information), and motor vehicle registrations may all fall within the penumbra of public information.

Governments deny access to sensitive or classified information often in order to protect the national interest. What constitutes the national interest may be defined quite widely, and what one government may consider sensitive another may deem harmless.

Governments may also seek to deny one branch of government information considered privileged or sensitive by another. In the United States there is frequent conflict between the legislative branch (the Congress) and the executive branch (the Presidency and the many offices that make up the executive branch). Congress, seeking to exercise its legislative oversight privileges, has often sought to extricate information from the executive. The executive branch, in its turn, has often sought to shield that information from Congressional or public scrutiny on the basis of executive privilege. Congress is often, but not always, successful in gaining access.

Many state and local governments have "sunshine laws." Such laws require public bodies to conduct the public business in an open and public forum. The theory is that public business should be conducted before the public to keep the process above reproach. Decisions therefore should not be taken *in camera*.

Ownership of Government Information

The second major dimension is ownership. In the United States, it is the prevailing theory that as the people paid for the information gathered or created by government, the public own it. With some significant exceptions, U.S. federal government documents are not copyrighted and are in the public domain. This means that any private citizen may use and republish government information at will and without royalty. For example, the Federal Aviation Authority (FAA) provides a procedure for the licensure of pilots. The licensing procedure includes a written, multiple answer examination. The questions and their answers are government information, considered to be in the public domain. As a result, there are any number of courses, videotapes, manuals, and books available to help prepare the aspiring pilot for the examination.

The approach taken by the U.S. government is not taken by many others. In the United Kingdom, government information is considered to be owned by the government and therefore copyright lies with the Crown. Before one can republish British government documents, one must have permission to do so and may be required to pay royalties on that copyright.

Freedom of Information Act. There are a limited number of laws of political science. These include (1) No one is permanent, people die and therefore must be replaced; (2) taxes are forever; and (3) information has value. Governments will seek to hoard what information they have. Perhaps this last statement is somewhat exaggerated, but there are often disagreements between government and those seeking government information over what should and should not be made public and when. To help define the what and when, Congress passed the Freedom of Information Act (5 USC § 552) or FOIA in 1966, which established the principle that absent reasons for restriction, information held by executive branch agencies should be made available. FOIA has been amended to include access to electronic records (the Electronic Freedom of Information Act Amendments of 1996 or E-FOIA). A number of states also passed their own legislation, sometimes called Little FOIAs. The FOIA legislation provides for access to nonsensitive information on request. In principle, government agencies are to provide copies of information. Moreover, citizens may also request copies of files the government may hold on them. Limitations and exemptions were added to the FOIA in the aftermath of the 9/11 tragedy and the escalated concerns over terrorism.

Other countries have similar acts, with varying degrees of coverage and restrictions, many of which have only very recently been enacted. For example, such legislation was passed

- in Australia and New Zealand in 1982
- in Canada in 1985
- in Ireland in 1997
- in Japan and the Czech Republic in 1999
- in the United Kingdom, Bulgaria, and South Africa in 2000
- in Bosnia, Poland, and Romania in 2001
- in Mexico, Jamaica, Peru, and Pakistan in 2002
- in Serbia, the Dominican Republic, and Ecuador in 2004
- in Germany, India, and Uganda in 2005

Although all of the Scandinavian countries have FOIA laws (some of which were passed long before the U.S. FOIA) and such legislation has been passed in most of Europe, the existence of such laws is still spotty in South America, Africa, and most of Asia. (For more complete information, see Privacy International.)

INFORMATION POLICY AND REGULATORY BODIES

As has already been noted above, there exists a large and growing number of societal institutions that formulate and implement information policy and serve to regulate information activities, including both governmental bodies at various levels and nongovernmental bodies. The discussion below illustrates some of the types of these institutions, focusing on agencies at the federal level in the United States and a selected sample of international intergovernmental and nongovernmental agencies. It should be noted again that there are parallel agencies in the other countries of the world that serve functions similar to those of the U.S. agencies that are described here.

U.S. Government Agencies

The following section discusses a sample of U.S. government agencies with responsibilities in the information environment. It could be argued that any and all government agencies participate in some way. This list is not meant to be exhaustive but rather to provide an idea of the depth and scope of government interest in information.

Agency for International Development. The Agency for International Development (USAID) is an arm of the State Department. It is concerned with promoting economic and social development in the Newly Industrializing Countries (NIC). Its mandate includes infrastructure building, including telecommunications, and other services. The American Centers, a part of U.S. Embassies abroad, provide library and often Internet access for interested people.

Central Intelligence Agency. The Central Intelligence Agency (CIA) was created in 1947 by the National Security Act. The CIA is one of several intelligence agencies in the United States and since 2004 has reported to the Director of National Intelligence. All countries maintain intelligence gathering and analysis capabilities.

The CIA has three parts to its mission:

- collecting intelligence that matters
- providing relevant, timely, and objective all-source analysis
- conducting covert action at the direction of the President to preempt threats or achieve United States policy objectives (U.S. Central Intelligence Agency, 2006)

Intelligence means information in the context of the CIA's mission. Counterintelligence can mean "disinformation." Intelligence includes both the original gathering of information and the gathering of information provided by others and the analysis of all information obtained. Intelligence/information can be gathered from a variety of sources, including both open and clandestine sources. Open source information is available from publicly available resources: official statements and statistics, newspapers, books, news broadcasts, Web sites, and so on. Clandestine resources include various forms of espionage from hidden listening devices to spy cameras and compromised officials, eye-in-the-sky spy satellites, and manned and unmanned reconnaissance flights to gather information.

The CIA provides a number of services to the public. Perhaps the best known is *The World Factbook.* For each country in the world, the *World Factbook* includes basic political, economic, and governmental structure data and provides a good summary introduction to a country.

Federal Communication Commission. The Federal Communications Commission (FCC) is an independent regulatory agency established in 1934 by the Communications Act. The FCC is charged with intrastate and interstate regulation of most aspects of telecommunications, including radio, television, cable, telephone, wire, and satellite communications.

The FCC administers the Telecommunications Act of 1996 (PL 104-104, 110 Stat. 56 (1996)), which liberalized entry into the broadcast, cable, and wire industry by deregulating earlier processes. The Act was designed to permit market forces to more actively "regulate" communications, replacing more stringent federal government regulation (see discussion in chapter 6).

The Telecommunications Act of 1996 affected regulation of broadband television broadcasting by increasing spectrum available to commercial broadcasters and reducing the public service requirement placed on commercial broadcasters. In addition, it liberalized rules for cable operators, including deregulating much of the rate setting.

The Act also contains *universal service* provisions requiring certain telecommunications companies to provide service to all potential subscribers at preferential, perhaps noneconomic rates. Further, it establishes the concept that schools, libraries, and health care providers are important institutions for the provision of telecommunications services. The universal service provisions require telephone companies to offer services to all potential customers, including those located remotely and those who could not otherwise afford service. The 1996 Act gave rise to the e-rate concept for Internet connection for certain public institutions (see previous discussion in chapter 9).

Federal Trade Commission. The Federal Trade Commission (FTC) is responsible for enforcement of consumer protection and antitrust regulations. Its mandate includes prevention of unfair and deceptive trade and marketing practices. It also includes regulation of e-commerce and related Internet activities. For example, the FTC undertakes to prevent e-auction fraud. It is the FTC that has had oversight of the formation of the media conglomerates discussed in chapter 6.

National Institute of Standards and Technology. The National Institute of Standards and Technology (NIST) is an agency of the U.S. Department of Commerce's Technology Administration. Under the Clinton administration it took lead responsibility to manage the U.S. National Information Infrastructure (NII) and to represent the United States in the Global Information Infrastructure (GII).

National Security Agency/Central Security Service. The National Security Agency (NSA) is another major intelligence agency in the United States. Its role is to provide protection for the U.S. government information systems, primarily through cryptology, and to provide intelligence derived from foreign signals transmission. The mission of the agency, stated in Executive Order 12333m, includes two aspects:

- The Information Assurance mission provides the solutions, products, and services, and conducts defensive information operations, to achieve information assurance for information infrastructures critical to U.S. national security interests.
- The foreign signals intelligence or SIGINT mission allows for an effective, unified organization and control of all the foreign signals collection and processing activities of the United States. NSA is authorized to produce SIGINT in accordance with objectives, requirements, and priorities established by the Director of Central Intelligence with the advice of the National Foreign Intelligence Board. (U.S. National Security Agency).

In recent years, particularly since 9/11, the agency has reportedly also been involved with surveillance of communication activities of U.S. citizens.

National Telecommunications and Information Administration. The National Telecommunications and Information Administration (NTIA) is an agency of the U.S. Department of Commerce. It is responsible for the executive branch's telecommunications policy, both domestically and internationally. The agency seeks to promote competition in the telecommunications and cable industries. It also promotes research and development and use of the high frequency spectrum.

Office of Management and Budget. The Office of Management and Budget (OMB) is in the Executive Office of the President. Under section 515 of the Treasury and General Government Appropriations Act of 2001 (PL 106-554), OMB is required to "provide policy and procedural guidance to Federal agencies for ensuring and maximizing the quality, objectivity, utility, and integrity of information (including statistical information) disseminated by Federal agencies."

OMB also has responsibility under the Paperwork Reduction Act (44 U.S.C. chapter 35) to promote paperwork reduction within the federal government and between the federal government and the citizenry.

Patent and Trademark Office. The Patent and Trademark Office (USPTO), an agency of the Department of Commerce, maintains a registry of patents, trademarks, and service marks to provide protection to the owners of intellectual property. The agency is responsible for administration of U.S. patent and trademark laws, issuing patents and registering trademarks in accordance with the requirements of the laws.

Other areas of government heavily involved in information control and regulation include the Departments of State, Defense, and Justice, as well as the U.S. Trade Representative. Beyond these, the national libraries, the Library of Congress, the National Library of Medicine, the National Agricultural Library, and the National Archives and Records Administration play important information roles at the federal level in the United States, although their function is to organize, manage, preserve, and distribute information, with lesser emphasis on control and regulation.

Information Ideas

The Hidden Role of the USPS as a Regulator of Information Flow
Under the United States Code Title 18 Section 1461, the sending of obscene material through the U.S. mail is prohibited. Specifically the code says:

> Every obscene, lewd, lascivious, indecent, filthy or vile article, matter, thing, device, or substance; and—
>
> Every article or thing designed, adapted, or intended for producing abortion, or for any indecent or immoral use; and
>
> Every article, instrument, substance, drug, medicine, or thing which is advertised or described in a manner calculated to lead another to use or apply it for producing abortion, or for any indecent or immoral purpose; and
>
> Every written or printed card, letter, circular, book, pamphlet, advertisement, or notice of any kind giving information, directly or indirectly, where, or how, or from whom, or by what means any of such mentioned matters, articles, or things may be obtained or made, or where or by whom any act or operation of any kind for the procuring or producing of abortion will be done or performed, or how or by what means abortion may be produced, whether sealed or unsealed; and
>
> Every paper, writing, advertisement, or representation that any article, instrument, substance, drug, medicine, or thing may, or can, be used or applied for producing abortion, or for any indecent or immoral purpose; and
>
> Every description calculated to induce or incite a person to so use or apply any such article, instrument, substance, drug, medicine, or thing—
>
> Is declared to be nonmailable matter and shall not be conveyed in the mails or delivered from any post office or by any letter carrier.

When someone is suspected of mailing obscene materials (for example, offering such materials for sale at a Web site), the U.S. Postal Inspection Service

(*Continued on p. 282*)

may be part of the team that investigates the alleged crime. This branch of the USPS is also involved in other areas in which distribution of information is considered illegal, such as child pornography and fraudulent offers. The full range of activities is described at the Service's Web site at www.usps.com/postalinspectors/jurislaw.htm.

Although the USPS is not generally thought of as a law enforcement agency, the U.S. Postal Inspection Service is one of the oldest such agencies in the country, having been established by Benjamin Franklin in 1772 as part of the colonial postal system. Thus the regulation and protection of the flow of information through the postal system is perhaps the earliest example in the United States of a regulatory agency for information.

Source

U.S. Postal Inspection Service. 2006. "Jurisdiction and Laws." Available: www.usps.com/postalinspectors/jurislaw.htm (accessed December 2006).

International Organizations

There are a growing number of international organizations to assist in the management and regulation of the information environment. It could be argued that all human endeavor includes some aspects of information; therefore all human organizations also have an information function. To address all of these organizations would be an overwhelming task. We will survey a short list of intergovernmental (IGO) and nongovernmental (NGO) organizations that have an explicit or strongly implicit information environment role.

International organizations have an interesting role to play in standardizing and rationalizing various information activities. It is important to remember that international intergovernmental organizations have countries as their members. The member states often accede to the authority of the organizations by virtue of a treaty. When properly adopted by each member, treaties have the force of law for each member in much the same way a statute has the force of law. The same is not true for the nongovernmental organizations, which can be defined as entities organized at the international level with nonstate members. Examples include the Internet Corporation for Assigned Names and Numbers (ICANN), the International Council for Science (ICSU), the Internet Society (ISOC), the International Olympic Committee (IOC), and the International Red Cross/Red Crescent, as well as the multinational enterprises (MNEs) like Disney, Coca Cola, or CNN.

From a regulatory perspective, the IGOs are preeminent. However, this is not to say that the NGOs do not have an important role to play in setting information policy. The World Wide Web Consortium (W3C), for example, has a very important standards setting function. It has, as well, taken the lead in pushing the limits of the Web, for example by promoting the development of the Semantic Web, proposed to improve information management and retrieval.

The multinational corporations have extensive economic and political power. A news system like the *Wall Street Journal, Le Monde*, the *New York Times*, CNN, Fox, the BBC, or CNBC has an important information gathering, processing, and transmission function. Consider the global reach of companies like Ford, Daimler Chrysler, Toyota, or Volkswagen. For those corporations whose primary products are in information, such as the parent companies of the aforementioned news systems, their role in international information activities is significant and extensive.

International organizations, whether IGOs or NGOs, represent a complex, interlinked web of organizations and interests. The following is not meant to be an exhaustive list of IGOs and NGOs that have a concern for or influence the information environment. To be exhaustive, one would have to list all such organizations. Our purpose here is but to highlight some of the key institutional players and to describe briefly their role in the information environment.

Representative IGOs

International Telecommunication Union. The International Telecommunication Union (ITU) is a Specialized Agency of the United Nations. The ITU establishes international telecommunications standards and provides a forum to remedy technical conflicts among its members. It has responsibility for regulating the international radio frequency spectrum as well as communications satellite orbits. It also provides a forum for governments and telecommunications companies to ameliorate differences and solve problems.

The ITU has important standardization functions: telecommunications to include mobile communications, numbering, and geographical coding; radio communications and spectrum management; and telecommunications development. These programs include assistance to developing countries in infrastructure development, rate structuring, and universal access issues. The ITU has undertaken an important development role, as defined by the Valletta Action Plan:

- Pay special attention to the requirements of the least developed countries.
- Work with governments to assist them in establishing appropriate telecommunication policies and regulatory structures.

- Play a creative and catalytic role in identifying and providing resource support, in the new telecommunication environment, to help meet the requirements of developing countries in close collaboration with global, regional and national organizations and agencies and the private sector.
- Maintain close cooperation with ITU-R and ITU-T.
- Include matters pertaining to information technology and broadcasting in its activities, as key factors in promoting economic, social and cultural development.
- Promote training in human resources development and human resources management. (International Telecommunication Union, 2003)

Organisation for Economic Cooperation and Development. The Organisation for Economic Cooperation and Development (OECD) is an organization representing developed countries. It has a particular interest in digital divide concerns and in how information and communication technologies relate to the economy and to societal change.

United Nations Educational, Scientific, and Cultural Organisation. The United Nations Educational, Scientific, and Cultural Organisation (UNESCO) is an agency of the United Nations created in 1945 with 191 member countries. UNESCO's purpose "is to contribute to peace and security by promoting collaboration among nations through education, science and culture in order to further universal respect for justice, for the rule of law and for the human rights and fundamental freedoms which are affirmed for the peoples of the world, without distinction of race, sex, language or religion, by the Charter of the United Nations" (UNESCO, UNESCO Constitution).

UNESCO has a significant interest in the information environment. It provides assistance to the Newly Industrializing Countries to develop their educational, scientific, and cultural infrastructure through grants, exchange programs, and access to information. UNESCO has also taken as part of its mandate the protection of "fragile cultures" in the face of a deluge of information, the result of the globalization of the information environment, to wit "social significance of the communication practices to which technological progress has given rise must be looked into" (UNESCO, *Ethics*). UNESCO maintains a number of programs to promote the information environment, including one to promote information ethics and another to help build library infrastructure in the NICs.

Universal Postal Union. The Universal Postal Union (UPU) was created in 1874 and represents a mechanism to facilitate the international exchange of mail. It also provides advice and assistance of a technical nature to the member nations. The international postal network represents some 430 billion letters mailed within and between countries per year (Universal Postal Union, 2001). The UPU is now a Specialized Agency of the United Nations.

World Bank and International Monetary Fund. The World Bank and the International Monetary Fund (IMF) have as part of their portfolio concern for the development of telecommunications and information infrastructures in developing countries. For example, a World Bank publication, *Telecommunications Policies for Sub-Saharan Africa* (Mustafa, Laidlaw, and Brand, 1997), explores how the World Bank telecommunications strategy can be applied in Sub-Saharan Africa and the funding needs to bring it to fruition.

The World Bank has taken an interest in protecting rural customers who may become disadvantaged vis-à-vis urban customers as telecommunications regimes undergo a shift from government to private-sector ownership. As we have seen, there is less profit and therefore less interest for private-sector entities to provide service in low population areas (Kayani and Dymond, 1997).

World Intellectual Property Organization. The World Intellectual Property Organization (WIPO) is an IGO with 183 member countries. Its stated purpose is "helping to ensure that the rights of creators and owners of intellectual property are protected worldwide and that inventors and authors are, thus, recognized and rewarded for their ingenuity." Further, "[t]his international protection acts as a spur to human creativity, pushing forward the boundaries of science and technology and enriching the world of literature and the arts. By providing a stable environment for the marketing of intellectual property products, it also oils the wheels of international trade" (World Intellectual Property Organization, 2001).

WIPO was not born de novo when it was established as a Specialized Agency of the United Nations in 1974. It is the successor to the United International Bureaux for the Protection of Intellectual Property (or BIRPI, its French acronym). In its beginning, BIRPI administered the Paris Convention for the Protection of Industrial Property of 1883 and the Berne Convention for the Protection of Literary and Artistic Works of 1886.

Since the late nineteenth century, there have been a number of additional new treaties and agreements to regulate intellectual property. In addition to the Paris and Berne Conventions, these include the Madrid Agreement (1891), the Hague Agreement (1925), the WIPO Convention (1967), the Patent Cooperation Treaty (1970), Madrid Agreement Protocol (1989), the WIPO Copyright Treaty (1996), the Patent Law Treaty (2000), and the Singapore Treaty on the Law of Trademarks (2006). These treaties cover the range of intellectual property regulation at the international level. The Paris Convention provides protection for inventions, patents, trademarks, and industrial design. The Berne Convention addresses copyright for a range of works including writing, music, works of art, and architectural design. The

Madrid and Hague Agreements provide protection for industrial design and the registration of trade and service marks. In total, WIPO administers some twenty international treaties on intellectual property and copyright.

WIPO also provides a classification framework for industrial design and trademarks. These are regulated by the Strasbourg Agreement (1971), the Nice Agreement (1957), the Vienna Agreement (1973), and the Locarno Agreement (1968). The body serves as one of the groups providing arbitration services for domain name disputes (see ICANN below).

WIPO has developed a Digital Agenda to regulate electronic commerce. One of its objectives is to integrate developing countries into the legal structures regulating electronic property rights.

World Trade Organization. The World Trade Organization (WTO) has succeeded its predecessor, the General Agreement of Tariffs and Trade, as one of the primary regulators of international economic intercourse. The WTO is closely related to WIPO, particularly its TRIPS program (trade-related aspects of intellectual property rights).

The WTO is designed to rationalize trade among nation-states. Its objective is to liberalize the rules of trade among its members, but it has encountered many barriers to liberalization, particularly as various groups—developing countries, the United States, the European Union—have sought to protect specific interests. Developing countries are, for example, critical of the developed countries and especially Europe for the many subsidies they provide domestic agriculture. The developed countries are critical of protectionist policies proposed by developing countries.

Under the Doha Mandate, various information-related provisions were adopted to provide assistance to developing countries to participate in the trade process. The objective of the WTO is to develop a "rules-based multilateral trading system."

The WTO is particularly active in the intellectual property sphere. The TRIPS, or Trade Related Aspects of Intellectual Property Rights, has participated in decisions on the importation of low-cost generic drugs by poor countries as well as general coordination of intellectual property regulation. The TRIPS Agreements specify minimum protections for each of the various types of intellectual property in coordination with the World Intellectual Property Organization (WIPO).

One interesting application of the TRIPS Agreements is the "geographical indications" understandings. Branding or naming that implies geographic source is to be protected—champagne should come from Champagne, cognac from Cognac, scotch whiskey from Scotland, and so on. By and large, geographical indications apply to wines and spirits but there is an effort to expand the protections more widely. Products, no matter how similar in manufacture or taste or application, should be called something else. Champagne from California is not "champagne"—it is sparkling wine; cognac from anywhere other than Cognac is brandy.

The WTO has been the subject of significant protest and criticism. It is seen as an engine to permit multinational companies to export employment from the developed world to the developing world while at the same time opening the developing world up for further exploitation of their natural resources by those same companies. A number of opposition groups have formed, opposed to the globalization of trade (see, for example, www.nadir.org/nadir/initiativ/agp/en/index.html).

A Sample of NGOs

International Federation of Library Associations and Institutions. The International Federation of Library Associations and Institutions (IFLA) is a consortium of national library associations, institutions, and, to a limited degree, individuals. IFLA has as its primary mission the promotion of libraries and librarianship globally.

Internet Corporation for Assigned Names and Numbers. The Internet Corporation for Assigned Names and Numbers (ICANN) was chartered by the U.S. Department of Commerce in 1998 as a not-for-profit NGO to oversee the Domain Name System (DNS). ICANN "is an internationally organized, non-profit corporation that has responsibility for Internet Protocol (IP) address space allocation, protocol identifier assignment, generic (gTLD) and country code (ccTLD) Top-Level Domain name system management, and root server system management functions" (ICANN, 2005).

The Domain Name System has inherent political and economic components (Koehler, 2000). The DNS consists of the two top domains—generic and country code (gTLD and ccTLD). These in turn are subdivided into separate top-level domains. The gTLD consisted of seven TLDs (.com, .edu, .gov, .int, .mil, .net, and .org) until a second set of seven (.aero, .biz, .coop, .info, .museum, .name, and .pro) was approved in 2001 (Koehler, 2001). The ccTLD describe regional or national domains and include .ar for Argentina, .bo for Botswana, .fr for France, .in for India, .nz for New Zealand, .tn for Tunisia, .us for the United States, .za for South Africa, and so on.

The ICANN predecessor organizations were either ad hoc, or, like the Internet Assigned Numbers Authority (IANA), too small to manage the increased demand placed upon them (Koehler, 1999). In 1998, the U.S. Department of Commerce undertook a study, and a series of recommendations resulted as part of its White Paper. The White Paper recommended, among other things, greater stakeholder representation to include the technical, business, and academic communities as well as greater international representation (U.S. Department of Commerce, 1998). ICANN, chartered as a not-for-profit NGO, lacks the ability to compel through the force of law.

Perhaps the most pressing and politicized areas where ICANN has competence is in assigning domain names. These are the unique names that precede the top-level domain name. In the gTLD space, the edu, gov, int, and mil TLDs are reserved for U.S.-based educational institutions (edu), U.S. government Web sites (gov), international organizations (int), and the U.S. military (mil). Similar space is reserved on the ccTLDs, for example, ac.au for academic institutions in Australia, mod.uk (Ministry of Defence) for military sites in Great Britain, and go.jp for Japanese government sites. The com space is considered "prime" for commercial and business enterprises and the org and net spaces have been "poached" for spillover from the com domain. Purists would like to see org space returned to the not-for-profit sphere and net space for Internet and other network enterprises. With the advent of the new gTLDs, there has been some movement toward restoring the original intent.

That said, there has been dispute over how the names are assigned and reassigned. Should the names be assigned on a first-come, first-served basis, or should some cognizance be taken of existing trademarks? Recall that domain names are unique whereas individuals and firms can coexist quite comfortably sharing the same name. Thus it is possible for Delta Airlines and Delta Faucet to share "Delta," but only one of them can own delta.com. ICANN has established a domain name dispute mechanism whereby these kinds of issues can be resolved. The process is quasi-legal in form and involves mediation of disputes by three NGOs and one IGO.

ICANN represents an interesting intermediate step between the adhocracy of the technical management of the Internet that existed before 1998 and some formalized regulatory regime. ICANN has many supporters and detractors. It has been careful to define and clarify its role. Nonetheless, it may yield to a more formal structure if demands for greater regulation of the name space continue.

International Council for Science. The International Council for Science (ICSU, previous name, International Council of Scientific Unions) is an organization of organizations representing national science bodies and single science international unions. Its purpose is to reduce barriers to scientific progress created by disciplinary specialization, and it is an example of an NGO that focuses more on promoting generation, standardization, and dissemination of information than on the more regulatory or management function of an organization such as ICANN.

The ICSU has established a number of scientific and special committees to address issues of global scale, the names of which illustrate the broad range of information activities that may be undertaken by an NGO of this type. The list includes Scientific Committee on Antarctic Research (SCAR), Programme on Capacity Building in Science (PCBS), Committee on Data for Science and Technology (CODATA), Scientific Committee on Problems of the Environment (SCOPE), Committee on Sciences for Food Security (CSFS), Steering Committee on Genetics and Biotechnology (SCGB), Scientific Committee for the International Geosphere-Biosphere Programme (SC-IGBP), Special Committee for the International Decade for Natural Disaster Reduction (SC-IDNDR), Special Committee on Oceanic Research (SCOR), Science Committee on Solar-Terrestrial Physics (SCOSTEP), Committee on Space Research (COSPAR), Scientific Committee on Water Research (SCOWAR), Commission on Frequency Allocations for Radio Astronomy and Space Science (IUCAF), and Scientific Committee on the Lithosphere (SCL).

The ICSU also supports the World Data Center System to assist in the coordination and sharing of data collected and stored by scientific groups in countries worldwide. It is also responsible for the Federation of Astronomical and Geophysical Data Analysis Services (FAGS), which coordinates efforts to collect, store, and disseminate data for the astronomy, geodesy, and geophysics disciplines.

World Wide Web Consortium. The World Wide Web Consortium (W3C) "develops interoperable technologies (specifications, guidelines, software, and tools) to lead the Web to its full potential. W3C is a forum for information, commerce, communication, and collective understanding" (World Wide Web Consortium, 2006). W3C plays an important role in developing technologies and standards for the World Wide Web. For example, it has promoted the adoption of Unicode as the standard including systems to support non-Roman alphabets and ideograms. The influence of W3C is seen in Web initiatives as far ranging as from style sheets to the Semantic Web concept (Berners-Lee, Hendler, and Lassila, 2001).

One very important undertaking is the Web Accessibility Initiative (WAI). WAI develops standards and processes for Web access for persons with disabilities (for more in-depth information see www.w3.org/WAI). The range of activity of the W3C in developing technologies and standards is indicated in figure 11-1.

Standards Organizations

The standards setting, maintaining, and regulating organizations are for the most part, but not exclusively, nongovernmental organizations (NGOs). There are also important governmental and international governmental organizations (IGOs) involved in standards setting and maintenance. These organizations

Accessibility	Improving Web accessibility for those with disabilities
Amaya	Web editor and browser
Annotea	Annotation software
Composite Capabilities/Preference Profiles—CC/PP	Device capability description profiles
Cascading Style Sheets—CSS	Style adaptor
Device Independence	Full Web access by all devices
Document Object Model—DOM	Platform/language neutral interface for document access
HyperText Markup Language—HTML	Standards evolution for HTML
HTML Tidy	HTML utility for error correction
HTML Validator	HTML "check" service
InkML	Electronic pen input formats
Internationalization	Support for UNICODE, use of various languages worldwide
Jigsaw	Web server platform
Libwww	W3C Protocol Library
MathML	Machine-machine math description
Multimodal Interaction	Various interaction standards
Patent Policy	Patents, standards, and the WWW
PICS	Metadata format
PNG	Raster image format
Privacy and P3P	Privacy control issues
Quality Assurance	Across W3C initiatives
RDF	Metadata format
Semantic Web	Metadata format
Synchronized Multimedia Integration Language—SMIL	Audiovisual presentation authoring
Style	Presentation definition
Scalable Vector Graphics—SVG	Graphics presentation
Technical Architecture Group—TAG	To build consensus around Web architecture
Timed Text	Real time text
URI/URL	Naming and addressing initiatives
Validators	Web document checks
Voice	Voice enabling
WAI	—see accessibility—
WebCGM	Electronic CGM standard
Web Ontology	Develop standard syntax and thesaurus
XForms	Web based form standards
XML	Markup language
XPath	Addresses points in an XML document
XSL and XSLT	XML Stylesheet standards

Figure 11-1   Selected W3C Standards Initiatives

Source: World Wide Web Consortium. 2006. "W3C A to Z." Available: www.w3.org/ (accessed December 2006).

and their work were discussed briefly in chapter 4 but are covered more expansively here.

What are standards? Standards are sometimes formal, sometimes informal agreements among individuals, corporations, and/or governments to accept amongst themselves an understanding, a process, a definition as a given.

Standards represent a consensus within a community that certain tools, processes, and products should function in some specified manner or meet some level of consistency.

These national and international organizations can be divided according to function and competence. There are general standards setting organizations in nearly all countries. There are several factors that are important to remember about these kinds of organizations. First, while many standards organizations cannot compel others to comply with the standards they issue, those affected have a strong interest in complying. For example, the ITU issued its V.90 56k modem standard in September 1998. Prior to that date there were two major competing and noncompatible 56k technologies in the marketplace. Adoption of a single standard stabilized both the marketplace and 56k Internet transmission.

The International Organization for Standardization (ISO). ISO is an NGO representing national standards organizations in 156 countries. ISO has three classes of membership: full members, correspondent members, and subscriber members. Full members are private or government agencies fully engaged in standards activities. Correspondent members are private or government agencies that do not yet have fully developed standards activities. Subscriber members represent countries with very small economies. The ISO is an unusual NGO in that some of its national members are national government agencies while others are private agencies. Full members are shown in figure 11-2.

The ISO catalog lists more than 14,000 standards. Of particular interest to the information domains are the 29, 31, 33, 35, and 37 ICS (International Classification for Standards) fields. These classification schemes are further disaggregated to individual ISO standards, each of which is given a unique number. The ISO 9000 and 14000 "generic management system standards" have been recognized as particularly important, especially for the newly industrializing countries. The ISO 9000 series is concerned with "quality management" while ISO 14000 addresses environmental management.

There are a number of ISO standards of specific interest to the information environment. A partial list of more significant ones is shown in figure 11-3.

*International Electrotechnical Commission (IEC).*The IEC prepares and publishes international standards in electronics and electrical technologies. These standards include testing and conformity, quality assessment of components, and certification in "explosive atmospheres."

NATIONAL STANDARDS ORGANIZATIONS

As noted previously, most countries have standards organizations, some of which are government agencies while others are private, as shown in the list of national members of the International Organization for Standards in figure 11-2. All

Algeria—Institut algérien de normalisation (IANOR)
Argentina—Instituto Argentino de Normalización (IRAM)
Armenia—Department for Standardization, Metrology and Certification (SARM)
Australia—Standards Australia International Ltd. (SAI)
Austria—Österreichisches Normungsinstitut (ON)
Azerbaijan—State Agency on Standardization, Metrology and Patents (AZSTAND)
Bahrain—Directorate of Standards and Metrology, Ministry of Commerce (BSMD)
Bangladesh—Bangladesh Standards and Testing Institution (BSTI)
Barbados—Barbados National Standards Institution (BNSI)
Belarus—Committee for Standardization, Metrology and Certification (BELST)
Belgium—Institut belge de normalisation (IBN)
Bosnia and Herzegovina—Institute for Standards, Metrology and Intellectual Property (BASMP)
Botswana—Botswana Bureau of Standards (BOBS)
Brazil—Associação Brasileira de Normas Técnicas (ABNT)
Bulgaria—Bulgarian Institute for Standardization (BDS)
Canada—Standards Council of Canada (SCC)
Chile—Instituto Nacional de Normalización (INN)
China—Standardization Administration of China (SAC)
Colombia—Instituto Colombiano de Normas Técnicas y Certificación (ICONTEC)
Costa Rica—Instituto de Normas Técnicas de Costa Rica (INTECO)
Croatia—State Office for Standardization and Metrology (DZNM)
Cuba—Oficina Nacional de Normalización (NC)
Cyprus—Cyprus Organization for the Promotion of Quality (CYS)
Czech Republic—Czech Standards Institute (CSNI)
Côte-d'Ivoire—Côte d'Ivoire Normalisation (CODINORM)
Denmark—Dansk Standard (DS)
Ecuador—Instituto Ecuatoriano de Normalización (INEN)
Egypt—Egyptian Organization for Standardization and Quality Control (EOS)
Ethiopia—Quality and Standards Authority of Ethiopia (QSAE)
Finland—Finnish Standards Association (SFS)
France—Association française de normalisation (AFNOR)
Germany—Deutsches Institut für Normung (DIN)
Ghana—Ghana Standards Board (GSB)
Greece—Hellenic Organization for Standardization (ELOT)
Hungary—Magyar Szabványügyi Testület (MSZT)
Iceland—Icelandic Standards (IST)
India—Bureau of Indian Standards (BIS)
Indonesia—Badan Standardisasi Nasional (BSN)
Iran, Islamic Republic of—Institute of Standards and Industrial Research of Iran (ISIRI)
Iraq—Central Organization for Standardization and Quality Control (COSQC)
Ireland—National Standards Authority of Ireland Glasnevin (NSAI)
Israel—Standards Institution of Israel (SII)
Italy—Ente Nazionale Italiano di Unificazione (UNI)
Jamaica—Bureau of Standards Jamaica (JBS)
Japan—Japanese Industrial Standards Committee Technical Regulation, Standards and Conformity Assessment Policy Unit, Ministry of Economy, Trade and Industry (JISC)
Jordan—Jordan Institution for Standards and Metrology (JISM)
Kazakhstan—Committee for Standardization, Metrology and Certification (KAZMEMST)
Kenya—Kenya Bureau of Standards (KEBS)
Korea, Democratic People's Republic—Committee for Standardization (CSK)
Korea, Republic of—Korean Agency for Technology and Standards, Ministry of Commerce, Industry and Energy (KATS)
Kuwait—Public Authority for Industry Standards and Industrial Services Affairs (KOWSMD)

Figure 11-2   National Standards Organizations

(*Continued on p. 293*)

Libyan Arab Jamahiriya—Libyan National Centre for Standardization and Metrology Industrial Research (LNCSM)

Luxembourg—Service de l'Energie de l'Etat, Organisme Luxembourgeois de Normalisation (SEE)

The former Yugoslav Republic of Macedonia—Standardization Institute of the Republic of Macedonia (ISRM)

Malaysia—Department of Standards Malaysia, Ministry of Science, Technology & the Environment (DSM)

Malta—Malta Standards Authority (MSA)

Mauritius—Mauritius Standards Bureau (MSB)

Mexico—Dirección General de Normas (DGN)

Mongolia—Mongolian Agency for Standardization and Metrology (MASM)

Morocco—Service de Normalisation Industrielle Marocaine, Ministère de l'industrie, du commerce et des télécommunications (SNIMA)

Netherlands—Nederlands Normalisatie-instituut (NEN)

New Zealand—Standards New Zealand (SNZ)

Nigeria—Standards Organisation of Nigeria (SON)

Norway—Norges Standardiseringsforbund (NSF)

Oman—Directorate General for Specifications and Measurements, Ministry of Commerce and Industry (DGSM)

Pakistan—Pakistan Standards and Quality Control Authority (PSQCA)

Panama—Comisión Panameña de Normas Industriales y Técnicas (COPANIT)

Philippines—Bureau of Product Standards, Department of Trade and Industry (BPS)

Poland—Polish Committee for Standardization (PKN)

Portugal—Instituto Português da Qualidade (IPQ)

Romania—Asociatia de Standardizare din România (ASRO)

Russian Federation—State Committee of the Russian Federation for Standardization and Metrology (GOST R)

Saudi Arabia—Saudi Arabian Standards Organization (SASO)

Serbia and Montenegro—Institution for Standardization (ISSM)

Singapore—Standards, Productivity and Innovation Board (SPRING SG)

Slovakia—Slovak Standards Institute (SUTN)

Slovenia—Slovenian Institute for Standardization (SIST)

South Africa—South African Bureau of Standards (SABS)

Spain—Asociación Española de Normalización y Certificación (AENOR)

Sri Lanka—Sri Lanka Standards Institution (SLSI)

Sweden—Swedish Standards Institute (SIS)

Switzerland—Swiss Association for Standardization (SNV)

Syrian Arab Republic—Syrian Arab Organization for Standardization and Metrology (SASMO)

Tanzania, United Republic of—Tanzania Bureau of Standards (TBS)

Thailand—Thai Industrial Standards Institute, Ministry of Industry (TISI)

Trinidad and Tobago—Trinidad and Tobago Bureau of Standards (TTBS)

Tunisia—Institut national de la normalisation et de la propriété industrielle (INORPI)

Turkey—Türk Standardlari Enstitüsü (TSE)

United States—American National Standards Institute (ANSI)

Ukraine—State Committee on Technical Regulation and Consumer Policy of Ukraine (DSSU)

United Arab Emirates—Emirates Authority for Standardization and Metrology (ESMA)

United Kingdom—British Standards Institution (BSI)

Uruguay—Instituto Uruguayo de Normas Técnicas (UNIT)

Uzbekistan—Agency for Standardization, Metrology and Certification (UZSTANDARD)

Venezuela—Fondo para la Normalización y Certificación de la Calidad (FONDONORMA)

Viet Nam—Directorate for Standards and Quality (TCVN)

Zimbabwe—Standards Association of Zimbabwe (SAZ)

Figure 11-2   National Standards Organizations (Continued)

ISO/IEC 646:1991	Information technology—ISO 7-bit coded character set for information interchange
ISO 843:1997	Information and documentation—Conversion of Greek characters into Latin characters
ISO 1001:1986	Information processing—File structure and labeling of magnetic tapes for information interchange
ISO 1004:1995	Information processing—Magnetic ink character recognition—Print specifications
ISO 1086:1991	Information and documentation—Title leaves of books
ISO 1155:1978	Information processing—Use of longitudinal parity to detect errors in information messages
ISO 1177:1985	Information processing—Character structure for start/stop and synchronous character oriented transmission
ISO 1681:1973	Information processing—Unpunched paper cards—Specification
ISO 1745:1975	Information processing—Basic mode control procedures for data communication systems
ISO/IEC 17462:2000	Information technology—3,81 mm wide magnetic tape cartridge for information interchange—Helical scan recording—DDS-4 format
ISO/IEC 17799:2000	Information technology—Code of practice for information security management
ISO/IEC 17875:2000	Information technology—Telecommunications and information exchange between systems—Private Integrated Services Network—Specification, functional model and information flows—Private User Mobility (PUM)—Registration supplementary service
ISO/IEC 17876:2003	Information technology—Telecommunications and information exchange between systems—Private Integrated Services Network—Inter-exchange signaling protocol—Private User Mobility (PUM)—Registration supplementary service
ISO/IEC 17877:2000	Information technology—Telecommunications and information exchange between systems—Private Integrated Services Network—Specification, functional model and information flows—Private User Mobility (PUM)—Call handling additional network features
ISO/IEC 17878:2003	Information technology—Telecommunications and information exchange between systems—Private Integrated Services Network—Inter-exchange signaling protocol—Private User Mobility (PUM)—Call handling additional network features
ISO/IEC 17913:2000	Information technology—12,7 mm 128-track magnetic tape cartridge for information interchange—Parallel serpentine format
ISO/IEC 18010:2002	Information technology—Pathways and spaces for customer premises cabling
ISO/IEC 18017:2001	Information technology—Telecommunications and information exchange between systems—Private Integrated Services Network—Mapping functions for the employment of Virtual Private Network scenarios
ISO/IEC 18051:2000	Information technology—Telecommunications and information exchange between systems—Services for Computer Supported Telecommunications Applications (CSTA) Phase III
ISO/IEC 18052:2000	Information technology—Telecommunications and information exchange between systems—Protocol for Computer Supported Telecommunications Applications (CSTA) Phase III
ISO/IEC TR 18053:2000	Information technology—Telecommunications and information exchange between systems—Glossary of definitions and terminology for Computer Supported Telecommunications Applications (CSTA) Phase III
ISO/IEC 18809:2000	Information technology—8 mm wide magnetic tape cartridge for information

Figure 11-3 ISO Information Standards

(Continued on p. 295)

	interchange—Helical scan recording AIT-1 with MIC format
ISO/IEC 18810:2001	Information technology—8 mm wide magnetic tape cartridge for information interchange—Helical scan recording AIT-2 with MIC format
ISO/IEC 18836:2001	Information technology—8 mm wide magnetic tape cartridge for information interchange—Helical scan recording—MammothTape-2 format
ISO/IEC 19058:2001	Information technology—Telecommunications and information exchange between systems—Broadband Private Integrated Services Network—Inter-exchange signaling protocol—Generic functional protocol (available in English only)
ISO 19101:2002	Geographic information—Reference model
ISO 19105:2000	Geographic information—Conformance and testing
ISO 19107:2003	Geographic information—Spatial schema
ISO 19108:2002	Geographic information—Temporal schema
ISO 19111:2003	Geographic information—Spatial referencing by coordinates
ISO 19113:2002	Geographic information—Quality principles
ISO 19114:2003	Geographic information—Quality evaluation procedures
ISO 19115:2003	Geographic information—Metadata
ISO/TR 19120:2001	Geographic information—Functional standards
ISO/TR 19121:2000	Geographic information—Imagery and grided data
ISO/IEC 19459:2001	Information technology—Telecommunications and information exchange between systems—Private Integrated Services Network—Specification, functional model and information flows—Single Step Call Transfer Supplementary Service
ISO/IEC 19460:2003	Information technology—Telecommunications and information exchange between systems—Private Integrated Services Network—Inter-exchange signaling protocol—Single Step Call Transfer supplementary service
ISO/IEC 20061:2001	Information technology—12,65 mm wide magnetic tape cassette for information interchange—Helical scan recording—DTF-2
ISO/IEC 20062:2001	Information technology—8 mm wide magnetic tape cartridge for information interchange—Helical scan recording—VXA-1 format
ISO/IEC 20161:2001	Information technology—Telecommunications and information exchange between systems—Private Integrated Services Network—Use of QSIG at the C reference point between a PINX and an Interconnecting Network
ISO/IEC 21407:2001	Information technology—Telecommunications and information exchange between systems—Private Integrated Services Network—Specification, functional model and information flows—Simple dialog supplementary service
ISO/IEC 21408:2003	Information technology—Telecommunications and information exchange between systems—Private Integrated Services Network—Inter-exchange signaling protocol—Simple dialog supplementary service
ISO/IEC 21409:2001	Information technology—Telecommunications and information exchange between systems—Corporate telecommunication networks—Signaling interworking between QSIG and H.323—Generic functional protocol for the support of supplementary services
ISO/IEC 21410:2001	Information technology—Telecommunications and information exchange between systems—Corporate telecommunication networks—Signaling interworking between QSIG and H.323—Call transfer supplementary services
ISO/IEC 21411:2001	Information technology—Telecommunications and information exchange between systems—Corporate telecommunication networks—Signaling interworking between QSIG and H.323—Call diversion supplementary services
ISO/IEC 21888:2001	Information technology—Telecommunications and information exchange between systems—Private Integrated Services Network—Specification, functional model and information flows—Call Identification and Call Linkage Additional Network Feature
ISO/IEC 21889:2001	Information technology—Telecommunications and information exchange between systems—Private Integrated Services Network—Inter-exchange

Figure 11-3   ISO Information Standards (Continued)

(*Continued on p. 296*)

	signaling protocol—Call Identification and Call Linkage Additional Network Feature
ISO/IEC TR 21890:2001	Information technology—Telecommunications and information exchange between systems—Interoperation of PISNs with IP networks
ISO/IEC 21989:2002	Information technology—Telecommunications and information exchange between systems—Private Integrated Services Network—Specification, functional model and information flows—Short message service
ISO/IEC 21990:2002	Information technology—Telecommunications and information exchange between systems—Private Integrated Services Network—Inter-exchange signaling protocol—Short message service
ISO/IEC 21991:2002	Information technology—Telecommunications and information exchange between systems—Corporate Telecommunication Networks—Signaling interworking between QSIG and H.323—Call completion supplementary services
ISO/IEC 21992:2003	Information technology—Telecommunications and information exchange between systems—Private Integrated Services Network—Mapping functions for the tunneling of QSIG through IP networks
ISO/IEC 22091:2002	Information technology—Streaming Lossless Data Compression algorithm (SLDC)
ISO/IEC 23270:2003	Information technology—C# Language Specification
ISO/IEC 23271:2003	Information technology—Common Language Infrastructure
ISO/IEC TR 23272:2003	Information technology—Common Language Infrastructure—Profiles and Libraries
ISO/IEC 23289:2002	Information technology—Telecommunications and information exchange between systems—Corporate telecommunication networks—Signaling interworking between QSIG and H.323—Basic services
ISO/IEC 23290:2002	Information technology—Telecommunications and information exchange between systems—Private Integrated Services Network—Mapping functions for the tunneling of QSIG through H.323 networks
ISO/IEC 23651:2003	Information technology—8 mm wide magnetic tape cartridge for information interchange—Helical scan recording—AIT-3 format
ISO 15706:2002	Information and documentation—International Standard Audiovisual Number (ISAN)
ISO 15707:2001	Information and documentation—International Standard Musical Work Code (ISWC)
ISO/IEC 15731:1998	Information technology—12,65 mm wide magnetic tape cassette for information interchange—Helical scan recording—DTF-1 format
ISO/IEC 15771:1998	Information technology—Telecommunications and information exchange between systems—Private Integrated Services Network—Specification, functional model and information flows—Common information additional network feature
ISO/IEC 15772:2003	Information technology—Telecommunications and information exchange between systems—Private Integrated Services Network—Inter-exchange signaling protocol—Common Information additional network feature
ISO/IEC 15773:1998	Information technology—Telecommunications and information exchange between systems—Broadband Private Integrated Services Network—Inter-exchange signaling protocol—Transit counter additional network feature
ISO 23950:1998	Information and documentation—Information retrieval (Z39.50)—Application service definition and protocol specification
ISO 2789:2003	Information and documentation—International library statistics
ISO/IEC TR 9573-13:1991	Information and documentation—International library statistics
ISO 14589:2000	Information and documentation—Records management

Figure 11-3   ISO Information Standards (Continued)

Source: International Organization for Standardization. 2006. ISO Standards. Available: www.iso.org/iso/en/CatalogueListPage.CatalogueList (accessed December 2006).

work to rationalize technical matters to promote development, commerce, and trade. The development of standards has proven particularly important in the many information-related fields.

In the United States there are two major general standards organizations—the American National Standards Institute (ANSI) and the National Institute of Standards and Technology (NIST). ANSI is a private-sector organization while NIST is an agency of the U.S. Department of Commerce. NIST has a focus on more "abstract" standards—measurement, time, generalized academic concerns—whereas ANSI provides a venue for more product-related standards to be developed by its participating parties. ANSI represents the U.S. standards community to ISO and IEC.

CONCLUSION

As this brief introduction to regulation and control of information and to a sampling of governmental, intergovernmental, and nongovernmental bodies involved suggests, the regulation and politics of information has become increasingly complex as information has become globalized through the changes in information technology. While information regulation and control is certainly not a new phenomenon, the structures for accomplishing such activities have proliferated and become increasingly broad in the collective overall scope of regulation. The globalization of information is also necessitating increased harmonization of national and international regulatory regimes, raising interesting potential conflicts in some of the policy areas, as will be seen in the next chapter.

QUESTIONS FOR CONSIDERATION

1. What factors influence whether or not information activity is regulated? What would determine the level of regulation? For example, why might or night not VoIP be regulated at international rather than national levels?
2. What kinds of information regulation occur at local levels? What are the bodies that enact and enforce such regulation?
3. What would be the effect on international information flow if there were no international regulatory bodies, such as WIPO and UPU?
4. In general, international policy and regulatory bodies affecting information are unknown to the average information user. How do these bodies affect the general use of information?
5. Which international NGOs are likely to have the most significant impact on regulation of information activities in the United States?

REFERENCES

Allison, Graham T. 1969. "Conceptual Models and the Cuban Missile Crisis." *The American Political Science Review* 63 (September): 689–718.

Benjamin, Stuart M., Douglas Lichtman, and Howard A. Shelanski. 2001. *Telecommunications Law and Policy.* Durham, NC: Carolina Academic Press.

Berners-Lee, Tim, James Hendler, and Ora Lassila. 2001. "The Semantic Web." *Scientific American* 284 (May). Available: www.scientificamerican .com/article.cfm?articleID=00048144-10D2-1C70-84A9809EC588 EF21&catID=2 (accessed December 2006).

Downes, Larry. 2004. "Internet Cleans Its Own House." *USA Today* (7 January). Available: www.usatoday.com/news/opinion/editorials/2004-01-08 -downes_x.htm (accessed December 2006).

Edwards, Lilian, and Charlotte Waelde, eds. 1997. *Law and the Internet: Regulating Cyberspace.* Oxford, UK: Hart Publishing.

International Organization for Standardization. n.d. "ISO Catalogue." Available: www.iso.org/iso/en/CatalogueListPage.CatalogueList (accessed December 2006).

International Telecommunication Union. 2003. "The Valletta Action Plan: A Strategic Plan for the ITU Development Sector." Available: www.itu .int/ITU-D/bdtint/Brochure00/VAP.html (accessed December 2006).

Internet Corporation for Assigned Names and Numbers. 2005. "ICANN Information." Available: www.icann.org/general (accessed December 2006).

Kayani, Rogati, and Andrew Dymond. 1997. *Options for Rural Telecommunications Development.* World Bank Technical Paper No. 359. Washington, DC: World Bank.

Koehler, Wallace. 1999. "Unraveling the Issues, Actors, and Alphabet Soup of the Great Domain Name Debates." *Searcher* 7 (May): 16–17.

———. 2000. "I Think ICANN: Climbing the Internet Regulation Mountain." *Searcher* 8 (March): 49–53.

———. 2001. "ICANN and the New 'Magnificent Seven.'" *Searcher* 9 (February): 56–58.

Mustafa, Mohammad, Bruce Laidlaw, and Mark Brand. 1997. *Telecommunications Policies for Sub-Saharan Africa.* World Bank Discussion Paper No. 353. Washington, DC: World Bank.

Privacy International. *Freedom of Information.* Available: www.privacy international.org/issues/foia (accessed December 2006).

United Nations Educational, Scientific and Cultural Organization. *Ethics of Scientific Knowledge and Technology.* Available: www.unesco.org/opi2/ ethics/information.htm (accessed December 2006).

———. n.d. "UNESCO Constitution." *About UNESCO.* Available: http:// portal.unesco.org/en/ev.php-URL_ID=15244&URL_DO=DO_ TOPIC&URL_SECTION=201.html (accessed December 2006).

U.S. Central Intelligence Agency. 2006. "CIA Vision, Mission, and Values." In

About the CIA. Available: www.cia.gov/cia/information/mission.html (accessed December 2006).

U.S. Department of Commerce. *Management of Internet Names and Addresses*. Docket Number 980212036-8146-02. U.S. National Telecommunications and Information Administration [1998]. Available: www.ntia .doc.gov/ntiahome/domainname/6_5_98dns.htm (accessed December 2006).

U.S. Postal Service. 2001. "Postal Service Announces National Roll-Out of FedEx Drop Boxes at Post Offices." USPS News: Press Releases (19 June), Release No. 01-059. Available: www.usps.com/news/2001/press/ pr01_059.htm (accessed December 2006).

Universal Postal Union. 2001. "UPU at a Glance." *About Us*. Available: www.upu.int/about_us/en/glance.html (accessed December 2006).

Wallace, Jonathan D., and Mark Mangan. 1996. *Sex, Laws, and Cyberspace*. New York: M&T Books.

World Intellectual Property Organization. 2001. "An Organization for the Future." In *About WIPO*. Geneva: WIPO, June. Available: www.wipo .int/about-wipo/en/gib.htm#P23_2347 (accessed December 2006).

World Wide Web Consortium. 2006. *Leading the Web to its Full Potential*. Available at: www.w3.org (accessed December 2006).

ADDITIONAL SOURCES

American National Standards Institute. "About ANSI Overview." Available: www.ansi.org/about_ansi/overview/overview.aspx?menuid=1 (accessed December 2006).

Borgman, Christine L. 2000. "The Premise and Promise of a Global Information Infrastructure." *First Monday* 5 (August). Available: www .firstmonday.org/issues/issue5_8/borgman/index.html (accessed December 2006).

International Council for Science. 2004. *About ICSU*. Available: www .icsu.org/5_abouticsu/INTRO.php (accessed December 2006).

International Electrotechnical Commission. 2006. Available: www.iec.ch (accessed December 2006).

International Federation of Library Associations and Institutions. 2006. "About IFLA." In *IFLANET*. Available: www.ifla.org/III/index.htm (accessed December 2006).

International Organization for Standardization. 2006. "About ISO." Available: www.iso.org/iso/en/aboutiso/introduction/index.html (accessed December 2006).

International Telecommunication Union. 2006. *Welcome to the International*

Telecommunication Union. Available: www.itu.int/home/index.html (accessed December 2006).

Organisation for Economic Co-operation and Development. *Information and Communications Policy.* Available: www.oecd.org/department/ 0,2688,en_2649_34223_1_1_1_1_1,00.html (accessed December 2006).

U.S. Agency for International Development. 2006. "This Is USAID." Available: www.usaid.gov/about_usaid (accessed December 2006).

U.S. Central Intelligence Agency. 2006. *The World Factbook 2006.* Available: www.cia.gov/cia/publications/factbook/index.html (accessed December 2006).

U.S. Federal Communications Commission. 2006. "About the FCC." Available: www.fcc.gov/aboutus.html (accessed December 2006).

U.S. Federal Trade Commission. 2006. "About the Federal Trade Commission." Available: www.ftc.gov/ftc/who.htm (accessed December 2006).

U.S. National Institute of Standards and Technology. 2006. Available: www.nist.gov (accessed December 2006).

U.S. National Security Agency. "Mission Statement." Available: www.nsa.gov/ about/about00003.cfm (accessed December 2006).

U.S. National Telecommunications and Information Administration. 1998. *NTIA.* Available: www.ntia.doc.gov/ntiahome/ntiafacts.htm (accessed December 2006).

U.S. Office of Management and Budget. *About OMB.* Available: www .whitehouse.gov/omb/organization/index.html (accessed December 2006).

U.S. Patent and Trademark Office. 2006. *About USPTO.* Available: www.uspto .gov/main/aboutuspto.htm (accessed December 2006).

U.S. Postal Service. *History of the U.S. Postal Service.* Available: www.usps .com/history/history/his1.htm (accessed December 2006).

World Intellectual Property Organization. *WIPO-Administered Treaties.* Available at: www.wipo.int/treaties/en (accessed December 2006).

World Trade Organization. *The WTO.* Geneva: World Trade Organization. Available: www.wto.org/english/thewto_e/thewto_e.htm (accessed December 2006).

Now that you have been introduced to some of the regulatory bodies and the areas in which they operate, can you identify what the basic categories and issues of information policy are? Based on your reading of the previous chapter, make a list of the areas of regulation that you learned about. Add to the list any additional policy concerns that you can think of from earlier chapters. Then when you have finished this chapter, see how well you did.

Chapter 12

The Areas and Issues of Information Policy

Learning Guide

After reading this chapter, you should be able to

- understand and define the following terms:
  - stakeholder
  - policy actor
  - *droit d'auteur*
  - open access
  - copyright
  - fair use
  - patent

  - trademark
  - service mark
  - trade secret law
  - transborder dataflow
  - e-government
  - public lending right

- identify the following acronyms and explain the relationship of each to information policy:
  - MPAA
  - RIAA
  - HAVA

  - HIPAA
  - USA PATRIOT Act

- describe the general processes of information policy development at national and international levels;
- identify key information policy actors and assess the significance of their activities;
- describe the various issues involved in the regulation of information within the United States;
- explain the effects of digital information on information policy;
- identify important aspects involved in both the access to and ownership of U.S. government information.

  When you have finished the chapter, return to this page to be sure you have learned what you need to know.

INTRODUCTION

The making of information policy in any political entity follows essentially the same process as policy making in any other area. In general, those interested in the area or affected by it, sometimes referred to as stakeholders, work to bring issues of concern to the attention of decision makers in the legislative arm of government. Policy is then enacted in the form of laws—but the formulation of policy really does not stop there. The implementation of the enacted legislation requires further policy making through the establishment of regulations, which specify the details of the policy, by the bodies charged with executing the laws (for example, by those governmental and intergovernmental regulatory bodies discussed in the previous chapter). In establishing those details, further policy making is occurring, sometimes beyond or at odds with what the legislative body thought it had enacted. In some political systems, policy determination continues in the judicial branch of government through the interpretation of the intent of the law or in consideration of whether the policy as enacted or implemented is in conflict with basic fundamental principles of the system, such as those articulated in a constitution.

For all policy, the process is complex, with many individuals, groups, and organizational entities involved (all of whom may be referred to as policy actors). For information policy, the process of formulation and implementation is even more complicated, primarily because information issues pervade nearly all other policy areas. Hence information policy formulation and implementation is diffused throughout multiple governmental, intergovernmental, and nongovernmental entities.

Although there are certainly many ways to think about the basic issues of information policy, one useful approach is to think of policy in three categories:

- policies related to generation and production of information
- policies on dissemination of and access to information
- policies on distribution of information

The first category includes policies that foster information creation and that encourage the recording of it in formats that can be reproduced. The second includes those policies that govern how information created and produced in some kind of information record is made accessible. This category would include policies that govern who may have access to information and under what conditions that access may be granted. The final category encompasses policies that govern how the distribution of information is accomplished—the economic aspects of how access is financed.

POLICIES ON GENERATION AND PRODUCTION

One major issue addressed by this set of policies is the role of government or the state in information generation and production. As we saw in the chapter on the economics of information, governments differ in how actively they are involved in developing information. For some, the role is primarily one of establishing a policy framework and regulatory infrastructure that will foster information development by the private sector. This approach would include legal provisions to protect intellectual property and to support a reward structure for information creators that will encourage their activities. In this area we find the laws related to copyright, patents, trademarks, and trade secrets. These legal structures serve to ensure that there is opportunity for financial reward from the intellectual labor of creating and producing information and to protect that intellectual property from theft, just as there are laws to protect individuals from theft of physical property. The structures are closely related, although they offer protection for different kinds of intellectual property and operate somewhat differently in terms of how they foster information generation.

Copyright is the concept applied to protection of expression of ideas from the unauthorized use by others and protects ownership rights for "transmittable" works—written, audio, video, etc. As we will see later in this chapter, there are differences in the concept and application of intellectual property rights between Eastern and Western intellectual property thought. However, in general, at least in Western nations, there is the concept that for some limited period of time (which varies) a right to control the reproduction of the expression of ideas (with some exceptions) resides with the creator of the information or a person or entity to whom that right has been transferred.

As technology advances, conflict escalates between the notion of copyright, which evolved in the print era, and the kinds of access to information that are possible in today's digital world. The Google Books Library Project (previously called Print for Libraries Project), which includes digitization of both in- and out-of-copyright materials, has brought forth concerns and direct challenge from publishers who see the project—at least the portion that includes the scanning and making available of copyrighted materials—as a threat to and violation of copyright. The Association of American University Presses (AAUP) has challenged Google's assertion that digitizing copyrighted materials can be done legally under the provisions of fair use (Section 107 of the Copyright Act) and by formal letter demanded a response from Google to sixteen questions that address various aspects of the Google claim. The AAUP view is that the project "is built on a fundamental, broad-sweeping violation of the Copyright Act" (Givler, 2005: 1–2). Both the Author's Guild and the Association of American Publishers (on behalf of five publishers: Wiley, Pearson Education, Simon & Schuster, Penguin Group USA, and McGraw-Hill) have filed suit against Google over this project.

Interestingly, the Google project has also raised concerns in Europe, but of a different policy nature. The perceived threat there is of increasing English-language domination (and particularly U.S. domination) of digital resources available via the Internet. In response, nineteen national libraries in Europe are supporting a European digital library project proposed to the European Commission and the European Council by heads of government in France, Germany, Hungary, Italy, Poland, and Spain.

Concerns related to copyright in electronic media are escalating. While there is activity on a number of fronts addressing copyright concerns, the most intense activity has been in the area of distribution of music files via the Web. With the failure of warnings to file swappers to significantly deter the illegal music file sharing activity, the Recording Industry Association of America (RIAA), which blames such activity for falling sales of CDs, mounted an aggressive campaign of lawsuits against individual violators who have shared copyright-protected music via the Web. The issuing of subpoenas to Internet Service Providers to force identification of violators, which has been upheld in federal court, spread to institutions of higher education, raising privacy of information concerns. The RIAA offered an "amnesty program" in return for copyright violators deleting their illegal files and promising not to engage in further such activity. Alternative, legal solutions to obtaining music files via the web are offered by the iTunes Music Store service from Apple Computer, RealNetworks' Rhapsody music service, and similar services, which provide for low-cost downloading of individual songs. This trend toward legal downloading is helping to restructure the entire music industry (see discussion in chapter 8). Even universities have entered into agreements with music companies to provide download rights for their students. Copyright issues related to the posting of videos via YouTube and other video sharing sites is another growing area of concern (Sandoval, 2006).

Patents, which also provide for protection for limited periods of time, protect an invention, a process or a product rather than expression of an idea, reserving to the inventor of the process or product the exclusive right to control its use. Patents are process designs that specify precisely how a new device is constructed and its application. The patent holder may make the process or product available for use by others through the granting of licenses, although the requirement to do this differs among countries. As with copyright, the protection is for intellectual creation that is unique and affords opportunity for financial gain as a means of encouraging intellectual effort.

Trademarks, a much more restricted form of intellectual property, protect a means of expression that is unique (as with copyright) and used to identify a specific good or family of goods. The trademark is identified with the specific company providing the good and conveys information about the presumed quality of the good. Trademarks do not have limited terms, although the exclusive use of a trademark may be lost if the trademark holder allows others to use it without challenge. For services there is a similar legal structure called a service mark. Trade and service marks may have no intrinsic value as such, but are valuable because they symbolize something else that has intrinsic value.

Trade secret law, which applies to confidential information not covered by patent or other intellectual property structures, provides protection from leakage or illegal transfer of information to competitors that could benefit financially from having such access. As with trademarks, the information so protected is not limited in term, but it must be guarded from loss and use by others in order to remain covered by trade secret law. The most famous trade secret, perhaps, is the Coca Cola recipe. Many have tried, but no one has yet succeeded in ferreting out the precise mixture. Once a process or concept is known it is never completely safe from the "competition." Although copyrights, patents, trademarks, and service marks are registered with governmental regulatory bodies and have at least the appearance of a regulatory and protection enforcement structure, trade secrets are not registered and enforcement is not through regulatory bodies.

Other aspects of policy that address the area of generation and production are those that speak to encouragement of diversity of sources of information content, that is, policies that attempt to ensure that content creation and production are not controlled by so few entities as to prevent market entry by others and to severely limit the diversity of information available. In the United States, this policy area is addressed both by the more general antitrust laws and by the regulations of the Federal Communications Commission, particularly those related to control of ownership of mass media, which is discussed in Part I and was also discussed in the chapter on societal institutions.

Intellectual property doctrine has evolved and continues to do so. Definitions of intellectual property vary from culture to culture and from time to time. Despite efforts to codify intellectual property at international (e.g., Berne Convention, World Intellectual Property Organization) and national (e.g., U.K. Copyright Designs and Patents Act of 1988, U.S. Digital Millennium Copyright Act of 1998) levels, national jurisprudence varies.

National and International Approaches

There are different traditions and approaches to the protection of intellectual property in different countries. These traditions and current approaches reflect the legal and ethical environments both within the various countries and at the international level. The French emphasis is on fairness and originality, so that the work must show something of the author beyond a restatement of the "obvious."

The idea that the author must be reflected in protected work developed into the very formalistic German approach, with the requirement of a high degree of creativity, which is "particularly severe in computer related/created works" (Lea, 1993a: 63). Such a stance contrasts with "the idiosyncratic United Kingdom copyright system" where "the standard of originality required of a would-be work is based more on labor expended (and costs incurred) than on questions of creativity" (Lea, 1993b: 127) and with the equally idiosyncratic U.S. system that focuses more on legal title to a protected work than on originality, creativity, or labor inputs. It is commonly thought that U.K. and American law primarily protect the interests of the investor and employer, while the civil law approach of continental Europe emphasizes the rights of individual authors: In France he or she who has made the greatest intellectual contribution to intellectual property is deemed to deserve the greatest protection.

European continental, U.K., and U.S. practices share a distinctly *individualist* ethos. This focus on individualist rights is largely a trans-Atlantic jurisprudence and one of fairly recent etiology. African and Asian thought are more *collectivist* in orientation. It has been shown (Hesse, 1996) that Western thinking on the source and ownership of intellectual creativity has undergone a perhaps not-too-subtle metamorphosis from one, still shared in Africa and Asia, where the producer of intellectual property is a conduit creating a shared social good to one where the producer/owner holds a private, exploitable economic good. Whatever the merits of intellectual property as a private good, the swing of the pendulum today tends to trump fair use and other access rights of the information user to the benefit of the rights owner.

Like the focus on the individual, emphasis on protecting the rights of the intellectual property owner over those of the user and creator is of recent development. Current practice as defined by the Berne Convention and maintained by the World Intellectual Property Organization is largely a North American and European twentieth-century phenomenon. A very different culture existed previously in Europe and North America, one that persists somewhat in other parts of the world today.

As noted, ideas and treatment of intellectual property differ over time and by country. Intellectual property issues are defined at the international level in community law ("common" international law) and by treaty. The World International Property Organization (WIPO) and related international governmental organizations (IGOs discussed in the previous chapter) regulate, implement, and (in the minds of some) create new law. WIPO is said to have concluded that copyright systems are better adapted to meet the challenge of technology than are *droit d'auteur* (rights of the author) systems.

The Berne Convention for the Protection of Literary and Artistic Works is recognized as guiding and defining international intellectual property issues. Article 6*bis* of the Berne Convention has been fundamental to the spread of explicit moral rights protection into the countries of the Anglo-Saxon or "common-law" tradition. It holds that

1. Independently of the author's economic rights, and even after the transfer of the said rights, the author shall have the right to claim authorship of the work and to object to any distortion, mutilation or other modification of, or other derogatory action in relation to, the said work, which would be prejudicial to his honor or reputation.
2. The rights granted to the author in accordance with the preceding paragraph shall, after his death, be maintained, at least until the expiry of the economic rights, and shall be exercisable by the persons or institutions authorized by the legislation of the country where protection is claimed. However, those countries whose legislation, at the moment of their ratification of or accession to this Act, does not provide for the protection after the death of the author of all the rights set out in the preceding paragraph may provide that some of these rights may, after his death, cease to be maintained.
3. The means of redress for safeguarding the rights granted by this Article shall be governed by the legislation of the country where protection is claimed. (Berne Convention, Article 6 (*bis*))

The advent of international regulation under the Berne Convention, WIPO, and the requirements imposed on members of the World Trade Organization (WTO) has caused member states to restructure their intellectual property law to be more consistent and to enforce more strictly existing legislation. (See for example, People's Republic of China. State Intellectual Property Office, 2004). The likely outcome of creating parallel national intellectual property regulation will certainly be a greater conformity and homogenization of law consistent with the Berne Convention and WIPO and WTO requirements. When the United States became signatory to the Berne Convention in 1988, American law was slowly modified to take greater recognition of European continentalist practices, particularly in regard to the rights of authors.

POLICIES ON DISSEMINATION OF AND ACCESS TO INFORMATION

What kinds of information may and many not be disseminated or accessed is the key focus of policies on dissemination of and access to information. This group of policies covers access to information produced by government, access to information in the private sector, and government access to personal information. The general policies related to access to government information have been discussed in chapter 11, including some of the policy considerations for access to personal information held by government, particularly as these concepts are structured in the United States. In summary, the U.S. policy in this area is in favor of open availability of information and wide dissemination. The overarching concept for access to information in the United States is that, absent specific reasons for restriction, information should be freely (that is, in an unrestricted manner) available to anyone wanting it. That said, there are areas of information that are commonly accepted as ones in which restriction of access or restriction of dissemination is appropriate. These areas include the following categories:

- information that is false or misleading
- information that may imperil or threaten national security
- information that is slanderous or libelous
- information that is obscene
- information that is personal

In all of these categories, there is an inherent intent to protect the individual or society from what are assumed to be the real or potential harmful effects of the information. There are legal structures and regulatory environments that seek to establish a framework in which protection is afforded, without undue violation of First Amendment rights. Such structures related to false and misleading information include laws and regulations prohibiting false advertising. For information that would affect national security there are regulatory structures that classify information, restricting access through various levels of controls. For slander (oral communication) or libel (published or broadcast communication), there are protections through tort law. Obscene information is generally not considered to have First Amendment protection, and laws exist at various levels of government that proscribe the dissemination of obscene information. Personal information, both personal information held by government and that held by the private sector, is protected by a complex, often confusing, set of laws. This category will be discussed more extensively later in this chapter.

In this policy area, issues arise, not so much on whether there should be limitations on access to or dissemination of information in these categories, but on what information actually falls within each of the categories. Here also arise considerable differences between U.S. interpretations of what information should fall into these categories of restriction and interpretations of other nations, including those of western Europe.

Beyond these categories, there are other categories of restrictions on dissemination of and access to information that relate not to the potential harm to the individual or society as a whole, but to perceived threats to the nation-state of either a political or an economic nature or threats to the national culture. Another way to describe this area would be limitations placed on availability of information when such limits are necessary to protect the nation's interests. Particularly for information that is exported outside of or imported into a country, and hence part of "transborder dataflow" (data or information crossing national borders), there are concerns about the harmful effects, with resulting policy frameworks and legal and regulatory structures that seek to control such information movement. The primary categories of restrictions would include the following:

- economic restrictions
- national sovereignty restrictions
- cultural heritage restrictions
- national security restrictions

Restrictions driven by concerns for a nation's economy, particularly that nation's development of its information industry, include export and import regulations, regulations on information technology transfer, tariffs, and immigration laws. This area may also encompass restrictions on dataflow outside of the country and restriction of access to foreign technology. National sovereignty restrictions include controls on the press, requirements for adherence to state approved interpretations in information products, and blocking of information that is politically contrary to the nation's government. Cultural heritage restrictions vary broadly but include such policies as requirements for specified percentages of information content originating in the country in television broadcasts, films shown in theaters, or other media; requirements restricting use of languages other than the national language or requiring preference for the national language in information products; restrictions on export of cultural material (paintings, sculpture, etc.); and blocking of information disseminated from other countries, either through import controls on printed materials or blocking of information disseminated electronically. National security restrictions, beyond those included above, encompass prohibitions of export of information technologies, requirements for processing of certain types of information within the country, and restriction of access to seemingly nonsecret information which, when aggregated, could provide information threatening to national defense, particularly if accessed by terrorist groups.

POLICIES ON DISTRIBUTION OF INFORMATION

How and under what auspices and at what costs charged to whom information can be obtained are the issues related to policies on distribution of information. As indicated in the introduction to this chapter, the complex of policies on distribution of information addresses issues of how access to information is financed. Who pays for the distribution and who pays for the access afforded to the individual? Although these issues have been addressed from an information economics point of view in chapter 9, there are policy aspects that go beyond what has been discussed. To a large degree, some of these additional issues are ethical ones, and further exploration of the ethical aspects will be included in the next chapter. Here, the policy areas will be identified and the basic concerns explored.

The major questions addressed in this area include the following:

How is access to information provided?
  —through the marketplace?
  —via some form of governmental or societal subsidy?
Is there a societal responsibility to equalize distribution mechanisms?
Are there any rights of society or individuals for information that counter the rights of the holders of intellectual property?

The answers to these questions, as with all of the policy issues considered thus far, vary among nations and are dependent in large measure on the political and economic structure of the country and on the value system.

In the United States, the prevailing framework for distribution of information and information products and services is the same as that for any other product or service: through the marketplace, with governmental interference, regulation, or control only as necessary to enable the market to work or in the interests of society as a whole. The issue of societal benefit from information and the resulting concept of public good provision of information were explored in chapter 9.

The answer to the question of the responsibility of society to equalize distribution mechanisms is one that, in the United States, changes as the political climate of the country changes. As noted previously (see the chapter on economics of information), concern for equalizing access to digital information currently appears to be waning, although important structures that support the concept of equalization of access through some form of societal (government) subsidy remain. The postal service, the public education system (including both K–12 and higher education), and the public library system do not appear under threat. The e-rate for telecommunications also continues, although its track record does not yet assure that it will reach the same level of integration into the societal fabric as the other institutions mentioned have achieved.

The rights of individuals and society to information that is the intellectual property of the creator is addressed through attempts to balance absolute ownership with a concept of limited right of use, known in U.S. copyright law as "fair use." This concept is discussed more expansively in the last section of this chapter. In other countries, including most other English-speaking nations, there is a further policy structure that addresses this balance, known as "public lending right." Under the public lending right (PLR) schemes, authors receive government payments for the lending of their books by public libraries. This approach goes far beyond any attempt in the United States to balance the governmental interference in the market for intellectual products with the rights of the creators of those products; but it is well established in a number of nations, including Australia, Austria, Belgium, Canada, Denmark, Estonia, the Faroe Islands, Finland, France, Germany, Greenland, Iceland, Israel, Liechtenstein, The Netherlands, New Zealand, Norway, Sweden, and the United Kingdom. It has recently been implemented in Latvia. During 2006, PLR was anticipated in Ireland, Lithuania, Luxembourg, the Slovak Republic, and Switzerland (Public Lending Right International Network, 2005).

There is another movement of importance addressing both the areas of intellectual property structure and policies for distribution of information, one that is something of a counter-culture challenge to the status quo. This challenge is occurring along several fronts. This movement includes national and international professional associations that find that current intellectual property regulations inhibit the free flow of ideas. It includes countries in development that tolerate the "one legal copy" (with all other copies being pirated from that copy) regime. It includes scholarly analysis, the "creative commons," (flexible copyright licenses) and open access initiatives. And it includes the unlawful and quasi-unlawful peer-to-peer services that try to ignore the intellectual property regulatory environment.

One of the most important aspects of this counter-culture challenge, the open access movement, has two basic orientations. The first is to provide online access to scientific and scholarly literature at little or no cost to users. The second is concerned with computer hardware and software access, again with little or no cost to end users and modifiers.

These challenges and the history of intellectual property theory change suggest that the current "exclusivist" interpretation of intellectual property doctrine may well undergo an evolution. Given emergent practice, the doctrine as modified may be more tolerant of end user and information creator rights and privileges.

There are any number of "collectivist" or "commons" initiatives that have been proposed to provide a less controlled environment for access to and use of information. A primary but by no means exclusive focus of the many open access initiatives concern access to and use of information provided over the Internet and the creation of code to present that information. The open access argument often includes issues of equity and fair use. For example, in October 2003, the Conference on Open Access to Knowledge in the Sciences and Humanities in Berlin concluded:

> Our mission of disseminating knowledge is only half complete if the information is not made widely and readily available to society. New possibilities of knowledge dissemination not only through the classical form but also and increasingly through the open access paradigm via the Internet have to be supported. We define open access as a comprehensive source of human knowledge and cultural heritage that, has been approved by the scientific community.
>
> In order to realize the vision of a global and accessible representation of knowledge, the future Web has to be sustainable, interactive, and transparent. Content and software tools must be openly accessible and compatible.

Further, the Conference declared:

> Open access contributions must satisfy two conditions:
>
> 1. The author(s) and right holder(s) of such contributions grant(s) to all users a free, irrevocable, worldwide, right of access to, and a license to copy, use, distribute, transmit and display the work publicly and to make and distribute derivative works, in any digital medium for any responsible purpose, subject to proper attribution of authorship (community standards will continue to provide the mechanism for enforcement of proper attribution and responsible use of the published work, as they do now), as well as the right to make small numbers of printed copies for their personal use.
> 2. A complete version of the work and all supplemental materials, including a copy of the permission as stated above, in an appropriate standard electronic format is deposited (and thus published) in at least one online repository using suitable technical standards (such

as the Open Archive definitions) that is supported and maintained by an academic institution, scholarly society, government agency, or other well-established organization that seeks to enable open access, unrestricted distribution, inter operability, and long-term archiving. (Berlin Declaration, 2006)

The Berlin Declaration is more individualistic than collectivistic, for it recognizes the rights of "author(s) and right holder(s)" who grant access to digital works. And to a large degree, the open access movement is concerned with access to and the use of digital works rather than all works, including print-based analog creations.

Recent commentators (e.g., Bollier, 2002, 2005; Lessig, 2001, 2004; Vaidhyanathan, 2001, 2004) have argued along an "information commons" metaphor. The bases of their arguments derive from the concept that we all share an information commons (a collectivist traditionalist approach) and that more legalistic, individualistic, and pro-right holder's jurisprudence has significantly eroded the collectivist-traditional rights we all held, resulting in perhaps the inevitable loss of fair use and other information access and use rights.

We do not begin to argue that the major trend in the regulation of intellectual property—that of individualistic ownership of intellectual property and the concomitant reduction of the rights of consumers and users of information—is on the wane. The legal environment is buttressed by the Berne Convention, the World Intellectual Property Organization, and the World Trade Organization, powerful, explicitly legal and implicitly ethical constructs. Nonetheless, we do suggest that however distant the voices and however far in the wilderness they may be, there are intellectual forces that recognize an ethical wrong in the development of intellectual property rights management. These voices may have begun to have an effect in moderating the overall impact of intellectual property rights management. Contrast if you will on the one hand the Digital Millennium Copyright Act of 1998 and the Sonny Bono Copyright Term Extension Act of 1998, both of which favor the rights holder, and on the other, the Technology, Education, and Copyright Harmonization Act (TEACH Act) of 2002, which defines certain fair use guidelines for intellectual property in the teaching and research environment and enhances the rights of the information user.

Finally, we would point out the obvious. For the most part the open access initiatives have been limited to the academic research and publication environment. Without question, the scholarly publications industry has become very centralized and expensive. To a large degree, open access publications advocate a much freer environment for the distribution, use, and derivative utilization of scholarly materials. Some might see this as a mechanism to break the oligopoly of publishers; others see it as a natural extension of scholarly activity. But again, for the most part, the open access movement does not extend to the entertainment market. Whither goest the scholarly market, the entertainment market will likely continue to remain highly centralized and more controlled to the benefit of the rights holder and to the detriment of the information consumer.

MAJOR AREAS OF CURRENT POLICY CONCERN

At the present time, there are three areas of information policy that are of pressing concern, both within the United States and worldwide. While there are other areas that are important, the changes that have been and are occurring as the result of developments in information technology have escalated attention to the areas of intellectual property, particularly the issue of copyright in electronic media; protection of information about individuals, which falls under the general rubric of privacy of information; and the digital information infrastructure, particularly the control of access to and use of the Internet, or as it is being called, "network neutrality."

Copyright

As indicated above, the structures of copyright afford protection to the owner of intellectual property and are balanced somewhat by attempts to provide for use of that property by others. Copyright and fair use are complex legal concepts. At their basis is the idea that the creators or innovators of new ideas should be able to protect the expression of their ideas or innovation against unauthorized use by others. At the same time, the consumers and users of information have rights to access information, to utilize information to create new information. While there is a legal regime established at the international level under the auspices of the World Intellectual Property Organization to administer the Berne Convention, copyright law is a matter of national jurisdiction. Until the United States became party to the Berne Convention, there were subtle but real differences between American practice and European practice.

As noted earlier in this chapter, there remain philosophical differences between approaches to Western and Eastern intellectual property thought, and hence in different systems copyright, patents, and other intellectual property rights are interpreted differently. In Western practice, copyright is an individual right, one that the creator of intellectual property can exercise, waive, or transfer at will. Civil law treatment of copyright is found in most continental European countries and other regions that have adopted those systems. In most civil law traditions, the artistic integrity of a work resides in the creator of the work. According to the Berne Convention, this integrity translates into rights inherent in the creator of the art or idea. In common law, largely Anglo-American, traditions, as in the United States, artistic rights can be transferred from one person or entity to another. Once waived or transferred, the rights to the intellectual property reside in the new owner. In Eastern practice, as in China and other Asian countries, the creation of intellectual property is seen as a social, collective exercise. The individual creator of intellectual property is merely a conduit through which the creative spirit of society is manifested, through which the artistic and intellectual expression of the community occurs (National Research Council, 2000). As a result, the creation is perceived to belong more to society than to the individual. Accordingly, the individual creator of the intellectual property has fewer rights in the product than in the West. We observed earlier in the chapter that this Eastern perception is not foreign to Western thought. Indeed, as late as the eighteenth century, the concept of individual intellectual property rights was not the norm in Europe. It was common practice for authors, playwrights, and artists to "borrow" liberally from one another without attribution or permission. Indeed, music composers often borrowed themes from one another, sometimes acknowledging the source, sometimes not. In fact, until the nineteenth century, authors generally did not profit significantly from their literary efforts. Ownership and profit was usually vested in the publisher. Authors had the honor and glory of fame, but to profit from such an endeavor simply was not "gentlemanly."

Before going further, let us dispel a common misconception. Ideas themselves cannot be copyrighted or patented. Even if ideas could be patented or copyrighted, in order to qualify for protection, the idea would have to be original. It is cliché but true that "nothing is new under the sun." All ideas and processes have a basis in ideas and processes that came before them. Can we distinguish between what is new and what has come before? Moreover, it is possible and in fact likely that several people could have similar ideas at the same or at different times. Scientists sometimes race to publish new ideas that emerge at the same time, because those ideas are based in part on the findings of others that make the new ideas possible. In science, as in other fields of human endeavor, the race goes to those who are first.

Under the Berne Convention and the U.S. Digital Millennium Copyright Act of 1998, copyright resides automatically in the creator of the work, whether artist, musician, or writer. To be copyrightable, a work must be "fixed in tangible form." Moreover, to be copyrighted, a work need only be "created"; it is no longer necessary for it to be "published." Nor is it now necessary for works to contain the copyright notice (copyright © year, name). These two requirements were part of the Copyright Law of 1909 but eliminated under the 1976 Copyright Act and after the United States became party to the Berne Convention in 1989. For works created after 1978, a copyright lasts the lifetime of the creator plus 70 years. For works copyrighted before 1978, the Sonny Bono Copyright Term Extension Act of 1998 extended the copyright term to 95 years.

The creator can assign the copyright to a second party for publication, reproduction, or for whatever other purpose. The copyright assignee then owns the rights to the work. Under U.S. law, a copyright transfer can be terminated after 35 years under specific circumstances.

In principle, once copyright lapses, it falls into the public domain. It can then be used without permission. Information creators almost always transfer their copyrights to publishers or producers. Sometimes the creator of a work may have never held the copyright. This happens when a creation is a "work for hire." This situation typically occurs when a writer or other creator is contracted to produce a specific intellectual product: a magazine article, a movie script, and so on. Copyrights for works for hire typically reside in the contractor rather than the contractee. Once the publisher or producer owns the copyright, those rights are held by them for the copyright term.

Fair Use

By fair use, we mean how someone may make use of the intellectual property of others. We have long accepted the idea that one may "borrow" the ideas and accomplishments of others so long as adequate attribution or citation is made. By borrowing the ideas of others, we do not necessarily arrogate their exact words, sounds, images, movements, but rather the underlying meaning. When we do copy their concepts, new intellectual property concerns are raised. Complex rules have evolved to help us to acknowledge the works of others. The taking of intellectual property at one level is plagiarism, at another, "piracy." Both plagiarism and piracy can have serious social and legal consequences.

Fair use is also concerned with the copying of text, images, sounds, etc., created by others for decorative, scientific, educational, and other uses. This was not a particularly major issue until the mid-twentieth century, when the advent of quick and inexpensive copying made it possible to duplicate intellectual property artifacts. It has always been possible to copy, but it has not always been possible to do it easily and accurately. For centuries, scribes copied and recopied manuscripts. And certainly, with the advent of the printing press, "unauthorized" copies of popular works were commonplace. But these practices required the expenditure of much time and effort.

Copy machines changed the time and effort equation. It is now a fairly recognized principle that one may make copies of material for personal or scholarly use. It is also generally recognized that the number of copies of the same work one may make is usually limited and limited perhaps to one copy. Under the Texaco rule resulting from a U.S. Federal Court decision (*American Geophysical Union v Texaco, Inc.*, 60 F.3d 913 (2d Cir. 1995)), it is clear that it goes beyond fair use to make multiple copies of articles for multiple uses, whether to avoid the need to buy multiple copies or to facilitate information dissemination. The rules for educational use of intellectual property have grown more complex. For example, except on a spontaneous basis, professors may not make multiple copies of scholarly articles and distribute them to their students; however, students individually may make those copies. There are also limits on the amount one may copy from a single work. One may not photocopy an entire book or journal, but one chapter or article is probably acceptable.

Fair use continues to be defined in statute law and court decisions. Fair use as a term of practice has moved from little or no regulation over the use of the intellectual property of others to an interesting morass of sometimes conflicting ideas and jurisdictions. Today, fair use is defined in the United States by the U.S. Copyright Act of 1976 and by federal court decisions that have interpreted it. The Act provides a four-part test for fair use. Under section 107:

> In determining whether the use made of a work in any particular case is a fair use the factors to be considered shall include
>
> 1. the purpose and character of the use, including whether such use is of a commercial nature or is for nonprofit educational purposes;
> 2. the nature of the copyrighted work;
> 3. the amount and substantiality of the portion used in relation to the copyrighted work as a whole;
> 4. the effect of the use upon the potential market for or value of the copyrighted work.
>
> The fact that a work is unpublished shall not itself bar a finding of fair use if such finding is made upon consideration of all the above factors. (U.S. Code Title 17 Chapter 1 § 107)

In the United States, defining case law includes *Basic Books, Inc. v Kinko's Graphics Corp* (1991); *Maxtone-Graham v Burtchaell*, (1987); *Encyclopaedia Britannica Educational Corp. v Crooks* (1982); and *American Geophysical Union v Texaco Inc.* (1994, 1995). The *Basic Books* case found that Kinko's infringed copyright when creating student course packs without appropriate payment of royalties. In *Burtchaell*, the court found that extensive quotations from another work did not per se represent an unfair taking. The use of appropriately cited material was, in fact, a fair use of copyrighted material. In the *Encyclopaedia Britannica Educational Corp.* case, the court held that wholesale copying and distribution of educational television programming, even for purely educational purposes, was beyond fair use and an illegal use of copyrighted material. As mentioned earlier, in the *Texaco* case the court found that the making of multiple copies of journal articles for distribution to Texaco researchers from a single subscription was an unfair taking of copyrighted materials.

The Purpose and Character test is an interesting one. It includes not only whether the fair use taking is for economic purposes but also why the taking was done. Thus Purpose and Character justifications include criticism, parody, and artistic expression.

The Nature of the Copyrighted Work test is concerned with the motive behind the creation of the copyrighted work. It also addresses the kind of work taken. Scholarly publications may have by their very nature a different level of protection from entertainment. "Sweat of the brow" is also important. Is the original work merely a collection of facts or does it represent a interpretative effort? In the United States, some intellectual effort is required (the *Feist* rule: *Feist Publications, Inc. v Rural Telephone Service Co.*, 499 U.S. 340 [1991]). In Australia, the mere effort of compiling a list (sweat of the brow) is sufficient to convey copyright protection (*Desktop Marketing* rule: *Desktop Marketing Systems Pty Ltd v Telstra Corporation Ltd* [2002] FCAFC 112).

The Amount Taken test is an argument that the taking of very small parts of a copyrighted work is fair use.

The Market Impact test addresses the economic damage a fair use taking might have on the copyright holder. Under U.S. law, market impact can be claimed as a fair use consideration. If a taking adversely impacts the value of the infringed work, then an unfair use may result. U.S. law differentiates between commercial and noncommercial takings. In "noncommercial" actions, the plaintiff (copyright holder) must demonstrate the damage, but in "commercial" action the burden lies on the defendant.

DIGITAL CONCERNS

The digital revolution has made the copying and transmission of intellectual property far easier. The Napster challenge underscored the inherent conflict between the owners and consumers of intellectual property. As a result, fair use rules are being revisited. The World Wide Web with its hypertext linking feature has raised a new concern. Are hypertext links a form of citation or do they represent an unfair taking of property? Are there some practices that are legitimate and some that are not? Based on court cases (*Ticketmaster v Microsoft* [1997], *Washington Post v Total News Inc.* [1997], *Ticketmaster v*

Tickets.com [2000]), we have something of an understanding of the limits of linking as citation or pointer. The "capture" of someone else's Web page within a frame may constitute an unfair taking. Linking with attribution may not be, particularly if used for scholarly or educational purposes. The policy on "deep linking" (a link bypassing the site's homepage) is still undergoing development, with positions on the legality of this practice varying from country to country. As of this writing, the most recent decisions in the United States and Europe have found deep linking not to be in violation of copyright (see, for example, *Denmark Maritime and Commercial Court, Home v Ofir*, decision of 24 February 2006). However, the opposite position has been taken by the Delhi High Court in India (Ott, 2006).

A struggle is currently under way on how intellectual property in digital form is to be protected. While the concept of copyright was more or less unquestioned as the appropriate means for protection in the print world (at least in the past century), protection of digital information increasingly includes two different approaches: (1) technological protections (for example, the CD playable only on a CD player, not on a computer) that restrict use of the purchaser of the information product and (2) migration from a copyright approach to a contract and licensing approach in the specification of the respective rights of the intellectual property owner and the user who wishes to purchase access to that property. This struggle is being played out in the United States in the consideration of various pieces of proposed federal and state legislation. At the federal level, database protection legislation pressures have been generated in part from the existence of the European Commission Database Directive (Directive 96/9EC), which provides specific copyright protection to databases. Other struggles have been between those pushing for federally mandated Digital Rights Management (DRM) standards and certified technologies and the groups pressing for consumer rights in digital media. At the state level, the Uniform Computer Information Transactions Act (UCITA) has been the primary vehicle but with success in only two states. However, pieces of the intent of UCITA appear from time to time in other state bills, particularly those dealing with spyware.

CURRENT ISSUES

The copyright, trademark, and patent questions have risen to a new level of intensity. As we have already seen, information has value. Moreover, information is treated in many quarters as a commodity that can be bought, sold, and bartered. These are complex matters about which volumes have been written. Suffice it to say that there are at least three major sides to the issues and numerous other positions.

First, copyright and other intellectual property is seen to be necessary in order to protect and provide adequate incentive for authors, composers, artists, and other creators to produce new intellectual goods. Without some means for reward (primarily financial reward), new information would not be created.

Second, most creators transfer their rights to second parties. Those second parties publish, package, market, and distribute intellectual goods. This is an inherently risk-laden enterprise, as most such ventures are not profitable. Although some are extraordinarily successful, for every Charles Dickens or Stephen King, Elvis or Madonna, Rembrandt or Peter Max, there are many, many more "also rans." Information creators may (or may not depending on contracts with the producers) share in the profit stream with royalties. These risk-taking entrepreneurs must also have adequate protection in the marketplace of ideas.

Finally, information products are consumed: they are also fodder for the creation of new information products. What we are now witnessing is an information environment where the owners of intellectual property seek more restrictive regulations on the use and transfer of information, while information users argue for the status quo ante or at least more liberal information use policy. Some critics argue that if information property protection regimes become too restrictive, those policies will stifle new information and knowledge creation (Vaidhyanathan, 2001). Others suggest that the information domain is part of our common heritage and that recent changes in intellectual property practice are draconian and analogous to fencing off open range (Lessig, 2001; Bollier, 2002). We are also being presented with new forms of intellectual property protection ranging from software licenses to broadcast flags.

Piracy

The content owners in the information industry, those to whom creators have transferred their rights, have become increasingly concerned about piracy. As noted previously, this concern has played out particularly in the lawsuits brought by the RIAA against those who have illegally downloaded music, but also in the actions of the Motion Picture Association of America (MPAA). The MPAA has had an aggressive campaign against pirating of movies, especially targeting downloads by college students through seeking assistance and support in the effort from the universities in which they are enrolled. These content owners, again particularly the MPAA, also have attempted to control use of digital television programming via the "broadcast flag," a coding embedded in the program to prevent copying and redistribution. This approach received a setback in May 2005 when the U.S. Court of Appeals for the District of Columbia Circuit found that the U.S. Federal Communications Commission (FCC) had exceeded its authority in issuing a 2003 ruling requiring all digital television receiver equipment sold after June 2005 to include technology to recognize such coding and to stop copying and redistribution. As of this writing, the pressures for legalizing this approach have moved to the U.S. Congress, where such legislation is under consideration. However, as with the online distribution of music, the legal distribution of digital TV programming and of movies is moving to the Web. Reruns of popular television programs are available for purchase through iTunes, and negotiations for purchasing legal downloading of movies through the same services are currently under way (Burrows and Grover, 2006).

Privacy

The concern for privacy of information about an individual, while more a concept of the twentieth century than one prevalent throughout history, has escalated in somewhat direct proportion to the increase in technological capacity to gather, store, aggregate, manipulate, transmit, and use information about a person without that individual's knowledge or consent. In earlier societies, there was less need for either government or the private sector to gather detailed information about individuals; but the complexity of life in the twenty-first century generates needs for record keeping on individuals that previous societies did not have. This increased need coupled with the vast increase in ability to collect and manipulate such information has brought privacy of information to the fore as perhaps the most critical information policy issue of the day.

Much of the current activity on privacy issues stems from the growing concern about the increased surveillance measures allowed by the USA PATRIOT (Uniting and Strengthening America by Providing Appropriate Tools Required to Intercept and Obstruct Terrorism) Act of 2001. In the United States, citizen awareness of privacy issues was significantly enhanced in 2003 as a result of implementation of the privacy regulations of the Health Insurance Portability and Accountability Act (HIPAA). At both the grassroots level and in Congress, measures to trim the effect of the PATRIOT Act were considered in the renewal of the provisions of the act that were due to sunset in 2005. Municipalities passed ordinances against the Act and several pieces of legislation were introduced into Congress that would restore some of the pre-PATRIOT Act protections against intrusion into privacy of individuals. However, as enacted, the renewal provided only minor relief from the more egregious privacy intrusions.

Other post-9/11 activities related to fighting terrorism that have raised privacy concerns include the now stalled Total—later Terrorism—Information Awareness Program that was under development by the Defense Advanced Research Projects Agency (DARPA) and the Computer Assisted Passenger Pre-screening System II (CAPPS II) and its successor Secure Flight of the

Transportation Security Administration. The activity of the National Security Agency, first reported in 2006, in maintaining a database of records of phone calls made by U.S. citizens and residents on home, business, and cell phones for the purpose of identifying potential terrorist activities is another recent example of extensive privacy intrusion by a government into the information activities of individuals.

The aspects of the privacy issue are complex, but there are two components that need to be highlighted in the context of this chapter:

- government access to and use of information about an individual, including information voluntarily provided or required by law and information gathered by surveillance without the individual's knowledge or consent
- commercial use of personal information, including information that has been provided as a necessary action in a purchase transaction and information that has been gathered by tracing an individual's movements in a Web environment

In regard to protection of privacy of individual information, there is a distinct divide between the concerns and approaches taken by European nations and those in the United States. While U.S. residents are becoming increasingly aware of and actively concerned about protection of personal information from improper use by the private sector, the thrust of privacy legislation and related regulatory protections has focused more on protecting individuals from governmental information misuse (Cate, 1997). The major federal privacy legislation addressing protection from governmental misuse, the Privacy Act of 1974, is restricted to protections from misuse by executive branch agencies of the federal government. In contrast to the U.S. approach, concern in European nations has been focused more on protection from misuse in the private sector. This difference in concern, as well as other differences in the policy environments of the countries, has resulted in substantially different approaches to protection of individual information privacy. In Europe, the approach has been an omnibus, comprehensive one, with legislation encompassing data collection and use in both the public and private sectors across various functional areas. In the United States, in contrast, but in keeping with the general approach to policy formulation, legislation has been much more incremental and piecemeal, particularly in its extension to the private sector. The result is a plethora of existing and proposed legislation at both federal and state levels addressing various areas of concern, from medical records (Health Insurance Portability and Accountability Act of 1996), educational records (Family Education Rights and Privacy Act of 1974), and video borrowing records (Video Privacy Protection Act of 1988) to financial information (Fair

Credit Reporting Act of 1970, Right to Financial Privacy Act of 1978, and Gramm-Leach-Bliley Act of 1999). (For a review of U.S. legislation, see *CDT's Guide to Online Privacy.*) While consistent with U.S. policy approaches in most areas, the upshot in privacy of information protection is that many loopholes still exist.

In general, European privacy laws (or, at least, those of countries in the European Union) have stricter requirements than those of the United States on such elements as consumer consent and notification for data gathering, confidentiality, security, and transnational data flow, in adherence with the European Union Directive on Data Privacy, which became effective in 1998. This Directive, although without force in the United States, has in practice had an influence in the development of further privacy protections for U.S. individual information, in that it prohibits sending of personal information to nations that do not have the same level of privacy protection for data. In order to prevent disruption of the conduct of international business by U.S. firms, an accord was reached to provide a means by which these companies can voluntarily comply with requirements equivalent to those of the directive (U.S. Department of Commerce).

The approach to information privacy protection in the United States has tilted more toward self-regulation for the private sector than government regulation and control. The Federal Trade Commission (FTC), which is the federal agency that oversees protection of consumer privacy, has changed its stance more than once on whether additional, explicit privacy legislation for the Internet is needed. However, the private sector itself, as represented by a diverse group of major corporations, has called for comprehensive consumer privacy legislation at the federal level (Consumer Privacy Legislative Forum, 2006).

IDENTITY THEFT

Another area of privacy concern relates to identify theft. The mass scale losses of identity information by federal agencies, universities, credit card companies, credit check companies, data brokers, and others, such as the loss of information on federal workers by the Bank of America, the loss of customer information by LexisNexis (Zeller, 2005a) and Ralph Lauren (Zeller, 2005b), the loss of employee data by Time Warner (Zeller, 2005c), the loss of credit information by ChoicePoint (Zeller, 2005a), the loss of student information by the University of California at Berkeley (Silverstein, 2005), and the loss of veterans' information and information on active-duty military personnel by the U.S. Department of Veterans Affairs (U.S. Department of Veterans Affairs, 2006) have escalated concern about protection of personal information to new heights. In the United States, there have been Congressional hearings on the matter, and the Federal Trade Commission at its Web site (www.consumer.gov/idtheft)

provides extensive advice on how to detect, protect against, and recover from identity theft. In the United Kingdom, the Home Office Fraud Steering Committee maintains a similar site (www.identitytheft.org.uk).

CORPORATE INFORMATION

Corporate information privacy and disclosure raise several complicated issues. With proprietary information there are protections against disclosure embedded in various mechanisms, including both laws and contracts. For example, the U.S. federal Freedom of Information Act exempts trade secrets and confidential business information from disclosure under the Act. There is further protection of trade secrets in other federal laws, as well as in state laws modeled after the Uniform Trade Secrets Act. Nondisclosure and noncompetitive clauses in contracts add further protection to proprietary information. At the same time there are requirements to disclose certain kinds of information, particularly financial information on which decisions to invest in publicly traded companies are made. And, there are laws and regulations that prevent the inappropriate sharing and use of such corporate information, such as the rules against insider trading promulgated by the U.S. Securities and Exchange Commission, which were prominent in the case of domestic mogul Martha Stewart (U.S. Securities and Exchange Commission, 2003).

Interest in corporate financial reporting has been increased in the United States and other developed countries following a number of scandals, Enron and WorldCom in 2001 and 2002 respectively among them. These scandals involved, among other issues, the relationship between the corporation and the independent auditor hired to provide scrutiny and oversight of corporate financial information. Under the securities legislation of many countries, public corporations are required to make public financial information developed and interpreted under generally accepted accounting rules. Too often the relationship between the company and its independent auditors has not been as independent as one might wish. New rules have been created to help ensure an arm's-length relationship between the audited and the auditor.

The Sarbanes-Oxley Act of 2002 (aka SOX and the Public Accounting Reform and Investor Protection Act) changed the ground rules for corporate accounting by increasing auditor independence and increasing oversight of the audit process. The Act resulted from the Enron scandals that involved Arthur Andersen, once a major accounting and consulting firm. Much of government oversight is provided by the Public Company Accounting Oversight Board (PCAOB). The Act makes corporate officers personally responsible for the accuracy of company information. The Act also extends "whistleblower protection" to employees of public companies who make public corporate delicts. It also requires financial officers to adhere to a code of ethics.

Similar legislation has been passed or is being considered in other countries. In 2003 in Canada, Ontario Bill 198 implemented regulations similar to SOX. A new European Union directive broadening oversight of the accounting industry in Europe was adopted in 2006 (European Commission, 2006).

Network Neutrality

Partly as a result of the continuing mergers in the telecommunication industry and partly due to the increasing scope of digital services offered by those who are providers of Internet access, the potential for a differential structure for broadband access, both in terms of speed and cost, is technically feasible and economically desirable on the part of the Internet providers. However, from the standpoint of many information service providers, particularly for the public sector providers (such as libraries and educational institutions), the establishment of such differential access, which would provide better Internet access for those who could afford to pay the broadband access providers for the higher levels, is detrimental. The conflict between these two approaches—neutrality in access versus control by the broadband providers—is at this writing being played out in various pieces of legislation proposed in the U.S. Congress, both legislation that would require network neutrality and legislation that would prohibit neutrality regulation and allow the giving of preferential treatment to specific content providers who could pay for it. The heart of the issue goes to whether one conceives of the Internet as part of the basic infrastructure of a nation, like roads (Wu, 2006) or as something else.

Information Ideas

E-Government as Information Policy in the Digital Age

E-governance is a concept that embraces all aspects of government functions that can be accomplished through electronic media. These functions encompass citizen initiated activities, such as filing tax forms or renewing licenses online. E-government is the process whereby government services are made available to the citizenry more easily and efficiently through online delivery mechanisms. Although the role of government as creator, generator, producer, and disseminator of information is discussed in chapter 11, the extent to which access to government services should be provided online, particularly for services involving information produced by or provided to government, is an area of information policy that is currently receiving increased attention, both in the United States and elsewhere.

(*Continued on p. 326*)

In large measure, the George W. Bush administration has adopted and expanded the e-government initiatives of the Clinton administration. Many information services previously managed in person or by mail can now be processed electronically. These range from renewing automobile license fees to voter registration. Forms and other documents can be and are downloaded from the Internet. For example, it is possible to download most Internal Revenue Service documents and forms and to file tax returns online. The Social Security Administration is working with local and state governments to facilitate online reporting and filing of death certificates. The Office of Citizen Services and Communications (OCSC) of the General Services Administration, created in July 2002, is one effort to promote e-government broadly at the federal level. The general approach of the Bush administration is defined in an OMB memorandum, short-titled *E-Government Strategy*, dated 27 February 2002.

The U.S. federal government is not alone in its support of e-government. Most of the state governments have adopted varying approaches to e-government. Likewise, many national governments worldwide are seeking e-government applications, ranging from, for example, New Zealand (see www.e-government.govt.nz) to South Africa (see www.gov.za).

Another aspect of e-governance, one that has experienced differing degrees of success, is the use of electronic balloting to replace other voting systems. In the United States, the Help America Vote Act (HAVA) of 2002 (PL 107-252) represents an effort to revise voting technology. HAVA was passed expressly "to provide funds to States to replace punch card voting systems" (HAVA preamble), no doubt in direct response to the "chads and dimples" that led to challenges to the outcome of the presidential election in 2000 in Florida. Electronic balloting and therefore electronic vote counting are seen as one possible replacement for paper punch ballots.

A number of countries are considering or have implemented electronic or Internet balloting. During 2000, the U.S. Department of Defense entertained the possibility of implementing electronic balloting for U.S. service personnel, the Voting Over the Internet Pilot Project. The idea was shelved as impractical because of implementation and fraud issues (see, for example, California Internet Voting Task Force, 2000).

Figure 12-1   U.S. Government Portal

Source: U.S. General Services Administration. Office of Citizen Services and Communication. Available: www.firstgov.gov/ (accessed December 2006).

(Continued on p. 327)

India in 2004 began extensive use of electronic voting machines (EVM) (India. Election Commission of India, n.d.). The Indian program was developed to reduce vote fraud and also to facilitate the electoral process in a country with an extremely large voting pool, more than 680 million people. Electronic voting is also used in Brazil (Mira, 2004).

E-governance raises some interesting questions and opportunities in a polity. It offers clear advantages for the technologically adept and for those with access. It offers little advantage in societies where there is limited online infrastructure or a citizenry without adequate skills to take appropriate advantage. There is therefore a parallel between the application of e-government technologies and digital divide concerns (see the discussion in chapter 13).

Some have seen the advent of e-governance as a vehicle for more than efficient delivery of government services to and by officials and citizens. It could lead in time to an expanded democratizing of society, perhaps a reinvigoration of the "New England Town Meeting" notion of individual participation in the political process. Others have suggested instead that a more open, electronic access to the political process might lead to a trivializing of the process.

E-government and its sister process e-commerce have only relatively recently been introduced as forces in our societies. It is as yet too early to conclude what the ultimate impact of the changes in practice will be and whether they will prove to be trivial or profound, but it is certain that change will follow.

Governments are also moving away from the physical publication of their public documents to an online information delivery system. For example, THOMAS (http://thomas.loc.gov) is a service of the U.S. Library of Congress to provide extensive information on Congressional activities.

Sources

California Secretary of State Bill Jones. California Internet Voting Task Force. 2000. *A Report on the Feasibility of Internet Voting, January 2000, Internet Voting Report.* Available: www.ss.ca.gov/executive/ivote/final_report.htm#final-1 (accessed December 2006).

India. Election Commission of India. "Electronic Voting Machine (EVM)." Available: www.eci.gov.in/Audio_VideoClips/presentation/EVM.ppt (accessed December 2006).

Mira, Leslie M. 2004. "For Brazil Voters, Machines Rule." *Wired News* (25 January). Available: www.wired.com/news/business/0,1367,61654,00.html?tw–newsletter_topstories_html (accessed December 2006).

U.S. Office of Management and Budget. 2002. *E-Government Strategy: Simplified Delivery of Services to Citizens, Implementing the President's Management Agenda for E-Government* (27 February). Available: www.whitehouse.gov/omb/inforeg/egovstrategy.pdf (accessed December 2006).

CONCLUSION

The information policy stream has always been changing and remains so. However, some of the most recent and proposed changes may be more revolutionary than evolutionary. Technological innovations over the past fifty years have most certainly undercut the ability of information creators and owners to protect their product. At the same time, current responses may overly limit the ability of information users and consumers to effectively occupy the information commons. A balance must be struck.

The areas of information policy discussed in this chapter and the regulatory bodies described previously constitute an introduction to these significant aspects of the information environment, but what has been covered here is really only the proverbial tip of the information policy and regulatory structure iceberg. As information has become increasingly central to society (as explored in earlier chapters), the diffusion of information policy concerns has broadened. No matter what policy area is under consideration, there is likely to be a significant information aspect that must be addressed. The key policy areas of generation and production, dissemination and access, and distribution help to illustrate the strong link between information policy and regulation and the political and economic structures and prevailing value system in a nation. It is this last aspect—the tie between values and information access and use—that will be explored in the next chapter on information ethics.

QUESTIONS FOR CONSIDERATION

1. How and why has digitization of information caused changes in policy related to distribution of information?
2. Why and how does information policy differ between countries, especially between developed and developing nations?
3. How is policy related to dissemination of and access to information produced by government affected by the prevailing political system of a nation?
4. How do the cultural values and political structures of a country influence which categories of information are likely to be accepted as ones in which restriction of access or restriction of dissemination is appropriate?
5. In what areas would changes in information policy affect your information-seeking behavior and the way you conduct your daily life?

REFERENCES

Association of American Publishers. 2005. "Publishers Sue Google over Plans to Digitize Books." *AAP Home Page* (19 October). Available: http://publishers.org/press/releases.cfm?PressReleaseArticleID=292 (accessed December 2006).

Association of American University Presses. "Google Book Search, née Google Print." *AAUP Issues in Scholarly Publishing.* Available: http://aaupnet.org/aboutup/issues/gprint.html (accessed December 2006).

Berlin Declaration. 2006. "Berlin Declaration on Open Access to Knowledge in the Sciences and Humanities." *Conference on Open Access to Knowledge in the Sciences and Humanities, 20–22 October 2003. Berlin.* Available: www.zim.mpg.de/openaccess-berlin/berlindeclaration.html (accessed December 2006).

Bollier, David. 2002. *Silent Theft: The Private Plunder of Our Common Wealth.* New York: Routledge.

———. 2005. *Brand Name Bullies: The Quest to Own and Control Culture.* Hoboken, NJ: John Wiley.

Burrows, Peter, and Ron Grover. 2006. "Apple's iTunes Movie Muddle." *BusinessWeek Online* (21 June). Available: www.businessweek.com/technology/content/jun2006/tc20060621_022435.htm?chan=technology_technology+index+page_today's+top+stories (accessed December 2006).

Cate, Fred H. 1997. *Privacy in the Information Age.* Washington, DC: Brookings Institution Press.

Cauley, Leslie. 2006. "NSA Has Massive Database of Americans' Phone Calls." *USA Today* (21 May). Available: www.usatoday.com/news/washington/2006-05-10-nsa_x.htm (accessed December 2006).

Center for Democracy and Technology. 2000. *CDT's Guide to Online Privacy.* Available: www.cdt.org/privacy/guide/introduction (accessed December 2006).

Consumer Privacy Legislative Forum. 2006. "Statement of Support in Principle for Comprehensive Consumer Privacy Legislation" (20 June). Available: www.cdt.org/privacy/20060620cplstatement.pdf (accessed December 2006).

European Commission. 2006. "Council Adopts New EU Rules on Audit of Company Accounts." Press Releases (25 April). Available: http://europa.eu.int/rapid/pressReleasesAction.do?reference=PRES/06/115&format=HTML&aged=0&language=EN&guiLanguage=en (accessed December 2006).

"European Digital Library Proposed." 2005. *eGovernment News* (4 May). Available: http://europa.eu.int/idabc/en/document/4239/194 (accessed December 2006).

Givler, Peter. 2005. Letter to Alexander Macgillivray, Senior Intellectual Property and Product Counsel, Google, Inc. (20 May). Available: www.aaupnet.org/aboutup/issues/0865_001.pdf (accessed December 2006).

Hesse, Carla. 1996. "Books in Time." In *The Future of the Book*, edited by Geoffrey Nunberg, 21–36. Berkeley, CA: University of California Press.

Lea, Gary. 1993a. "Databases and Copyright—Part I—The Problems." *Computer Law and Security Report* 9, no. 2: 68–73.

———. 1993b. "Database Law—Solutions Beyond Copyright—Part II: The Solutions. *Copyright Law and Security Report* 9, no. 3: 127–129.

Lessig, Lawrence. 2001. *The Future of Ideas: The Fate of the Commons in a Connected World*. New York: Random House.

———. 2004. *Free Culture: How Big Media Uses Technology and the Law to Lock Down Culture and Control Creativity*. New York: Penquin Press.

National Research Council. 2000. *The Digital Dilemma: Intellectual Property in the Information Age*. Washington, DC: National Academy Press.

Newman, Simon, and Wallace Koehler. 2004. "Copyright: Moral Rights, Fair Use, and the Online Environment." *Journal of Information Ethics* 13, no. 2: 38–57.

Ott, Stephen. 2006. "News: Update 40." *Links & Law—Information about Legal Aspects of Search Engines, Linking and Framing* (1 June). Available: www.linksandlaw.com/news.htm (accessed December 2006).

People's Republic of China. State Intellectual Property Office. 2004. "Report on the Protection of Intellectual Property Rights in China in 2003 (Abstract)." Available: www.sipo.gov.cn/sipo_English/gfxx/zyhd/t20040414 _33974.htm (accessed May 8, 2007).

Public Lending Right International Network. 2005. "New PLR Systems Expected in 2006." *What's New* (November). Available: www.plrinternational .com/news/news.htm (accessed December 2006).

Sandoval, Greg. 2006. "YouTube Dances the Copyright Tango." *CNET News.com* (24 July). Available: http://news.com/com/YouTube+dances+ the+copyright+tango/2100-1025_3-6097365.html (accessed March 2007).

Silverstein, Stuart. 2005. "UC Berkeley Looks into Laptop Theft." *Los Angeles Times* (29 March): B 4.

United Kingdom. Home Office Fraud Steering Committee. 2006. *Identity Theft*. Available: www.identity-theft.org.uk (accessed December 2006).

U.S. Court of Appeals for the District of Columbia Circuit. 2005. No.

04-1037. *American Library Association et al. vs. Federal Communications Commission.* Decided 4 May 2005. Available: http://pacer.cadc.uscourts.gov/docs/common/opinions/200505/04-1037b.pdf (accessed December 2006).

U.S. Department of Commerce. "Welcome to the Safe Harbor." *Export.gov.* Available: www.export.gov/safeharbor (accessed December 2006).

U.S. Department of Veterans Affairs. 2006. "Secretary Nicholson Provides Update on Stolen Data Incident: Data Matching with Department of Defense Providing New Details" (6 June). Available: www1.va.gov/opa/pressrel/pressrelease.cfm?id=1134 (accessed December 2006).

U.S. Federal Trade Commission. n.d. *Deter, Detect, Defend: Avoid Against Identity Theft.* Available: www.consumer.gov/idtheft (accessed December 2006).

U.S. Securities and Exchange Commission. 2003. "SEC Charges Martha Stewart, Broker Peter Bacanovic with Illegal Insider Trading" (4 June). Available: www.sec.gov/news/press/2003-69.htm (accessed December 2006).

Vaidhyanathan, Siva. 2001. *Copyrights and Copywrongs: The Rise of Intellectual Property and How It Threatens Creativity.* New York: New York University Press.

———. 2004. *The Anarchist in the Library: How the Clash Between Freedom and Control Is Hacking the Real World and Crashing the System.* New York: Basic Books.

Wu, Tim. 2006. "Why You Should Care about Network Neutrality." *Slate* (1 May). Available: www.slate.com/id/2140850/fr/rss/#ContinueArticle (accessed December 2006).

Zeller, Tom, Jr. 2005a. "Another Data Broker Reports a Breach." *New York Times* (10 March): C 1.

———. 2005b. "Polo Warns of Possible Problem with Credit Card Information." *New York Times* (15 April): C 6.

———. 2005c. "Time Warner Says Data on Employees Is Lost." *New York Times* (3 May): C4.

ADDITIONAL SOURCES

Chissick, Michael, and Alistair Kelman. 2002. *Electronic Commerce: Law and Practice.* 3rd ed. London: Sweet & Maxwell.

Fernandez-Molina, J. Carlos, and Eduardo Peis. 2001. "The Moral Rights of Authors in the Age of Digital Information." *Journal of the American Society for Information Science and Technology* 52, no. 2: 109–117.

Stern, Christopher. 2006. "The Coming Tug of War over the Internet." *Washington Post* (22 January): B01.

Weiss, Peter N., and Peter Backlund. 1997. "International Information Policy in Conflict: Open and Unrestricted Access versus Government Commercialization." In *Borders in Cyberspace: Information Policy and the Global Information Infrastructure*, edited by Brian Kahin and Charles Neeson, 300–321. Cambridge, MA: MIT Press.

What do ethics mean for you? What about information ethics? Do ethics principles change as technology changes? Are we more attuned, more sensitive to information ethics because many of the stakes have been raised? Before you begin reading this chapter, write a statement that reflects your ethical positions on access to and use of information. When you complete the chapter, consider whether you wish to revise your statement.

Chapter 13

Information Ethics

Learning Guide

After reading this chapter, you should be able to

- understand and define the following terms:
  - value
  - morals
  - ethics
  - code of ethics
  - digital divide
- identify the following acronyms and explain the relationship of each to information ethics:
  - COPA
  - CIPA
  - FERPA
  - HIPAA
  - USAPA
  - WSIS
- explain the historical and current issues in information ethics;
- assess the impact of changing information technologies on ethical issues related to information;
- discriminate among the varying ethical positions of different segments of the information profession;
- analyze the influence of cultural values and political structures on the ethical stances related to information.

When you have finished the chapter, return to this page to be sure you have learned what you need to know.

INTRODUCTION

Considering information ethics is somewhat like considering technology ethics. For information, as for technology, the ethics issues are not so much embedded in the entity itself (the information or the technology), but in the context—cultural, political, economic—and in the use. Information ethics are extremely complex and have become more complex with changes in technology. There are challenges to privacy. Computer hackers with their worms and viruses can create havoc and cause untold damage. New professions have been created and new ways to do old tasks discovered.

Changes in the information environment have led to a new awareness of ethics, values, and legal obligations and responsibilities among the information professions. This chapter touches upon the differences among the information professions and the ethical and moral responses of these information professionals in an expanding environment.

The discussion in this chapter on information ethics is closely related to the chapter on information regulation. It might be argued—and argued correctly—that much of what is presented here is appropriate for and might have been developed in the information regulation discussion.

The new information technologies have created new conditions that require different and, if not different, more intense, responses from information professionals. As we have already seen, the information environment has brought information in its many manifestations more easily and faster to the desktops, laptops, notebooks, PDAs, portable media players, and other information devices of the information user and consumer. It has also made it far easier to create and disseminate information, again in its many manifestations.

One recurring theme throughout this work has been

does the information environment of today represent a revolutionary change or is it business as usual, only more so?

The question can be answered both ways. How one answers depends in part on perspective and in part on where one decides the revolution began. We might argue that the information revolution began when human beings gained the ability to think and to speak. Or it may have begun when humans began painting on walls, reading, scratching letters into clay, using printing presses, communicating instantaneously by telegraph or telephone, being entertained and educated at a distance with radio and television, or, finally, being intimately networked by the Internet.

A second theme has been

are the social challenges posed by any technological innovation in any era fundamentally different from those posed by earlier technologies?

For example, the pornography industry has been forever a part of the publishing industry. Because pornography is now much easier to distribute, and more importantly, more easily accessed, has there been a revolutionary change?

A third theme, as we saw in chapter 7, is that new information professions are created as new information technologies are developed. The sixteenth century had new printing professionals; the nineteenth century saw the emergence of the photography, telegraph, and telephone professions; the early twentieth century witnessed recording and moving pictures experts; and the last half of the twentieth century began with the emergence of computer programmers and ended with Webmasters. In the early years of the twenty-first century, the information architect and the knowledge manager are increasingly prominent professionals. Again, we ask

> *do these new professionals represent a revolution, or are they performing similar tasks in a different environment?*

Perhaps the answer to all of the questions is that it is both a bit revolutionary and a bit a continuation of the past in new dress. If that is the case, we may find that our current ethical concerns related to information are both a continuation of concerns from the past and new ethical issues resulting from the revolutionary effects of technological change.

ETHICS AND CULTURE

As suggested in the introduction, the cultural context is a major component of the grounds in which information—and all other—ethics are embedded. How information is interpreted, valued, even identified as such, depends in large measure on the culture in which it is found.

We know that different cultures have different moral, ethical, and legal systems. These differences are reflected in national, regional, and sectoral differences. Margaret Mead in *Coming of Age in Samoa* (1928), for example, demonstrated that different cultures practice different sexual mores. One culture can impose its ethics and mores on others, just as missionaries influenced the sexual practices of far more than one culture. Technology can shift values as well. Sexual mores underwent change in the West, particularly so in the 1960s, after the introduction of effective contraception controlled by women.

We have suggested in these pages that changes in information and information systems also change—or, at a minimum, influence—cultures and their ethics. As discussed in chapter 10, the Academie française has as one of its major functions the protection of French culture against outside influences. The Canadian government requires broadcasters to include "Canadian content" in their programming mix. The Government of Quebec has tried to require that much of the business conducted there be done in French, including store signs. Many states in the United States have proposed "English only" legislation. At the U.S. federal level, legislation was introduced in the 109th Congress to make English the official language of the United States. On the other hand, some countries, India and South Africa among them, have sought to accommodate the multiplicity of languages and cultures by making many languages "official."

Nothing cuts more deeply than division driven by religion. As we have seen already, religion can be influenced by information and can itself be promoted by information. The argument has been made that the printing press fueled the Protestant Reformation and the growth of nationalism. Protestantism advocated the use of local languages and the publication of vulgate Bibles. These practices reduced the globalizing impact of Latin as the language of the Church and among elites (Eisenstein, 1983). It might, in fact, be argued that without printing, Protestantism might easily have failed. Early Protestantism needed, even required, the propagandizing force provided by enhanced information dissemination. It also required a literate population.

The spread of Islam has also changed the face of many cultures. To give but one example, Muslims consider the depiction of humans as profane idolatry. As Islam spread into Southern and Eastern Europe and across Asia, so did cultural influences. As late as 2001, the Taliban rulers of Afghanistan destroyed the famous giant stone statues of the Buddha. The Taliban is not alone in this: the Mogul conquerors of India removed the faces of gods from Hindu figures in the sixteenth century. Lest we point fingers at Muslims, let us also remember that Protestants removed the images of saints from churches that were once Catholic or Orthodox. The Spanish conquistadors melted golden Aztec artifacts for the bullion. And in the early nineteenth century, it was proposed to break up the Taj Mahal for its marble. In reality, it has only been in very recent years that the artifacts of one culture (or of the past) have been valued for anything more than their monetary value in the present.

ETHICS SOURCES

We as human beings have grappled with issues of right and wrong, morality and law, and ethics and duty ever since human beings began to engage in abstract thinking. Philosophers and ethicists have identified at least two metasources for these norms: they are either somehow transcendent to human beings or they are human based and have an individual or social basis.

Some thinkers posit a transcendent source for some norms and a more human one for others. We can divide these approaches into two distinct models: the "multiple-source" model and the "single-source" model, as illustrated in

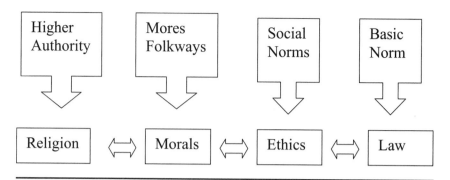

Figure 13-1   Multiple-Source Model

figures 13-1 and 13-2. The multiple-source model suggests that each of the four systems that define good and evil, right and wrong, or just and unjust have separate etiologies. That is to say, our systems of religion, morals, ethics, and law are at their sources independent of one another. They in turn, however, both affect and effect one another.

The single-source model provides that each of the four systems has a single, unified source. That source can be and has been defined in many ways. Many have ascribed it to a deity. Others look to social theory. Still others have ascribed a biological basis.

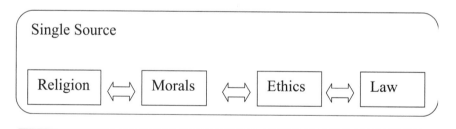

Figure 13-2   Single-Source Model

ON THE DIFFERENCES: LAW, ETHICS, AND MORALS

There are two approaches to the question of the differences between and relationships among law, ethics, and morals. The first is to argue that legal, ethical, and moral norms are, in the main, equal. The second is to suggest that there is a hierarchy among the three, with morality at the pinnacle, followed in descending order of importance by ethics and law.

Morality is an outgrowth of custom, of practice, of established habit. It is "known" but rarely codified. Once codified, morality ceases to be morality per se, but is transmuted through the codification process into law. We find the most formal recognition of this transmutation in the Anglo-American common law and international community law traditions. Hugo Grotius (1925) was perhaps first to express the community law concept in his 1625 work *De Jure Belli Ac Pacis*. It might also be noted that Grotius distinguished between primary and secondary laws of nature. Primary laws of nature are immutable and have a divine source. Secondary laws of nature can be discovered through reason, and reason is the root of community law.

MORALS, VALUES, AND ETHICS

Morals represent a set of mores, customs, and traditions that may have been derived from social practice or from religious guidance. Values are a subset of morals. Milton Rokeach offers the following definitions:

> A *value* is an enduring belief that a specific mode of conduct or end-state of existence is personally or socially preferable to an opposite or converse mode of conduct or end-state of existence. A *value system* is an enduring organization of beliefs concerning preferable modes of conduct or end-states of existence along a continuum of relative importance. (1973: 5)

The application of values is ethics. Michael Gorman defines the application of values:

> In application values are useful and usable because they are standards by which we assess what we do; measure how near we are to, or how far we are from, an objective; and compare our actions and our state of being to those of others and to ideals represented by our values. (2000: 7)

As Martha Smith (1997) argues, information ethics are perceived to be a subset of applied ethics, or ethical principles that are both broad and theoretical but also have specific application. Ethics necessarily, at least in their applied form, undergo metamorphosis as underlying conditions change. Thus, for example, as technology changes the conditions of practice (see Negroponte, 1995), these change the ethics that guide the practice.

Our professional organizations are one set of sources for both values and ethical principles. Many professional organizations have published codes of ethics, although codes of ethics and value statements are very recent phenomena for the information professions. The American Library Association (ALA) took an early lead in defining a set with its Code of Ethics, first enunciated in 1938. In the United States, with the signal exception of the ALA, information professional associations did not begin developing codes until 1969; in fact, more than 80 percent of American information association codes of ethics were created after 1980. For example, the Associated Press Managing Editors promulgated their code in 1995.

Codes of ethics of the information professional associations vary in content and purpose, dependent in large part on the responsibilities of the organization and the purposes the organization addresses (Koehler and Pemberton, 2000). For a list of professional organizations with links to ethics codes, mission statements, and statutes, see Koehler, *Ethics Links to Librarian and Information Manager Associations WWW Pages*.

Statements of values are perhaps more difficult to articulate than ethical codes, although they are assumed as the bases of the codes. The International Federation of Library Associations and Institutions (2005) has defined a set of core values, articulated in its statutes. In the United States, the library profession witnessed a debate within the ALA over the identification and adoption of a Core Values Statement (CVS) as both a guide for training practitioners and as a standard for its members. At its July 2000 meeting, the ALA Council declined to accept the proposed CVS draft; but in June 2004 the body approved a statement listing the core values and referring for definition of them to existing policy documents (ALA, 2004).

ETHICS, MORALS, AND INFORMATION

Rafael Capurro (2001) defines for us the challenges for information ethics and the imperatives before us:

- the development of moral values in the information field
- the creation of new power structures in the information field
- information myths
- hidden contradictions and intentionalities in information theories and practices
- the development of ethical conflicts in the information field

We distinguish between moral and ethical considerations. Part of that process is a necessary awareness that the two, ethics and morality, are related and that the one builds upon and reflects the other. From one perspective, ethics, morals, and legal norms differ from one another in the degree to which they are formalized and in the form that sanctions, if any, are applied. Moral values in general, and more specifically in the information field, evolve in part as a consequence of our ethical, legal, and religious beliefs. They also result from changing social and technological realties.

INFORMATION AS PRACTICE

Before we can wrestle with the ethics and values of the information professions, we must acknowledge issues of definition in the information disciplines. Schrader (1986) argues that there are more than 100 definitions of information in the information field. For each definition of information, each category of the information professions, and each information discipline, do we need different sets of ethics and values? Or does a single set cover all? Rafael Capurro has raised for us some very challenging questions at the nexus of the information professions and ethics. For example, he argues:

> The question "what is information?" asks for substantial characteristics of something. But information, taken as a dimension of human existence, is nothing substantial. Instead of asking: "what is information?" we can ask: "what is information (science) for?" . . . The aim of information science is to thematize this con-*textual* dimension taking into consideration primarily all technical forms of communication as parts of other forms of life. . . .
>
> Taking into consideration the unity of boths [*sic*] aspects, the methodological and the pragmatic, information heuristics and information hermeneutics, information science can be considered a sub-discipline of rhetoric. (2003)

As Capurro points out for us, the intersection of Aristotelian rhetoric, politics, and ethics underpin the information professions. Capurro argues further:

> The question "what is information for?" leads to the question "what is information science for?" since information science, conceived as a hermeneutic-rhetorical discipline, studies the con-*textual* pragmatical dimensions within which knowledge is shared *positively* as information and *negatively* as misinformation particularly through technical forms of communication. These are not just an instrument but a "way of being." This conception of information science is important if we want information systems to become part of the background of various forms of living. (2003)

Our value systems and ethical practices become a part of "the background of various forms of living." We must also understand the well-known dictum that "where you stand depends on where you sit." Values and ethics may be colored by one's perceptions of information and the professions.

CODES OF ETHICS AND VALUES: WHAT THE PROFESSIONALS TELL US

Where do information ethics come from? That is to say, within a given cultural context, what are some of the sources that form the bases for ethical decision making by information professionals?

Legal theoreticians tell us that there are three basic sources of law discovery and creation. These are legislation, practice, and the writings of experts. Ethical systems, however, are not legislated. That results in an inherent contradiction. Once legislated, the norm set becomes law. For potential sources of professional ethics and values, we can identify

- writings of experts;
- provisions of codes of ethics;
- values information professionals report they hold.

Expert Commentary

To consider an example of expert commentary as the source of ethics and values, we can review several recent papers that seek to enumerate core values and ethical precepts in the library professions: Rubin and Froehlich (1996), Koehler and Pemberton (2000), and Gorman (2000). While these studies varied in their emphasis and in the terminology used to name the values and the ethical principles, the chart in figure 13-3 shows the commonality of their findings. Values and principles that appear across the studies include privacy, intellectual freedom, intellectual property rights, access, and various social issues, such as literacy. Other values that appeared in additional papers by Froehlich (2000), Koehler (2003), and Koehler et al. (2000) included, among others, diversity, equality of opportunity, preservation of the intellectual record, information literacy, confidentiality, and observance of the trust placed in the professional by society.

Professional Codes of Ethics

The Koehler and Pemberton (2000) study reflected in the chart in figure 13-3 derived the principles and values enumerated from examination of the

Koehler and Pemberton 2000	Gorman 2000	Rubin and Froehlich 1996
Client/Patron Rights and Privileges	Privacy Service Rationalism	Privacy
Selection Issues	Intellectual Freedom	Selection and Censorship
	Stewardship	Reference
Professional Practice	Stewardship	Intellectual Property Rights
		Administration
Access Issues	Equity of Access	Access
		Technology
Employer Responsibility		Loyalties
Social Issues	Democracy Literacy and Learning	Social Issues

Figure 13-3   Mapping of Ethical Principles and Values

codes of ethics of more than thirty information professional associations and found that six general areas of concern (listed in the chart) could be abstracted from them. These six correspond with the ethical and moral values often described in the literature of the field. Many writers have identified some or all of the following values as core professional values (see Intner and Schement, 1987; Stichler and Hauptman, 1998; Hauptman, 1991; Rubin, 1991; Baker, 1992; Peterson, 1992; Miller, 1995; Johnson, 1994; Hisle, 1998; Symons Stoffle, 1998; Gorman, 2000):

- intellectual freedom
- protecting users' right to privacy/confidentiality
- intellectual property rights
- professional neutrality
- preservation of the cultural record
- equity of access

These six issues correspond well to the six Koehler and Pemberton report and to those that Rubin and Froehlich (1996) have described. With the exception of intellectual property rights, they also reflect core values articulated by the American Library Association and by IFLA.

Several professional codes of ethics are provided in figures 13-4 to 13-7, taken from organizations in journalism, computing, and librarianship. By examining these codes, it becomes clear that while there are common elements, such as some of those reflected in the list above, there are specific tenets that differ because the professions differ. Journalism codes of ethics include a strong focus on accuracy, objectivity, and fairness. The library codes stress service. Computer science codes concern themselves with avoidance of harm and with service.

If we abstract the various codes of ethics for the information professions, we find that they can be reduced to two basic concepts. The first is, "do what you do well." The second is, "while doing it well, avoid harming others." The computer science codes proscribe the development and dissemination of viruses and worms. They also proscribe computer hacking. These practices

---

Seek Truth and Report It
Journalists should be honest, fair and courageous in gathering, reporting and interpreting information.
Journalists should:

- Test the accuracy of information from all sources and exercise care to avoid inadvertent error. Deliberate distortion is never permissible.
- Diligently seek out subjects of news stories to give them the opportunity to respond to allegations of wrongdoing.
- Identify sources whenever feasible. The public is entitled to as much information as possible on sources' reliability.
- Always question sources' motives before promising anonymity. Clarify conditions attached to any promise made in exchange for information. Keep promises.
- Make certain that headlines, news teases and promotional material, photos, video, audio, graphics, sound bites and quotations do not misrepresent. They should not oversimplify or highlight incidents out of context.
- Never distort the content of news photos or video. Image enhancement for technical clarity is always permissible. Label montages and photo illustrations.
- Avoid misleading re-enactments or staged news events. If re-enactment is necessary to tell a story, label it.
- Avoid undercover or other surreptitious methods of gathering information except when traditional open methods will not yield information vital to the public. Use of such methods should be explained as part of the story.
- Never plagiarize.
- Tell the story of the diversity and magnitude of the human experience boldly, even when it is unpopular to do so.
- Examine their own cultural values and avoid imposing those values on others.
- Avoid stereotyping by race, gender, age, religion, ethnicity, geography, sexual orientation, disability, physical appearance or social status.
- Support the open exchange of views, even views they find repugnant.
- Give voice to the voiceless; official and unofficial sources of information can be equally valid.
- Distinguish between advocacy and news reporting. Analysis and commentary should be labeled and not misrepresent fact or context.
- Distinguish news from advertising and shun hybrids that blur the lines between the two.
- Recognize a special obligation to ensure that the public's business is conducted in the open and that government records are open to inspection.

Figure 13-4 Society of Professional Journalists' Code of Ethics

Source: Society of Professional Journalists. 2006. Code of Ethics. Available: www.spj.org/ethics-code.asp (accessed December 2006). From Society of Professional Journalists, 3909 N. Meridian St., Indianapolis, IN 46208, www.spj.org. Copyright © 2007 by Society of Professional Journalists. Reprinted by permission. (Note: Preamble not included.)

(Continued on p. 344)

Minimize Harm

Ethical journalists treat sources, subjects and colleagues as human beings deserving of respect.

Journalists should:

- Show compassion for those who may be affected adversely by news coverage. Use special sensitivity when dealing with children and inexperienced sources or subjects.
- Be sensitive when seeking or using interviews or photographs of those affected by tragedy or grief.
- Recognize that gathering and reporting information may cause harm or discomfort. Pursuit of the news is not a license for arrogance.
- Recognize that private people have a greater right to control information about themselves than do public officials and others who seek power, influence or attention. Only an overriding public need can justify intrusion into anyone's privacy.
- Show good taste. Avoid pandering to lurid curiosity.
- Be cautious about identifying juvenile suspects or victims of sex crimes.
- Be judicious about naming criminal suspects before the formal filing of charges.
- Balance a criminal suspect's fair trial rights with the public's right to be informed.

Act Independently

Journalists should be free of obligation to any interest other than the public's right to know.

Journalists should:

- Avoid conflicts of interest, real or perceived.
- Remain free of associations and activities that may compromise integrity or damage credibility.
- Refuse gifts, favors, fees, free travel and special treatment, and shun secondary employment, political involvement, public office and service in community organizations if they compromise journalistic integrity.
- Disclose unavoidable conflicts.
- Be vigilant and courageous about holding those with power accountable.
- Deny favored treatment to advertisers and special interests and resist their pressure to influence news coverage.
- Be wary of sources offering information for favors or money; avoid bidding for news.

Be Accountable

Journalists are accountable to their readers, listeners, viewers and each other.

Journalists should:

- Clarify and explain news coverage and invite dialogue with the public over journalistic conduct.
- Encourage the public to voice grievances against the news media.
- Admit mistakes and correct them promptly.
- Expose unethical practices of journalists and the news media.
- Abide by the same high standards to which they hold others.

Figure 13-4   Society of Professional Journalists' Code of Ethics (Continued)

harm others and destroy property. Some aspects of computer hacking may also violate the privacy of others. Journalists too are directed to avoid harming others as they seek the truth. Librarians place service above all other responsibilities, but they too are to avoid harm.

The Society of Professional Journalists Code of Ethics, adopted in 1996 but based on a 1926 code, calls upon journalists to seek and report truth, minimize harm, act independently, and be accountable and gives specific dicta for the application of the code by professional journalists (see figure 13-4).

The computing profession is also deeply concerned with ethical practice.

1. **GENERAL MORAL IMPERATIVES.**

1.1 Contribute to society and human well-being.

1.2 Avoid harm to others.

1.3 Be honest and trustworthy.

1.4 Be fair and take action not to discriminate.

1.5 Honor property rights including copyrights and patent.

1.6 Give proper credit for intellectual property.

1.7 Respect the privacy of others.

1.8 Honor confidentiality.

2. **MORE SPECIFIC PROFESSIONAL RESPONSIBILITIES.**

2.1 Strive to achieve the highest quality, effectiveness and dignity in both the process and products of professional work.

2.2 Acquire and maintain professional competence.

2.3 Know and respect existing laws pertaining to professional work.

2.4 Accept and provide appropriate professional review.

2.5 Give comprehensive and thorough evaluations of computer systems and their impacts, including analysis of possible risks.

2.6 Honor contracts, agreements, and assigned responsibilities.

2.7 Improve public understanding of computing and its consequences.

2.8 Access computing and communication resources only when authorized to do so.

3. **ORGANIZATIONAL LEADERSHIP IMPERATIVES.**

3.1 Articulate social responsibilities of members of an organizational unit and encourage full acceptance of those responsibilities.

3.2 Manage personnel and resources to design and build information systems that enhance the quality of working life.

3.3 Acknowledge and support proper and authorized uses of an organization's computing and communication resources.

3.4 Ensure that users and those who will be affected by a system have their needs clearly articulated during the assessment and design of requirements; later the system must be validated to meet requirements.

3.5 Articulate and support policies that protect the dignity of users and others affected by a computing system.

3.6 Create opportunities for members of the organization to learn the principles and limitations of computer systems.

4. **COMPLIANCE WITH THE CODE.**

4.1 Uphold and promote the principles of the Code.

4.2 Treat violations of this code as inconsistent with membership in the ACM.

Figure 13-5   ACM Code of Ethics and Professional Conduct
Source: Association for Computing Machinery. ACM Code of Ethics and Professional Conduct. 2003. Available: www.acm.org/constitution/code.html (accessed December 2006). Copyright © Association for Computing Machinery, Inc. Reprinted with permission. (Note: Preamble and commentary not included.)

The Association for Computing Machinery has developed a complex code of ethics, adopted in 1992 (see figure 13-5).

The Computer Ethics Institute has developed a somewhat less complex Ten Commandments of Computer Ethics (see figure 13-6).

The 1995 Code of Ethics of the American Library Association holds as seen in figure 13-7.

1. Thou shalt not use a computer to harm other people.
2. Thou shalt not interfere with other people's computer work.
3. Thou shalt not snoop around in other people's computer files.
4. Thou shalt not use a computer to steal.
5. Thou shalt not use a computer to bear false witness.
6. Thou shalt not copy or use proprietary software for which you have not paid.
7. Thou shalt not use other people's computer resources without authorization or proper compensation.
8. Thou shalt not appropriate other people's intellectual output.
9. Thou shalt think about the social consequences of the program you are writing or the system you are designing.
10. Thou shalt always use a computer in ways that insure consideration and respect for your fellow humans.

Figure 13-6   Ten Commandments of Computer Ethics

Source: Computer Ethics Institute. Ten Commandments of Computer Ethics. *1992. Available: www.brook.edu/its/cei/overview/Ten_Commanments_of_Computer_Ethics.htm (accessed December 2006). Copyright © 1991: Computer Ethics Institute. Reprinted with permission.*

I. We provide the highest level of service to all library users through appropriate and usefully organized resources; equitable service policies; equitable access; and accurate, unbiased, and courteous responses to all requests.

II. We uphold the principles of intellectual freedom and resist all efforts to censor library resources.

III. We protect each library user's right to privacy and confidentiality with respect to information sought or received and resources consulted, borrowed, acquired or transmitted.

IV. We recognize and respect intellectual property rights.

V. We treat co-workers and other colleagues with respect, fairness and good faith, and advocate conditions of employment that safeguard the rights and welfare of all employees of our institutions.

VI. We do not advance private interests at the expense of library users, colleagues, or our employing institutions.

VII. We distinguish between our personal convictions and professional duties and do not allow our personal beliefs to interfere with fair representation of the aims of our institutions or the provision of access to their information resources.

VIII. We strive for excellence in the profession by maintaining and enhancing our own knowledge and skills, by encouraging the professional development of co-workers, and by fostering the aspirations of potential members of the profession.

Figure 13-7   ALA Code of Ethics

Source: American Library Association. 2006. Code of Ethics of the American Library Association. *Available: www.ala.org/ala/oif/statementspols/codeofethics/codeethics.htm (accessed December 2006). Reprinted with permission. (Note: Preamble omitted.)*

Reported Values

As an example of reported values as sources of ethics, the work of Koehler is useful. Koehler et al. (2000) polled approximately 1900 information workers worldwide and found a near unanimity of opinion. Almost all information workers identified "service to patron or client" among the top three of their values and many indicated it as the first. Equality of access issues and information literacy were also among the first tier of values identified.

Where does this take us? These values discussed in the literature, generalized from the ethics codes of our professional organizations, and reported by practitioners represent a starting point from which we can begin to identify the moral perspectives of information professionals.

Information Ideas

Changing Contexts Change Information and the Ethics of Its Use

Take a careful look at the image below. Where does it come from and what do the symbols represent? This pillar stands outside Birla House in Delhi, India. On 30 January 1948, Mahatma Gandhi was shot dead near this site.

Figure 13-8   Swastika Symbol I: Birla House, Delhi, India
Source: Photograph by Wallace C. Koehler, Jr.

(*Continued on p. 348*)

One symbol is Sanskrit for Om, the meditation sound. The other, the swastika, is in some ways a much more interesting symbol. For Hindus and Buddhists, the swastika symbol is a representation of good.

Compare the symbol above with the one below.

Figure 13-9   Swastika Symbol 2: Flag of Germany
Source: Photograph by Wallace C. Koehler, Jr.

In this changed context, the benign symbol from the Birla House becomes a representation of evil incarnate, immediately bringing to mind Hitler and the Third Reich, the Holocaust, and the worldwide devastation of World War II. The same symbol in this context conveys an information environment that was unethical and reprehensible.

Between these two extremes we can find examples of the symbol, such as the one in figure 13-10, that do not, at least for the twenty-first century viewer, convey any ethically laden information.

The symbol has appeared in such diverse contexts as the floor of the Amiens Cathedral (see http://commons.wikimedia.org/wiki/Image:Amiens-pavement-swastika.jpg), on Minoan pottery on the island of Crete (see http://commons.wikimedia.org/wiki/Image:Kretominoisches_Hakenkreuz_asb _2004_PICT3431.JPG), and on the temple of Bulgugsa in Korea (see http://commons.wikimedia.org/wiki/Image:1974_Korea_Bulgugsa.jpg).

Thus, the context of the information artifact, as well as the culture in which it exists, changes the ethics of its use and of the information conveyed.

(Continued on p. 349)

Figure 13-10   Swastika Symbol 3: "Love Bird," American Sheet Music, 1911

Source: Historic American Sheet Music Collection (1910–1920, Justin Herman; Music A-951), Rare Book, Manuscript, and Special Collections Library, Duke University. Available: http://scriptorium.lib.duke.edu/sheetmusic. Used by permission.

ISSUES IN INFORMATION ETHICS

In the introduction to this chapter we suggested that the ethical concerns faced today are in part new issues generating from the effects of technological change. The impact of technological change is to a substantial degree being heightened by the geopolitical context, which is affecting how the changes are used. Although the political context has always shaped the deployment of information technology, and hence the ethics of information, such influence, from the close-up perspective of today, appears exaggerated over that of previous times. With distance, the effects may not loom as large.

Within our current field of vision, however, we find ourselves in a period of transition. Information is the new currency. The new information environment has heightened the potential for conflict and has provided new tools to both widen and constrict the application of ethical practice. Many of these issues have received greater concern and emphasis in light of 9/11 and subsequent policies. Governments, private organizations, and individuals are involved in the reexamination and sometimes redefinition of practice and ethical principles. If the aftermath to the events of 9/11 brings home any lesson, it is the essential tension between social and individual rights.

The first question we need to ask is whether the new information realities have created a new moral and ethical environment for us all, for information professionals, and/or for individuals. At minimum, new technology creates new challenges to the moral order. In the United States we accept as a given that access to universal electrical and telephone service has risen to the level of right. It would be morally incomprehensible to deny anyone access to these services based on location or economic status. We have begun to consider whether an equivalent right exists for access to medical care and medical information. New technology carries with it inherently the ability to modify or create expectations as well as moral concerns and legal and ethical rights. We must recognize that different cultures maintain different moral, ethical, and legal traditions. The following provides brief examples of some of those differences.

Privacy

Privacy rights are frequently balanced against the rights of the state or some other organization (employers, the press, for example) to penetrate personal privacy. Personal privacy is not an absolute. Public figures, by virtue of the public nature of their personae, have fewer rights than do not-so-public figures. What propels an individual into that status is not always clear. Notoriety is sometimes claimed as the test. There is an inherent tautology that sometimes creates public figures. If the press makes you notorious, you are a public figure and therefore you are notorious. Was Monica Lewinsky a public figure before or after the press made her one? And if you do not know who Monica Lewinsky is, is she still a public figure?

CULTURAL DIFFERENCES

The private person/public person concept has different treatments in different cultures. In the United States, in order for a public person to bring a libel action against the media, it is necessary for the plaintiff to demonstrate that false statements were knowingly made by the defendant. In the United Kingdom, the rules are much tighter. It is only necessary to demonstrate that the allegations are false. The media are held to a higher standard when media reports concern private persons.

WORKPLACE PRIVACY

Do privacy rights extend to the workplace? We might distinguish between privacy of person and privacy of communications. Courts and statutes protect the rights of privacy of the person in some cases and not in others. For example, it is unlawful for employers and others to place cameras in lavatories, showers, and dressing rooms. Employers may require employees and potential employees to submit to background and drug tests, particularly when hiring for sensitive positions. There may be differential tests. School officials may require athletes to submit to drug testing when the student body as a whole may not be so required. Students under a certain age are compelled to attend school; participation in organized sports is voluntary. The voluntary nature of athletics represents implicit acceptance of school policy.

Several important ethical principles are raised when employees use employer-supplied communications. Should employers monitor that use? If they should, is monitoring limited only to logging that use, or can employers read or listen to those communications? As a general rule, statutes and courts have held that employees do not have privacy rights when using equipment provided by employers. Employers may monitor the telephone, mail, and Internet use of employees, including reading or listening to the communications. Misuse of company-owned communications may be grounds for dismissal. In effect, it could be argued that the right to private communication is abridged for an employee when he or she uses the employer's property improperly.

Do the rights of the employer extend beyond the workplace? Employers have few rights to monitor the private speech of their employees, particularly when the employee is acting outside the workplace, as a private person, and using his or her own means of communication. There may be exceptions to this rule, particularly when private utterances become public, or when statements in some way harm the employer. False statements that cause stock price fluctuations may be both unethical and unlawful, for example.

INTERNET PRIVACY ISSUES

The Internet, particularly the World Wide Web and e-mail, have raised new privacy issues. Because of the way the Internet works, privacy can easily be breached. The Internet is built on the movement of information packets through nodes along various communications routes. As messages are routed through nodes, messages can be copied and read. Web queries can be traced back to the sending computer from its IP (Internet protocol) and its logon addresses. In addition, it is possible to create logs of the Web movements of users.

The Internet has also made it easier to search for and find information about individuals. There are Web-based search engines that can locate and provide maps to the residences of many people. Many of these personal finding tools are telephone-book–based. It can be argued that the Web search engine does little more than what an individual can do with a set of telephone book white pages. In fact, the Web engines consolidate the many phone books into a single, easily searchable database. Because we are easier to find, it is easier to penetrate our privacy.

However, with the advent of the online social networking phenomenon, in which individuals share in publicly accessible space (or space accessible to members of the network, such as MySpace.com or Facebook) what would in a pre-Internet era have been considered the intimate details of a private life, the privacy boundaries and expectations are being reshaped. While concerns have escalated about the privacy of information related to minors, general expectations of the young, Internet-bred generations are different, with less concern for privacy of information (see Aftab, 2004).

PRIVACY OF RECORDS

There are a number of proprietary databases that provide access to information gleaned from public records. Births, marriages, deaths, arrests, convictions, and real property transfers are both public record and very often published in newspapers. Other public records—driver's licenses, professional licenses, sale and purchase of aircraft, automobile registrations, probated wills, and so on—are also a matter of public record. These records are not typically published by newspapers but may be available on demand from the federal, state, or local governments. Some jurisdictions place limits on to whom and how these records are provided. In some states, it is possible to build comprehensive databases built on these records. These databases are, in turn, available to anyone willing to pay the price to access them.

Other records are considered confidential and are often protected by law. These include medical and health records, grades and other education records, many government records like census data or tax returns, and financial records. There are legal regimes designed to protect these records from unauthorized public view. For example, the Family Educational Rights and Privacy Act of 1974 (FERPA), 20 USC S. 1232g, protects student records. See the previous chapter for other privacy laws.

The Hippocratic Oath, dating to the fourth century BCE, holds, in part

> Whatever I see or hear in the lives of my patients, whether in connection with my professional practice or not, which ought not to be spoken of outside, I will keep secret, as considering all such things to be private. (U.S. National Library of Medicine, History of Medicine Division, 2002)

In April 2003 the rules regarding protection of privacy in health records, implemented as part of PL 104-191 Health Insurance Portability and Accountability Act (HIPAA), went into effect. As noted in chapter 12, implementation of this legislation has heightened awareness of privacy issues in the United States.

Protection of privacy of financial records, reviewed in the previous chapter, is currently in question in the United States as revealed in the reports of the monitoring of financial transactions by the CIA and the U.S. Treasury Department through access to transactions processed through SWIFT, the Society for Worldwide Interbank Financial Telecommunication, located in Belgium (Aversa and Shrader, 2006).

COMMUNICATION PRIVACY

Our rights to protection of privacy, particularly in communications, are under challenge. The USA PATRIOT Act of 2001 (USAPA) expanded the authority of the federal government to legally monitor electronic communications, including telephone and the Internet. The provisions of the USAPA are partly in response to the events of 9/11, but they also stem from technology changes. Cellular telephones and the Internet have changed the environment in which electronic surveillance takes place. But, it is the "war on terror" that, at least in the United States, is the underlying rationale for the expanded intrusion by government into the communication of individuals, such as that described in chapter 12.

Intellectual Freedom

The American Library Association defines intellectual freedom as

> the right of every individual to both seek and receive information from all points of view without restriction. It provides for free access to all expressions of ideas through which any and all sides of a question, cause or movement may be explored. Intellectual freedom encompasses the freedom to hold, receive and disseminate ideas. (American Library Association, 2006b)

Recent U.S. legislation has been seen to limit intellectual freedom and to constitute a form of de facto and de jure censorship. These recent laws include the Child Online Protection Act (COPA), the Children's Internet Protection Act (CIPA), and the Neighborhood Children's Internet Protection Act (NCIPA). The CIPA and NCIPA regulations place restrictions on the distribution of e-rate funds to public institutions (public libraries and schools) that decline to filter Internet content or otherwise limit access for minors to certain Internet materials. This legislation followed on the heels of the Communications Decency Act (CDA) and the 1997 Supreme Court decision in *Reno v ACLU* holding many of the CDA provisions unconstitutional. COPA and CIPA were both challenged (*Ashcroft v ACLU, ALA v United States*). On 23 June 2003, the U.S. Supreme Court ruled in *ALA v the United States* that the filtering requirements of the Children's Internet Protection Act (CIPA) are constitutional and do not violate First Amendment rights since adult patrons of libraries may request that filters be turned off. By 1 July 2004, all public libraries receiving e-rate funds were required to comply with the CIPA requirement for blocking software to prevent access to obscene or pornographic images and to materials harmful to minors and by 2005 to certify compliance or efforts to achieve compliance in order to receive funds supporting Internet access through the Library Services and Technology Act.

The other case in this area, *Ashcroft v ACLU*, which challenged the constitutionality of the Child Online Protection Act, had a different outcome. It was returned by the Supreme Court to the lower court for a decision on constitutionality, with the injunction against enforcement continued pending further action on the case. The Appeals Court again found the law unconstitutional, and the Supreme Court upheld the decision of the Appeals Court in June 2004 but returned the case to the lower courts. As of this writing, the law is again in federal court (*ACLU v Gonzales*).

It seems certain that the new technology, the World Wide Web, will continue to prompt legislative challenges to harness its excesses and legal challenges to those constraints. The CDA attempted to define those limits broadly. When those efforts were unsuccessful, COPA, CIPA, and NCIPA sought narrower definitions and restrictions, with differing results.

Can we argue that there are legitimate limitations on intellectual freedom? Most societies accept some degree of censorship. Intellectual freedom and privacy rights are sometimes at odds. FERPA, for example, places severe limits on our ability to delve into educational records. Medical and financial records have also been protected.

Censorship can be imposed for other purposes. Most frequently it is imposed to protect national security. As counterweight to the classification of information (in government at least) are the FOIA laws (see chapter 12). Many governments impose draconian censorship in order to protect the regime, to maintain elites in power, and to limit the circulation of information. Some censorship is imposed to maintain cultural value systems or to preserve moral and religious beliefs.

Free speech is a corollary to intellectual freedom. We may censor inflammatory speech, at least in the context meant by Supreme Court Justice Oliver Wendell Holmes in *Schenck v United States*, 249 U.S. 47 (1919), who held that "The most stringent protection of free speech would not protect a man in falsely shouting fire in a theatre and causing a panic."

Religious speech sponsored by public institutions in the United States is unconstitutional, particularly in public schools (see *McCollum v Board of Education*, 333 U.S. 203 (1948), *Engel v Vitale*, 370 U.S. 421 (1962), *Lee v Weisman*, 112 SCt. 2649 (1992)). On the other hand, religious groups may use public buildings for religious purposes under limited circumstances (see *Lamb's Chapel et al. v Center Moriches Union Free School District*, 508 U.S. 384 (1993) and *Good News Club v Milford Central School* (2001)).

Catherine MacKinnon (1993) has raised the interesting argument that certain kinds of speech are more than only words (the title of one of her books). Certain words (and we include images in this) are acts. Pornography and hate speech are incendiary and are antisocial behavior that may well be actionable in the law. For MacKinnon, to view a film depicting a rape or a lynching is to participate in the rape and the lynching. Verbal and visual sexual harassment, mere words perhaps, are more than words. They are acts (MacKinnon, 1993).

Equitable Access and Information Literacy

We suggest first that equality of access can be defined in the context of three fundamental information ethics concerns: the right of access, literacy, and information literacy. Generally, "literacy" is defined as the ability to read and process intellectually the information acquired through reading. Reading, of course, is defined in its broadest sense. Information literacy includes information technology competence, for it implies the ability to use existing technology at a certain ability level in order to compete successfully with others who can take advantage of information and information technologies.

These literacy issues and concerns predate any thought of digital information processing and transmission by thousands of years. To have equitable access one must be both literate and information literate. Information literacy is the ability "to recognize when information is needed and . . . the ability to locate, evaluate and use effectively the needed information" (Burnheim, 1992: 192).

The information literacy concept is not confined to a particular format, as Lenox and Walker note:

> Whether information comes from a computer, a book, a government agency, a film, a conversation, a poster, or any number of other possible sources, inherent in the concept of information literacy is the ability to dissect and understand what you see on the page or the television screen, in posters, pictures, and other images, as well as what you hear. If we are to teach information literacy, we must teach students to sort, to discriminate, to select, and to analyze the array of messages that are presented. (Lenox and Walker, 1992: 4–5)

There are at least three levels of responsibility for access and information literacy that need to be addressed: (1) individual responsibilities, (2) societal responsibilities, and (3) governmental responsibilities. We will examine these levels briefly below.

HISTORY OF ACCESS

Consider that 150 years ago most people never ventured more than fifty miles from their homes, that fifty years ago only 20 percent of the American population had ever ridden in an airplane, and by the beginning of the third millennium in some countries only 20 percent of the population had ever made a telephone call. Does the new digital reality create a new set of information "haves" and "have-nots" that is somehow more perfidious than existed before? Or are we looking at "business as usual"?

To put the question in other words, have we experienced a Kuhnian paradigm shift in the information environment and therefore perhaps in society? Is that paradigm shift limited to the information environment, information science, or information theory? Or has nothing nearly so dramatic taken place, and do we continue to face and address the same set of questions in new dress?

Or to put the question in a somewhat different way, engineers speak of plateau changes. Plateau changes occur where a parameter change affects in some fundamental way the behavior of some object or some thing. For example, when an aircraft exceeds the speed of sound, there is a fundamental aerodynamic change. The physics change. Airplanes fly differently. We see this by wing configurations, among other things. Another example is superconductivity. Electricity flows through certain materials with no resistance once temperatures are reduced beyond certain critical levels, or plateaus, if you will.

Can we argue that the new realities in information access, transfer, and management in some way represent a paradigm shift, a plateau change? If so, does this create a rift so profound and of such a magnitude between information haves and have-nots that it cannot or will not be overcome?

It should be remembered that access to information has often been seen as a two-edged sword. New information systems and efficient access and publication are correctly perceived as threats to the existing social order. The printing press, the public library, and other technologies and information institutions not only inform and educate; they raise expectations. Consider the ramifications of the invention of moveable type by Johannes Gutenberg in the fifteenth century. It has been argued that there must have been a confluence of a number of forces for any given set of technologies to impact society in a meaningful way. Consider the social and intellectual forces of the day. The fifteenth and sixteenth centuries were to witness significant reform and to include Martin Luther's 95 Theses in 1517. Luther was further to argue the importance of biblical translation in 1530. Bibles translated into local languages and in the hands of the general population proved to be a powerful tool and often the undoing of the status quo ante.

Improvements in printing technologies, including papers, metallurgy, energy, and distribution systems, all led to reduced costs and a proliferating demand for the printed book. These changes went hand in hand with increased literacy. And in the end, all of these forces may well have contributed to not only a better informed and socially broader populace but also to redefinitions in the political, social, moral, and economic structures and beliefs. The pen is indeed mightier than the sword.

DIGITAL DIVIDE

The term "digital divide" has been coined to describe a gap in understanding, capability, and access to technology in order to exploit the digital revolution in information. The digital divide has been identified to have two topographies. The first is a domestic one—countries both developed and in development have found that there are at least two groups in their societies. One group—the "haves"—has access to information technology (computers, software, high-speed Internet access) and the information to use that information technology (education, training, technical sophistication). The other group—the "have nots"—lacks access to any or all of the facilities and abilities held by the haves. It is posited that the gap between the "haves" and "have-nots" may be so deep and so wide that the have-nots cannot achieve the same degree of competence and therefore access to social and economic goods that the haves control unless there is active intervention by various elements of society. These elements or groups include governments, schools, libraries, and other agents. Unless social agents intervene, it is further argued, have-nots may be relegated to a second-class knowledge status and be unable to pull themselves from that condition even with future intervention by governments or other agents.

The second definition is similar, except that it is focused on countries or regions rather than individuals. Unless countries build their information infrastructures—and here infrastructures include not only physical infrastructure like telephone and optical cable systems, satellite access, cell phone networks, and so on; computing systems; and access to software but also the training and education of human resources—these countries are destined to fall ever farther behind. Again, at some point, the digital divide may become so wide that the barriers the divide erects may become insurmountable.

Mossberger, Tolbert, and Stansbury (2003) argue that the digital divide should be described as four different divides rather than as a single phenomenon. These four divides are the access divide, the skills divide, the economic opportunity divide, and the democratic divide. These four divides, at least as they are manifested within the United States, can be understood in terms of gender, ethnicity, race, education, and income level. Where once the digital revolution was thought to be the harbinger of democracy and equality or as the great leveler, it has perhaps contributed to a widening of the gap rather than closing it (see, for example, Carter, 1997). Even where government and nongovernmental actors seek to close the digital divide, many observers conclude that the process is complex and difficult (Papazafeiropoulou and Pouloudi, 2004; Organisation for Economic Co-operation and Development, 2001).

If we accept the hypothesis that the digital divide at the individual, national, and international levels is indeed an accurate description of a current social dynamic, do we then have ethical, moral, and/or legal obligations to respond to it? Do we have an obligation to ameliorate the consequences of the digital divide; and, if so, what steps must we take?

The digital divide raises once again a number of fundamental equity and ethical questions:

- Is the digital divide simply another manifestation of social, economic, and other cultural divisions that, in time, will recede in importance? Recall that various groups in various cultures at various times have long debated access to education, to books, to information.
- Will an enlightened self-interest or public policy close the digital rift just as it has in a broad way provided access to literacy through education in most societies?
- Or is digital literacy of such import that to be left behind now is to be left behind forever?

There is an assumption underlying the digital divide issue that the digital divide is a social ill and should be eliminated. We accept that as a given. But, is the digital divide a separate issue, or is it part of a larger concern? Stephen Foster has argued that "the underlying concerns surrounding the issue of the digital divide are actually more about the nature and future of education than about the current distribution of technology" (Foster, 2000: 439). We suspect Foster is right. But we need to explore the assumption.

If the digital divide is, in fact, a social ill, then some interesting questions are raised. The one often raised first is who should pay for reducing the divide. Part of that answer is governments and part is foundations, but certainly part has to be individuals. If governments, and we can include under governments many schools, libraries, and other institutions, are to narrow the digital divide, are they to do it with training, equipment, infrastructure, funding, regulation, or some combination of all of these? How quickly is this task to be accomplished?

Inherent in all such questions is the belief that narrowing the domestic or international digital divide would be a social good. We ought to consider this question carefully. Or, to put it a little differently, are there social and infrastructure changes that must take place before narrowing the digital divide makes sense? Consider the much-quoted statistic that in many places in the world, nearly 80 percent of the population has never made a telephone call, much less used a computer. In many places, vast majorities of the population cannot read or write. Before we concern ourselves with digital literacy, should we not first concern ourselves with literacy?

The "serial" answer to the question is "first one then the other." The "parallel" answer is that both can occur simultaneously. It is possible to close both the literacy and the digital divides at the same time. It may well be that as one focuses on the digital divide, it will spill over into the literacy area.

Another set of problems involves the disproportionate distribution of goods and services between elites and everyone else. The digital divide, in fact, is nothing new. Societies have almost always debated distribution and redistribution policies for a wide range of social goods, including quality education, information access, literacy training, health care, infrastructure development, and so on. Many countries have used public policy either to divide populations or to bring them together. The use of public policy leverage is inherent in the digital divide debate.

In the United States, there has been a several-pronged response to the digital divide. The Clinton administration, the first American government to have had to be concerned with the digital divide, responded with e-rates and other support for increased public school and public library Internet access. State and local governments also invested heavily in wiring schools.

It should perhaps be pointed out that this is by no means a unique public policy response. Federal and state governments have long supported an equality of access to public utilities. Consider universal telephone access requirements and the rural electrification programs begun in the 1930s. There are interesting differences as well. The government required electric and telephone companies to make their services available everywhere to everyone. These policies had, in part, a residential focus: households were to have electric and telephone service, and in the United States today most do.

This approach has not been the one taken for digital services. The Clinton administration focused on public schools and libraries. Moreover, cable television companies have never been required to provide universal service, in part because cable is perceived to offer entertainment rather than serve a public need and in part because there are alternative delivery systems, like broadcast television and satellite service.

If the digital divide is to be closed, there is a need to ensure that

- an adequate network infrastructure is developed;
- people are trained to use Internet facilities and to understand the Internet and its limitations;
- hardware and software are made available and usable without unreasonable hardship.

Finally, let us ask the most dangerous of questions:

Is there an inherent right to access to information?

Take, for example, government publications. In the United States, most (but not all) government publications and many publications underwritten with government funds are considered to be in the public domain. From an intellectual property and copyright perspective, this body of information is freely accessible and may be copied at will. In the United Kingdom, the Crown holds the copyright and can limit the right to copy and access. A higher order question that might be asked is "do we have a right to be informed?" Well, perhaps not (Wellman, 1999; Morehead, 1995); or can we distinguish between passive rights "to be informed" and active rights to seek information?

PLAYERS

In the United States, the U.S. Department of Commerce's National Telecommunications and Information Administration (NTIA) was given the responsibility by the Clinton administration to address the digital divide in the United States. Beginning in 1995, the NTIA published a series of reports on the digital divide in the United States. These are as follows:

Falling Through the Net: A Survey of the "Have Nots" in Rural and Urban America (1995), a survey of telephone, computer, and modem penetration, shows the rural and central city poor are more likely to lack connectivity than are other Americans and identifies the disparities in connectivity and access related to race, age, income, education level, and geographic location.

Falling Through the Net II: New Data on the Digital Divide (1998) updated the 1995 study and confirmed the continued existence of a digital divide based on ethnic, income, racial, and other characteristics.

Falling Through The Net: Defining the Digital Divide (1999) examines households for telephones, computers, and Internet connectivity. The digital divide is described as a civil rights issue:

> Households with incomes of less than $20,000 and Black households, for example, are twice as likely to get Internet access through a public library or community center than are households earning more than $20,000 or White households. Similarly, low-income households and households with lower education levels are obtaining access at schools at far higher rates. (U.S. NTIA, 1999)

Falling Through The Net: Toward Digital Inclusion (2000) continues the same analysis but also explores quality of connectivity (speed) and disability issues.

The George W. Bush administration has downplayed both the term and the concept of the digital divide. It has not ignored it, however. The report under the Bush administration, published jointly by the NTIA and the Economics and Statistics Administration (also part of the U.S. Department of Commerce) changed the character of the dialogue.

A Nation Online: How Americans Are Expanding Their Use of the Internet (2002) reports changes in U.S. household computer and Internet use. The report concludes that there has been a substantial narrowing in the domestic digital divide as households and schools in all segments of society become more wired. The result has been substantially reduced federal funding for technology and training initiatives that fell under the digital divide initiatives.

INTERNATIONAL PERSPECTIVES

The digital divide may be receding as an issue in the United States, but it remains recognized as a major international development issue. Substantial barriers to narrowing the international digital divide persist. Ross Shimmon (2001), then Secretary General of the International Federation of Library Associations and Institutions (IFLA), argued that households in OECD countries typically had some 72 access pathways per 100 inhabitants to digital information in 1998, whereas in developing countries the figure was 7.8 pathways per 100 inhabitants, and in the poorest countries it was as few as

1.6 per 100 inhabitants. Relative access costs remain exorbitant as well. Peter Lor (2003), South Africa's National Librarian, takes an equally pessimistic view on the possible role of national libraries and other national institutions in developing countries in bridging the digital divide—too big a problem and too few resources with which to address them.

The first meeting of the World Summit on the Information Society (WSIS, see www.itu.int/wsis) addressing many of the issues surrounding use of information in development met in Geneva, Switzerland, 10–12 December 2003, with a second meeting in Tunis, 16–18 November 2005. The Geneva meeting promulgated a Declaration of Principles entitled Building the Information Society: a Global Challenge in the New Millennium (WSIS, 2003). The document recognizes the centrality of information and information technologies for development and human advancement in the information society. It identifies the importance of information for furtherance of the United Nations' Millennium Declaration and exhorts the member states to promote information and information technology for the world's poorest countries consistent with the Universal Declaration of Human Rights. The Declaration calls upon the member states to recognize cultural diversity, to promote international and regional cooperation, and to consider establishment of a voluntary "Digital Diversity Fund." The concept of "shared knowledge" undergirds the WSIS philosophy. The Tunis meeting added to the other concerns a recognition that there exists a gender divide as part of the digital divide.

Also in the international arena, there are a number of organizations addressing digital divide issues by supporting and promoting information and communication technologies (ICT), chiefly in the developing countries. Examples include the World Bank Group's Global Information & Communication Technologies Department (GICT) and the United Nations Information and Communication Technologies (UNICT) Task Force. The GICT helps focus private, donor, and public financing onto ICT projects. The UNICT Task Force is charged to support the Millennium Development Goals of the United Nations through application of ICT. These goals include reduction of extreme poverty, sustainable growth, promoting health and combating HIV, reducing slums, developing global solidarity, and "bridging the digital divide" (Annan, 2000).

The United Nations Development Programme (UNDP) perceives that ICT has a major component for the democratization of societies (United Nations Development Programme, n.d.a). It has incorporated elements of ICT into its projects, for example e-society and e-governance components in its initiatives in Armenia (United Nations Development Programme, n.d.a) and in Slovakia (United Nations Development Programme, n.d.a). The Digital Opportunity Initiative (DOI), a UNDP initiative together with Accenture and the Markle Foundation had as its objective "to provide a strategic framework that will help developing countries, communities, and supporting organizations leverage the unique benefits of information and communications technologies (ICT) to further sustainable human development" (United Nations Development Programme, 2001). Accenture is a private-sector consulting firm, and the Markle Foundation is a philanthropic organization.

There are a number of other programs to provide public access to the digital environment, both within the United States and worldwide. These include the following:

Public Institutions, Such as Libraries, Schools, Other Public Agencies

In the United States, public libraries have taken much of the load for closing the digital divide. Since 1994, there have been regular reports made every year or two on public library Internet access. The 2004 study reports that nearly all U.S. public libraries now have public access Internet connections—98.9 percent, up from 95.3 percent in 2002. Even for areas defined as in poverty, over 90 percent of public libraries provide public Internet access (Bertot, McClure, and Jaeger, 2005: 17). One might conclude that the digital divide in the United States has narrowed to parity with the whole country.

Public libraries can be important vehicles for providing Internet access to all segments of a society. The public library movement is strong in the United States, but the public library as a major public institution is not a universal one. Where the public library is not a major social actor, alternatives must be found.

Nongovernmental Not-for-profits

Foundations can play a role in addressing the digital divide. For example, the Bill and Melinda Gates Foundation has supported technology grants to public libraries in the United States and Canada, targeting low-income communities as the first recipients of Gates grants. The Gates Foundation has extended its reach outside North America with grants to libraries in Chile and Mexico to provide hardware, software, and training (Bill & Melinda Gates Foundation, 2006b). In July 2000, the Helsinki (Finland) Public Library was the recipient of the first Access to Learning Award for its work in increasing Internet access in the library, followed by awards to public library Internet access projects in Argentina and Guatemala (2001), Colombia (2002), South Africa (2003), Denmark and China (2004), Bangladesh (2005), and Nepal (2006) (Bill & Melinda Gates Foundation, 2006a). With the addition of the Buffet billions to the Gates Foundation coffers (see Hauser, 2006), this foundation will likely be the most influential player in both the NGO and IGO arenas in addressing digital divide concerns.

The Benton Foundation has funded several studies and helps support the Digital Divide Network. The studies sponsored or featured by the Benton Foundation argue for a variety of strategies to close the digital divide, from social organizations like youth or faith-based organizations to more residential connectivity.

The Internet Society (ISOC) has developed programs to assist countries in development. ISOC's journal, *On the Internet*, frequently publishes articles from or about Internet development in the NICs. It also sponsors training. The Internet Society Network Training Workshop for Countries in the Early Stages of Internetworking has conducted workshops to provide training in network management in both English and French to meet the needs of peoples in anglophone and francophone countries and also holds workshops in Spanish. The Internet Society has taken the view that through training and other assistance, countries in development can overcome the digital divide (Internet Society, 2006).

A final interesting example is the WorldSpace Direct Media Service (DMS). It now provides or seeks to provide L-band radio and simplex high bandwidth Internet service from its two satellites to much of Africa, Asia, and Europe. It has not begun an Americas service because, according to Wikipedia (2006), its intended frequencies have been claimed by the U.S. Air Force.

This section has touched on the digital divide issue by raising questions. It has been suggested that the digital divide as a concern is not something new, but rather a new manifestation of an old problem: access and literacy. Information professionals of all kinds have been concerned with whether and how to address access and literacy since there were information professionals. We have had different premises and different answers, but the questions have been similar.

There is a new concern, but one that again re-echoes earlier concerns, that those on the wrong side of the digital divide are destined to second-class status unless something is done and done soon. This question is still debated. If there is a need for intervention, then what kind of intervention is needed, by which social institutions, with what degree of emphasis and concern?

Intellectual Property

Although we have considered intellectual property issues in the previous chapter, they are reviewed here in the context of the ethical considerations entailed. Intellectual property issues revolve along a number of axes. The first set is concerned with the producers/owners' rights to protect information from inappropriate use against the rights of users to consume and reuse information. The right to protect information from inappropriate use (whatever that may be) is balanced by the right of users to make *fair use* of that intellectual property. We recognize that some forms of information use are wrong. Plagiarism is the taking not only the ideas but also the words (sounds, images) of others without attribution. Plagiarism does not include the use of the information of others in whole or in part so long as the source of the information is appropriately attributed. There is, as ever, a debate as to what constitutes appropriate attribution, and some of that debate is an issue of form rather than substance (e.g., which citation system to use).

Second, we distinguish between types of intellectual property and the means we use to protect that property. As discussed earlier, there are three basic forms of intellectual property protection: (1) the copyright, (2) the patent, and (3) registration of trade and service marks.

The purpose behind copyright, patent, and service and trademark protection is to reserve the economic benefits for the information creator or the property owner for a specific period in order to reward information creation. It is also seen as an incentive for new information creation. If information creators, the arguments holds, were not compensated for their ideas and efforts, few would expend the time, trouble, and expense to create new works and processes. In turn, information distributors would be reluctant to assume risks associated with the purchase of information rights were they also not adequately protected.

Copyrights and patents were invented to protect against the inevitable migration of ideas and know-how. However, as we have seen, information and information systems have become truly globalized. Ideas and processes have never been confined within any border for any protracted period. For example, in the beginning of the nineteenth century, the British textile industry sought to protect manufacturing processes by prohibiting the export of milling and weaving plans. The plans were carried out in one man's head and formed the basis of the American industry. Similarly, French pineapple interests prohibited the export of a particular plant strain, until plants were smuggled to Hawaii to form the basis of the industry there.

Restricting the use of ideas and know-how to those who initially created them raises issues related both to national security and to digital divide concerns. A few examples help to illustrate:

- As a general rule, many processes can be "reverse engineered." Once it is known that something is possible, particularly when one has a working model of the end product, it can be copied. The Soviet nuclear weapons program is a good example. Following the famous letter from Albert Einstein to President Franklin Roosevelt in 1939, the United States began a crash program (the Manhattan Project). In early 1945, the Trinity Test proved the process, followed by the use of the weapon against Japan in August 1945. It is important to remember that until 1945, the A-bomb was theoretical. Several approaches had been proposed in an environment of uncertainty. The Soviets exploded their first device in 1948. They were not working in a theoretical void; they knew that it was possible to build a bomb. They were perhaps assisted by espionage. But in the end, they "reverse engineered" the process more quickly than did the Americans, working from scratch.

- The pharmaceutical industry is experiencing "reverse engineering." Many firms find that either their patented drugs are copied by other firms or similar but not quite exact formulations are produced as generic drugs. For national benefit reasons, many countries tolerate, even promote, copying. India, for example, has had many pharmaceutical companies producing drugs for domestic consumption based on proprietary formulations in other countries, although recent tightening of Indian patent laws will diminish this practice. Drug companies claim they are losing a return on investment; the governments of developing nations point to the needs of their populations for the medicines. In Uganda and other African countries, establishment is under way of domestic pharmaceutical companies that will be able to copy and produce patented drugs, a practice which is allowed under World Trade Organization rules for the poorest of countries (Anderson, 2006).

- The Chinese have until recently followed an "adoptive" policy, which is to say they have not always honored patents and copyrights. They have begun to move into mainstream practice in return for World Trade Organization membership and most favored nation trade treatment by the United States.

These examples point to the need for balance between social and individual rights and needs. Before any society breaks convention, there must be a clear and compelling need to do so. Often there are many legal, ethical, and moral issues that must be resolved before property rights are abridged or before significant changes are made.

Because intellectual property may be easy to reproduce, is it ethical to do so? Do situational ethics apply to intellectual property? That is to say, in one set of circumstances it may be ethical, but in another it may not? Does technological change drive ethical change? For example, until music was recorded in digital format it could not be copied that way. Until the technology was developed to capture digital signals, it was equally impossible to record it. Because the status of the industry changed, together with "capture technology," have intellectual property rules changed as well?

Fair use is another aspect of intellectual property that raises ethical issues. It is concerned with the rights of others to use protected information, including the right of access to information and the amount of that information that may be taken and used without substantial reworking. All too often the decision of how much may be used and by whom is left to the copyright owner and not to the end user. There is evolving jurisprudence (see the previous chapter) to help us understand the parameters of rights and privileges on both sides of the issue.

Why are we so preoccupied with intellectual property rights? There are two basic reasons. The first is to protect and acknowledge the ideas of others. But second, intellectual property has value, some of it a great deal of value. Let us keep in mind (as discussed in the information economics chapter) that information is very expensive to produce but very inexpensive to reproduce. Take the Napster situation as an example. Music must be conceived, written, performed, and recorded. The cost of the first recording is therefore very high, but subsequent copies are not. The same can be said for software, films, books, and so on. Any material in digital format is inherently easier to copy and to copy exactly from the original. Intellectual property concerns therefore have become more intense as the ability to copy and to copy exactly has become easier. This is not to say that we have not been concerned before with the making of unauthorized copies; we have. But prior to the advent of photography and later photocopying, the copying of a work was very labor intensive. Those labor costs alone were often a disincentive against inappropriate taking of intellectual property.

The makers of intellectual property fully recognize the principle of the expensive first copy and the very inexpensive second and subsequent copies. They also recognize the principle that they cannot recoup costs on the sale of the first copy but must redistribute costs and profits on the sale or licensing of subsequent copies.

Digital divide issues have raised an interesting set of questions for information producers. Should the market price of digital and other information goods be varied according to the customer? Some information producers, for example the publishers of scholarly journals, have already adopted different scales for library and individual subscribers. Based on the idea that library-owned copies will be read by more people than individual subscriptions, libraries are charged more for their subscriptions. The same idea is used for software licensing. Software licenses are often negotiated on the basis of the number of potential uses or installations. The greater the number of installations, the higher is the price for the license. E-book producers license their materials on the basis of the maximum number of users at any given time.

You may have noted that we have again introduced the notion of "license" versus "ownership." There are subtle but very important differences between these two concepts. Information producers have traditionally sold "information containers." When you own a book, for example, you own the physical object but not the words contained therein. You may resell the object, you may destroy it, or you may deface it. You may keep it and reread it whenever you wish, and you may lend it to others to read and reread.

Licenses place limits on these rights of ownership. These limits depend in large part on the terms of the license. Through licensing, the information copyright or patent holder (note, we do not say information creator) may limit the extent to which the information is used or transferred.

Licenses may expire. They may be limited to a specific device or machine. What licenses achieve, from an ethical point of view, is an increased measure of control, not only over the reproduction of information in a particular expressed form, but also over all access to and use of that information, tipping the scales in the intellectual property equation in favor of the intellectual property owner and away from the notion of balance between user and creator that the idea of copyright (as set forth in the U.S. Constitution) was intended to protect.

As discussed in the previous chapter, the differing cultural traditions of countries result in differing ethical stances toward intellectual property, with ownership of creative expression perceived on a more collective societal basis in the Eastern tradition than is the case in Western thought. However, even in the United States, there is a limited sense of collective intellectual property. In the United States, most government publications are in the public domain. They are in the public domain because they are conceived, written, published, and distributed using taxpayer monies. The public has paid for them; therefore, the public owns them. This is not so in the United Kingdom. For the most part, Her Majesty's Stationary Office (HMSO), an agent of government, owns these copyrights. HMSO-owned materials may not be copied without permission.

Information beyond Borders

Finally, the last information issue we will examine concerns how countries are dealing with information originating beyond their borders. At present, we are witnessing an extension of extraterritorial authority by courts to regulate electronic commerce.

In the United States, the concept of community standards—moral standards—can be applied to prosecute pornographers. In *Miller v California* [413 U.S. 15, 23 (1973)], the U.S. Supreme Court argued that obscene or vulgar speech does not necessarily have Constitutional protection. The Court applied a three-part test:

(a) whether the average person, applying contemporary community standards, would find that the work, taken as a whole, appeals to the prurient interest

(b) whether the work depicts or describes, in a patently offensive way, sexual conduct specifically defined by the applicable state law
(c) whether the work, taken as a whole, lacks serious literary, artistic, political, or scientific value

Part (a) of the test, the "contemporary community standards" test, has been interpreted to mean that the moral standards of one community can be used to set the standards for prosecution of offenses committed in jurisdictions where indeed they may not violate contemporary community standards.

In *U.S. v Thomas* [*U.S. v Thomas*, 74 F.3d 701 (6th Cir. 1996), cert. denied, 117 S.Ct. 74 (1996)] the owners of a sexually explicit electronic bulletin board maintained in California were successfully prosecuted in a federal court in Tennessee. It was successful because the bulletin board could be and was accessible from Tennessee and because community standards are different in Tennessee from those in California.

By implication, *U.S. v Thomas* could extend outside the United States. We have already seen parallel cases in Germany when in 1997 (the Felix Somm case [Amtsgericht München, Geschäftsnummer: 8340 Ds 465 Js 173158/95]) the court sought to regulate pornography provided through CompuServe. The second "famous case" arose in France in 2000 [*UEJF et Licra c/ Yahoo! Inc. et Yahoo France,* Tribunal de Grande Instance de Paris, Ordonnance de référé, 22 mai 2000] where the court sought to bar the advertisement and sale of Nazi paraphernalia through the Web portal Yahoo!

Harold Thimbleby (1998) observes that many of our ethical and moral perspectives are in conflict with global commercial realities. The *Thomas, CompuServe,* and *Yahoo!* cases raise some interesting questions and moral and ethical dilemmas. What are the rights of producers or managers of wikis or blogs, successors to the electronic bulletin boards? What are the moral implications of the dissemination of what one society defines as obscene or inflammatory materials? Do extraterritorial rights inhere in governments to regulate such material? Thimbleby and others concern themselves with the "commons," our collective rights, our collective morality. Others may see the promotion of the commons as the diminution of the rights of the individual. Is there an inherent conflict between collective and individual rights, between collective and individual morality? Is it morally acceptable to find technical solutions to these conflicts?

CONCLUSION

In information ethics, the continuing concerns from the past—balancing of rights in intellectual property, intellectual freedom, equitable access to information, and protection of information about individuals—have been and are being transformed by the effects of technological change. If the new information technologies have created new challenges, those new ethical challenges might be based upon the

- enhanced ability to monitor and gather aggregate data on individuals
- enhanced ability to ignore intellectual property rights
- failure of transmission of ethical values to the new environment
- ethical, social, and cultural conflict resulting from globalization of access to information
- loss of common value systems

We are brought back around to Capurro's six points and the development of moral values in the information field and the development of ethical conflicts in the information field. We see that defining morality, much less identifying specific ethical and moral values, is a complex undertaking. There are conflicting forces that are prompting a reexamination and a redefinition of moral and ethical values. Some of the conflict results from cultural differences as the information environment becomes more ubiquitous. We see this, for example, in different interpretations of intellectual property rights.

Some of the conflict results from clashes exacerbated by the ease of access that technology brings us. We have always had sexually explicit materials in our cultures. The mosaics at Pompeii, museums in Amsterdam and Berlin, the *Kama Sutra*, or Japanese pillow books are more than ample examples. Are these obscene? Printing and now the Internet have made access to such materials much easier than it once was.

The concern over the increasingly restrictive regulations on use and transfer of information (discussed in chapter 1 and again in chapter 12) is at base an ethical issue that addresses the balance of the rights of the individual and the rights of society. As technology has enabled increased access to and use of information within and across societies, it has also made possible increasing restrictions, controls, and monitoring of use and access. How to manage these two divergent directions is an ethical issue that will be decided in the political arena.

In the final analysis, perhaps what we now witness are three trends. The first is a conflict between traditional moral and ethical norms across cultures brought together by the new information technologies. Intellectual property rights are a case in point. The second is a reemphasis on once quiescent concerns now made more important again by the new information technologies. Concerns with privacy, access, and censorship are examples. Finally, perhaps we are also witnessing the emergence of new moral and ethical issues. These are more difficult to document but may include preservation of the record, greater concerns with information overload, and the implications of the loss of personal insularity.

QUESTIONS FOR CONSIDERATION

1. Are ethical issues related to information different from ethical issues in other areas, for example, health care?
2. If, as this chapter argues, ethics related to information are embedded in the cultural context in which they are found, are there any universal ethical principles on information use that might be found across all cultures? Why or why not?
3. Changing information technology has affected how information is used. What ethical issues exist today related to information use that would not have existed 50 years ago?
4. Why do the codes of ethics of various sectors of the information professions emphasize different aspects of ethical information behavior?
5. How can the conflict between ethical positions related to information and values in other areas (for example, protection of information privacy and responsibility of government to protect citizens from terrorists) be resolved? Does one value have to be sacrificed for another?

REFERENCES

Aftab, Parry. 2004. "The Privacy Lawyer: From the Mouths of Babes." *Information Week* (19 July). Available: www.informationweek.com/story/showArticle.jhtml?articleID=23901422 (accessed December 2006).

American Library Association. 2004. "Core Values of Librarianship." Available: www.ala.org/ala/oif/statementspols/corevaluesstatement/corevalues.htm (accessed December 2006).

———. 2006a. *Code of Ethics of the American Library Association.* Available: www.ala.org/ala/oif/statementspols/codeofethics/codeethics.htm (accessed December 2006).

———. 2006b. *Office for Intellectual Freedom.* Available: www.ala.org/ala/oif/Default622.htm (accessed December 2006).

Anderson, Tatum. 2006. "Africa Rises to HIV Drug Challenge." *BBC News* (8 June). Available: http://news.bbc.co.uk/1/hi/business/5027532.stm (accessed December 2006).

Annan, Kofi A. 2000. "We the Peoples, The Role of the United Nations in the 21st Century. Millennium Report of the Secretary-General to the United Nations." New York: United Nations. Available: www.un.org/millennium/sg/report/full.htm (accessed December 2006).

Association for Computing Machinery. 2003. *ACM Code of Ethics and Professional Conduct*. Available: www.acm.org/constitution/code.html (accessed December 2006).

Aversa, Jeannine, and Katherine Shrader. 2006. "U.S. Gets Access to Worldwide Banking Data." *WashingtonPost.com* (22 June). Previously available: www.washingtonpost.com/wp-dyn/content/article/2006/06/22/AR2006062201583_pf.html (accessed June 2006).

Baker, Sharon L. 1992. "Needed: An Ethical Code for Library Administrators." *Journal of Library Administration* 16, no. 4: 1–17.

Bertot, John Carlo, Charles R. McClure, and Paul T. Jaeger. 2005. *Public Libraries and the Internet 2004: Summary Results and Findings*. For Bill and Melinda Gates Foundation and American Library Association. Tallahassee: Florida State University College of Information, Information Use Management and Policy Institute. Available: www.ii.fsu.edu/projectFiles/plinternet/2004.plinternet.study.pdf (accessed December 2006).

Bill & Melinda Gates Foundation. 2006a. "Access to Learning Award." Available: www.gatesfoundation.org/GlobalDevelopment/GlobalLibraries/AccessLearningAward/default (accessed December 2006).

———. 2006b. "Global Libraries." Available: www.gatesfoundation.org/GlobalDevelopment/GlobalLibraries (accessed December 2006).

Burnheim, Robert. 1992. "Information Literacy—A Core Competency." *Australian Academic and Research Libraries* 23 (December): 188–196.

Capurro, Rafael. 2001. "Ethics and Information in the Digital Age." LIDA 2001 Annual Course and Conference: Libraries in the Digital Age, Dubrovnik, Croatia, 23–27 May, 2001. Available: www.capurro.de/lida.htm (accessed December 2006).

———. 2003. "Foundations of Information Science Review and Perspectives." Available: www.capurro.de/tampere91.htm (accessed December 2006). Originally published as "What Is Information Science For? A Philosophical Reflection." In *Conceptions of Library and Information Science: Historical, Empirical and Theoretical Perspectives*, edited by Pertti Vakkari and Blaise Cronin, 82–98. London: Taylor Graham, 1992.

Carter, Dave. 1997. " 'Digital Democracy' or 'Information Aristocracy'? Economic Regeneration and the Information Economy." In *The Governance of Cyberspace: Politics, Technology and Global Restructuring*, edited by Brian D. Loader, 136–152. London: Routledge.

Computer Ethics Institute. 1992. *Ten Commandments of Computer Ethics*. Available: www.brook.edu/its/cei/overview/Ten_Commanments_of_Computer_Ethics.htm (accessed December 2006).

Digital Opportunity Initiative. Available: www.opt-init.org (accessed December 2006).

Eisenstein, Elizabeth. 1983. *The Printing Revolution in Early Modern Europe.* Cambridge, UK: Cambridge University Press.

Foster, Stephen P. 2000. "The Digital Divide: Some Reflections." *International Information & Library Review* 32 (September/December): 437–451.

Froehlich, Thomas. 2000. "Intellectual Freedom, Ethical Deliberation, and Codes of Ethics." *IFLA Journal* 26, no. 4: 264–272.

Gorman, Michael. 2000. *Our Enduring Values: Librarianship in the 21st Century.* Chicago: American Library Association.

Grotius, Hugo. 1925. *The Law of War and Peace: De Jure Belli Ac Pacis.* Translated by Francis W. Kelsey. Indianapolis, IN: Bobbs-Merrill.

Hauptman, Robert, ed. 1991. "Ethics and the Dissemination of Information. Special Issue." *Library Trends* 40 (Fall): 199–375.

Hauser, Christine. 2006. "Buffet to Give Billions to Gates Charity and Others." *New York Times* (25 June).

Hisle, W. Lee. 1998. "Values for the Electronic Age: Crossroads of Profession." *College and Research Libraries News* 59 (July/August): 504–505.

International Federation of Library Associations and Institutions. 2005. "Core Values, Article 6." In *IFLA Statutes and Rules of Procedures*, 3. The Hague: IFLA. Available: www.ifla.org/III/IFLAstatutes.pdf (accessed December 2006).

Internet Society. 2006. "Education and Training: Network Training Workshops." Available: www.isoc.org/educpillar/ntw.shtml (accessed December 2006).

Intner, Sheila, and Jorge Schement. 1987. "The Ethic of Free Service." *Library Journal* 112 (1 October): 50–52.

Johnson, Wendall G. 1994. "The Need for a Value Based Reference Policy: John Rawls at the Reference Desk." *Reference Librarian* no. 47: 201–211.

Koehler, Wallace. *Ethics Links to Librarian and Information Manager Associations WWW Pages.* Valdosta, GA: Valdosta State University. Available: http://books.valdosta.edu/mlis/ethics/EthicsBibOrg.htm (accessed December 2006).

———. 2003. "Professional Values and Ethics as Defined by 'The LIS Discipline.'" *Journal of Education for Library and Information Science* 44 (Spring): 99–119.

Koehler, Wallace, Jitka Hurych, Wanda Dole, and Joanna Wall. 2000. "Ethical Values of Information and Library Professionals—An Expanded Analysis." *International Information & Library Review* 32 (September/December): 485–507.

Koehler, Wallace, and J. Michael Pemberton. 2000. "A Search for Core Values: Towards a Model Code of Ethics for Information Professionals." *Journal of Information Ethics* 9 (Spring): 26–54.

Lenox, Mary F., and Michael L. Walker. 1992. "Information Literacy: Challenge for the Future." *International Journal of Information and Library Research* 4, no. 1: 1–18.

Lor, Peter. 2003. "National Libraries and the Digital Divide." Conference of Directors of National Libraries, August 2003, Berlin, Germany. National Library of Australia. Available: www.nla.gov.au/initiatives/meetings/cdnl/2003/09digdiv.pdf (accessed December 2006).

MacKinnon, Catherine. 1993. *Only Words.* Cambridge, MA: Harvard University Press.

Mead, Margaret. 1928. *Coming of Age in Samoa.* New York: Morrow.

Miller, Heather S. 1995. "Ethics in Action: The Vendor's Perspective." *Serials Librarian* 25, nos. 3/4: 295–300.

Morehead, Joe. 1995. "The Myth of Public Access to Federal Government Information as a Constitutional Right." *Serials Librarian* 26, no. 2: 1–26.

Mossberger, Karen, Caroline J. Tolbert, and Mary Stansbury. 2003. *Virtual Inequality: Beyond the Digital Divide.* Washington, DC: Georgetown University Press.

Negroponte, Nicholas. 1995. *Being Digital.* New York: Knopf.

Organisation for Economic Co-operation and Development. 2001. *Understanding the Digital Divide.* Available: www.oecd.org/dataoecd/38/57/1888451.pdf (accessed December 2006).

Papazafeiropoulou, Anastasia, and Athanasia Pouloudi. 2003. "The Digital Divide Challenge: How Stakeholder Analysis Can be used to Formulate Effective IT Diffusion Policies." In *Social and Economic Transformation in the Digital Era,* edited by Georgios Doukidis, Nikolaos Mylonopoulos, and Nancy Pouloudi, 47–55. Hershey, PA: Idea Group.

Peterson, Kenneth G. 1992. "Ethics in Academic Librarianship: The Need For Values." In *The Information Environment: A Reader,* edited by Geraldene Walker, 298–310. New York: G. K. Hall.

Rokeach, Milton. 1973. *The Nature of Human Values.* New York: Free Press.

Rubin, Richard. 1991. "Ethical Issues in Library Personnel Management." *Journal of Library Administration* 14, no. 4: 1–16.

Rubin, Richard, and Thomas Froehlich. 1996. "Ethical Aspects of Library and Information Science." *Encyclopedia of Library and Information Science* 58, supplement 21: 33–52. New York: Marcel Dekker.

Schrader, Alvin M. 1986. "The Domain of Information Science: Problems in Conceptualization and in Consensus-Building." *Information Services & Use* 6, nos. 5/6: 169–205.

Shimmon, Ross. 2001. "Can We Bridge the Digital Divide?" *Library Association Record* 103, 11. Available: www.la_hg.org.uk/directory/record/r200111/article2.html

Smith, Martha M. 1997. "Information Ethics." *Annual Review of Information Science and Technology* 32: 339–366.

Society of Professional Journalists. 2006. *Code of Ethics*. Available at: www.spj.org/ethics_code.asp (accessed December 2006).

Stichler, Richard N., and Robert Hauptman, eds. 1998. *Ethics, Information and Technology: Readings*. Jefferson, NC: McFarland.

Symons, Ann K., and Carla J. Stoffle. 1998. "When Values Conflict." *American Libraries* 29 (May): 56–58.

Thimbleby, Harold. 1998. "Personal Boundaries/Global Stage." *First Monday* 3 (March). Available: www.firstmonday.org/issues/issue3_3/thimbleby/index.html (accessed December 2006).

United Nations Development Programme. *ICT for Democracy: Support to Information Society and Democratic Governance*. Available: www.ict.am/?go=info&view=090307 (accessed December 2006).

———. "Information & Communications Technologies for Development: Regional ICTD Initiatives." Available: http://sdnhq.undp.org/it4dev/docs/regional.html (accessed December 2006).

———. 2001. "Digital Opportunity Initiative Final Report." Available: www.undp.org/surf-panama/egov/docs/programme_activities/evalreports/doi_Discussion_session_Introductory_presentation.pdf (accessed December 2006).

———. 2006. "Information & Communications Technologies for Development." Available: http://sdnhq.undp.org/it4dev (accessed December 2006).

U.S. National Library of Medicine. History of Medicine Division. 2002. "The Hippocratic Oath." Translated by Michael North. *Greek Medicine*. Bethesda, MD: National Library of Medicine. Available: www.nlm.nih.gov/hmd/greek/greek_oath.html (accessed December 2006).

U.S. National Telecommunications and Information Administration. 1995. *Falling Through the Net: A Survey of the "Have Nots" in Rural and Urban America*. Available: www.ntia.doc.gov/ntiahome/fallingthru.html (accessed December 2006).

———. 1998. *Falling Through the Net II: New Data on the Digital Divide*. Available: www.ntia.doc.gov/ntiahome/net2 (accessed December 2006).

———. 1999. *Falling Through The Net: Defining the Digital Divide*. Available: www.ntia.doc.gov/ntiahome/fttn99/contents.html (accessed December 2006).

————. 2000. *Falling Through The Net: Toward Digital Inclusion.* Available: www.ntia.doc.gov/ntiahome/fttn00/contents00.html (accessed December 2006).

U.S. National Telecommunications and Information Administration and the Economics and Statistics Administration. 2002. *A Nation Online: How Americans Are Expanding Their Use of the Internet.* Available: www.ntia.doc.gov/ntiahome/dn/index.html (accessed December 2006).

Wellman, Carl. 1999. *The Proliferation of Rights: Moral Progress or Empty Rhetoric?* Boulder, CO: Westview.

Wikipedia. 2006. "WorldSpace." Available: http://en.wikipedia.org/wiki/ WorldSpace (accessed December 2006).

World Summit on the Information Society. 2003. "Declaration of Principles, Building the Information Society: A Global Challenge in the New Millennium." Document WSIS-03/GENEVA/DOC/4-E, 12 December. Available: www.itu.int/dms_pub/itu-s/md/03/wsis/doc/S03-WSIS-DOC-0004!!PDF-E.pdf (accessed December 2006).

ADDITIONAL SOURCES

Belsey, Andrew, and Ruth F. Chadwick, eds. 1992. *Ethical Issues in Journalism and the Media.* New York: Routledge.

Biegel, Stuart. 2001. *Beyond Our Control? Confronting the Limits of Our Legal System in the Age of Cyberspace.* Cambridge, MA: MIT Press.

Crawford, Nelson A. 1970. *The Ethics of Journalism.* New York: Knopf. St. Clair Shores, MI: Scholarly Press. First published 1929.

Digital Divide Network. Benton Foundation. Available: www.digitaldividenetwork.org (accessed December 2006).

Dole, Wanda V., Jitka M. Hurych, and Wallace C. Koehler. 2000. "Values for Librarians in the Information Age: An Expanded Examination." *Library Management* 21, no. 6: 285–297.

Foley, Theresa. 1999. "The Battle for Bandwidth." *Air Force Magazine* 82 (October). Available: www.afa.org/magazine/Oct1999/1099bandwidth.asp (accessed December 2006).

Hausman, Carl. 1992. *Crisis of Conscience: Perspectives on Journalism Ethics.* New York: HarperCollins.

Metz, Cade. 2006. "MySpace Nation." *PC Magazine* (July): 76–87.

U.S. ENGLISH, Inc. 2006. "Making English the Official Language." Available: www.usenglish.org/inc/default.asp (accessed December 2006).

World Bank Group. Global Information & Communication Technologies. 2006. "About GICT." Available: http://info.worldbank.org/ict (accessed December 2006).

WorldSpace. 2005. *About WorldSpace.* Available: www.worldspace.com/about/
index.html (accessed June 2006).

World Summit on the Information Society. 2006. Available: www.itu.int/
wsis (accessed December 2006).

The preceding chapters have a purpose. That purpose is to explore "information" and the "information environment" from various perspectives and in various contexts. In this last chapter we consider where the future of information may be leading us and how what has gone before helps us to understand what our information future(s) may be. Before you read this final chapter, write your own scenario of the information future.

Chapter 14

Information Future(s)

Learning Guide

After reading this chapter, you should be able to

- envision a possible scenario for the state of information access and use five years from now;
- understand how the past development of the information environment may (or may not) help to predict the future;
- discuss the potential of literature to contribute to how we understand our information past and future;
- identify the major themes of this book.

When you have finished the chapter, return to this page to be sure you have learned what you need to know.

INTRODUCTION

In this book we have traversed the landscape of the information environment, looking at it from various perspectives ranging from theoretical to political, from individual to governmental, and from past to present. To conclude we venture into the unknown and speculate on whether our journey can inform us on what lies ahead.

We have developed several themes throughout this work. One theme that has permeated our discussions is that dependence on information devices is not new; rather, it is the form, nature, and capacity of these devices that have changed and that will continue to do so. As a result of technological changes, there has been an escalating speed in the transmission and dissemination of information to the point that it now can be instantaneous. Moreover, the reach of that dissemination has extended to encompass the entire world and beyond, across all future time, as we presently understand it.

At the same time that the speed and reach have increased, there has been a concomitant increase in our capacity for creating, storing, retrieving, and managing information; and both the devices and the structures that accomplish these activities have become increasingly complex. These changes have simultaneously necessitated and been supported by progress from a state of disorganization to standardization in the processes for information activities.

From a societal perspective, we have seen the broadening of access to the technology of the time from a restricted elite to a much wider segment of the population and increases in the speed with which each new information technology becomes available for inclusion into the daily life of a broad spectrum of individuals. At the same time, and particularly recently, we are witnessing the commodification of information in all of its forms, which is accelerating ethical concerns related to information.

In the societal institutions that create and distribute information the recent trend has been toward increasing concentration of ownership across all the categories of information activities, resulting in horizontal and vertical integration of the information production and distribution industries. The previous separation and independence of the various agencies that function to create, distribute, and manage information has declined. The lines between previously separate information delivery systems are blurring. Convergence is also seen among the social institutions involved, with both government and private institutions offering similar information products and services.

As information technology has become more diversified, the professions that deal with information have similarly seen diversification, as well as expansion in number. As new information technology develops, new information professions are created, at the same time that previously existing professions adapt and migrate to new forms and formats for long-standing information functions.

Information policy has likewise been affected by the changes in technology. Rights of information creators are in a state of change. New technologies are escalating the digital divide concerns related to access and literacy. There is some evidence that the policy changes related to and social challenges posed by today's technology are perhaps more fundamental, maybe even revolutionary, in effect than what happened in response to earlier technological development. What is certain is that conflict between traditional moral and ethical norms across cultures is being brought to the fore by the new information technologies and that there are new moral and ethical issues emerging as a result of the globalization of information.

As we have seen, information changes have led to or facilitated social changes. What can we say about the current set of information changes and their implications for society? Social, economic, and environmental policy of the 1970s was much influenced by the publication of *The Limits to Growth: A Report for the Club of Rome's Project on the Predicament of Mankind* in 1972. Marshall McLuhan (1964, 1967) added another and different dimension when he suggested that we live in a *global village*, interconnected by the electronic arteries of telephony, television, radio, cable, and other mechanisms.

E. F. Schumacher and Barry Commoner were among the first to prescribe the decentralization of society, technology, and the economy for ecological, democratization, and equity goals. Both were major advocates of renewable and sustainable technologies and economies. Commoner (1990), for example, sees the need for pro-environmental technology if positive global environmental, economic, and social outcomes are to emerge. Schumacher (1973), through his opus magnus *Small is Beautiful*, argued for environmentally benign and decentrally managed "appropriate technologies." Implicitly or explicitly, part of the solution to the impending environmental, population, and/or resource crisis lay in social restructuring and decentralization made possible in part by the growing sophistication of the global telecommunication networks. Keep in mind that when *The Limits to Growth* was published, the WWW would not be conceived for another twenty years, ARPANET was less than ten years old, the Communications Satellite Act of 1962 had been law for a decade, and the first telecommunications satellites had been placed in orbit in 1964.

Commoner (1971) foresaw and prescribed the erosion of the city. Given highly efficient telecommunications and transportation networks, the raison d'être for the city no longer exists: the facilitation of communications and commerce. Commoner's concept has been reincarnated as the "telecity" (Pelton, 2004), a decentralized global village infrastructure based on state-of-the-art telecommunications. The telecity, it is theorized, reduces the impact on society of terrorism, natural disasters, environmental degradation, and other calamities because of its decentralized nature.

We have begun to see aspects of decentralization, if you will, and of the rise of the telecity. These include not only more efficient telecommunications, the Internet and the World Wide Web, and enhanced transportation networks, but also applications of these technologies in the social, economic, and government spheres. Workers telecommute and teleconference. Students attend classes online. Companies like eBay and Amazon.com have created new markets and new marketing. E-government and e-governance are emerging. Virtual communities have been established.

We have seen that information changes have both an upside and a downside. These changes often threaten the status quo, which, depending upon your perspective, is an upside or downside effect. Humans are social beings. Do we become more or less "humanized" at distance? What of privacy or intimacy? Does globalization threaten cultural identity or expand it? Are the political and intellectual commons expanded or contracted?

LOOKING BACK AND LOOKING FORWARD

In chapter 1, a key concept was introduced. While dependence on information devices is not a new phenomenon, information over time has come to us in an ever increasing array of processes and with ever increasing speed. We no longer have the luxury of the insulation that time brings between event and response. Until the middle of the nineteenth century, events occurring in one place were either never known in other places or became known only with the passage of days, weeks, months, and sometimes years. The assassination of Julius Caesar in 44 BCE without a doubt had very little import at the time for China, the Americas, and most of Africa. Aside from dynastic struggles in Rome itself, it probably meant very little for the rest of Europe. The assassinations of the Archduke Ferdinand, the Mahatma Gandhi, President Kennedy, and Dr. Martin Luther King in the twentieth century all had immediate consequences all over the world.

In chapter 3 we considered how individuals behave in their information interactions, looking at what we know—and what we do not know—about information needs and wants and how individuals seek and use information. We observed that the systems established for managing information influence that behavior, which led us to explore, in chapters 4 and 5, first the history of information technology, then current late twentieth century and early twenty-first century information technologies. We saw that it was change in information technology that enabled the extension of access to and the sphere of human communication from the immediate to the extended here and now. We found that changes in information technology were the engines that made it possible for information to be created, processed, re-processed, transmitted, disseminated, and consumed at ever increasing speeds and at ever decreasing economic costs to the end user. In chapters 5 and 6 we also saw that our information creation, dissemination, and consumption institutions changed alongside the changes in technology and in the changes in the speed of the movement of information. In many cases, particularly in the late twentieth century, we saw a vertical and horizontal convergence among the information institutions.

In chapter 2, we undertook to survey the various meanings of the "information" concept. If we learned anything from that exercise, it is that there are many meanings of "information," and not all of them are congruent and some are contradictory. Theodore Roszak, in his very interesting book *The Cult of Information*, originally published in 1986, makes the point that the Shannon-Weaver definition of information turns all other definitions of information on their heads, for it is not concerned with the content or meaning of the message, but rather with the clarity of transmission (1994: 11–12).

At about the same time that Shannon was working, Norbert Wiener (1948, 1950) coined the term *cybernetics* to mean automated information technologies in feedback loops. Adequate information, according to Wiener, was necessary if one were to "live effectively." Cybernetics, information processing and feedback, could define life itself. Artificial intelligence or AI was to become one child of cybernetics. AI has yet to live up to expectations; but it, in turn, gave rise to expert systems. Both AI and expert systems use automated, sometimes autonomous, databases and processes to replace or augment human decision making.

Herbert Simon, one of the fathers of artificial intelligence, expounded in an interview for *Omni Magazine* in 1994:

> AI can have two purposes. One is to use the power of computers to augment human thinking, just as we use motors to augment human or horse power. Robotics and expert systems are major branches of that. The other is to use a computer's artificial intelligence to understand how humans think. In a humanoid way. If you test your programs not merely by what they can accomplish, but how they accomplish it, then you're really doing cognitive science; you're using AI to understand the human mind. (Stewart, 1997)

Thus at the beginning of the second half of the twentieth century, the New Testament definition of information ("In the beginning was the word and the word was with God and the word was God," [John 1:1]) was replaced by information as process. This idea of information as process led to one vision of the future described by the novelist Kurt Vonnegut (1952) as a totalitarian economic despotism managed by machines, technocrats, and capitalists or, if you will, "Process as demigod."

A second vision of the future in an information-rich society is that of George Orwell in his novel *1984,* first published in 1949. Orwell describes a society in which information is manipulated to meet political needs and one in which personal freedoms and privacy cease to exist. To continue the biblical analogy, if you will, the Orwellian vision for the future reverses John 8: 32: "and you shall know the truth, and the truth shall make you free."

A third way of looking at the future in the context of information has been to explore the ethical, political, and social characteristics and consequences of technology. Lewis Mumford (1964) argued, for example, that some technologies are more anarchic and some more totalitarian than others. David Lilienthal (1944), at one time chairman of the Tennessee Valley Authority (TVA) and an author of the Acheson-Lilienthal report on nuclear nonproliferation, saw TVA and its multipurpose dams as an engine for democracy. Langdon Winner (1986) entitles his first chapter "Technologies as Forms of Life" and his second "Do Artifacts Have Politics?" Jacques Ellul (1964) is perhaps the most pessimistic of the commentators on technology and society. He suggests that the rise of the technocratic society has led to an erosion of social mores and ethics, that the technological society is amoral.

Some observers argue that certain technologies are inherently good or evil, political or nonpolitical, and so on. Let us take, for example, some energy technologies. We have already noted that David Lilienthal believed that the multipurpose dams and the TVA model promoted democracy. Others see more sinister "designs" in some technologies. During the 1970s, it was decided that the United States would not develop the liquid metal fast breeder reactor (LMFBR) technology, because that technology was more prone to nuclear weapons proliferation than other reactor designs. Indeed, it has been argued that the light water reactor (U.S. design) used for electricity generation is worse than the heavy water reactor (Canadian design) for the same reason. Few of us would argue that nuclear weapons nonproliferation is a desirable end (although according to General Pierre Gallois [1961], the father of French nuclear weapons policy, proportional deterrence is a strategic good). Denis Hayes (1977) was to reject almost out of hand most conventional energy sources and nuclear power in particular as an "authoritarian" technology. The array of solar energy technologies was more consistent with democratic society and more environmentally benign as well. E. F. Schumacher (1973) probably took the concept of technology as a good or evil the farthest. He was a major advocate of small technologies. He was to argue that big technology was inherently dehumanizing in its size and demand for specialization. Big technology is the product of big business and big government. These breed and are bred by a quest for profit to the point that profit becomes an end in itself.

What, then, of the information technologies? Tim May, with a "sort of" Marxian introduction—"A specter is haunting the modern world, the specter of crypto anarchy"—informed us that "Computer technology is on the verge of providing the ability for individuals and groups to communicate and interact with each other in a totally anonymous manner" (May 1992). The Internet as a crypto-anarchic tool suggested a breakdown of social and legal controls and perhaps the beginning of the decline of big government and big business and an end to intrusions into our privacy.

On the other hand, David Shenk (1997) has offered the interesting hypothesis that the Internet—once called the Wild Wild Web—is really a "Republican" technology because it promotes big business and small government. Moreover, information overload is bad for the health. Clifford Stoll (1995) offers a popular critique of the Web. He finds that it replaces—in fact, usurps—many social functions that may best be left alone. Moreover, the technology itself is replete with problems. Michael Dertouzos (1997) sees the information revolution contributing to the globalization of business. And, if left unchecked by regulation, the rift between the haves "North" and the have-nots "South" will grow.

There is a growing literature to suggest that the Internet provides both social goods and social ills. Remember the argument by Nicholas Negroponte that current information technology is leading to the breakdown of the nation-state. For the sake of argument, let us assume he is correct (although as we have pointed out, it just is not so, at least for the time being). Depending on your perspective, the breakdown may or may not be a good thing or a bad thing. More porous borders may promote increased economic exchange, but again they may not. If history teaches us anything, we are likely to see even more localized violence, perhaps terrorism, as micro-groups compete with one another to fill the void left by the state. On the other hand, the collapse of the nation-state could lead us to some form of libertarian utopia.

Howard Rheingold (2000) reminds us that the digital revolution began in the nineteenth century with Charles Babbage and the Lady Lovelace, George Boole, and others who prepared the way for John von Neumann, Vannevar Bush, J. C. R. Licklider, Vinton Cerf, Tim Berners-Lee, and many others. Rheingold (1993) has also argued for the growth of virtual communities. He provides an immense bibliography on virtual communities on the Web (at www .rheingold.com/vc/book/biblio.html). Virtual communities, as Rheingold and many others argue, are groups of individuals, located wherever they may be, with like interests. These virtual communities, which have come to replace physical communities, find their strength in the fact that people sharing interests can find one another and join together to further those interests.

The virtual community may, in fact, promote all sorts of interests and may have a democratizing force. It may also work in the opposite direction. Critics of virtual communities have pointed out that the Internet serves to bring people with "socially aberrant" beliefs together just as efficiently as it does for those with socially benign or positive ends.

Regardless of the direction of the development of virtual communities enabled by information technologies, information remains, as it has always been, a source of power in society. As we explored in chapter 10, the relationship between information and power (and power and information) is complicated. But because of this relationship, information and the flow of information is a serious matter and has been regulated by government, as was examined in chapters 6, 8, 11, and 12. Information regulation is a complex undertaking (see, for example, Schement and Curtis, 1995). How information transmission and information content is or should be regulated is a matter of major debate. There is continuing concern over the intrusion of government and nongovernmental bodies in censorship, individual privacy, intellectual freedom, and other information related values (see, for example, National Academy of Sciences, 2006). These issues were introduced in chapter 13, with its focus on information ethics.

Well, where does this leave us? We saw in chapter 4 and throughout that changes in information and information delivery and social change go hand in hand. Without doubt, the information revolution of the latter half of the twentieth century has led and will lead to social change; and those changes will affect information and information delivery. It could be that information is the new communism and that Negroponte is right: the nation-state may wither away. It could be that virtual communities will lead to a new global democratization and fraternal communication. It is also possible that Vonnegut or Orwell is right and information and information technology will lead to a more malignant totalitarianism.

Jacques Ellul (1964) may also be right. An amoral society accepts the proposition that "once the genie is out of the bottle," it is neither possible nor necessary to put it back in. We are no longer concerned with ideas but with the suppression of fear and anxiety resulting from the uncertainties new technologies bring. History has shown us that new information systems lead to new social, political, and economic configurations.

We debate possible futures in the academic and popular literatures. Science fiction writers, for example, have sometimes predicted events to come.

They can provide us with a glimpse into the possibilities of the future. Some paint a dark picture; others are more optimistic. Some are technology based, others more humanistic and sometimes extra-humanistic.

Jules Verne, for example, in his 1865 travelogue *From the Earth to the Moon* (*De la Terre à la Lune*) describes the beginnings of manned space travel and the advent of submarines in *Twenty Thousand Leagues under the Sea* (*Vingt Mille Lieues sous les mers*, 1869). Others, like *Journey to the Center of the Earth* (*Voyage au centre de la Terre*, 1864), describe events that have yet to come to pass.

H. G. Wells wrote a number of interesting works including *The Time Machine* (1895), *The Invisible Man* (1897), and *The War of the Worlds* (1898). In a nonfiction work, *World Brain* (1938), Wells discussed the merits of an encyclopedic resource that some have come to identify with the World Wide Web.

In 1945, the science fiction author Arthur C. Clarke proposed that geostationary satellites could provide comprehensive global telecommunications coverage. The first geostationary earth satellite, Intelsat I or Early Bird, was launched on April 6, 1965, fully twenty years after Clarke's prescient letter. There are now at least 300 satellites in Clarke Orbit (for a list see www.satsig .net/sslist.htm). These satellites provide telecommunications coverage as well as television programming. The Clarke Orbit is an equatorial orbit, some 42,164 km from the center of the earth or 35,787 km mean sea level above the earth. These satellites are in geostationary orbits, that is, they orbit with the earth so that they remain constantly above the same spot.

The mathematician and science fiction author Isaac Asimov proposed some interesting laws of information in the science fiction he wrote. For example, an "uncertainty principle in information" could be defined as "the farther you go back, the less reliable the information becomes—no matter what you do" (Asimov, 1991: 272).

> Records don't last forever. . . . Memory banks can be destroyed or defaced as a result of conflict or can simply deteriorate with time. Any memory bit, any record that is not referred to for a long time, eventually drowns in accumulated noise. Dors Venabili c. 12,050 Galactic Era (Asimov, 1991: 150)

Others would take more contemporary and more political interpretation. George Orwell in *1984* (1949) was highly critical of the use of language as a means of political control. In *Animal Farm* (1945), Orwell denounced the Soviet prescription of utopia. In *Brave New World* (1932), Aldous Huxley was highly critical of genetic manipulation to achieve utopian ends. The psychologist B. F. Skinner suggested in *Walden Two* (1948) that utopian society could be achieved through applied psychology. He followed that with *Beyond Freedom and Dignity* (1971), defending his premises by defining what he termed the *mentalistic constructs* of "freedom" and "dignity" in psychological terms. Ray Bradbury in *Fahrenheit 451* (1953) analyzes the impact of censorship and social control on society.

Of a more positive nature, Robert Heinlein in *Stranger in a Strange Land* (1961) developed utopian notions of social construct. These included gender relationships and interpersonal understanding, as well as concepts of truth and observation.

We have long been struck by the role of fiction to bring issues to the fore because it may help define our technological malaise. Consider the Frankenstein phenomenon, from Mary Wollstonecraft Shelley's creation in the nineteenth century to the Boris Karloff films of the first half of the twentieth century. Two technologies were addressed: medical sciences and electricity. Electricity and evil were subjects of many films during the 1930s. In the 1950s through the 1980s, nuclear energy was made the focus in such films as *Them*, *Dr. Strangelove*, and the *China Syndrome*. Biology and DNA manipulation succeeded as the new concern in the 1990s with such films as *The Fly* and the *Jurassic Park* series. And with the approach of the new millennium, we concerned ourselves with artificial intelligence and computers (*2001: A Space Odyssey*). A striking example is the Douglas Adams novel, first a BBC radio series, *The Hitchhiker's Guide to the Galaxy* (later also a BBC television series and a motion picture). Its computer knew the answer (42) but was never too certain of the question—revealed to us in the end as the answer to the question of the meaning of Life, The Universe, and Everything.

Information Ideas

The Dangers of Predictions of the Information Future
It is always risky to try to predict the future, regardless of the area. The history of information and information technology is littered with a plethora of forecasts that, in retrospect, range from amusing in their naiveté, to frightening in their caution, and to astounding in their correctness. In a 1983 work, Ithiel de Sola Pool analyzed the forecasts that were made about the telephone and its impact on society between 1876 and 1940, trying to determine what factors contributed to making correct guesses. What he found, for the telephone, was that accuracy was achieved when the forecasters used both assessment of the technology and its potential and analysis of the market for the technology (Pool, 1983: 1–2).

(Continued on p. 389)

In a project modeled on Pool's work conducted by faculty and students at Elon University and the Pew Internet & the American Life Project, predictions about the Internet made from 1990 to 1995 were gathered and examined, resulting in a book (Anderson, 2005) and a database of predictions. A related Web site, *Imagining the Internet: A History and Forecast*, continues to gather predictions about networked communication as well as providing access to the database and to predictions about other, earlier technologies (Elon University/Pew Internet Project).

Exploring the site and reading Pool's book are good ways to explore how forecasting, or pre-assessment of the future, has fared over roughly the last century and a half. As an indication of what can be found—and how widely ranging predictions can be—consider the following examples from the *Imagining the Internet* site:

Radio

> I have anticipated radio's complete disappearance ... confident that the unfortunate people, who must now subdue themselves to listening in, will soon find a better pastime for their leisure. (H. G. Wells, "The Way the World is Going," 1925, quoted in *Forward 150/Back 150*, "1890s–1930s Radio")

Telephone

> A system of telephony without wires seems one of the interesting possibilities, and the distance on the earth through which it is possible to speak is theoretically limited only by the curvature of the earth. (John J. Carty, AT&T engineer, "Prophets Column," *Electrical Review*, 1891, quoted in *Forward 150/Back 150*, "1870s–1940s Telephone")

Television

> Television won't be able to hold on to any market it captures after the first six months. People will soon get tired of staring at a plywood box every night. (Darryl F. Zanuck, 20th Century Fox, 1946, quoted in *Forward 150/Back 150*, "1920s–1960s Television")

Sources

Anderson, Janna Quitney. 2005. *Imagining the Internet: Personalities, Predictions, Perspective.* Lanham, MD: Rowman & Littlefield.

Elon University/Pew Internet Project. *Imagining the Internet: A History and Forecast.* Available: www.elon.edu/predictions (accessed December 2006).

Pool, Ithiel de Sola. 1983. *Forecasting the Telephone: A Retrospective Technology Assessment of the Telephone.* Norwood, NJ: Ablex.

INFORMATION, SOCIETY, AND THE FUTURE

If indeed this is the information age and ours is a society based on the use, production, and consumption of information, where are we going? Prognostication is a dangerous business. Undoubtedly the digital revolution will result in social changes just as the information revolutions that have preceded it. The digital revolution will promote other social revolutions and be promoted by them.

We have already considered some of these changes. We have also looked at some of the grim, as well as optimistic, possible futures that may result from a technologically rich information environment. Alvin Toffler (1980) suggested two decades ago that we are embarking on a *Third Wave* in human history. The first wave was the agricultural revolution, the second the industrial revolution, and now the third the information revolution. In *Future Shock*, Toffler (1970) explained and predicted social dislocation and disruptions as a result of the "shock" from a new superindustrial revolution and from information overload.

The previous information revolutions have resulted in the emergence of new elites and the displacement (and sometimes replacement) of old elites. Power relationships and organizational structures changed. Tim May (1992) suggests a new crypto-anarchism arising from the new information vehicles. But David Shenk (1997) sees it as supporting the status quo and even a little perhaps the status quo ante. We saw predictions in the 1990s that libraries would disappear or undergo significant redefinition (for example, Hirsch and Weber, 1999) followed by a recognition that libraries (in some format) continue to have relevance (for example, Beagle, 2000). F. W. Lancaster (1999) predicted, then recanted, on his predictions for a paperless society.

As we saw in chapter 7, the information revolutions have brought changes in the information professions, with the increasing diversity of information technology leading to greater diversity in the information professions. However, as we observed, some basic roles for information professionals migrate across technologies. As the information future evolves, while the specifics of information positions will change, there will continue to be a need for those who can work in society to create, transmit, manage, manipulate, interpret, store, and help others use information.

Some see evidence of an Orwellian use of information technology to increase the power of government and big business, particularly in the aftermath of 9/11. Others see these efforts as a necessary response to the threat to the public good. In the United States, legislation has been introduced, and some passed, that further limits certain privacy, civil liberties, and free speech rights. Whether such legislation is constitutional is a matter for the U.S. Supreme

Court. Examples include the USA PATRIOT Act of 2001 (PL 107-56), amended in 2006, that expands the ability of law enforcement to use electronic surveillance. The Children's Internet Protection Act (CIPA) and the Neighborhood Children's Internet Protection Act (NCIPA) of 2000 (PL106-554) tie library and school Internet e-rates to filtering and, in the eyes of some, represent an attempt at Internet censorship. The Communications Decency Act of 1996 sought to regulate Internet content but was successfully challenged in *Reno v ACLU*. The Child Online Protection Act of 1998 (14 USC 231) was passed to limit access by minors to commercial pornography via the Internet. The Digital Millennium Copyright Act (DMCA) has been interpreted to favor copyright holders (usually big business) to the detriment of the information creator and of information users. International organizations like the World Intellectual Property Organization (WIPO) and the World Trade Organization (WTO) have been accused of furthering the interests of the multinational corporation to the detriment of everyone else.

Bill Joy took us a step further with his eloquent essay, "Why the Future Doesn't Need Us." Joy was no joy when he suggested that human beings will yield to machines, that humans will be rendered redundant. Joy states:

> The twenty-first-century technologies—genetics, nanotechnology, and robotics (GNR)—are so powerful that they can spawn whole new classes of accidents and abuses. Most dangerously, for the first time, these accidents and abuses are widely within the reach of individuals or small groups. They will not require large facilities or rare raw materials. Knowledge alone will enable the use of them. (Joy, 2000)

Joy is not alone in his prediction of the victory of technology over life (Leslie, 1996). Robert Oppenheimer, one of the creators of the A-bomb, is said to have quoted the god Vishnu in the *Bhagavad-Gita* on the explosion of the first weapon in 1945: "Now I am become Death, the destroyer of worlds" (Los Alamos National Laboratory, 2001). Yet we have also witnessed technological changes that may herald something of a victory over death, or at least a postponement of death. Olshansky et al. (2006), writing in *The Scientist*, note that pharmaceuticals and other biological and medical advances may slow the aging process, enhance biological functions, and extend life expectancy. Other "man-machine" interfaces are with us. These range from eyeglasses first invented in the tenth century to the heart pacemakers of the twentieth. There will be no doubt be more "cyborgnetic" advances that incorporate information technologies. And there will continue to be concern over ethical and equity matters. Chris Gray (2001) in his book *Cyborg Citizen: Politics in the Posthuman Age* covers the many ramifications of cyborg culture from artificial insemination and cloning to mind-machine interactions.

We should not end on a pessimistic note. Theodore Roszak, whose book *The Cult of Information* is subtitled *A Neo-Luddite Treatise* . . . leaves us this in his closing paragraph:

> The art of thinking is grounded in the mind's astonishing capacity to create beyond what it intends, beyond what it can foresee. We cannot begin to shape that capacity toward humane ends and to guard it from demonic misuse until we have first experienced the true size of the mind. (Roszak, 1994: 244)

We have two choices. We can quit, for if we buy into the defeat of humanity, well, why try; we will die. The other choice is to recognize that the information environment poses some extraordinary challenges that can and must be mastered by experiencing "the true size of the mind."

QUESTIONS FOR CONSIDERATION

1. What do you predict will happen to the institutions, like educational institutions, that transmit information to future generations over the next ten years? What are some indicators that point in the direction you predict?
2. What role will information professionals have in society in the medium-term future (ten years out)? What evidence can you suggest to support your prediction?
3. Will information technology continue to be an important force in how society develops over the next century? Looking back over changes in the last 100 years, what would you predict for the next 100 years in societal change stemming from information technology developments?
4. Will information and information activities dominate historical development longer than agriculture and industrialization did in earlier times? What specifics support your response?
5. What current ethical issues related to information will continue to be a concern in the future? Why?

REFERENCES

Adams, Douglas. 1979. *The Hitchhiker's Guide to the Galaxy*. New York: Harmony Books.

Asimov, Isaac. 1991. *Prelude to Foundation.* New York: Bantam Reissue.

Beagle, Donald. 2000. "Web-based Learning Environments: Do Libraries Matter?" *College & Research Libraries* 61 (July): 367–379.

Bradbury, Ray. 1953. *Fahrenheit 451.* New York: Ballantine.

Clarke, Arthur C. 1945a. "Extra Terrestrial Relays: Can Rocket Stations Give World-wide Radio Coverage?" *Wireless World* 51 (October): 305–308.

———. 1945b. "Peacetime Uses for V2." *Wireless World* 51 (February): 58.

Commoner, Barry. 1971. *The Closing Circle: Nature, Man, and Technology.* New York: Knopf.

———. 1990. *Making Peace with the Planet.* New York: Pantheon Books.

Dertouzos, Michael L. 1997. *What Will Be: How the New World of Information Will Change Our Lives.* San Francisco: HarperEdge.

Ellul, Jacques. 1964. *The Technological Society.* Translated by John Wilkinson. New York: Vintage Books.

Gallois, Pierre. 1961. *The Balance of Terror: Strategy for the Nuclear Age.* Boston, MA: Houghton Mifflin.

Gray, Chris. 2001. *Cyborg Citizen: Politics in the Posthuman Age.* New York: Routledge.

Hayes, Denis. 1977. *Rays of Hope: The Transition to a Post-Petroleum World.* New York: Norton.

Heinlein, Robert A. 1961. *Stranger in a Strange Land.* New York: Putnam.

Hirsch, Werner Z., and Luc E. Weber, eds. 1999. *Challenges Facing Higher Education at the Millennium.* Phoenix, AZ: Oryx Press.

Huxley, Aldus. 1932. *Brave New World.* New York: Harper.

Joy, Bill. 2000. "Why the Future Doesn't Need Us." *Wired* 8.04 (April). Available: www.wired.com/wired/archive/8.04/joy_pr.html (accessed December 2006).

Lancaster, F. Wilfrid. 1999. "Second Thoughts on the Paperless Society." *Library Journal* 124 (15 September): 48–50.

Leslie, John. 1996. *The End of the World: The Science and Ethics of Human Extinction.* London: Routledge.

Lilienthal, David. 1944. *TVA: Democracy on the March.* New York: Harper.

Los Alamos National Laboratory. 2001. "The Manhattan Project" (10 January). Available: http://set.lanl.gov/programs/cif/Curriculum/Past/BM5.htm (accessed December 2006).

May, Timothy C. 1992. "The Cryptoanarchist Manifesto." Activism.net, 22 November. Available: www.activism.net/cypherpunk/crypto-anarchy.html (accessed December 2006).

McLuhan, Marshall. 1964. *Understanding Media: The Extensions of Man.* New York: McGraw-Hill.

McLuhan, Marshall, and Quentin Fiore. 1967. *The Medium is the Massage.* New York: Bantam.

Mumford, Lewis. 1964. "Authoritarian and Democratic Technics." *Technology and Culture* 5 (Winter): 1–8.

National Academy of Sciences. Computer Science and Telecommunications Board. 2006. *Privacy in the Information Age.* Available: www7.national academies.org/cstb/project_privacy.html (accessed December 2006).

Olshansky, S. Jay, Daniel Perry, Richard A. Miller, and Robert N. Butler. 2006. "In Pursuit of the Longevity Dividend." *The Scientist* 20, no. 3. Available: www.the-scientist.com/article/display/23191 (accessed December 2006).

Orwell, George. 1945. *Animal Farm.* London: Secker & Warburg.

———. 1949. *1984.* New York: Signet.

Pelton, Joseph N. 2004. "The Rise of Telecities: Decentralizing the Global Society." *Futurist* 38 (January–February): 28–33.

Rheingold, Howard. 1993. *The Virtual Community: Homesteading on the Electronic Frontier.* New York: HarperPerennial.

———. 2000. *Tools for Thought: The History and Future of Mind-Expanding Technology.* 2nd ed. Cambridge, MA: MIT Press.

Roszak, Theodore. 1994. *The Cult of Information: A Neo-Luddite Treatise on High-Tech, Artificial Intelligence, and the True Art of Thinking.* 2nd ed. Berkeley, CA: University of California Press.

Schement, Jorge Reina, and Terry Curtis. 1995. *Tendencies and Tensions of the Information Age: The Production and Distribution of Information in the United States.* New Brunswick, NJ: Transaction Publishers.

Schumacher, E. F. 1973. *Small Is Beautiful: Economics as if People Mattered.* New York: Harper and Row.

Shenk, David. 1997. *Data Smog: Surviving the Information Glut.* San Francisco: HarperEdge.

Skinner, B. F. 1948. *Walden Two.* New York: Macmillan.

———. 1971. *Beyond Freedom and Dignity.* New York: Knopf.

Stewart, Doug. 1997. "Herbert A. Simon: Thinking Machine." Interview June 1994. *The Unexpurgated Interviews. Omni* Archives. Omni Publications. Available: http://web.archive.org/web/20021010004638/http://www.omnimag.com/archives/interviews/simon.html (accessed December 2006).

Stoll, Clifford. 1995. *Silicon Snake Oil: Second Thoughts on the Information Highway.* New York: Doubleday.

Toffler, Alvin. 1970. *Future Shock.* New York: Random House.

———. 1980. *The Third Wave.* New York: Morrow.

Verne, Jules. 1865. "De la Terre à la Lune. Trajet direct en 97 heures." [*From the Earth to the Moon*] *Journal des Débats politiques et littéraires* (14 September–14 October).

———. 1869. "Vingt Mille Lieues sous les mers. Tour du monde sous-marin." [*Twenty Thousand Leagues under the Sea*] *Magasin* 11, no. 121 (20 March 1869): 13, no. 151 (20 June 1870).

———. 1874. *Journey to the Center of the Earth* (*Voyage au centre de la Terre*). New York: Scribner, Armstrong.

Vonnegut, Kurt. 1952. *Player Piano*. New York: Delacort Press.

Wells, H. G. 1895. *The Time Machine, an Invention*. London: W. Heinemann.

———. 1897. *The Invisible Man: A Grotesque Romance*. New York: E. Arnold.

———. 1898. *The War of the Worlds*. New York: Harper & Brothers.

———. 1938. *World Brain*. New York: Doubleday, Doran.

Wiener, Norbert. 1948. *Cybernetics; Or Control and Communication in the Animal and the Machine*. New York: Wiley.

———. 1950. *The Human Use of Human Beings: Cybernetics and Society*. Boston, MA: Houghton Mifflin.

Winner, Langdon. 1986. *The Whale and the Reactor: A Search for Limits in an Age of High Technology*. Chicago: University of Chicago Press.

ADDITIONAL SOURCES

Barber, Benjamin R. 1996. *Jihad v. McWorld*. New York: Ballantine Books.

Brown, Lester R., Christopher Flavin, and Sandra Postel. 1991. *Saving The Planet: How to Shape an Environmentally Sustainable Global Economy*. New York: W. W. Norton.

Appendix I

Glossary of Terms

Note: The acronym associated with the term is given in italics before the term. The entries are alphabetized using the acronyms.

AI **artificial intelligence:** computer-based decision systems, often in "tree" configuration, that seek to replicate the intelligence of human beings. AI is concerned with the machine application of human knowledge as well as with machine learning systems and is a concept related to expert systems.

Analog: the representation of information in some continuous systematic medium, as opposed to "digital," or the representation of information in discrete sets. For example, information carried on an alternating frequency electromagnetic wave or through symbolic representation is in analog form.

ASK **anomalous state of knowledge:** term originated by Nicholas J. Belkin to denote an information need. ASKs underlie information needs, are states of mind that affect end information needs and therefore search strategies.

Baby Bells: the regional Bell telephone operating systems formed as a result of the divestiture (breakup) of American Telephone & Telegraph (AT&T) and the Bell System by court order in 1984; related to the term "Ma Bell," which was used to refer to AT&T and the Bell System.

Bandwidth: the range or band of frequencies available to carry a message. The greater the bandwidth, the greater is the carrying capacity and/or speed of the system.

Bibliographic utility: an entity, such as OCLC, formed to supply bibliographic information to libraries through sharing or purchase of such information from one or more sources.

Blog: short for Weblog. Both a noun and a verb. A form of online journal for discussion purposes both by the blog owner and often by respondents.

BPL **Broadband over Power Lines:** a technology that permits Internet transmission over utility power lines. BPL in principle can provide symmetric (both receiving and sending) and full duplex (two-way) communication at a rate greater than one gigabyte per second.

ccTLD **country code Top-Level Domain:** Internet top-level domain that indicates the country of registry in a URL address. The country code follows the ISO 3166 two-letter country abbreviation standard. For example, a URL might take the form http://aaa.bbb.us for a U.S. registered domain name. See gTLD.

CDA **Communications Decency Act:** a part of the 1996 U.S. Telecommunications Act (PL 104-104,110 Stat. 56 (1996)), which made it illegal to transmit or display to anyone under 18 "indecent" or "patently offensive" material on the Internet and which was found unconstitutional by the U.S. Supreme Court in 1997.

CES **Corpus Encoding Standard:** one of several XML-based systems developed to mark up archived digitized documents.

CIO **chief information officer:** a corporate officer or official in an organization responsible for the management and maintenance of the information technology of the enterprise.

CIPA **Children's Internet Protection Act:** federal legislation passed and signed in December 2000 (PL106-554) that requires use of filters on computers accessing the Internet in public libraries and schools in order for those entities to qualify for federal funding through the Library Services and Technology Act, the Elementary and Secondary Education Act Title III, and the Universal Service discount or e-rate program. The constitutionality of portions of the act related to public libraries was challenged in the courts. The Supreme Court upheld the constitutionality of the challenged portions in June 2003, resulting in enforcement of the filtering requirement for public libraries.

CKO **chief knowledge officer:** a corporate officer or official in an organization responsible for knowledge management in the organization, including the development and maintenance of the knowledge management infrastructure, the development of an organizational culture that promotes knowledge sharing, and the use of knowledge resources to further the goals, both financial and otherwise, of the organization.

Codex: an information record in the form of separate leaves (pages) of writing or printing on parchment or paper that have been bound together with stitching or through some other means.

Codices: plural of codex.

COPA **Child Online Protection Act:** federal legislation passed in October 1998 (included in PL 105-277 signed in 1999, 47 U.S.C. Sec. 231(a)(1)) prohibiting distribution for commercial purposes of material harmful to minors through the World Wide Web to any minor. The constitutionality of the law was challenged in *Ashcroft v ACLU*. In 2002, the Supreme Court heard the case and referred it back to the appeals court level, letting stand an injunction against its enforcement until the case was resolved.

CORC **Cooperative Online Resource Catalog:** a completed OCLC initiative to provide cooperative cataloging by libraries of WWW-based content. Replaced by OCLC Connexion in 2002.

CPO **chief privacy officer:** a corporate officer or official in an organization responsible for developing and implementing privacy guidelines within an organization and between the organization and its clients that ensure adherence to legal and technical requirements and consistency with the goals and contractual obligations of the entity.

Cryptography: the art of encoding or encrypting a message. See steganography.

Cybernetics: a term coined by Norbert Wiener to imply biological and mechanical control systems. Both closed and open systems with positive and/or negative feedback or circular regulatory loops are included in the definition.

Data drilling: a methodology used to search for and locate specific information in one or more sets of digital data. Data drilling is closely related to data mining, except that data mining implies a more general exploration. Both data drilling and mining employ computer-based search and retrieval algorithms for information retrieval.

Data mining: a methodology used for discovering unanticipated and previously unidentified patterns in or relationships with or among sets of data through use of various techniques, including statistical and vector analysis.

DBS **direct broadcast satellite:** a method for delivering broadcast content directly to individual receiving sites (such as homes) through the use of satellites and small receiving dishes mounted at the receive site. The methodology is used as an alternative to cable as a delivery system for televised material.

Digital: the representation of information in discrete units, as contrasted with analog, the representation of information in some continuous systematic medium.

Digital divide: a term used to denote the differences in access to and facility to use digital information technology and content among various demographic and geographic groups. The term is applied both at a group level within countries and at a country level and refers to the gap between those who have access and those who do not.

DMCA **Digital Millennium Copyright Act:** federal legislation passed in 1998 (PL 105-304), amending the U.S. Copyright Act, that added new rules prohibiting circumvention of technological protection measures, i.e., technology embedded in digital products by copyright owners to limit or control use, and made equipment or services designed for such circumvention illegal.

DNS **domain name system:** system by which alphanumeric or mnemonic URLs that serve as aliases for numeric Internet protocol addresses are translated from the URL to the IP address.

Documentalist: term used, primarily in Europe, for a person who is a specialist in or practices documentation, which is the study of the management and communication of information.

DOI® **Digital Object Identifier:** a propriety markup language and symbol set for the identification and exchange of digital information as well as intellectual property protection.

DPL **digital power line:** A broadband technology that can carry signals over low-voltage power lines. It is capable of carrying Internet traffic up to 2 Mbps. One advantage that DPL has over other "wired" systems is effective access for rural users. Telephony and television can be DPL supported. Also known as BPL (see above).

DRM **digital rights management:** technical and legal systems to protect the intellectual property inherent in digital documents while developing a mechanism of the fair use of the content.

DSL **digital subscriber line:** a technology for use of existing copper wire telephone lines for delivery of digital information content that provides a constant Internet connection. The speed of transmission of content for DSL varies but can reach 1.5 megabytes per second, making it a preferable transportation medium.

EAD DTD **encoded archival description document type definition:** One of several XML-based systems developed to mark up archived digitized documents.

Expert systems: machine-based decision systems that are based on human knowledge and emulate human expert decision processes; related concept to artificial intelligence.

Extranet: a closed nonpublic Internet connection between two or more independent organizations.

FERPA **Family Educational Rights and Privacy Act:** federal legislation (§ 513 of PL 93-380), also known as the Buckley Amendment, passed in 1974, that limits access to education records held by education institutions receiving funds from the U.S. Department of Education, except as required for the conduct of the educational enterprise, unless permission is given by the student (or parents in the case of minors). The Act also provides for access to the education records by parents (in the case of minors) and students and for correction of inaccuracies in the records.

FOIA **Freedom of Information Act:** U.S. federal legislation passed in 1966 that made information held by agencies of the executive branch of the federal government available on written request with certain exclusions and exemptions to protect individual privacy, proprietary and financial information, classified information related to national security, and certain information pertaining to law enforcement. The legislation has been amended several times. The term is also used to refer to similar legislation in other countries and state-level legislation in the United States (called "little FOIAs").

GII **global information infrastructure:** term used to denote the conglomerate information infrastructures that exist across the world, encompassing all national information infrastructures as well as all of the equipment, personnel, and organizations that constitute them.

GILS **global (or government) information locator service:** mark up language, software, and system for information retrieval of government documents.

GNP **gross national product:** the total economic activity of a country, measured on some time-defined (usually annually or quarterly) basis.

GPS **global positioning system:** satellite-based navigation system developed originally by the U.S. Department of Defense for military applications. GPS is now in wide use for commercial and private navigation and geographic purposes.

gTLD **generic Top-Level Domain:** "functional" top-level Internet domain (e.g., .com). Seven gTLDs were originally introduced with an additional seven approved in 2001. Between 2003 and 2007, the list grew to 20 gTLDs. See ccTLD.

GUI **graphical user interface:** term used for an interface with a computer application or system that displays information and links to other information on the monitor screen using visual icons and graphics rather than all text and special symbols, such as those in a programming language.

HAVA **Help America Vote Act of 2002:** (PL 107-252) HAVA provides for simplified registration processes. It is also interpreted to promote electronic voting.

HDTV **high-definition television:** a system for use of compressed digital signals to transmit television content, which provides a higher quality of visual display.

HIPAA **Health Insurance Portability and Accountability Act of 1995:** (PL 104-191) Title I provides portability of health care provisions. Title II addresses the portability of medical records in electronic format. It also addresses the security and privacy of medical records.

HTML **hypertext markup language:** the coding, or special language using symbols called tags, that is used to provide instructions for formatting or layout of information and linking to other sites in documents placed on the World Wide Web.

IGO **intergovernmental organization:** an international organization that has countries, or more precisely, official governments, as its members.

Informatics: the discipline or study of systems and algorithms, and structures to manage and improve information transmission and communications.

Internet-2: second-generation high-bandwidth Internet system designed for government, industry, academic, and educational applications. Internet 2 utilizes advanced networking systems.

Intranet: closed, private Internet within any given organization or entity.

IP **Internet protocol:** any one of a number of "rules" or algorithms that standardize Internet operation and communication.

ISDN **integrated services digital network:** ISDN is a POTS-based digital telephone connection system. ISDN provides "higher speed" digital connectivity for Internet and other purposes than V90 56k modem service. ISDN takes two forms: Basic Rate Interface (BRI) and Primary Rate Interface (PRI). BRI provides two 64 kbs B channels and one 16 kbs D channel for 144 kbs service. In the United States PRI provides 23 B channels and one D for 1.36 Mbs. In Europe, PRI service adds seven B channels for 1.984 Mbs.

ISP **Internet service provider:** an entity that provides access to the Internet for individuals and/or companies, usually, although not exclusively, on a monthly fee basis. Services of an ISP usually include access to the World Wide Web and an e-mail account.

IT **information technology:** general term applied to any technology used in creating, recording, storing, displaying, retrieving, or managing information. Used with capital letters, the term usually applies to computer and communication systems and associated hardware and software, as in the IT department of a company.

Knowledge discovery: a series of techniques for extraction of previously unknown information from digital collections; a variation of data mining.

LAN **local area network:** a set of computers sharing a common dedicated line and often a single set of software and hardware peripherals.

Librarianship: the knowledge, skills, and attitudes that form the practice of providing library service.

LIS **library and information science:** the discipline that encompasses the knowledge and methodologies for creating, selecting, organizing, storing, retrieving, accessing, managing, providing, and using information in a specific setting or for specific users.

MARC **machine readable cataloging:** a set of similar Z39.50 compatible codes and formats designed for cataloging traditional and electronic documents for OPACs and data exchange.

Markup language: a system of coding using symbols called tags to indicate the structure and relationships of a text file.

Mashup: a digital application, product, or service created by mixing together two or more previously existing applications, products, or services.

MEP **Model Editions Partnership:** one of several XML based systems developed to mark up archived digitized documents.

Metamessage: in communication, an interpretation of a message by a receiver of the message that is beyond the actual literal meaning of the message conveyed. It may be different from the message that was intended by the sender and may be related to the relationship between the sender and the receiver. Metamessages are implicit, rather than explicit, and deal with attitudes and feelings.

MIS **management information systems:** the discipline that studies systems and methodologies for use and management of digital information in business environments for decision making in support of the goals of the enterprise.

MNE **multinational enterprise:** a company or organization that operates in more than one country.

Modem: modulator/demodulator, a device that enables data from a computer (digital format) to be translated into a form that can be carried over phone lines (analog format) and then translated back into a form that the computer can manipulate.

NCIPA **Neighborhood Children's Internet Protection Act:** federal legislation passed and signed in December 2000 (PL106-554) that requires that public libraries and schools have an Internet safety policy in order to qualify for federal e-rate discount.

NGO **nongovernmental organization:** an organization, often at the international level, in which the members may be other organizational entities but are not official governments.

NIC **newly industrializing countries:** countries that are in the stage of rapidly developing domestic industries for the first time, formerly called "developing countries" and "less developed countries."

NII **national information infrastructure:** the complex of equipment, personnel, organizations, protocols, and systems that exist within a country to facilitate the movement of information both into and within the country.

OCR **optical character recognition:** a system that recognizes printed or otherwise written information or images and translates them into digital format that can be manipulated or interpreted by a computer.

OPAC **online public access catalog:** generic name for a library catalog that is in digital format and available online to the public for use in determining the holdings of the library.

PDA **personal digital assistant:** any of a number of small, handheld computers that provide for the recording, storage, retrieval, receipt, and transfer of information in digital format.

Peer-to-peer: term used to indicate sharing of information or files directly from one computer to another without a server or other centralized source.

PICS **Platform for Internet Content Selection:** a system for labeling the content of information in Web pages, either by the creator of the page or by some third party, along dimensions established by the labeler, such as degree of violence or sexual content, that will allow retrieval of information matching the desired content levels of the user.

Pictographs: representation of objects through the use of graphic symbols or pictures.

PLC **Power Line Communication:** another name for Broadband over Power Lines. See BPL. Also Packet Loss Concealment, a technique to statistically reduce the impact of packet loss via VoIP.

POTS **plain old telephone service:** term used to distinguish the basic two-way voice communication service using copper wire from other added or more sophisticated services, such as data transfer.

PTT **post, telegraph, telephone:** the generic name used for the national ministry of a country in which the three major communication systems are owned and operated through a single governmental agency.

PURL **Persistent Uniform Resource Locator:** an OCLC initiative to resolve the problem of moving or changing URLs. PURL is a redirect service that provides an alias for the "old" URL and redirects it to its newer form.

R&D: research and development.

RDF **Resource Description Framework:** one of several XML-based systems developed to mark up digitized documents, primarily for document or information cataloging and retrieval.

RFID **radio frequency identification:** a low-power broadcasting chip that can be attached to any object (humans, animals, goods) and used to identify or trace the movement of the chip and the object to which it is attached. RFIDs may be powered (contain a power source, typically a battery) or passive (no power source).

RSS **Really Simple Syndication** or **Rich Site Summary:** an XML-based Internet information "pull" technology that permits users to receive information feeds to which they have subscribed.

SDI **selective dissemination of information:** a proactive service providing current information to users, based on their profiles of interest.

Search engine: a set of computer programs designed to index keywords and other terms to enable the retrieval of documents containing specified information.

Semantic Web: an abstract ontology-based system to represent Web-based information. Meaning is represented and mapped through a series of ontologies to provide greater precision.

SGML **Standard Generalized Markup Language:** a generalized markup language designed to apply identifiers or "term markers" to digital documents. It is used to tag and therefore organize document terms, thereby lending to content definition.

SLMS **school library media specialist:** title of a person who designs and implements library services in a K–12 setting.

Steganography: the art of hiding a message by use of invisible inks to embedding messages in graphic and audio computer and Internet files. See cryptography.

T1: a digital data stream capable of running at 1.544 megabits/second (Mbs). The European equivalent is E1 with a carrying capacity of 2.048 Mbs.

T3: a digital data stream capable of running at 44.746 megabits/second (Mbs). The European equivalent is E3 with a carrying capacity of 34 Mbs.

TEI **Text Encoding Initiative:** one of several XML-based systems developed to mark up archived digitized documents.

Telnet: an Internet protocol permitting a client computer to logon to a host computer and emulate one of its terminals.

TLD **top-level domain:** the primary or first-level Internet addressing element of a domain name level below the root. There are two variants: the generic (gTLD) and country code (ccTLD).

TREC **Text Retrieval Conference:** a National Institute of Standards and Technology (NIST) and the Defense Advanced Research Projects Agency (DARPA) initiated standardized testbed project to support information retrieval research.

UCITA **Uniform Computer Information Transactions Act:** proposed uniform state contract legislation, developed through the National Conference of Commissioners on Uniform State Laws and to date passed in two states (Virginia and Maryland, both in 2000), that would govern the licensing and use of computer information, such as software and other digital information products, including particularly those in which the transactions occur online, and which would allow for enforceable contract terms that do not include the rights of use granted under copyright law.

URC **Uniform Resource Classification:** an experimental form of URI; a collection of information about or defining a Web resource.

URI **Universal** or **Uniform Resource Indicator:** short strings that identify Internet resources so that they can be retrieved via a variety of protocols. Resources may include text, images, multimedia, and other objects.

URN **Uniform Resource Name:** an Internet resource, e.g., Web site, with a permanent associated identifier. PURLs are a variant.

USA PATRIOT **Act:** Uniting and Strengthening America by Providing Appropriate Tools Required to Intercept and Obstruct Terrorism Act, U.S. legislation passed in October 2001 in reaction to the terrorist attacks of 9/11 that provides broad powers to federal law enforcement and intelligence agencies to investigate possible or suspected terrorist activity, including monitoring of electronic communication and electronic surveillance.

VoIP **voice over Internet protocol:** protocol that permits duplex (two-way) telephone-like conversation over the Internet.

VR **virtual reality:** a representation of the "real world" in a computer-generated environment.

WAI **Web accessibility initiative:** a W3C initiative designed to develop WWW software to support use by persons with disabilities.

WAIS **wide area information server:** a system providing for search and retrieval of Internet information.

WAN **wide area network:** a multilocation network, typically covering an extensive geographic area and typically consisting of two or more LANs. Unlike in LANs, software and peripherals are not shared.

WSIS **World Summit on the Information Society:** a set of international meetings held in 2003 and 2005 under the general sponsorship of the United Nations' International Telecommunication Union to address issues and processes for developing an information society in all nations.

XML **eXtensible Markup Language:** a W3C-developed and simplified form of SGML used for Web documents.

Appendix 2

Glossary of Acronyms of Organizations

ALA	American Library Association
ANSI	American National Standards Institute
ARPA	Advanced Research Projects Agency
ARPANET	Advanced Research Projects Agency Network
BIRPI	United International Bureaux for the Protection of Intellectual Property
CIA	Central Intelligence Agency (U.S.)
ERIC	Educational Resources Information Center
FAA	Federal Aviation Administration (U.S.)
FCC	Federal Communications Commission (U.S.)
FTC	Federal Trade Commission (U.S.)
HMSO	Her Majesty's Stationery Office (U.K.)
IANA	Internet Assigned Numbers Authority
ICANN	Internet Corporation for Assigned Names and Numbers
ICSU	International Council for Science
IEC	International Engineering Consortium
IEEE	Institute of Electrical and Electronics Engineers
IETF	Internet Engineering Task Force
IFLA	International Federation of Library Associations and Institutions
IMF	International Monetary Fund
IOC	International Olympic Committee
ISO	International Organization for Standardization
ISOC	Internet Society
ITU	International Telecommunication Union

MPAA	Motion Picture Association of America
NIST	National Institute of Standards and Technology (U.S.)
NSFnet	National Science Foundation network
NTIA	National Telecommunications and Information Administration (U.S.)
OCLC	Online Computer Library Center
OECD	Organisation for Economic Cooperation and Development
OMB	Office of Management and Budget (U.S.)
RIAA	Recording Industry Association of America
UNESCO	United Nations Educational, Scientific, and Cultural Organisation
UPU	Universal Postal Union
USAID	U.S. Agency for International Development
USPTO	U.S. Patent and Trademark Office
W3C	World Wide Web Consortium
WIPO	World Intellectual Property Organization
WTO	World Trade Organization

Index

About the Authors

June Lester is a professor in the University of Oklahoma School of Library and Information Studies, where she has been on faculty since 1993, serving from 1993 to 2000 as Director of the School. Prior to joining the OU faculty Lester was Associate Dean, School of Library and Information Sciences, University of North Texas, 1991–1993, and Director, Office for Accreditation, American Library Association, 1987–1991. Before that she was Associate Professor, Division of Library and Information Management, Emory University. She holds a B.A. and a M.Ln. from Emory University and the C.A.L. and D.L.S. from Columbia University. She teaches graduate courses in the foundations of information studies and user information behavior and the introduction to the information environment for the Bachelor of Arts in Information Studies degree. Special areas of interest include education for library and information studies, distance education, and information policy.

Lester served as Treasurer of the American Society for Information Science and Technology in 2004–2007 and as President of the Association for Library and Information Science Education (ALISE) in 1995–1996. Other professional activities have included two terms on the ALISE Board of Directors, a term on the Editorial Board of the *Journal of Education for Library and Information Science*, membership on the Editorial Board of the *Journal of Academic Librarianship*, various positions in the Council on Postsecondary Accreditation (1987–1991), membership on the ALA Committee on Accreditation (1985–1987), service as an external review panel chair for the Committee on Accreditation, chair of the ALA Office for Library Personnel Resources Advisory Committee (1996–1998), and a term on the ALA Council (1986–1987). In the American Society for Information Science and Technology she served three terms as chair of the Information Science Education Committee (2000–2003) and also served on the Technical Program Committee and chaired several award juries.

Wallace C. Koehler, Jr., is Director and Professor in the Department of Information Studies at Valdosta State University, Valdosta, Georgia. Prior to moving to VSU in 2001, he was Assistant Professor on the faculty at the

University of Oklahoma School of Library and Information Studies (1998–2001). He has taught in the areas of government, politics, foreign policy, and international law at the University of Tennessee, Vanderbilt University, Maryville College, and Temple University. His other experience includes work as a senior researcher and consultant for Information International Associates; as staff associate of Aspen Systems Corporation Applied Management Sciences Division; as head of the Technology and Policy Assessment Division of the Center for Energy and Environment Research, University of Puerto Rico; and as assistant director for Policy Analysis and International Studies at the University of Tennessee Energy, Environment and Resources Center. He holds a Ph.D. and M.A. in government from Cornell University, and an M.A. in political science and an M.S. in information science from the University of Tennessee. He teaches in the areas of foundations of information studies, government information sources, online searching, public libraries, information ethics, information policy, research methods, and web organization. His areas of research include bibliometrics, professional and information ethics, and webmetrics.

Koehler is active in committee service in IFLA, ALA, and ALISE and serves on the editorial boards of the *Journal of Internet Cataloging*, *CyberMetrics*, and *Information Research*. He is an External Examiner for the East African School of Library and Information Science, Makerere University, Kampala, Uganda, and a member of the University of Tennessee School of Information Sciences Advisory Board. In 2004–2007 he chaired both the Lowndes County Library Board and the Southeast Georgia Library Board.